First World War
and Army of Occupation
War Diary
France, Belgium and Germany

32 DIVISION
Divisional Troops
161 Brigade Royal Field Artillery
30 December 1915 - 24 September 1918

WO95/2380/4

The Naval & Military Press Ltd
www.nmarchive.com
Published in association with The National Archives

Published by

The Naval & Military Press Ltd

Unit 10 Ridgewood Industrial Park,

Uckfield, East Sussex,

TN22 5QE England

Tel: +44 (0) 1825 749494

www.naval-military-press.com

www.nmarchive.com

This diary has been reprinted in facsimile from the original. Any imperfections are inevitably reproduced and the quality may fall short of modern type and cartographic standards.

© **Crown Copyright**
Images reproduced by permission of The National Archives, London, England, 2015.

Contents

Document type	Place/Title	Date From	Date To
Heading	WO95/2380-4		
Heading	32nd Division Divl Artillery 161st Bde R.F.A. Jan 1916-1919 Oct.		
Heading	32nd Divisional Artillery. 161st Brigade R.F.A. January 1916 Dec 1918		
War Diary	Fovant. Southampton	30/12/1915	30/12/1915
War Diary	Havre	31/12/1915	31/12/1915
War Diary	Argoeuves	01/01/1916	03/01/1916
War Diary	St. Gratien.	04/01/1916	04/01/1916
War Diary	Albert.	05/01/1916	05/01/1916
War Diary	Baizieux	06/01/1916	06/01/1916
War Diary	Albert	07/01/1916	31/01/1916
Heading	32nd Divisional Artillery. 161st Brigade R.F.A. February 1916		
War Diary	Albert	01/02/1916	29/02/1916
Heading	32nd Divisional Artillery. 161st Brigade R.F.A. March 1916		
War Diary	In The Field	05/03/1916	26/03/1916
Heading	32nd Divisional Artillery. 161st Brigade R.F.A. April 1916		
War Diary	In The Field	03/04/1916	29/04/1916
Heading	32nd Divisional Artillery. 161st Brigade R.F.A. May. 1916		
War Diary	In The Field	05/05/1916	26/05/1916
Heading	32nd Divn. Arty. Headquarters 161st Brigade R.F.A. June 1916.		
War Diary	In The Field	03/06/1916	30/06/1916
Heading	War Diary Headquarters, 161st Brigade. R.F.A. (32nd Division) July 1916		
War Diary	In The Field	01/07/1916	29/07/1916
Heading	32nd Divisional Artillery. 161st Brigade R.F.A. August 1916		
War Diary	In The Field	01/08/1916	31/08/1916
War Diary	In The Field.	06/09/1916	30/09/1916
Heading	32nd Divisional Artillery. 161st Brigade R.F.A. October 1916		
War Diary		04/10/1916	28/10/1916
Heading	32nd Divisional Artillery. 161st Brigade R.F.A. November 1916		
War Diary	In The Field	01/11/1916	28/11/1916
Heading	32nd Divisional Artillery. 161st Brigade R.F.A. December 1916		
War Diary	In The Field	04/12/1916	30/12/1916
Heading	161st. (Yorks.) Brigade R.F.A. War Diary For Period 1st to 31st January 1917. Vol		
War Diary	In The Field	03/01/1917	27/01/1917
Heading	161st (Yorks.) Brigade R.F.A. (32nd Divisional Artillery) War Diary Covering Period 1st February to 28th February 1917 Vol 14		
War Diary	In The Field	01/02/1917	27/02/1917

Heading	32nd Divn 161st. (Yorks.) Brigade R.F.A. War Diary for period 1st to 31st March 1917 inclusive		
War Diary	In The Field.	01/03/1917	31/03/1917
Heading	161st (Yorks.) Brigade R.F.A. War Diary for period 1st to 30th April 1917 Vol 16		
War Diary	In The Field	01/04/1917	29/04/1917
Heading	161st (Yorks.) Brigade R.F.A. War Diary for the Period-1st to 31st May 1917. Vol 17		
War Diary	In The Field.	02/05/1917	31/05/1917
Heading	161st (Yorks.) Brigade R.F.A. War Diary-For period 1st to 30th June 1917 Vol 18		
War Diary	In The Field.	01/06/1917	30/06/1917
Heading	161st (Yorks,) Brigade R.F.A. War Diary. for period. 1st to 31st July 1917.		
War Diary	In The Field	02/07/1917	31/07/1917
Heading	161st (Yorks,) Brigade R.F.A. War Diary for period 1st to 31st August 1917. Vol 20		
War Diary	In The Field	01/08/1917	31/08/1917
Heading	161st (Yorks.) Brigade R.F.A. War Diary 1st September 1917 to 30th September 1917 Vol 21		
War Diary	In The Field.	02/09/1917	30/09/1917
Heading	161st (Yorks.) Brigade R.F.A. War Diary (A.F.C. 2118) for period 1st to 31st October 1917 Vol 22		
War Diary	In The Field	01/10/1917	04/10/1917
War Diary	Night	05/10/1917	06/10/1917
War Diary	Night	05/10/1917	11/10/1917
War Diary	In The Field	12/10/1917	31/10/1917
Miscellaneous	Officer Commanding. /161st Brigade R.F.A.	11/10/1917	11/10/1917
Heading	161st (Yorks) Brigade, R.F.A. War Diary. 1st to 30th November 1917. Vol 23		
War Diary	In The Field	01/11/1917	30/11/1917
Heading	161st (Yorks.) Brigade R.F.A. War Diary for period 1st to 31st December 1917. Vol 24		
War Diary	In The Field	02/12/1917	31/12/1917
Heading	161st (Yorks.) Brigade R.F.A. War Diary Covering period 1st to 31st January 1918 Vol 25		
War Diary	In The Field	01/01/1918	31/01/1918
Heading	161st (Yorks.) Brigade R.F.A. War Diary Covering period- 1st to 28th February 1918 Vol 26		
War Diary	In The Field	01/02/1918	28/02/1918
Heading	32nd Divisional Artillery. 161st (Yorks) Brigade Royal Field Artillery. March 1918		
Heading	161st (Yorks) Brigade R.F.A. War Diary for period-1st to 31st March 1918. Vol 27		
War Diary	In The Field	01/03/1918	31/03/1918
Heading	32nd Div. VI. Corps. War Diary Headquarters, 161st Brigade, R.F.A. April 1918		
Heading	War Diary April 1918. 161st Brigade R.F.A. Vol 28		
War Diary	In The Field	01/04/1918	30/04/1918
Heading	161st (Yorks.) Brigade. R.F.A. War Diary Covering Period 1st May, 1918-31st May, 18 Vol 29		
War Diary	In The Field	01/05/1918	31/05/1918
Heading	161st (Yorks.) Brigade, R.F.A. War Diary From 1st June, 1918 To 30th June, 1918.		
War Diary	In The Field	01/06/1918	30/06/1918

Heading	161st (Yorks) Brigade, R.F.A. 32 Div. War Diary Covering Period 1st July, 1918, 31st July, 1918 Vol 31		
Miscellaneous	Cover for Documents. Nature of Enclosures.		
War Diary	In The Field.	01/07/1918	30/07/1918
Heading	161st (Yorks.) Brigade, R.F.A. War Diary-Covering Period From 1st Aug. 1918 To 31st Aug. 1918. Vol 32		
Miscellaneous	Cover for Documents. Nature of Enclosures.		
War Diary	In The Field.	01/08/1918	31/08/1918
War Diary	In The Field	01/09/1918	30/09/1918
Miscellaneous	Casualties During Month of September 1918	02/10/1918	02/10/1918
Miscellaneous	Headquarters, 32nd D.A. War Diary	09/09/1918	09/09/1918
Miscellaneous	O.C., A/161st Bde. R.F.A.	08/09/1919	08/09/1919
Operation(al) Order(s)	161st (Yorks.) Brigade R.F.A. Operation Order No. 8.	10/09/1918	10/09/1918
Operation(al) Order(s)	161st (Yorks.) Brigade Operation Order No. 11.	12/09/1918	12/09/1918
Operation(al) Order(s)	161st (Yorks.) Brigade R.F.A. Operation Order No. 12	13/09/1918	13/09/1918
Operation(al) Order(s)	161st (Yorks.) Brigade R.F.A. Operation Order No. 13	16/09/1918	16/09/1918
Miscellaneous	161st Bde. R.F.A. Instructions No. 2	16/09/1918	16/09/1918
Operation(al) Order(s)	161st (Yorks.) Brigade R.F.A. Operation Order No. 14.	17/09/1918	17/09/1918
Miscellaneous	161st (Yorks.) Brigade R.F.A. Artillery Instructions No. 38	18/09/1918	18/09/1918
Miscellaneous	161st (Yorks.) Brigade R.F.A. Artillery Instructions No. 39	19/09/1918	19/09/1918
Miscellaneous	161st (Yorks.) Brigade R.F.A. Artillery Instructions No. 40.	20/09/1918	20/09/1918
Miscellaneous	H.Q., 32nd Divisional Artillery. War Diary	21/09/1918	21/09/1918
Miscellaneous	H.Q. 32nd Divisional Artillery.	21/09/1918	21/09/1918
Miscellaneous	161st (Yorks.) Brigade R.F.A. Artillery Instructions No. 41.	22/09/1918	22/09/1918
Miscellaneous	161st Bde. R.F.A.	22/09/1918	22/09/1918
Operation(al) Order(s)	161st (Yorks.) Brigade R.F.A. Operation Order No. 15	23/09/1918	23/09/1918
Heading	161st (Yorks.) Brigade. R.F.A. War Diary Covering Period from 1st October 1918 to. 31st October. 1918 Vol 34		
War Diary	In The Field	01/10/1918	31/10/1918
Miscellaneous	161st (Yorks.) Brigade R.F.A. Artillery Instrution No. 47	05/10/1918	05/10/1918
Operation(al) Order(s)	161st (Yorks.) Brigade R.F.A. Operation Order No. 18	07/10/1918	07/10/1918
Operation(al) Order(s)	161st (Yorks.) Brigade R.F.A. Operation Order No. 19.	07/10/1918	07/10/1918
Miscellaneous	161st (Yorks.) Brigade R.F.A. Artillery Instructions No. 49.	08/10/1918	08/10/1918
Operation(al) Order(s)	161st (Yorks.) Brigade R.F.A. Order No. 20	09/10/1918	09/10/1918
Miscellaneous	161st (Yorks.) Brigade R.F.A. March Table.	09/10/1918	09/10/1918
Miscellaneous	161st (Yorks.) Brigade R.F.A. Artillery Instructions No. 50.	14/10/1918	14/10/1918
Miscellaneous	161st (Yorks.) Brigade R.F.A. Artillery Instructions No. 51.	15/10/1918	15/10/1918
Miscellaneous	6th Divisional Artillery Instructions No. 5	16/10/1918	16/10/1918
Miscellaneous	Addendum To 6th Divisional Artillery Instructions No. 5	16/10/1918	16/10/1918
Miscellaneous	Instructions No. 2	16/10/1918	16/10/1918
Operation(al) Order(s)	161st (Yorks.) Brigade R.F.A. Operation Order No. 21.	16/10/1918	16/10/1918
Miscellaneous	Right Group Instructions No. 3		
Operation(al) Order(s)	161st (Yorks.) Brigade R.F.A. Operation Order No. 22.	22/10/1918	22/10/1918
Miscellaneous	O.C., A/161. War Diary	22/10/1918	22/10/1918
Miscellaneous	O.C., A/181. War Diary 38	22/10/1918	22/10/1918
Miscellaneous	Warning Order. War Diary 39	23/10/1918	23/10/1918

Type	Description	Start	End
Miscellaneous	Appendix "A" Extract from 32nd Divnl. Routine Orders dated 18.10.18	18/10/1918	18/10/1918
Miscellaneous	Cover for Documents. Nature of Enclosures.		
Heading	161st (Yorks.) Brigade, R.F.A. War Diary Covering Period. From. 1st November. 18. To 30th November, 18 Vol 35		
War Diary	In The Field.	01/11/1918	30/11/1918
Miscellaneous	Appendix "A" Casualties During Month Of November, 1918		
Miscellaneous	161st (Yorks.) Brigade, RFA Artillery Instruction No. 1	02/11/1918	02/11/1918
Miscellaneous	161st (Yorks.) Brigade, RFA Artillery Instruction No. 2	03/11/1918	03/11/1918
Miscellaneous	161st (Yorks.) Brigade, RFA Artillery Instruction No. 3	03/11/1918	03/11/1918
Miscellaneous	Report Of Operations Of 161st (Yorks.) Brigade. R.F.A. from November 4th 1918 to November 10th 1918.	10/11/1918	10/11/1918
Miscellaneous	Pace of Report On Advance.		
Miscellaneous	Diary Of Advance Of A/161 Brigade R.F.A. from St. ORS to Semmries	04/11/1918	04/11/1918
Miscellaneous	Report On Advance Of B/161 In Operation From November 4th to 10th 1918.	04/11/1918	04/11/1918
Miscellaneous	Report Of C/161 On Advance 4th Novr. to 10th Novr. 1918.	04/11/1918	04/11/1918
Miscellaneous	Report Of D/161 On Advance 4th Novr. to 10th Novr. 1918.		
Miscellaneous	Lessons Learnt.		
Miscellaneous	Cover for Documents. Nature of Enclosures.		
Heading	161st (Yorks.) Brigade R.F.A. War Diary Covering Period 1st December 1918 to 31st December 1918 Vol 36		
War Diary	Honours & Awards The Distinguished Conduct Medal		
War Diary	In The Field.	01/12/1918	31/12/1918
Operation(al) Order(s)	161st (Yorks.) Brigade R.F.A. March Order No. 4.	11/12/1918	11/12/1918
Operation(al) Order(s)	161st (Yorks.) Brigade R.F.A. March Order No. 5.	12/12/1918	12/12/1918
Operation(al) Order(s)	161st (Yorks.) Brigade R.F.A. March Order No. 6.	13/12/1918	13/12/1918
Heading	Lancashire Division (Late 32nd Divn) 161st Brigade R.F.A. Jan-Oct 1919		
Heading	161st (Yorks.) Brigade R.F.A. War Diary. For Period. From. 1st January. 1919 to. 31st January. 1919 Vol 37		
War Diary	In The Field.	03/01/1919	05/01/1919
War Diary	Nameche Area	06/01/1919	28/01/1919
War Diary	In The Field.	30/01/1919	30/01/1919
Miscellaneous	Cover for Documents. Nature of Enclosures.		
War Diary	Samson, Belgium.	03/02/1919	04/02/1919
War Diary	Germany.	05/02/1919	26/02/1919
War Diary	Namur	02/02/1919	02/02/1919
War Diary	Ramesdorf, Germany.	03/02/1919	03/03/1919
Operation(al) Order(s)	War Diary. 161st (Yorks.) Brigade R.F.A. from. 1/3/19. to 31/3/19 Vol 39		
War Diary	Germany.	01/03/1919	30/03/1919
Heading	161st (Yorks.) Brigade. R.F.A. War Diary Covering Period From. 1st April. 1919. to. 30th April, 1919.		
War Diary	Beuel Germany.	01/04/1919	20/04/1919
War Diary	Beuel, Germany.	22/04/1919	30/04/1919
Miscellaneous	Cover for Documents. Nature of Enclosures.		
Heading	161st (Yorks.) Brigade. R.F.A. War Diary Covering Period. From. 1st May 1919. To 31st May 1919		

War Diary	Beuel. Germany.	01/05/1919	31/05/1919
Miscellaneous	Cover for Documents. Nature of Enclosures.		
War Diary	Beuel Germany.	01/06/1919	18/06/1919
War Diary	Nieder Pleis.	20/06/1919	25/06/1919
War Diary	Nieder Pleis. Germany.	27/06/1919	28/06/1919
War Diary	Beuel.	29/06/1919	30/06/1919
War Diary	Beuel. Germany.	01/07/1919	30/07/1919
War Diary	Beuel. Germany.	15/08/1919	15/08/1919
War Diary	Beuel Germany.	28/10/1919	28/10/1919
Heading	War Diary 161st Brigade RFA 25 Sept 1918-13 Aug 1919		
Heading	War Diary Army Book 152, Correspondence Book. (Field Service.) 161st Bde R.F.A.		
Operation(al) Order(s)			
Heading	War Diary 161st Brigade RFA 1 April 1917-24 Sept 1918		
Miscellaneous	War Diary April to Dec 1917 Feb to Dec 1918 Jan to Aug 1919 Army Book 152, Correspondence Book. (Field Service.) 161st Bde R.F.A.		
Miscellaneous	Opened on Closed On		
War Diary		01/04/1917	31/12/1917
Miscellaneous	Honours & Awards December 1917.	00/12/1917	00/12/1917
War Diary		01/01/1918	24/09/1918
Miscellaneous			

WPS 1 / 2380 (4)

WPS 5 / 2380 (4)

32ND DIVISION
DIVL ARTILLERY

161ST BDE R.F.A.
JAN 1916-DEC 1918
1919 OCT

32ND DIVISION
DIVL ARTILLERY

32nd Divisional Artillery.

161st BRIGADE R. F. A.

JANUARY 1 9 1 6

1

Dec 1918

Army Form C. 2118

WAR DIARY
INTELLIGENCE SUMMARY
(Erase heading not required.)

HQ 1/6, 1/18T (YORKS.) BDE, R.F.A.
FEB 2 1916

Place	Date	Hour	Summary of Events and Information	Remarks and references to Appendices
FOVANT. SOUTHAMPTON	30.12.15		The Whole Brigade (4 Batteries and Ammunition Column) marched out from FOVANT and entrained without mishap at SALISBURY. Arrived at SOUTHAMPTON and embarked. Entraining, detraining and embarkation arrangements worked without a hitch, and the Brigade was well up to time.	
HAVRE	31.12.15		Arrived at HAVRE and entrained for LONGEAUX same day.	
ARGOEUVRES	1.1.16.		Arrived at LONGEAUX where Bde detrained. Marches through AMIENS to ARGOEUVRES where Brigade was billeted that night.	
	2.1.16.		Brigade resting at ARGOEUVRES.	
	3.1.16.		Brigade resting at ARGOEUVRES.	
ST. GRATIEN	4.1.16.		Brigade marched to ST. GRATIEN and billeted there.	
ALBERT	5.1.16.		Headquarters proceeded to ALBERT. The right Section of each Battery went into action relieving 1st Lowland Brigade (T). Ammunition Column at BAIZIEUX.	
BAIZIEUX				
	6.1.16.		The left Sections of Batteries went into action relieving the left Sections of 1st Lowland Brigade (T). Wagon lines of "A","B" and "C" Batteries at BRESLE, "D" at WARLOY, Ammunition Column at BAIZIEUX.	
ALBERT	7.1.16.		All Batteries registering.	

WAR DIARY
or
INTELLIGENCE SUMMARY

(Erase heading not required.)

Instructions regarding War Diaries and Intelligence Summaries are contained in F.S. Regs., Part II. and the Staff Manual respectively. Title Pages will be prepared in manuscript.

HDQS. 161ST (YORKS.) BDE. R.F.A.
No. ....
FEB 2 1916

Place	Date	Hour	Summary of Events and Information	Remarks and references to Appendices
ALBERT	8.1.16.		Nothing of note to report.	Reference Map 57 D S.E. 4
	9.1.16.		Enemy trenches shelled at various points. The Hun seems sleepy.	
	10.1.16.		Quiet day.	
	11.1.16.		Machine Gun Emplacement demolished at X.7.6.96. (Ref 57 D S.E. 4). Amm. Col. moved to Warloy.	
	12.1.16.		"D" Battery and Howitzers shelled enemy trenches West of X.1.a. 68. Considerable damage was reported to have been done.	
	13.1.16.		"B" and "C" Batteries and Howitzers bombarded new enemy trench between X.7.6.95 and X.8.a.02, results appeared good.	
	14.1.16.		Quiet day.	
	15.1.16.		Quiet day.	
	16.1.16.		Quiet day.	
	17.1.16.		"B" and "D" Batteries cooperated with Howitzers and Trench mortars and bombarded Enemy Salient X.7.6.9092. "B" Battery dispersed working party at same point during the night. The salient was severely damaged.	
	18.1.16.		Quiet day.	
	19.1.16.		Trench along bottom of valley about R.31.d.90, was bombarded by "B" and "D" Batteries and Howitzers; results appeared to be good.	

WAR DIARY
INTELLIGENCE SUMMARY
(Erase heading not required.)

Instructions regarding War Diaries and Intelligence Summaries are contained in F.S. Regs., Part II. and the Staff Manual respectively. Title Pages will be prepared in manuscript.

Place	Date	Hour	Summary of Events and Information	Remarks and references to Appendices
ALBERT	20.1.16.		"B" Battery, 4.5 and 8" Howitzers and Trench Mortars had a combined 'Strafe' of enemy salient X 7 b 9092. Considerable damage was done. "B" Battery fires a few rounds during the night to disperse working parties at same point.	Reference Map 57 (D) SE 4
	21.1.16.		"B" Battery fired a few rounds into salient X 7 b 9092 during the day to prevent working parties repairing the damage done on the previous day.	
	22.1.16.		"A" "B" and "C" Batteries cooperated with Howitzers and Trench Mortars in firing two rounds gun fire into the village of Thiepval. Nothing worthy of record.	
	23.1.16.		One gun from "C" Battery was taken forward to East Edge of Authuille Wood in preparation for the morrow's shoot.	
	24.1.16.		One gun of "C" Battery under CAPT. CHISHOLM went into position near Wood Post. AUTHUILLE WOOD and made excellent practice on 'THE MOUND' X.7.B.9092. 43 H.E. shell were fired and open sights used at a range of 700x and 25 direct hits were obtained. "A" Battery, 164 Brigade were also firing and made 9 direct hits on 'THE MOUND'.	
	25.1.16		Nothing worthy of record.	
	26.1.16.			

WAR DIARY or INTELLIGENCE SUMMARY

Place	Date	Hour	Summary of Events and Information	Remarks and references to Appendices
ALBERT	27.1.16		Kaiser's Birthday. A shoot was arranged at suspected gun emplacement X.14.B.05.65, this was fixed originally for 11 a.m. (but by request of O.C. XI Border Regt. was put forward to 9 a.m. as it was thought that the Hun might be preparing an early surprise packet in celebration of the great day. In the evening a combined shoot took place at the village of THIEPVAL.	Reference Map 57 D SE 4.
	28.1.16		Rumours of gas attacks to the North are rife.	
	29.1.16 Snow		In the early morning shells and rumours filled the air. One section of "A" Battery was temporarily moved forward and proceeded to cut a lane about 4 yards wide in German wire about X.B.C.15. 152 rounds of Shrapnel, fuze 85, were used at a range of about 1750. Adjacent wire was considerably damaged.	
	30.1.16		Quiet day.	
	31.1.16		"B" Battery fired several rounds Shrapnel to cover Trench Mortar firing on wire in front of THE MOUND. About dusk enemy was heard heavily bombarding the front of the 18th Division immediately on our right.	

32nd Divisional Artillery.

161st BRIGADE R. F. A.

FEBRUARY 1 9 1 6

Army Form C. 2118

WAR DIARY
—or—
INTELLIGENCE SUMMARY
(Erase heading not required.)

Instructions regarding War Diaries and Intelligence Summaries are contained in F. S. Regs., Part II. and the Staff Manual respectively. Title Pages will be prepared in manuscript.

Place	Date	Hour	Summary of Events and Information	Remarks and references to Appendices
ALBERT	1.2.16.		In the morning "A" Battery in conjunction with "A" 164 Howitzer Battery fires successfully on suspected emplacement at X.14.B.0567, the shape of which was considerably altered. In the afternoon "A" Battery cut wire about X 8 a 15 and fired at intervals during the night in the hopes of catching the repairing party. Both these shoots took place from a forward position range about 1700.	All 10/2/16 to sheet 57 D SE 4.
	2.2.16		Quiet day.	
	3.2.16.		Quiet day.	
	4.2.16.		From 11 a.m. to 1 p.m. and from 3 p.m. to 5 p.m. slow bombardments were conducted against the enemy trenches and OVILLERS - LA - BOISSELLE. This shoot was under Corps arrangements and all Batteries were engaged. Wire was cut by "C" Battery at X 8 A 0500. Batteries were well pleased with the effect of their own fire.	
	5.2.16		In the morning a slow prolonged bombardment of OVILLERS and enemy trenches was carried out to support counter-attack of French at FRISE.	

WAR DIARY
INTELLIGENCE SUMMARY
(Erase heading not required.)

Place	Date	Hour	Summary of Events and Information	Remarks and references to Appendices
ALBERT	5.2.16		In the afternoon "C" Battery cut wire at X 8 a 0500. "C" Battery was unable to fire in the morning owing to faulty communications. The Hun began to retaliate rather more and the valley between B and C Battery seems to be marked down.	All references to Sheet 57 D S.E. 4
	6.2.16		Quiet day. A few rounds only were fired at a working party and for registration purposes. Building of O.Ps and improvement of others is in full swing.	
	7.2.16		Only a few rounds were fired at working parties and a ration party. On the night of the 7th-8th a flashlight was used by the Germans for the first time on this front. Its exact position was not located but a few rounds were fired in search of it. Its object was probably to prevent work being continued on a new Infantry Trench.	
	8.2.16		An advanced gun of B/161 engages Twin mounds at X 2 b 0 b, at a range of about 1600x. Covering fire was provided by B, C, and D batteries and 4.5" Howitzers were also turned onto the mound. Results were disappointing; after 26 rounds bore fires the advanced gun jammed after obtaining 12 direct hits. It was noticed that the	

WAR DIARY
or
INTELLIGENCE SUMMARY

(Erase heading not required.)

All references to Sheet 57D. S.E. 4.

Place	Date	Hour	Summary of Events and Information	Remarks and references to Appendices
ALBERT	8.2.16.		Delay fuze H.E. were of little use for a target of this description as they burst in air after hitting the mound and did no damage. Enemy artillery was rather more active, shells falling round A, B, and C Batteries in the course of the day.	
	9.2.16		AUTHUILLE WOOD was shelled intermittently all day and several casualties occurred in F2 Sector. The Infantry were persistent in asking for retaliation and a few rounds were fired at enemy trenches and farms from 5 to 6 p.m. Our front line trenches in X 7 B & D and especially the trenches around AUTHUILLE WOOD were violently bombarded and the whole Artillery group responded along trenches opposite with a slow rate of fire. Lacrimatory and gas shells were freely fired, and both A and C Battery were shelled. After 6 p.m all was quiet. It is believed that a small raiding party entered our trenches at the point of AUTHUILLE WOOD and that two green rockets were the signal for them to cross their parapet.	
	10.2.16		B and D Batteries took part in a Divisional shoot at 2, 3, and 4.30 p.m. Two rounds gunfire were fired on each occasion.	

WAR DIARY
or
INTELLIGENCE SUMMARY

(Erase heading not required.)

Instructions regarding War Diaries and Intelligence Summaries are contained in F.S. Regs., Part II. and the Staff Manual respectively. Title Pages will be prepared in manuscript.

Place	Date	Hour	Summary of Events and Information	Remarks and references to Appendices
ALBERT	11.7.16		Quiet day	
	12.7.16		Quiet day.	
	13.7.16		Enemy artillery fairly active. We retaliated with only a few rounds.	
	14.7.16		Quiet day.	
	15.7.16		From 3 to 3.30 p.m. two Batteries of the Brigade in conjunction with two Batteries 4.5" Howitzers carried out a combined shoot on trenches N.E. of AUTHUILLE WOOD. The shooting was fairly but no material damage was done. Enemy retaliated feebly.	
	16.7.16		In conjunction with 4.5" Howitzers a bombardment of OVILLERS was carried out from 4 to 4.50 p.m. with an interval of ten minutes at 4.20 p.m. One Battery of 83rd Brigade (18 Pr) also cooperated. The Howitzers also fired a few rounds at POZIERES and FARME DU MOUQUET	
	17.7.16		Quiet day.	
	18.7.16			
	19.7.16		Enemy shelled AUTHUILLE WOOD intermittently, our guns retaliated.	
	20.7.16			
	21.7.16		Quiet day.	

WAR DIARY
or
INTELLIGENCE SUMMARY

(Erase heading not required.)

Place	Date	Hour	Summary of Events and Information	Remarks and references to Appendices
ALBERT	22.2.16		B and C Batteries in conjunction with 4.5" Howitzers took part in several bursts of fire on enemy trenches. The programme was arranged by the Division.	
	23.2.16 24.2.16 25.2.16		Quiet days. Operations were hindered by snow and bad light.	
	26.2.16		A combined shoot took place between 6 and 7 p.m. at roads and tracks behind the enemy lines	
	27.2.16 28.2.16		Quiet days.	
	29.2.16		A combined shoot with Howitzers and Trench Mortars took place at 11 a.m. objective being the enemy front line trenches at points where they were of earth. It was hoped that the parapets had been weakened by the thaw and that considerable damage would be done. The shooting, especially of Trench Mortars was accurate but less damage to parapets than had been anticipated was done.	

A.S.Cotter
161 Brigade, R.F.A.

32nd Divisional Artillery.

161st BRIGADE R. F. A.

MARCH 1 9 1 6

WAR DIARY
or
INTELLIGENCE SUMMARY

(Erase heading not required.)

Army Form C. 2118

Instructions regarding War Diaries and Intelligence Summaries are contained in F. S. Regs., Part II. and the Staff Manual respectively. Title Pages will be prepared in manuscript.

Place	Date	Hour	Summary of Events and Information	Remarks and references to Appendices
In the Field	5/3/16		Enemy front line trenches effectively bombarded by Howitzers and 18 pdr Batteries. The whole country to north show working movements of infantry and work in new ground the batteries dangerous.	
	6/3/16		Enemy heavily bombarded our front line trenches. In response to infantry and for retaliation our batteries bombarded with effect the enemy front line. Bombardment lasted 3 hours	
	9/3/16		Combined shoot on enemy front line trench all batteries Division participating. Enemy trenches were seen to be considerably damaged. Many heavy shell falling in front line trench.	
	10/3/16		About 11pm enemy heavily bombarded C2 to D1 front line trench. All batteries employed in retaliation warning having been previously arranged in reference to strength of enemy bombardment of enemy front line trench. Strength was very heavy. No damage to our trenches by enemy being fired. Enemy used to shells very shortly after the battery position. No artillery casualties reported. The Enemy casualties were effectively repulsed by the Warwickshire Avenues	
			1 Officer killed	
			1 Officer wounded	
			2 " killed	
			13 " wounded	

1875 Wt. W593/826 1,000,000 4/15 J.B.C. & A. A.D.S.S./Forms/C. 2118.

Army Form C. 2118

WAR DIARY
or
INTELLIGENCE SUMMARY

(Erase heading not required.)

Instructions regarding War Diaries and Intelligence Summaries are contained in F. S. Regs., Part II. and the Staff Manual respectively. Title Pages will be prepared in manuscript.

Place	Date	Hour	Summary of Events and Information	Remarks and references to Appendices
In the Field	14/3/16		Enemy Howitzer battery heavily bombarded C/161 Hows battery the casualties being a gunner's arm. 96 to 100 18.5cm shells were fired forcing one C/161 to remove to new position	
	17/3/16		A continued bombardment C161B on heavy front line & communication trenches was carried out with fair results	
	24/3/16		After Tilman wounded while acting in hearing officer in El outer	

A. S. Coly LT.-COL.
CMDG. 161ST (YORKS.) BDE...

1875 Wt. W593/826 1,000,000 4/15 J.B.C. & A. A.D.S.S./Forms/C. 2118.

32nd Divisional Artillery.

161st BRIGADE R. F. A.

APRIL 1 9 1 6

WAR DIARY or INTELLIGENCE SUMMARY

Army Form C. 2118

161 R.F.A Vol 4

Place	Date	Hour	Summary of Events and Information	Remarks and references to Appendices
In the Field	3-4-16		The following Officers joined the Brigade and were attached as follows – 2/Lieut A.J. Davis to C/161 Bde R.F.A. 2/Lieut A.B. Heinemann R.F.A to C/161 Bde R.F.A	
"	8-4-16		2/Lieut H.L. Games R.F.A to D/161 Bde R.F.A. 2/Lieut A.J. Davis R.F.A posted to C/161 Bde R.F.A	
"	9-4-16		Lieut R Smith posted to 161 Brigade R.F.A and attached to A. Battery	
"	10-4-16		2/Lieut B. Bakewell posted to 161 Bde R.F.A, and attached to Ammn Column – 2/Lieut E Turnbull posted to 161 Bde R.F.A and attached to C Battery	
"	22-4-16		The Brigade took part in a bombardment on Thuylval Redoubts, when a successful raid was carried out by our Infantry. Lieut R. Crew was wounded when observing from O.P. in Pendrille Wood street and evacuated – 2/Lieut P.R. Lowater who was sent up to observe our Artillery fire from our French line trenches was hit, went down to the Linn and evacuated	
"	29-4-16		2/Lieut E. Roberts attached to D. Battery 161 Bde R.F.A was posted to 155 Bde R.F.A	

*17411. who took 15 prisoners (the party largest in front) one was not located but our bombardment was so accurate that by now and over it was to great extinction.

O. S. Cato LT-COL.
CMDG. 161ST (YORKS.) BDE. R.F.A.

32nd Divisional Artillery.

161st BRIGADE R. F.A

MAY 1916

Army Form C. 2118

XXXX Vol 5

WAR DIARY
or
INTELLIGENCE SUMMARY
(Erase heading not required.)

Instructions regarding War Diaries and Intelligence Summaries are contained in F.S. Regs., Part II. and the Staff Manual respectively. Title Pages will be prepared in manuscript.

HQRS. 161ST (YORKS.) BDE R.F.A.
No.
JUN 2 1916

Place	Date	Hour	Summary of Events and Information	Remarks and references to Appendices
In the Field	5-5-16		2/Lieut E. Bueller posted to Head Quarters as O.O. from C Battery 161 Bde R F A	
"	6-5-16		A reece was carried out at Pilckem by the German on the German front line trenches. Our Artillery bombarded the Enemy's front trenches and then lifted their fire, for the infantry to enter. Five prisoners was brought back and many reported killed. Many reported Enemies or Brigade on Artillery was inflicted as being particularly severe.	
"	7-5-16		Lieut R. Crews & 2/Lieut R R Hunt struck off Strength of Brigade	
"	8-5-16		At 10.0 p.m. the Enemy opened Heavy bombardment on our trenches in "An Crock" Sub Sector, during which a raid was carried out on trenches held by the Devons. One Officer killed & 25 men reported missing. Lieut L.W. Fortune attached to 161 Bde R F A) posted to 161 Bde and attached to A Battery	
"	10-5-16		Group handed over to Colonel Allcard, and Hend Quarters changed with 164 Bde R F A	
"	11-5-16		Colonel Cotton takes over C.R.A. and changes his Quarters to Linkes (General Tyler proceeds on leave)	
"	13-5-16		2/Lieut Roberts R F A posted from 155" Bde R F A to D/Battery 161 Bde R F A	

Army Form C. 2118

WAR DIARY
or
INTELLIGENCE SUMMARY
(Erase heading not required.)

Instructions regarding War Diaries and Intelligence Summaries are contained in F. S. Regs., Part II. and the Staff Manual respectively. Title Pages will be prepared in manuscript.

Place	Date	Hour	Summary of Events and Information	Remarks and references to Appendices
In the Field	15.5.16		Lieut C Dickson R.A.M.C transferred to 90th Field Ambulance. Lieut F. Cant R.A.M.C transferred from 90th Field Ambulance	
"	24.5.16		Colonel Cotton assumes his Command	
"	25.5.16		2/Lieut G. M. Taylor died of "Action" when on daily return of Trenches	
"	26.5.16		Captain H Cottee O/C D Battery 161 Bde R.F.A to B Battery 164 Bde R.F.A on reorganisation of 18 Howitzer Batteries	
			2/Lieut B. Groves from D/161 to B/164 as for above	
			2/Lieut E. Roberts ditto	
			2/Lieut J. Betley ditto	
			2/Lieut H. Jones ditto	
			B Battery under the command of Captain Roan-Watkins joined the Brigade in place of Captain Cottee's Battery.	

A. S. Cotton Lt-Col.
CMDG. 161ST (YORKS.) BDE. R.F.A.

32nd Divn. Arty.

Headquarters

161st BRIGADE R. F. A.

J U N E

1 9 1 6.

WAR DIARY or INTELLIGENCE SUMMARY

Army Form C. 2118

161 R FA Vol 6

Place	Date	Hour	Summary of Events and Information	Remarks and references to Appendices
In the Field	3.6.16		The wagon lines of A, C & D Batteries were inspected G.O.C. Division and were afterwards reviewed in front of them.	
"	5-6-16		A successful raid was carried out at 11.0 p.m. on the Enemy's trenches just north of the Sabisch. A party of four Officers & 80 men from the 11th Borders entered the Enemy's trenches and returned with 13 prisoners - 5 others gave trouble when on the way over, so were dealt with on the spot. Unfortunately Scout Prowse who was in command of the party was killed - At 11.0 p.m. an artillery and Trench Mortar bombardment on the German trenches, a fuze being made at 11.15 to allow our Infantry to see their line was being lifted for them to enter. The wire hung from trench to trench, the infantry report that the artillery fire was excellent, and that the T.M's succeeded in cutting the wire. The infantry raiding party had completely wrecked the trenches reached. Congratulations were afterwards received from both the Army & Corps Commanders for the very excellent work carried out by our Artillery. A belt of wire was found by an Infantry patrol close to the Enemy's parapet which had not been cut by the T.M's, this however was successfully dealt with by a Bangalore Torpedo.	
"	6-6-16		Very wet & cold. Operations quiet	
"	8-6-16		A Tactical Exercise was carried out at 6.30 a.m. on the Belmont Bangers training ground - Three objectives were given to the Infantry to be taken representing an advance of about two miles, these being carried out by a schedule of time taking in all two hours & forty minutes. Smoke was used to screen the attack made against the first and fourth objectives, and Stokes T.M's opened - The artillery barrage was admirably worked, it being represented by the Cavalry canopy and flags, they moving forward in front of the Infantry, and showing the lifts of our guns.	
"	10.6.16		A Divisional horse show was held at Guelin consisting of 10 classes, all of which was well filled in spite of the bad weather. The two most interesting classes were perhaps those	

WAR DIARY
or
INTELLIGENCE SUMMARY
(Erase heading not required.)

Army Form C. 2118

Instructions regarding War Diaries and Intelligence Summaries are contained in F. S. Regs., Part II. and the Staff Manual respectively. Title Pages will be prepared in manuscript.

Place	Date	Hour	Summary of Events and Information	Remarks and references to Appendices
In the Field	10-6-16		An Artillery Lunch and Officers Charges & the former A/18r saw the Artillery 18th and 19th on entailed team of Stalls ready built board out on Charges heir is recommended that to look the judges some time to make up their minds, the French Liaison was a popular entry. For General Tylis own bay gelding. C Battery 184 Brigade merged from American Ice 2 to 4 per winter	
"	12-6-16		Another Tactical Exercise was held in the Belmont Training ground, when the same scheme was carried out as on the 8-6-16. Colonel Middleton commander the 245 Brigade R.F.A. found our head quarters	
"	13-6-16		Captain Gordon Adjutant of the 245th Brigade R.F.A. and some of his staff came to our head quarters. 2/Lieut Currey joined Head Quarters as Liaison Officer. An Officer from Each of our Batteries visited the 4th Squadron Flying Corps Hounsworth, and was instructed in registering targets in conjunction with Aeroplanes, on the musketry range	
"	21-6-16		2/Lieut Currey moved up into Battle Head Quarters	
"	23-6-16		Colonel Cotton Colonel Middleton and Captain Gordon Left Albert and moved into Battle Head Quarters — the wagon lines went up to Cardes new and horses being in the open. Being British storm sprung up at 4 p.m. when Lightning struck the cable of the Hounsworth Balloon and it's five, fortunately, the two occupants were able to descend to safely using the parachute.	

WAR DIARY
or
INTELLIGENCE SUMMARY

(Erase heading not required.)

Army Form C. 2118

Instructions regarding War Diaries and Intelligence Summaries are contained in F. S. Regs., Part II. and the Staff Manual respectively. Title Pages will be prepared in manuscript.

Place	Date	Hour	Summary of Events and Information	Remarks and references to Appendices
In Field	24-6-16		"V" Day. Wire cutting started at 6.A.M and continued all day. The enemy replying very little.	
"	25-6-16		"V" Day. Own artillery continued the 18 pounders along there wire well. Also the heavies started their bombardment which continued all day. The enemy replied vigorously on our front line & communicating trenches	
"	26-6-16		"W" Day. During the night became more active generally. At 3.20 p.m. gas was successfully discharged by us, the enemy replying at once with a heavy barrage on no-man's-land. Wire cutting continued by the 18 pounders, and all the artillery used to destroy enemy's trenches and strong points.	
"	27-6-16		"X" Day. Our bombardment and wire cutting continued, the enemy's reply at times being heavy, their artillery also again paid annual attention to our front line and communication trenches, also registering their own front line. At 7-10 a.m. smoke was discharged by no volunteers. At ---- hours heavy fire from the Boches. It was observed that the enemy always the night had some men manner repairs to wire	
"	28-6-16		"Y" Day. Owing to our artillery having successfully cut the wire, fire was not so active, this change was also obtained in the enemy's reply. At 3.20 p.m. smoke was again discharged by us, the enemy putting up at once a heavy barrage. At night the 2.D.R.D.Y.L.I. sent out a patrol with a view to view the state of enemy's wire, in most places where it had been dealt with by the 18 pounders it was completely cut and	

1875 Wt. W593/826 1,000,000 4/15 J.B.C. & A. A.D.S.S./Forms/C. 2118.

WAR DIARY
or
INTELLIGENCE SUMMARY

(Erase heading not required.)

Army Form C. 2118

Place	Date	Hour	Summary of Events and Information	Remarks and references to Appendices
2/1th Field	28-6-16		Quite a revival to our Infantry	
"	29-6-16		"Z" Day hoped for 48 hours, the Bombardment however being continued	
"	30-6-16		The Bombardment Continued. Congratulatory message was received from G.O.C. 97 Infantry Brigade on the manner in which the 7 trench Mortar Brigade) demolished the enemy's strong points [?] 1 & 2 &c	

A.S. Esta
Lt Col
Cmdg 7/6/ Fd RFA

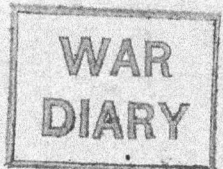

Headquarters,

161st BRIGADE, R.F.A.

(32nd Division)

J U L Y

1 9 1 6

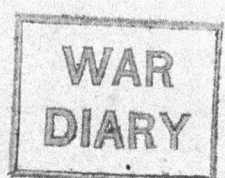

Headquarters,

161st BRIGADE, R.F.A.

(32nd Division)

J U L Y

1 9 1 6

Army Form C. 2118

WAR DIARY
or
INTELLIGENCE SUMMARY
(Erase heading not required.)

Instructions regarding War Diaries and Intelligence Summaries are contained in F.S. Regs., Part II. and the Staff Manual respectively. Title Pages will be prepared in manuscript.

Place	Date	Hour	Summary of Events and Information	Remarks and references to Appendices
In the Field.	1-7-16		After 7 days bombardment of the German trenches, and the wire being successfully cut, July 1st was chosen as the day to launch our attack on the front covered by the Fourth Army. The 32nd Division - consisting of 96th, 97th and 14th Brigades, and commanded by Br-Gen. Compton, 14th, Br-Gen. Jardine 97th and Br-Gen. Yatman 96th - were to attack the German front from the North of THIEPVAL to the Valley opposite the NAB. Four objectives were to be taken in two hours and 40 minutes, the last being the German second line, in front of which were situated the strong points GOAT REDOUBT and FARM MOUQUET.

Previous to Zero time - which was 7-30 a.m. - all our Artillery, except the Heavies, carried out an intense bombardment of an hour on the enemy's front line and communicating trenches.

From observation, and also the reports which the Infantry of 97th Brigade brought back, our Right Group of Artillery - commanded by Lieut-Col. A.S.Cotton, D.S.O. - had very successfully cut the wire; in fact, on no occasion did I hear that, our Infantry had been held up by it.

The Right Group, 32nd Divisional Artillery, consisted of 161st Brigade, R.F.A. complete, A/164 and B/164 and 245th W.R.,R.F.A.,T.F.,Bde. complete supported the attack of 97th Infantry Brigade. The 16th and 17th H.L.I. were told off to attack, with 2/K.O.Y.L.I. in support, and 11th Border Regiment in reserve - the reserve Battalion was to move up under cover of smoke across NO MAN'S LAND to the S. of LIEPSIG SALIENT, but owing to very heavy M.G. fire from the flank, could make no progress. Lieut-Col. P.W.MACHELL, C.M.G., D.S.O. was killed and every Officer of the Battalion either killed or wounded. Similarly on the left, 16th H.L.I. were held up, but 17th H.L.I. carried the point of the salient and established themselves firmly in LIEPSIG REDOUBT - their further advance was held up by M.G. fire, and, in spite of repeated efforts, no further progress could be made. The Artillery Barrage was laid down strictly to time, and owing to the thick smoke and dust, it was not until 8 a.m. that the O.C. was able to make out what was happening when 2 Batteries were clearly seen leaving the parapets and holding up with hostile M.G's and Infantry who could be clearly seen leaving the parapets and holding up the advance. Or these batteries opening fire, the enemy took cover, but M.G's on the left, i.e. enfilading the advance, could not be made out owing to lie of the ground and were unable to be dealt with.

96th Infantry Brigade on the left, opposite THIEPVAL, met with even less success and at no point were able to establish themselves in enemy's lines. | |

Army Form C. 2118

WAR DIARY
or
INTELLIGENCE SUMMARY
(Erase heading not required.)

Instructions regarding War Diaries and Intelligence Summaries are contained in F. S. Regs., Part II. and the Staff Manual respectively. Title Pages will be prepared in manuscript.

Place	Date	Hour	Summary of Events and Information	Remarks and references to Appendices
In the Field	2-7-16		At 5-30 a.m. a further attack was made on our front by the 14th Brigade, this being supported by our Artillery; they were, however, unable to advance and hold any further ground.	
"	3-7-16		The day was spent in consolidating our position on the Salient. The 2nd Battn. of the Manchester Regiment, who had been holding the salient since the 1st, being relieved by the Wilts. 2/Lieut. R.V.Corle, C/161, was wounded when at the advanced report dug-out.	
"	4-7-16		At 1 a.m. the enemy made a stubborn attack on the Salient. Owing to the excellent barrage put up by our Artillery, the Wilts had little difficulty in driving them back with heavy losses. A shell burst over Group Headquarters, causing eight casualties to men and killing two horses.	
"	5-7-16.		At 7 p.m. our Infantry holding the point of salient attacked the enemy's trenches on their right and left. The objective on the right was obtained, but on the left failed. Our Artillery, assisted by heavy shell fire which was lifted the moment the attack went forward.	
"	6-7-16.		At 12 midnight a further desparate attempt was made by the enemy to recover the salient trenches captured the previous day, but again our Artillery were at once ready with their barrage. The Infantry reported that had it not been for the prompt response of our Artillery, they could not have held the trenches. I would here add that from July 1st, practically all the messages from the Salient had come through our advance report dug-out, instituted by the Right Group Artillery (this report dug-out also supplied all information to the Infantry).	
"	7-7-16.		OVILLERS was taken by us but lost later in the day. At 9-30 a.m. an Aeroplane flying low was brought down close to the Right Group Headquarters, the two occupants being killed (4th Squadron). The accident was thought to be a direct hit from one of our own guns.	
"	8-7-16.		The outskirts of OVILLERS were re-taken by us. CONTALMAISON was taken and lost twice.	
"	9-7-16.		Our Artillery from 9-30 a.m. shelled the enemy's trenches all day with a view to preventing them reinforcing the attack we were making on our right. CONTALMAISON was reported to be in our hands in the evening.	

1875 Wt. W593/826 1,000,000 4/15 J.B.C. & A. A.D.S.S./Forms/C. 2118.

Army Form C. 2118

WAR DIARY
or
INTELLIGENCE SUMMARY
(Erase heading not required.)

Instructions regarding War Diaries and Intelligence Summaries are contained in F. S. Regs., Part II. and the Staff Manual respectively. Title Pages will be prepared in manuscript.

Place	Date	Hour	Summary of Events and Information	Remarks and references to Appendices
In the Field.	10-7-16.		CONTALMAISON again lost and re-taken by us. At 11-0 p.m. S.O.S. Signals were sent up from the Salient (6th West Yorks; 146 Brigade) Barrage "A" being at once put on by our Artillery. Previous to this our Infantry had in the early part of the night attacked the enemy's trenches joining us at the Salient.	
"	11-7-16.		The 7th West Yorks; relieved the 6th in the Salient. Lieut-Colonel A.S.Cotton, D.S.O. was wounded by a premature from our own guns when outside Headquarters. He left his command to Colonel Middleton, Lieut; & Adjutant S.P.Hannam was killed when in our forward trenches. The following report was received at 12-45 p.m. :- CONTALMAISON captured and 5 officers - including a Battalion Commander and 200 O.R. prisoners At MAMETZ WOOD we took 300 prisoners, including 13 Officers, 3 field guns and one large Howitzer. Heavy counter-attack on CONTALMAISON repulsed. At 11-0 p.m. the enemy attacked the salient, barrage "A" being called for from our Infantry.	
"	12-7-16.		At midnight a further attempt was made by the enemy to recover his lost trenches at the Salient. With the assistance of our Artillery the 7th West Yorks; were able to drive them back, inflicting heavy losses. Lieut; S.P.Hannam was buried at AUTHUILLE Cemetery.	
"	13-7-16.		Quiet day.	
"	14-7-16.		At 2-15 a.m. all our Artillery bombarded the enemy's trenches behind the salient and at 2-25 a.m. our Infantry attacked with a view to taking further trenches. The enemy were, however, met in force and prepared, so that desperate fighting took place. After taking about fifty yards of these trenches, our Infantry were compelled to retire. Time after time, however, our troops renewed the attack, but could not establish a footing.	
"	15-7-16.		At 3-55 a.m. S.O.S. Signals were reported from the salient, in reply to which our Artillery opened with a heavy barrage. It appears that the enemy attacked our trenches from the left and also NO MAN'S LAND, using Flammenwerfers, but met with such a hot reception from Stokes and M.G's, that they were compelled to retire with heavy losses. Our Batteries at CRUCIFIX CORNER were heavily shelled by gas shells and had to work the guns for hours in their helmets. Unfortunately, Lieut; Lupton of C/245 Bde.R.F.A. was killed.	

Army Form C. 2118

WAR DIARY
or
INTELLIGENCE SUMMARY
(Erase heading not required.)

Instructions regarding War Diaries and Intelligence Summaries are contained in F. S. Regs., Part II. and the Staff Manual respectively. Title Pages will be prepared in manuscript.

Place	Date	Hour	Summary of Events and Information	Remarks and references to Appendices
In the Field.	16-7-16.		At 12-0 a.m. our Artillery fire was called for by S.O.S. signals, and replied at once, A further attack having been made on the salient by the enemy. Lieut: P.Crow and Lieut: L.G.Firth joined 161 Bde. and were posted to "A" and "C" Batteries respectively. Again our Batteries at CRUCIFIX CORNER were shelled all night by gas shells and had to use their helmets.	
"	17-7-16.		At 2-0 a.m. the Gloucesters on our right attacked and captured the enemy's front line for two hundred yards, Our artillery supported the attack by shelling the trenches on their left and preventing reinforcements getting up.	
"	18-7-16.		At 2 p.m. our Brigade received orders to hand over to the 245th Brigade R.F.A.,T.F. and be out of action by 8-0 p.m.	
"	19-7-16.		At 6-0 a.m. the first Battery marched out of SENLIS, followed by the rest of the Brigade at quarter of an hour's interval. The road taken was through ACHEUX-WARLINS-ORVILLE and on to AUTHIEULE, where we halted for the night. An easy march of about 12 miles. Billets poor. Lieut-Colonel R.Fitzmaurice took command of the Brigade.	
"	20-7-16.		The Brigade left at 6-0 a.m. for FILLIEVRES via DOULLENS-FROHEN LE GRAND & BOFFLES. The march was about 18 miles through a fine country and the billets were very good.	
"	21-7-16.		At 9-0 a.m. we left FILLIEVRES for PETIT ANVIN via LINZEUX - BAUVOIS -and PUIREMONT. The march was about 13 miles and again through fine fertile country.	
"	22-7-16.		Next march was to LIERES. About the same distance as yesterday. Here the Brigade halted until the 29th.	
"	23-7-16.		Lieut-Colonel R.Fitzmaurice inspected the 4 Batteries in their lines.	
"	25-7-16.		The D.D.R. inspected the Brigade horses at 10-30 a.m. and Lieut-Col:R.Fitzmaurice left afterwards to take over C.R.A., 32nd Div.	
"	27-7-16.		Lieut-Colonel A.S.Cotton, D.S.O. returned to his command of 161st Brigade, R.F.A.	
"	29-7-16.		The Brigade left LIERES at MARIES LES MINES, where they went into billets.	

31-7-16.

O.S.Co. Lieut-Colonel,
Commanding 161st (Yorks.) Brigade, R.F.A.

32nd Divisional Artillery.

161st BRIGADE R. F. A.

AUGUST 1 9 1 6

Army Form C. 2118

WAR DIARY
INTELLIGENCE SUMMARY
(Erase heading not required.)

Instructions regarding War Diaries and Intelligence Summaries are contained in F.S. Regs., Part II. and the Staff Manual respectively. Title Pages will be prepared in manuscript.

Place	Date	Hour	Summary of Events and Information	Remarks and references to Appendices
In the Field.	1-8-16		The 161st Brigade R.F.A. was at MARLES-LES-MINES. "B" and "C" Batteries sent Officers forward to see the positions they were to occupy on the LA BASSÉE front.	
	2-8-16		Riding School for Officers commenced.	
	3-8-16		The Brigade left MARLES-LES-MINES at 7-0 a.m. for BEUVRY - about 9 miles. Sections of "B" "C" & "D" Batteries went up into action.	
	4-8-16		The remaining sections of "B" "C" & "D" Batteries went up into action.	
	5-8-16		Lieut-Col; R.Fitzmaurice came back to the Brigade.	
	7-8-16		BETHUNE was shelled by 15 inch gun and considerable damage done.	
	9-8-16		At 10-30 p.m. "D" Bty's wagon line was shelled, one horse being killed and 7 injured.	
	11-8-16		Lieut-Colonel R.Fitzmaurice left 161 Bde. and took over command of 156th Bde.R.F.A. & Right Group.	
	12-8-16		Church Service held in Wagon lines.	
	14-8-16		A Divisional Artillery School of Instruction was commenced by 161st Brigade R.F.A. - under Lieut-Colonel A.S.Cotton, D.S.O., 6 Officers and 12 N.C.O's being detailed to attend. Lieuts; Taylor & Bottomley from 155 Bde. Lieut;Buckley from 161 Bde. Lieut; Drury from 164 Bde. Lieut; Hastings from 168 Bde. and Lieut; Monk from 32nd D.A.C. The day's instruction started with Riding School at 7-0 a.m.; 9-30 Section Gun Drill; 11-0 Stables ; 2-30 p.m. a Lecture by Lieut-Col; Cotton; stables 4-30; Section Gun Drill 6-0 and Stables at 7-30 p.m. was the basis of the day's work.	
	17-8-16		G.O.C. Division inspected Wagon Lines.	
	18-8-16		The Officers & N.C.O's attending Artillery School visited the 32nd Infantry School at FERNAY.	
	20-8-16		Lieut; L.C.Firth posted from C/161 to D/164. 2/Lieut; J.Felthess attached to D/161 posted to D/161.	

Army Form C. 2118

WAR DIARY or INTELLIGENCE SUMMARY

(Erase heading not required.)

Instructions regarding War Diaries and Intelligence Summaries are contained in F. S. Regs., Part II. and the Staff Manual respectively. Title Pages will be prepared in manuscript.

Place	Date	Hour	Summary of Events and Information	Remarks and references to Appendices
In the Field	23-8-16.		The Artillery School broke up, the Officers and N.C.O's returning to their units. 2/Lieut; A.A.Drury posted to D/161 from D/164.	
	25-8-16.		Right Section of "A" Bty; 161 went up into action at PHILOSOPHE.	
	26-8-16.		Left Section of "A" Bty; 161 ditto	
	27-8-16.		Lieut-Colonel A.E.Cotton,D.S.O. proceeded on 10 days leave.	
	28-8-16.		Capt; Birkin A.V.C. posted to Base Veterinary Hospital.	
	28-8-16.		Capt; J.W.Richardson,A.V.C. attached 161 Bde. vice Capt; Birkin.	
	28-8-16.		Lieut; H.R.Cameron, A/161, posted to 1st Division (iii Corps)	
	28-8-16.		Lieut; G.E.Samuels, D/161 ditto.	
	31-8-16.		Captain F.W.Carr, R.A.M.C., M.O.i/c 161 Bde.R.F.A. returned off leave.	

In the Field,
31st August 1916.

Adjutant for Lieut-Colonel,
Commanding, 161st (Yorks.) Brigade, R.F.A.

WAR DIARY

INTELLIGENCE SUMMARY

(*Erase heading not required.*)

Army Form C. 2118

Instructions regarding War Diaries and Intelligence Summaries are contained in F.S. Regs., Part II. and the Staff Manual respectively. Title Pages will be prepared in manuscript.

Place	Date	Hour	Summary of Events and Information	Remarks and references to Appendices
In the Field.	6-9-16		Lieut-Col; A.S.Cotton, D.S.O., returned off leave. Major W. Weatherbe, B/161, left Headquarters and rejoined B/161. C/161 has one N.C.O. killed and 1 N.C.O. and 1 man wounded.	
"	7-9-16		Lieut-Col; A.S.Cotton, D.S.O. left 161 Bde. Hqrs. to take command of the HULLUCH Group Artillery.	
"	10-9-16		A successful raid was carried out by the 16th Lancashire Fusiliers, on the enemy's front line South of AUCHY. Previous to our Infantry going over, the enemy's trenches were heavily shelled by our Artillery, the fire being lifted for them to enter. The enemy appeared to have been holding this line very thinly, as apart from 4 prisoners brought back, only a few wounded were found. The Infantry report the Artillery fire was excellent, and that they were able to move behind it with confidence.	
	17-9-16		Lieut-Colonel A.S.Cotton, D.S.O. handed over command of the HULLUCH Group Artillery to the 3rd Division. The 18 Pdr. Batteries of the 161 Bde. were made into 6 gun batteries, A/161 receiving a section from A/164, B/161 receiving a section from A/164 and C/161 receiving a section from C/168. 2/Lieut; T.F.J.I. Massey posted from A/164 to A/161 Bde. R.F.A. 2/Lieut; G.W.Ward, posted from A/164 to B/161 Bde. R.F.A. 2/Lieut; S.G.Drappes-Lomax posted from Hqrs. 168 to C/161 Bde. R.F.A. 2/Lieut; C.H.Morton posted from C/168 to C/161 Bde. R.F.A. 2/Lieut; C.L.W.Haffenden, D/161 – attached to D/164 – rejoined D/161.	
	18-9-16		Right Section of D/161 went into new position at East edge of PHILOSOPHE.	
	20-9-16		Left Section of D/161 went into new position at PHILOSOPHE.	
	21-9-16		Left Section of B/161 went into new position at GARONS-DU-RUTOUI.	
	22-9-16		Right Section of B/161 went into new position at GARONS-DU-RUTOUI. & 1 gun of A/164	
	23-9-16		Lieut-Colonel A.S.Cotton, D.S.O., and Hqrs. 161 Bde. R.F.A. went back to PHILOSOPHE to take over HULLUCH Group Artillery.	

30th September 1916

Lieut-Colonel,
Commanding 161st (Yorks;) Brigade, R.F.A.

32nd Divisional Artillery.

161st BRIGADE R. F. A.

OCTOBER 1 9 1 6

Army Form C. 2118

WAR DIARY
or
INTELLIGENCE SUMMARY

(Erase heading not required.)

(1).

Instructions regarding War Diaries and Intelligence Summaries are contained in F. S. Regs., Part II. and the Staff Manual respectively. Title Pages will be prepared in manuscript.

Place	Date	Hour	Summary of Events and Information	Remarks and references to Appendices
	4/10/16		The Brigade which was covering the HULLUCH front and formed part of the 8th Divisional Artillery with Colonel Cotton D.S.O. as Group Commander, handed over to the 8th Division and returned to their Wagon Lines at BETHUNE.	
	7/10/16		Colonel Cotton D.S.O. moved up to LOCON and took over C.R.A. of the 5th Composite Artillery from 31st Division, Captain Ellis acting as his Brigade Major and Lieut Creasy as his Staff Captain. Batteries of the Brigade forming part of three Groups, Right, Centre and Left under the command of Captain Pease-Watkins, Major Weatherbe and Major Hill and covering GIVINCHY, FESTUBERT and FERME DE BOIS Fronts.	
	10/10/16		Lieut Creasy who was suffering from fever went on leave, 2/Lieut Filtness of D Battery taking his place, Captain Cant, Medical Officer, left the Brigade owing to sickness.	
	14/10/16		Captain Gibson, Medical Officer, joined the Brigade.	
	15/10/16		Colonel Cotton D.S.O. Handed over C.R.A. of the 5th Composite to the 5th Divisional Artillery and returned to his Head Quarters at BETHUNE, his Staff also going. The Batteries of the Brigade were also relieved on the night of the 15/16 with the exception of a Section of each Battery which came out on the night of the 16/17. 2/Lieut Lomax took over the duties of Adjutant until the return of Lieut Creasy who was granted an extension of three weeks leave on medical grounds.	
	16/10/16		The Brigade marched from the Wagon Lines at BETHUNE to MARLES LES MINES and occupied the billets as they were in on the march up. Units moved off in the following order Head Quarters 11.30a.m. A Battery 3p.m. B Battery 3.10p.m. C Battery 3.20p.m. and D Battery 3.30p.m. The march was an easy one of about 7 miles and the day fine. Sections left behind in action joined the Brigade in the evening.	
	17/10/16		The Brigade left MARLES LES MINES for HOUVELIN via BRUAY and HOUDAIN in the following order Head Quarters 9.30a.m. B Battery 9.40a.m. C Battery 9.50a.m. and D Battery 10a.m. and A Battery 10.10a.m. Billetting parties with the Orderly Officer left at 8 o'clock. Guides for the Supply Wagons were at Cross Roads DUVAL at 2 o'clock.	
	18/10/16		The Brigade marched from HOUVELIN to ETREE WAMIN via BAILLEUL-AUX-CONAILLES, MAIZIERES, and	

Army Form C. 2118

WAR DIARY
or
INTELLIGENCE SUMMARY

(2)

(Erase heading not required.)

Instructions regarding War Diaries and Intelligence Summaries are contained in F.S. Regs., Part II. and the Staff Manual respectively. Title Pages will be prepared in manuscript.

Place	Date	Hour	Summary of Events and Information	Remarks and references to Appendices
	19/10/16		MAGNICOURT Units moving off in the following order Head Quarters 9.25a.m. C Battery 9.30a.m. D Battery 9.40a.m. A Battery 9.50a.m. and B Battery 10a.m. Billetting Parties leaving at 8a.m. and Guides for Supply Wagons being at Cross Roads at N in MAGNICOURT at 3p.m. The distance from HOUVELIN to ETREE WAMIN is almost 13 miles and the road undulating.	
	20/10/16		The Brigade left ETREE WAMIN for ORVILLE via BEAUUDRICOURT, IVERGNY, and HALLOY moving off as follows Head Quarters at 11.25a.m. D Battery 11.30a.m. A Battery 11.40a.m. B Battery 11.50a.m. C Battery 12 noon. The Brigade to be formed up in column of rout 500 yards between Batteries the head of the column to be halted at Cross Roads 1 mile N.E. of IVERGNY Church at 12 noon. Billetting Parties left at 9a.m. and Guids for Supply Wagons to be ORVILLE CHURCH at 4p.m. The Brigade marched under the command of Major Weatherbe as Colonel Cotton D.S.O. went forward in the early morning to see G.O.C. 51st Division at BERTRAMCOURT. Upon arriving at ORVILLE cit was found that the Infantry had not moved out and that no lines or billets were vacant, arrangements were, however, ultimately made for the Brigade to come into AMPLIERS. Day very wet and march of 12 miles on hilly road. Th	
			The Brigade marched from AMPLIERS to LOUVENCOURT via SARTON and MARIEUX in the following order A Battery 7.30a.m. B Battery 7.35a.m. C Battery 7.40a.m. D Battery 7.45a.m. and Head Quarters afterwards. Colonel Cotton D.S.O. and O.C. Batteries with an Officer proceeded at 8.30a.m. In Motor Bus to chosen positions for Batteries. Billetting Parties left at 9a.m. Batteries then halted outside LOUVENCOURT until instructions were sent back to them regarding Billets. Guides to meet, Supply Wagons 200 Yards S.W. of L in LOUVENCOURT No Billets procurable for men so shelters and tents were served out to Batteries. In the evening the Batteries moved up into action in the open at ENGLEBELMER AND CAME UNDER THE 51st Division. Head Quarters remained at LOUVENCOURT until the following day.	
	21/10/16		Colonel Cotton D.S.O. and his Staff moved up into action at ENGLEBELMER joining 51st Division and under No. 2 Group. Captain Gibson, Medical Officer, remaining at LOUVENCOURT.	
	22/10/16		2/Lieut Hook joined the Brigade and was attached to B Battery.	
	26/10/16		The 153rd Infantry Brigade supported by our Artillery carried out a successful raid at 5.30p.m. A Party 6th Black Watch and afterwards one from the 7th Gordon Highlanders took part in the	

WAR DIARY
or
INTELLIGENCE SUMMARY

(Erase heading not required.)

Instructions regarding War Diaries and Intelligence Summaries are contained in F. S. Regs., Part II. and the Staff Manual respectively. Title Pages will be prepared in manuscript.

(3).

Place	Date	Hour	Summary of Events and Information	Remarks and references to Appendices
	28/10/16		raid, the Black Watch was unable to enter the enemy's trenches owing to machine gun fire and lost their Officer when in the act of trying to lift a wire entanglement. The Gordon Highlanders were however more successful and returned with one prisoner, four other Germans were taken but gave so much difficulty in no man's land that they had to be shot. Four men of C Battery were wounded by a premature when returning from the trenches.	

1st November 1916.

2/lieut.
for Lieut Colonel
Commanding 161 Brigade R.F.A.

32nd Divisional Artillery.

161st BRIGADE R. F. A.

NOVEMBER 1 9 1 6

Army Form C. 2118

WAR DIARY
—or—
INTELLIGENCE SUMMARY
(Erase heading not required.)

Instructions regarding War Diaries and Intelligence Summaries are contained in F.S. Regs., Part II. and the Staff Manual respectively. Title Pages will be prepared in manuscript.

Place	Date	Hour	Summary of Events and Information	Remarks and references to Appendices
In the Field	1/11/16	4.30am	Captain R.P. Ellis A/161, was wounded by a premature from an 18 Pdr battery when walking up to the trenches. Lieut H. Maxwell, A/161, fortunately was with Capt Ellis and rendered excellent assistance.	
"	4/11/16		The Brigade commenced to set up in the right of our Sector.	
"	7/11/16		Lieut-Col J.G. Gaston D.S.O. proceeds to Guremount and inspected Brigade Wagon Lines. The weather had been very bad and as the men were all in the open the conditions were anything but good. They however, with one or two exceptional days no complaints. At 5.45 p.m. a raid was attempted by the 9th Royal Scots. The attack was made in three waves, the first lot of 30 creeping close up to the enemy's wire to give two time. As soon as the barrage lifted they made a rush for the front line, but were so impeded by the state of the ground that it was impossible to rush them and give in cordingue exposed to enemy machine gun fire. The following waves came up but met with no mire success. The Artillery Barrage was excellent, and the Infantry were able to approach within 25 yards of it.	
"	9/11/16		Lieut + N/I. Lebleay returned off leave, and 2/Lt R. Stroppul came returned to 6/11/16.	
"	10/11/16		"X" Day - Our Batteries were busy destroying enemy wire. Captain Gibson Ran. B left the Brigade for the 5 Army Infantry School and Lieut. McCormick joined since Capt. Gibson	
"	12/11/16		"Y" Day - More Cutting and Registering of guns. Lieut McCormick Ran. 6 came up to G.B.	
"	13/11/16		"Z" Day - Zero time was 5.45 am. At the morning very dark with a thick fog. Our Artillery Gune covered the 5th Division, whose objective was Yellow Line this being	

WAR DIARY or INTELLIGENCE SUMMARY

Place	Date	Hour	Summary of Events and Information	Remarks and references to Appendices
	13/11/16 (continued)		an advance of about 1000 yards, which included the capture of BEAUMONT HAMEL and the Y Ravine. The reports which came in during the day as to our success were very meagre and also most conflicting. It was therefore impossible to gather where our Infantry had got to. The enemy's front line appeared to give little trouble, as a very few Blue & many prisoners were captured on Nov: 13th. Y section of BEAUMONT was not captured until the night, and it was not until it was later on the day the Y Ravine & so-called Station Road (about 100 yards north of the Ravine) that our troops working from the direction of our objective and was captured during the day. Our troops working from the direction of Hamel on the captures of about 300 prisoners. "A" Coy on our left is supposed to be holding the objective on 999 Road. Had not been reported, but the Infantry were holding FRANKFORT TRENCH and had captured about 1000 prisoners.

On our right, the 63rd Division appears to have been most successful and captured Men at Beauce bridge, going in about 1200 prisoners. The attack by the 2nd Division on our left was also carried on well towards the HOW Line, and resulted in the capture of many prisoners. The Infantry supported by the 99th so to most land in the preparation of the Artillery fire, the barrage appearing to have been so accurate that it was possible for them to keep quite close to it. V. W. The Divisional Comdr L.s.t of Bn of position, 99th asked for volunteers to accompany him in the firing line in the afternoon. Four men from each Bty were taken, with 2 Officers, in addition to a party of men from the Canadian Y. M.s, and an officer. The above |

Instructions regarding War Diaries and Intelligence Summaries are contained in F.S. Regs., Part II. and the Staff Manual respectively. Title Pages will be prepared in manuscript.

Army Form C. 2118

Sheet 3

WAR DIARY
or
INTELLIGENCE SUMMARY
(Erase heading not required.)

Place	Date	Hour	Summary of Events and Information	Remarks and references to Appendices
	13/11/16 (Continued)		troops proceeded direct to No man's land and Y. Ravine and during the night succeeded in bringing in 2 Officers and 21 men. Much difficulty was experienced in carrying in the wounded owing to the ground being so cut up by shell fire, a heavy barrage in rear.	
	14/11/16		The day was spent in consolidating our positions. The following notice appeared in S.R.O's:— "The Army Commander wishes to thank all ranks of Fifth Army which accomplished yesterday's great victory. When troops have now withstood the fatigues of prolonged effort to which they were subjected to the utmost of their endurance, and have been more fortunate than others, but this is always the case in war and is to be expected. Great results have been achieved, and the Army Commander is confident in the 'Troops under his command'. His confidence has been more than justified." From information received, it appeared that new infantry were not holding FRANKFORT and MUNICH Trench.	
	15/11/16		Owing to Heavy Artillery fire, our infantry had to retire to behind the MUNICH Trench. Lieut A. Drury 8/R.I., was shot dead by a sniper when got on parapet. Lineup Copt. F.H. O'Neill Martin D/161 in the evening the Captain brought in Lieut Drury's body.	
	16/11/16		Lieut A. Drury, 9/161, was buried at ENGLEBELMER Military Cemetery by Father A. Grant.	
	17/11/16		2 Brigades of the 32nd Division (the 94th & 97th) came up into position and were in the open all night. It was bitterly cold with snow falling & a sharp frost.	
	18/11/16		A.C. and these two Brigades were just forward to attack. The objective being to capture the MUNICH and FRANKFORT trenches. Enemy when can be gathered blackened that the enemy were found to be holding their lines very strongly and that in the place of heavy	

WAR DIARY
INTELLIGENCE SUMMARY

(Erase heading not required.)

Army Form C. 2118

Shell H

Place	Date	Hour	Summary of Events and Information	Remarks and references to Appendices
	18/6 (continued)		Machine Gun & Rifle fire was now unable to capture their first objective. Some of the portions, and the K.O.Y.L.I. however, succeeded in entering their objective but not being supported on their flanks were unable to take advantage of it and had by nightfall to fall back. The K.O.Y.L.I were cut off in FRANKFORT trench and RIDEAU REDOUBT. A., B., and C. Batteries moved their guns up forward into a position S. of AUCHONVILLERS. In the evening Capt. & R. Christie & 2/Lieut A. Harkness & 1/101 with a party of men from each Battery went out to assist the wounded and did good work. A party from the 161 Brigade R.F.A. (under Lieut E.H. Morton, B/161) arrived but too up to the troops in BEAUMONT HAMEL.	
	20/6		The 10th Infantry Brigade relieved the 91st Infantry Brigade who were holding the line.	
	21/6		Information was brought in by a boy of the K.O.Y.L.I. that a party of his men — about 100 strong — with 9 Officers, were still holding out in FRANKFORT trench. Every effort was made to get them out. An attempt was made in the evening to bring food & water was, unfortunately very bad. He filled every bottle he had, but the allied army to the enemy being so alert, at the break through.	
	22/6		Lieut J. Hope R. Creasy M.C. was wounded close to the O.P. in Carlisle Street. Lieut E. Humble A/161 joined HQ as Adjutant. In the afternoon an attempt was made to rescue the men of the K.O.Y.L.I. from FRANKFORT trench. Under a heavy barrage the 10 Lancs crept close up to MUNICH trench and succeeded in throwing it, which the barrage lifted they were however unable to get as far as FRANKFORT trench as they were met by heavy machine gun fire	

Sheet 5   War Diary

22/11 — Orders were received for our Brigade to relieve the 245 Brigade, who were in action S. of COLINCAMPS.

23/11 — A section of each of our Batteries - with the exception of 21/161 who remained in their old position - moved up to take over from the 245 Brigade, the 124th Brigade relieving us.

24/11 — The remaining sections of our Batteries moved up into the positions previously occupied by the 245 Brigade.

25/11 — H.Q. & staff of our Brigade handed over to the I.H. Brigade and moved up into a position S. of COLINCAMPS.

28/11 — 2/Lieut G.D. Hogben joined the Brigade from A 32 T.M.B.Ty & was posted to A/161.

In the Field,
1st December 1916.

[signature]
Lieut Colonel,
Comdg 161st (York) Brigade R.F.A.

32nd Divisional Artillery.

161st BRIGADE R. F. A.

DECEMBER 1 9 1 6

Army Form C. 2118

WAR DIARY
INTELLIGENCE SUMMARY

(Erase heading not required.)

Instructions regarding War Diaries and Intelligence Summaries are contained in F. S. Regs, Part II. and the Staff Manual respectively. Title Pages will be prepared in manuscript.

Place	Date	Hour	Summary of Events and Information	Remarks and references to Appendices
In the Field	4-12-16		The 32nd Divisional Artillery was relieved by 37th Divisional Artillery. 18 Pdr.Batteries of 161st (Yorks;) Bde.R.F.A. were relieved by 126th Brigade R.F.A. and D/161 (How.) by D/123 Bde. R.F.A.	
	5-12-16.		Headquarters and Batteries of 161st Bde.R.F.A. moved down to Wagon Lines at LOUVENCOURT, where they stayed the night. The 161st (Yorks;) Bde.R.F.A. complete - under the command of Lieut-Colonel A.S.Cotton,D.S.O marched to ST: OUEN via VAUCHELLES - MARIEUX - SARTON - AUTHIEULE - DOULLENS - CANDAS - MONTRELET - FIEFFES - CANAPLES - HALLOY - BERTAUCOURT - ST: OUEN, stating the night of the 5/6th at AUTHIEULE and arriving at ST: OUEN on the 6th.	
	7-12-16.		Lieut; & Adjutant R.L.CREASY, M.C., transferred to England (wounded) and struck off strength accordingly with effect from this date.	
	14-12-16.		Capt; H.L.McCORMICK, R.A.M.C., Medical Officer i/c 161st Bde.R.F.A. proceeded on 14 days leave, he being relieved by Capt; C. DICKSON, R.A.M.C., Medical Adviser to Town Major,ST: OUEN.	
	16-12-16.		2/Lieut; E.H.BINDLOSS, Orderly Officer, proceeded on 10 days leave.	
	17-12-16.		Brigade Headquarters complete, together with a working party consisting of 4 Officers and 120 O.R. from 161st Bde.R.F.A. and also a party of 2 Officers and 78 O.R. from 32nd D.A.C. - the whole under the command of Lieut-Colonel A. S. COTTON, D.S.O., proceeded to MARIEUX via BERTAUCOURT - HALLOY - HAVERNAS - NAOURS - VERT GALAND FARM - BEAUQUESNE - MARIEUX, for the purpose of constructing Horse Standings and Huts on the MARIEUX-RAINCHEVAL and MARIEUX-SARTON Roads respectively. The remainder of 161st Brigade R.F.A. remained at ST: OUEN and came under the orders of Officer Commanding 168th Brigade R.F.A.	
	18-12-16.		Lieut-Colonel A.S.COTTON, D.S.O., proceeded on 10 days leave, the command of the working party at MARIEUX passing to Major W. Weatherbe, B/161. Holiday.	
	25-12-16.		Half Holiday. Major W. Weatherbe proceeded on 10 days leave, he being relieved by Major E.H.P.PEASE-WATKIN, D/161.	
	26-12-16.		Lieut-Colonel A.S.COTTON, D.S.O., returned off leave.	
	28-12-16.		Advance parties - consisting of 1 Officer and 20 O.R. from each 18 Pdr.Bty. and 1 Officer and 15 O.R. from the Howitzer Bty; of the Brigade - left MARIEUX to get positions near AUCHONVILLERS ready for occupation by Batteries of the Brigade on the 3rd January 1917.	
	30-12-16.		Remainder of working party at MARIEUX (with exceptin of 161st Bde. H.Q. complete which remained at MARIEUX) proceeded to rejoin respective units of Bde. and D.A.C. at ST: OUEN. Lieut; P.C.Hunt (a/Adjutant) proceeded on 10 days leave and Lieut; C.W.Ward, B/161 took over duties of a/Adjutant.	

A.S.Cotton LT.-COL.
C.O. 161ST (YORKS.) BDE, R.F.A.

SECRET

161st (Yorks.) Brigade R.F.A.

War Diary

— for —

Period 1st to 31st January 1917.

Army Form C. 2118

WAR DIARY
INTELLIGENCE SUMMARY
(Erase heading not required.)

Instructions regarding War Diaries and Intelligence Summaries are contained in F.S. Regs., Part II. and the Staff Manual respectively. Title Pages will be prepared in manuscript.

Place	Date	Hour	Summary of Events and Information	Remarks and references to Appendices
In the Field.	3-1-17.		The Brigade - under command of Lieut-Col: A.S.Cotton, D.S.O. - left SARTON as follows:- H.Q. 9-10 a.m., "B" Bty. 9-15 a.m., "C" Bty. 9-30 a.m., "D" Bty. 9-45 a.m. and "A" Bty. at 10 a.m. and proceeded to ACHEUX WOOD, less Brigade Headquarters which proceeded to MAILLY MAILLET.	
"	4-1-17.		One section of each of the Batteries went into action in positions South of AUCHONVILLERS.	
"	5-1-17.		Remaining sections went into action.	
"	6-1-17.		2/Lieut; G.D.Hogben, A/161, admitted into hospital. - cut hand.	
"	7-1-17.		Major E.H.P.Pease-Watkin, D/161, awarded D.S.O.	
"	10-1-17.		2/Lieut; W.G.Launder posted to A/161.	
"	11-1-17		At 6-0 a.m. the 91st Infantry Brigade made a successful attack upon MUNICH TRENCH, capturing their objectives, Batteries of the 161st Brigade R.F.A. supporting the operation by a heavy barrage from Q.6.a.6.3. to Q.6.c.6.5. which lifted in front of the Infantry to Q.6.b.1.5. to Q.6.c.9.6. 2/Lieut; H.W.TILMAN, C/161, went forward to the captured position to lay a telephone line and was wounded. He, however, continued with his work until communications were established. For this service he was awarded the M.C.	
	11-1-17.		2/Lieut; E.B.Hastings posted to C/161.	
	12-1-17.		2/Lieut; C.H.MORMON, C/161, evacuated to England sick, and struck off strength.	
	16-1-17.		The 32nd Divisional Artillery relieved the 3rd Divisional Artillery. One section of each Battery went into action in positions North of MAILLY MAILLET on the night of 16/17, remaining sections on night of 17/18th.	
	17-1-17.		The 161st Brigade R.F.A. relieved the 42nd Brigade R.F.A. and formed "A" Group of 32nd Divisional Artillery. Headquarters of Brigade established at COURCELLES. No; L/12326 Sgt. Dunlop W.H., A/161; L/12177 Gnr Cammish T.R., C/161 and L/13669 Gnr Moody F. D/161 awarded Military Medal.	
	17-1-17.		No; 32508 B.S.M. Harvey C.W.; B/161 awarded Military Cross. 2/Lieutenants N.G.Gorrod, F.S.Harper, R.T.Peacop and R.H.Thompson posted to A. B. C. & D. Batteries respectively.	
	5-1-17.		2/Lieut; H.W.Tilman, C/161, Evacuated to England wounded and struck off strength.	
	18-1-17.		D/161 received a section from C/155, completing them to a 6-gun Battery.	
	20-1-17.		2/Lieut; E.S.Robinson posted to D/161, from C/155.	
	22-1-17.		Brigade Headquarters moved from COURCELLES to MAILLY MAILLET. Section received by D/161 from C/155 came into action.	
	25-1-17		Lieut-Colonel A.S.Cotton, D.S.O., granted one month's leave to England; Major J.F.K.Lockhart A/161, taking over command of the Brigade during his absence.	

Army Form C. 2118

WAR DIARY
or
INTELLIGENCE SUMMARY

(Erase heading not required.)

Instructions regarding War Diaries and Intelligence Summaries are contained in F. S. Regs., Part II. and the Staff Manual respectively. Title Pages will be prepared in manuscript.

Place	Date	Hour	Summary of Events and Information	Remarks and references to Appendices
In the Field	27-1-17.		At 5-0 p.m. the enemy commenced to shell MAILLY MAILLET. A quantity of shell fell near Brigade Headquarters. 1 Dvr. was wounded and 2 horses killed and 2 horses wounded. Shelling ceased at about 5-30 p.m.	

J.D.M............
Major,
Commanding 161st (Yorks;) Brigade, R.F.A.

161st (Yorks.) Brigade R.F.A.
(32nd Divisional Artillery)

War Diary

Covering period 1st February to 28th February 1917.

Vol 14

Army Form C. 2118

WAR DIARY
INTELLIGENCE SUMMARY
(Erase heading not required.)

Instructions regarding War Diaries and Intelligence Summaries are contained in F. S. Regs., Part II. and the Staff Manual respectively. Title Pages will be prepared in manuscript.

Place	Date	Hour	Summary of Events and Information	Remarks and references to Appendices
In the Field.	1-2-17.		Attached Officers and men of 310th Bde.R.F.A. (62nd Division) left Headquarters and Batteries to take over from the 7th Divisional Artillery on our right.	
	4-2-17.		Our Infantry during the night pushed forward and established strong points close up to TEN TREE ALLEY, meeting with little opposition.	
	5-2-17.		On our right the 63rd Division successfully attacked PUISIEUX Trench from the ANCRE to ARTILLERY ALLEY, capturing the whole of their objectives.	
	6-2-17.		The enemy counter-attacked strongly the trench captured the previous day, but was caught in the Artillery barrage and compelled to retire with heavy losses.	
	7-2-17.		Lieut-Col; F.E.L.Barker took over command of the Brigade, Major J.F.K.Lockhart returning to his Battery, A/161.	
	8-2-17.		During the night, 2/Lieut; W.E.Mead, A/161, went forward to TIKE POST to register our barrage for the attack on TEN TREE ALLEY. Communications were most difficult, as a line had to be laid back to GOUGH POST and then carried via WAGON ROAD to BURN WORK and on to the Batteries. By means of a trabsmitting station in WAGON ROAD, messages were sent through and registration carried out successfully.	
	10-2-17.		The 7th Division improved their position North of the ANCRE by the capture of MIRAUMONT ALLEY. At 8-30 a.m. the 97th Infantry Brigade attacked TEN TREE ALLEY from WAGON ROAD to point R 1 a 8.6. The attack proved most successful and only slight losses were incurred, the Infantry capturing the whole of the ground with the exception of two small posts, 3 Officers and 219 O.R. being taken prisoners. The barrage put up by this Brigade and registered from TIKE POST on the 8th was highly praised by the Infantry.	
	12-2-17.		The enemy counter-attacked the captured positions in TEN TREE ALLEY at 7-30 p.m. He was, however, easily driven back by our Artillery and Machine Guns.	
	13-2-17.		At, 7-30 a.m. the 97th Infantry Brigade attacked the two posts still held by the enemy in TEN TREE ALLEY, the attack being supported by a heavy barrage by our Artillery, which was carefully registered from a forward post the previous day. Our Infantry appeared to have been met by heavy Machine Gun Fire and were compelled to retire, followed up by the enemy, as at 8-45 a.m. "S.O.S" Signals were sent up by our Infantry. During the whole of	

1875 Wt. W593/826 1,000,000 4/15 J.B.C. & A. A.D.S.S./Forms/C. 2118.

Army Form C. 2118

WAR DIARY
—or—
INTELLIGENCE SUMMARY
(Erase heading not required.)

Instructions regarding War Diaries and Intelligence Summaries are contained in F.S. Regs., Part II. and the Staff Manual respectively. Title Pages will be prepared in manuscript.

Place	Date	Hour	Summary of Events and Information	Remarks and references to Appendices
In the Field.	13-2-17. (Contd;)		the day our Artillery was kept very active, the enemy replying very vigourously. At 6-30 p.m. and 8-0 p.m. "S.O.S" Signals were again sent up by the Infantry (97th Bde.), and our Artillery opened fire. These operations necessitated an expenditure of 5,000 rounds by the 161st Bde.R.F.A. The 311th Bde.R.F.A. (62nd Division) came into the Left Group, 32nd Divnl;Arty;, prior to taking over our front.	
	14-2-17.		The 161st Brigade R.F.A. came out of action and proceeded to Wagon lines at BUS.	
	17-2-17.		The 161st Bde.R.F.A. left Wagon lines at BUS at 9-0 a.m. "A" Bty; leading, remaining	
	19-2-17.		Batteries following at 10 minutes interval apart, and proceeded to HAVERNAS, a distance of 18 miles. Lieut-Col; F.E.L.Barker did not march with the Brigade, but handed over command to Major J.F.K.Lockhart, A/161.	
	22-2-17.		Brigade marched out of HAVERNAS at 9-50 a.m. in the following order for ARGOEUVRES:- Headquarters 9-50, B/161 10 a.m., C/161 10-15 a.m., D/161 -10-30 a.m., and A/161 at 10-45 a.m. Route:- FIEFFLERS and VAUX. Roads very poor in places.	
	23-2-17.		At 10 a.m. the Brigade left ARGOEUVRES for DEMUIN via AMIENS, Headquarters leading, followed by "C" "D" "A" and "B" Batteries respectively. The march was about 18 miles on very heavy roads Two Officers per Battery and 2 officers from Headquarters went forward by motor to see the new Battery positions and returned to DEMUIN at night.	
	24-2-17.		Brigade left DEMUIN for LE QUESNEL at 10 a.m. In the following order - Hdqrs., followed by "D" "A" "B" "C" Batteries respectively. The march was an easy one of 8 miles on good roads. The Batteries took over covered horse lines and huts from the French, whom we were relieving. Headquarters were established at BEAUFORT.	
	25-2-17		The Brigade moved up into action after dark, occupying the gun pits out of which the French had moved their guns into the open. Brigade Headquarters were established at FOLIES.	
	26-2-17		Registration was commenced by the Batteries of 161st Bde.R.F.A., the French Batteries still remaining in action alongside the Bties of 161st Bde R.FA.	
	27-2-17.		Registration was completed and at 7-0 p.m. the French pulled out of action and handed over to the 161st Bde.R.F.A. Lieut-Colonel A.S.Cotton, D.S.O., returned from England.	

Commanding 161st (Yorks;) Brigade R.F.A.
Lieut-Colonel,

32nd Divn

161ST (Yorks;) Brigade R.F.A.

War Diary
for period
1st to 31st March 1917 inclusive.

Army Form C. 2118

WAR DIARY
or
INTELLIGENCE SUMMARY
(Erase heading not required.)

161st (Yorks;) Brigade R.F.A.

Instructions regarding War Diaries and Intelligence Summaries are contained in F.S. Regs., Part II. and the Staff Manual respectively. Title Pages will be prepared in manuscript.

Place	Date	Hour	Summary of Events and Information	Remarks and references to Appendices
In the Field.	1-3-17		The 14th Infantry Brigade who occupied Headquarters at LE QUESNOY were heavily shelled and an ammunition Dump close by blown up. At 6-45 p.m. S.O.S. Signals were sent up on our left and Batteries opened fire at once on their protective barrage. It appears, however, that the Signals were sent up by the enemy. "C" Battery from their forward position cut wire. Wire cutting could not be continued as observation poor.	
	2-3-17		Under cover of a heavy bombardment the enemy attacked our trenches in the ROUVROY Sector. At two points they momentarily obtained a footing. We captured one wounded prisoner of 69th R.I.R.	
	3-3-17		The following telegrams were published for information of all ranks:- (1) FROM His Majesty The King to Field-Marshall Sir Douglas Haig:- 1-3-17 - I wish to express my admiration of the splendid work of all ranks under your command in forcing the enemy by a steady and persistent pressure to quit carefully prepared & strongly fortified positions. These successes are a fitting sequel to the fine achievements of my Army last year in the Battle of the SOMME, and reflect great credit on those responsible for drawing up the plans of this campaign. (2) FROM Field Marshall Sir Douglas Haig to His Majesty The King:- 2-3-17 - On behalf of all ranks I beg leave to express our very respectful thanks for your Majesty's most gracious message of approval of what has been recently accomplished by the Forces under my command, as a sequel to the SOMME Battle. It is a deep satisfaction to those responsible for drawing up the plans of the Campaign to know that their work has been so generously commended by your Gracious Majesty.	12-3-17. 2/Lieut: A.W.Denniston rejoined the Brigade and was posted to "A" Battery.
	4-3-17.		"B" & "C" Batteries wire-cutting. During the night our Artillery fired on enemy approaches and communication trenches.	
	6-3-17.		Batteries commenced work on their forward positions.	
	12-3-17		A French raiding party on our right entered the enemy's first and support line trenches, which were found unoccupied. The 161st Brigade R.F.A. supported the attack with 12, 18-Pdrs and 6, 4.5" Hows.	
	13-3-17.		Wire-cutting by "B" & "C" Batteries. The camouflage O.P. erected by 161 Bde. R.F.A. in June 1916 on the SOMME was taken down and conveyed to FOLIES by motor lorry.	
	15-3-17.		A section of "A", "B" & "C" Batteries moved up to forward positions.	

Army Form C. 2118

Instructions regarding War Diaries and Intelligence
Summaries are contained in F. S. Regs., Part II.
and the Staff Manual respectively. Title Pages
will be prepared in manuscript.

WAR DIARY
INTELLIGENCE SUMMARY
(Erase heading not required.)

161st Bde.R.F.A.

Place	Date	Hour	Summary of Events and Information	Remarks and references to Appendices
In the Field.	16-3-17		The remaining sections of "A", "B" & "C" Batteries moved up to forward positions. Light being good, wire-cutting was continued in afternoon. Enemy very quiet, and it appears by the almost absence of his Artillery fire that the persistent reports of his preparation to retire must be correct.	
	17-3-17. 18-3-17.		Every indication of the enemy retiring, which was confirmed later in the day. × See orders and The 161st Bde.R.F.A. advanced from FOLIES to LIANCOURT, a distance of about 6 miles beyond our old front line. The point of assembly was "No man's land" where the LE QUESNOY-PARVILLIERS road crosses it. Here a considerable halt had to be made, as the bridges over the German trenches were not completed until 2 p.m. The going was very bad up to PARVILLERS, but after this point the roads were in excellent order through FRESNOY and on to the main ROYE-PERONNE Rd. where Batteries halted in the open for the night. In places a little delay was caused by barricades and broken glass. Material left behind by the enemy was practically nil and his retirement must have been carried out very orderly. Headquarters, which were to be established for the night at LIANCOURT, were not so fortunate, as all roads leading to the village from the South and East were temporarily blocked by trenches across them or trip wire, with the result that our transport could not get through until 11 p.m. In the morning Lieut-Col: A.S.Cotton,D.S.O. accompanied by the Brigade Major & Orderly Officer, 32nd Divisional Artillery, went forward to reconnoitre for our advance. There were no signs of the enemy.	
	19-3-17.		Brigade Headquarters left LIANCOURT at 10-30 a.m. and picked up the Batteries where they had halted for the night. We then advanced through ETALON, HERLY and on to NESLE, where Headquarters remained for the night, Batteries pushing on to QUIQUERY and covered our Infantry who were holding the line VOYENNES and South West of OFFOY. Practically all villages passed through had been destroyed by the enemy and in places were still burning. Fruit trees everywhere were cut down and bridges blown up. The roads, however, were in excellent order and the enemy appears to have carried out a very orderly retreat, as no material was left behind. In NESLE the few remaining inhabitants, who were either the very old or young children, were unable to express their delight at seeing our troops, and produced flags which had been carefully hidden away for so long.	
	20-3-17.		Headquarters moved up to BACQUENCOURT in the morning and occupied house out of which French Cavalry were moving. Batteries went forward to the Mill on the main HAM Road about 1000 yds N.E. of Headquarters. "C" Bty remained in reserve at BILLANCOURT. The same destruction of villages was to be found everywhere, and the railways made useless by removing the rails and sleepers and blowing up bridges.	
	21-3-17.		In the afternoon, Headquarters moved to LANGUEVOISIN and occupied the Chateau, Batteries going forward and occupied a position close to OFFOY Station covering our Infantry, who had /pushed	

1875 Wt. W593/826 1,000,000 4/15 J.B.C. & A. A.D.S.S./Forms/C. 2118.

Army Form C. 2118

WAR DIARY

161st Bde. R.F.A.

(3)

INTELLIGENCE SUMMARY

(Erase heading not required.)

Place	Date	Hour	Summary of Events and Information	Remarks and references to Appendices
In the Field.	21-3-17 (Contd).		pushed/ on, to a line MATIGNY - TOULLE Roads on our right.	
	22-3-17.		"B", "C" & "D" Batteries moved back to the previously occupied positions at the Mill on the HAM Road, covering the line the 96th Infantry Brigade were holding, VOYENNES-OFFOY, with advance posts at MATIGNY-TOULLE. "A" Battery remained in action at OFFOY Station. Capt; H.L.McCormick R.A.M.C. left Headquarters and was attached to "C" Battery.	
	23-3-17.		Telephone Communication was established between Headquarters and all Batteries and also with the two Liaison Officers. An O.P. was also chosen N.W. of TOULLE and connected up with "A" Bty. All Battery horses were sent back to FOLIES except 20 per Battery, which remained with the guns.	
	24-3-17. 25-3-17.		Lieut; R.L.CREASY, M.C. arrived at Wagon Lines. 2/Lieut; W.F.MEAD, A/161, was awarded the Military Cross. On the night of 8th February 1917, when the Brigade was in action on the BEAUMONT HAMEL front, he wentforward to TIKE POST, and in the early morning of the following day registered the Brigade barrage for the capture of TEN TREE ALLEY.	
	26-3-17.		Lieut; R.L.CREASY M.C. arrived at Headquarters. Lieut-Colonel A.S.COTTON, D.S.O. with his Battery Commanders went forward and reconnoitred positions at FORESTE. 2/Lieut; T. Campbell joined the Brigade and was attached to "C" Battery.	
	28-3-17.		Bde. Headquarters advanced to AUROIR and Batteries came up to FORESTE during the night, covering the 97th Infantry Brigade who had outposts holding a line ETRAILLERS-ROUPY. Wagon Lines were established at DOUILLY.	
	29-3-17.		2/Lieut; E.S.ROBINSON, D/161 and 2/Lieut; E.B.HASTINGS, C/161, were slightly wounded when with a working party at VAUX, and admitted into hospital.	
	30-3-17.		"A" & "C" Batteries moved up into action at VAUX and "B" and "D" Batteries at FLEUQUERES.	
	17.3.17		at 7 am The Bde. put a barrage on N & ROYE-AMIENS Road to Coor an attack by 62 French Divn on our Right. North Trench forced to the wire front - Scharnelleup & R.F. pushed forward into Sanskrit Suptin & Patrols GRANLIERS OYES. Tank Gallois moved forward & came into action in No Mans land covering Infy attacking DARNULLERS. DAMERY	

A. J. Colton Lt.-Col.

CMDG. 161st (YORKS.) BDE. R.F.A

161st (Yorks.) Brigade R.F.A.

War Diary

— for period —
1st to 30th April 1917.

Instructions regarding War Diaries and Intelligence Summaries are contained in F. S. Regs., Part II. and the Staff Manual respectively. Title Pages will be prepared in manuscript.

WAR DIARY

~~or~~

~~INTELLIGENCE SUMMARY~~

(Erase heading not required.)

Army Form C. 2118

Place	Date	Hour	Summary of Events and Information	Remarks and references to Appendices
In the Field.	1-4-17.		In the early morning the 97th Infantry Brigade attacked and captured the Village of SAVY with the 11th Border Regt and 17th H.L.I. Artillery support to this operation was given by the 159th, 161st and 168th Brigades R.F.A., consisting of a heavy barrage on the Village lifting to the far side as our Infantry advanced. From information received, as well as the number of enemy's dead lying out in the open, it appears that they suffered heavy losses when retiring from the Village. The 161st Brigade R.F.A. sent forward an Officer with the 17th H.L.I. who kept in communication with the Brigade sending back the progress of the enemy. Later in the day the 96th Infantry Brigade went through the 97th and captured SAVY WOOD, under cover of a creeping barrage from Artillery. They, however, failed to occupy point 138 their final objective, where fighting went on throughout the night. At 10-0 p.m. the 161st Brigade R.F.A. moved their Headquarters from CHATEAU DE POMMERY to SAVY Village, and during the night the Batteries moved forward and came into action at 2-0 a.m. South of the Village, opening fire at 5-0 a.m. in support of attack of 14th Infantry Brigade.	
	2-4-17.		The 14th Infantry Brigade came up during the night of 1st, and at 5-0 a.m. sent forward the 2nd Manchester Regt; and 16th H.L.I., their objectives being to capture the Villages of HOLNON, SELENCY and FRANCILLY. Support to these operations was given by the 3 Brigades of Artillery and consisted of a creeping barrage lifting as the Infantry advanced. Little resistance appears to have been given by the enemy, the three villages falling into our hands without heavy losses, point 138 also being taken by two Companies of the Dorsets Regt. East of FRANCILLY a German Field Gun Battery 77 cm was captured by the 2nd Manchester Regt; the enemy refusing to surrender and fighting the guns until the detachments were shot down. With a view to recapturing these guns, the enemy counter attacked at this point forcing our Infantry to retire a few hundred yards and leaving the guns in the open. The enemy was, however, unsuccessful, as the position we held commanded the guns and made it impossible for the enemy to approach the Battery. In the evening an attempt was made by the 161st Brigade R.F.A. to bring in the guns. At 8-30 p.m. a party of four men from each Battery - under Lieut: C.W.WARD - were to man-handle the guns out of their pits ready for teams which were timed to arrive a few minutes later. It appears, however, that the enemy had a listening post close by, as our party was met with a heavy barrage as soon as they attempted to approach. It was throught advisable to withdrew until the following night.	

1875 Wt. W593/826 1,000,000 4/15 J.B.C. & A. A.D.S.S./Forms/C. 2118.

Army Form C. 2118

WAR DIARY
INTELLIGENCE SUMMARY
(Erase heading not required.)

Instructions regarding War Diaries and Intelligence Summaries are contained in F. S. Regs., Part II. and the Staff Manual respectively. Title Pages will be prepared in manuscript.

Place	Date	Hour	Summary of Events and Information	Remarks and references to Appendices
In the Field.	3-4-17.		Under Major LUMSDEN, D.S.O. and Lieut. C.W. WARD a further party from the 161st Brigade R.F.A. went out at 8-30 p.m. to bring in the guns. From the experience of the previous night it was thought advisable to approach the position from a different direction and that a covering party from the Infantry was also necessary. In spite of heavy shelling, the party pushed on and reached the guns, which were pulled out of the pits and ready for the teams (under Lieut. R. C. TRAFFES-TOMKIN M.C.) to hook in and away as soon as possible. In this wayfour of the guns had been successfully removed and got back. Just as No. 5 gun was being withdrawn a large party of the enemy appeared over the crest, and breaking through the covering party rushed the position, forcing our men to abandon the gun half out and the ore not yet removed from its pit. Desperate fighting took place in the dark, and the enemy after destroying the breech block of No. 6 gun, was forced to retire with heavy losses. Both guns were then withdrawn.	
	4-4-17.		Battery Commanders went forward during the day to reconnoitre positions for their Batteries to move forward into during the night. Unfortunately the day was most unfavourable, visibility being impossible owing to snow falling heavily all day. Positions chosen were "A" two sections in HOLNON to the N.E. of the village, with the remaining section about half a mile away to the South. "B" and "C" Batteries Cross Roads South East of HOLNON and "D" Bty. on the Railway where it cuts the HOLNON-SAVY Road. During the night, Batteries moved forward into these positions and came into action the following morning.	
	6-4-17.		Headquarters of the 161st Bde. R.F.A. — which were still in SAVY — moved up to and occupied dug-outs in the Railway Embankment close to "D" Bty. "A" Bty when registering was heavily shelled, losing 1 Officer and 5 men. It was, therefore, thought advisable for the two sections to move back, where they had more cover, as soon as possible. "B" Bty had two telephonists wounded.	
	7-4-17.		In the evening Lieut-Col. A.S. Cotton D.S.O. with a party of men from Headquarters assisted in the man-handling of "A" Battery guns through the Village of HOLNON to where the detached section were in action. The withdrawal was accomplished without loss in spite of hostile fire. 2/Lieuts; E. COKE, R.G. JOHNSON and W.R. GOODMAN joined from 3.C. Reserve Bde. R.F.A. and were posted to "A" "B" and "C" Batteries respectively.	
	8-4-17.		Lieut; E.F.J. SHINER and 2/Lieut; M. JONES were posted from 32nd D.A.C. to 161 Bde. and were posted to D/161.	
	12-4-17.		a/Captain P. CROW, Commanding A/151 was wounded.	
	13-4-17.		An Officers patrol went out at night to see if FAYET was occupied, and returned with the loss of one Officer, finding the enemy holding the village.	

Army Form C. 2118

WAR DIARY
INTELLIGENCE SUMMARY
(Erase heading not required.)

Instructions regarding War Diaries and Intelligence Summaries are contained in F. S. Regs., Part II. and the Staff Manual respectively. Title Pages will be prepared in manuscript.

Place	Date	Hour	Summary of Events and Information	Remarks and references to Appendices
In the Field.	14-4-17.		At 4-30 a.m. the 97th Infantry Brigade - using the 16th H.L.I. and K.O.Y.L.I. who were in the line - attacked and captured the village of FAYET without much resistance. Lieut-Colonel A.S.COTTON, D.S.O. who was in Liaison with the Infantry had at his disposal three Brigades of Artillery, the 159, 161 and 168th Brigades, and had arranged a barrage in support of the attack consisting of 12 lifts, which had previously been most carefully registered. The success of the Infantry in capturing this village with such small losses, appears to be greatly due to the excellent support of the Artillery, as it held a point of great advantage. After capturing the village the Infantry pushed on to their second objective, which included the taking of CEPY FARM, and also the Sunken Road running North from it. After hard fighting the Farm fell into our hands, but the troops on the left were not so fortunate as heavy enfilade M.G. fire caught them from the TWIN COPSE. It was therefore thought advisable to retire our Infantry and deal with the Woods first. In the afternoon after all the Artillery had bombarded the TWIN COPSE for half an hour, the 11th Border Regt advanced and occupied the two Woods. It appears that the enemy had been greatly shaken by our bombardment, as little or no resistance was offered, the enemy either running away on the far side or coming out to meet our men with their hands up. During the day's operation 379 prisoners fell into our hands including 4 Officers. All reports received from the Infantry speak with the highest praise of the support given by the Artillery, and say the fire was so accurate and prompt that it gave the troops the greatest confidence. At night the 161st Bde. R.F.A. moved forward, the Batteries coming into action in the following positions:- "A" Bty N.E. of HOLNON, "B" Bty in the Village of SELENCY, "C" Bty in the Valley West of BOIS DES ROSES and "D" Bty in HOLNON Village, and opening fire in the morning of the 15th.	
	16-4-17.		"C" Battery who were occupying a very forward position had one Gunner killed and two wounded and a gun knocked out of action.	
	17-4-17.		2/Lieut: R.A.WYRLEY-BIRCH joined the Bde. from the Royal Military Academy, Woolwich, and was posted to A/161.	
	20-4-17.		The 32nd Divisional Infantry were relieved by the 61st Division and went out of the line to rest. C.R.A., 32nd Division handed over to C.R.A. 61st Division and went back to VOYENNES. The 161st Brigade R.F.A. covered the 184th Infantry Brigade. "C" Battery wired themselves in, with two M.G. posted close to Battery in case of an enemy attack.	

Army Form C. 2118

WAR DIARY
or
INTELLIGENCE SUMMARY

(Erase heading not required.)

(4)

Instructions regarding War Diaries and Intelligence
Summaries are contained in F. S. Regs., Part II.
and the Staff Manual respectively. Title Pages
will be prepared in manuscript.

Place	Date	Hour	Summary of Events and Information	Remarks and references to Appendices
In the Field.	23-4-17.		Lieut: C.W. WARD, B/161, awarded Military Cross, the work described. D/161 sent a section forward to the BOIS DE ROSES for Counter-Battery work	
	26-4-17.		At 7-20 p.m. "S.O.S" Signals were sent up by one of our posts close to GEPY FARM. In response the Artillery opened fire at once on their protective barrage. The enemy, it appears, tried to rush a post but were held up by the barrage and M.G. fire, having to retire with considerable loss and leaving six prisoners in our hands. Later in the evening a report was received from our Liaison Officer that the enemy were in GEPY FARM. The Artillery were therefore turned on it from 10 to 10-10 p.m. and then lifted for the Infantry to enter. No enemy, however, were found. The Infantry report that they were very pleased by the prompt support they received from the Artillery and the accuracy of the fire.	
	28-4-17.		At 4-20 a.m. a successful raid was carried out by a Company and two Platoons of the 4th Oxfords in the crater at N.31.a.0.6., enemy's trenches and CURANTE WOOD. Supported by an artillery barrage from the 161st and 160th Brigades R.F.A. the Infantry entered the Crater, where a machine gun was captured, the detachment and occupants shewing little fight and escaping capture by running away. At the same time a further party of our Infantry were working north and attacking CURANTE WOOD, where two more Machine Guns were captured. Here also the enemy left hurriedly and appears to have been quite taken by surprise at our flank attack. After completing the operations, our Infantry returned with two of the M.G's and one prisoners. Lieut; B.C. TRAPPES-LOMAX, M.C., C/161, was wounded at 9-30 p.m.	
	29-4-17.		At 9-30 p.m. 161st Bde.R.F.A. bombarded GEPY FARM for 10 minutes, after which a patrol was sent out by the Infantry and found it unoccupied. Later in the night our Infantry listening post reported that the enemy had sent out a party which were then occupying the Farm. Again the Artillery were called upon to shell it for 10 minutes, after which a further patrol was sent out, but returned not having found the enemy. a/Capt; P. CROW (Lieut;T.F.) R.F.A. on 7th, 8th & 9th April 1917 near HOLNON observed fire throughout the day in a most exposed part of our line within 250 yards of enemy under heavy shelling and M.G. fire; displayed the greatest gallantry and resolution and furnished most valuable reports as to work and movements of enemy throughout this period. For this work he has since been awarded the Military Cross.	

Lt. Col.
CMDG. 161ST (YORKS.) BDE. R.F.A.

1875 Wt. W593/826 1,000,000 4/15 J.B.C. & A. A.D.S.S./Forms/C. 2118.

161st (Yorks.) Brigade R.F.A.

War Diary

– for the period –
1st to 31st May 1917.

Army Form C. 2118.

WAR DIARY
or
INTELLIGENCE SUMMARY.
(Erase heading not required.)

Instructions regarding War Diaries and Intelligence Summaries are contained in F. S. Regs., Part II. and the Staff Manual respectively. Title pages will be prepared in manuscript.

Place	Date	Hour	Summary of Events and Information	Remarks and references to Appendices
In the Field.	2-5-17		The 184th Infantry Brigade – whom the 161st Brigade R.F.A. were covering – were relieved by the 183rd Infantry Brigade. C/161 Bde. R.F.A. moved a section back to the position previously occupied by B/168th Bde. R.F.A.	
	3-5-17		Night firing by A/161 on RIFLE PITS. Lt; a/Capt; P. CROW invalided to England (wounded) and struck off strength of Brigade.	
	4-5-17		C/161st Bde. R.F.A. withdrew to wagon line at GERMAINE to rest.	
	5-5-17		The 183rd Infantry Brigade relieved by the 184th Infantry Brigade. During the night the 161st Brigade R.F.A. were called upon to bombard CEPY FARM for 5 minutes, after which Infantry patrols were sent out. 2/Lieut; T. JONES, D/161, proceeded on leave.	
	7-5-17		A Section of A/161 and a section of D/161 were brought out of action after dark, and proceeded to their Wagon Lines at GERMAINE and FORESTE respectively, having been relieved by sections of 168th Brigade R.F.A. Lieut; R. SMITH posted from 32nd Divisional Ammunition Column and attached C/161.	
	8-5-17		During the night of 8/9th, the two remaining sections of D/161 were relieved by D/168 Brigade R.F.A. and B/161 by C/168th Bde. R.F.A.	
	9-5-17.		Hdqrs. 161st Bde R.F.A. were relieved by Hdqrs. 168th Bde. R.F.A. and withdrew to Wagon Line at AUROIR.	
	10-5-17		The two remaining sections of A/161 were relieved by C/161, and returned to wagon lines at GERMAINE. Major J.F.K. LOCKHART, A/161, posted to 32nd Divisional Ammunition Column. Lieut; E. H. BINDLOSS proceeded on leave.	
	11-5-17		Lt.a/Major T. KAY returned off leave.	
	14-5-17		The 161st Brigade R.F.A. (less "C" Battery), with Headquarters leading (together with a Section of 32nd D.A.C. and a portion of Divisional Train A.S.C.) marched to CURCHY-ETALON area via VOYENNES and NESLE, where they were billeted for the night.	
	15-5-17		The 161st Brigade R.F.A. together with Section of 32nd D.A.C. and portion of Divisional Train A.S.C. left CURCHY-ETALON area and marched to BOUCHOIR-FOLIES area via CREMERY, where it was billeted for the night.	
	16-5-17.		The 161st Brigade R.F.A. left BOUCHOIR-FOLIES area and marched to HAILLES near AMIENS. During the above marches the Brigade marched as a Brigade and the weather was cool and fine.	
	17-5-17		2/Lieut; T. JONES returned off leave.	
	21-5-17		2/Lieut; F.G. STEVENS posted from 32nd D.A.C. and attached A/161.	
	20-5-17		C/161st Brigade R.F.A. rejoined Brigade, having been relieved on the night of 17th by the French. Brigade sports were held at HAILLES.	

Army Form C. 2118.

WAR DIARY
INTELLIGENCE SUMMARY.
(Erase heading not required.)

Instructions regarding War Diaries and Intelligence
Summaries are contained in F. S. Regs., Part II.
and the Staff Manual respectively. Title pages
will be prepared in manuscript.

Place	Date	Hour	Summary of Events and Information	Remarks and references to Appendices
In the Field.	23-5-17.		During the day the 161st Brigade R.F.A. left HAILLES and marched to MARCELCAVE, where it entrained for CAESTRE, travelling via AMIENS, ABBEVILLE, BOULOGNE, CALAIS and ST: OMER. Units of Brigade entrained at following times:- A/161 at 9-40 a.m., H.Q/161 - 1-50 p.m., B/161 - 5-40 p.m., C/161 - 9-40 p.m. and D/161 - 1-50 a.m., 24-5-17. The journey occupied about 12 hours.	
	24-5-17.		2/Lieut; H. W. TILMAN, M.C. rejoined C/161. The 161st Brigade R.F.A. reached CAESTRE, detrained and marched to a Camp close to BAILLEUL. Lieut; E.H.BINDLOSS returned off leave.	
	25--5-17		The 161st Brigade R. F. A. commenced work on Battery positions - which were in the open and only about 700 yards behind the German front line.	
	28-5-17		1 Gun per Battery went up into action.	
	30-5-17		2 further Guns of C/161 went up into action.	
	31-5-17		All remaining Guns and Howitzers of the Brigade went up into action. The undermentioned N.C.O's and men have been awarded the Military Medal:-	

```
            L/5525  Sgt. Waring R.          A/161
            L/12130 Bdr. Preston L.         H.Q/161
            L/19391 Bdr. Hughes J.          B/161
            34222   Gnr King F.J.           H.Q/161
            L/12205 Gnr Jobling G.A.          "
            L/19429 Gnr Midgley S.            "
            L/27674 Gnr Jobling F.W.        A/161
            L/5647  Gnr Slater B.             "
            L/5677  Dvr Lawrence J.           "
            L/12180 Dvr Hanby G.            C/161
            L/19998 Gnr Hodges W.           D/161.
```

| | 15-5-17. | | Lieut-Col; A.S.Cotton, D.S.O.; Lt.e/Capt; P.Crow, Major W.Weatherbe, Major E.H.P.Pease-Watkin, D.S.O., Capt;& Major E.A.Chisholm, and Lieut; E.H.Bindloss, all mentioned in despatches. | |

1st June 1917.

A. S. Cotton
Lieut-Colonel,
Commanding 161st (Yorks;) Brigade R. F. A.

161st (Yorks.) Brigade R.F.A.

War Diary

for period

1st to 30th June 1917

Army Form C. 2118.

WAR DIARY
or
INTELLIGENCE SUMMARY.
(Erase heading not required.)

Instructions regarding War Diaries and Intelligence Summaries are contained in F. S. Regs., Part II. and the Staff Manual respectively. Title pages will be prepared in manuscript.

Place	Date	Hour	Summary of Events and Information	Remarks and references to Appendices
In the Field.	1-6-17		Bombardment of MESSINES-WYTSCHAETE Ridge. 2/Lieut; A.S.BLACKLAWS posted to Brigade from 32nd D.A.C. and attached to D/161.	
	2-6-17		Batteries carried out registration.	
	3-6-17		Further registration carried out. At 3-0 p.m. under heavy artillery fire, a raid was carried out on the German front line, resulting in the capture of 16 prisoners. Capt; H.L.McCORMICK, R.A.M.C., M.O. 1/c 161st Brigade R.F.A. left Headquarters and joined C/161.	
	5-6-17		Headquarters, 161st Brigade R.F.A. moved up to their Battle H.Q. in NEWPORT DUG-OUTS.	
	6-6-17		Final bombardment of MESSINES-WYTSCHAETE Ridge.	
	7-6-17		Attack by 2nd Army at 3-10 a.m. Capture of MESSINES-WYTSCHAETE Ridge by 12 noon. Further attack at 3-10 p.m. and capture of OOSTAVERNE LINE. 36th Divisional Artillery, supported by 32nd Divisional Artillery and 4 Army Field Artillery Brigades supported the attack by 2 Infantry Brigades, each with 2 Battalions in front, 1 in support and 1 in reserve. 4 Mines were exploded immediately before zero hour. Very little resistance was experienced during these attacks, in which Tanks were employed. 2/Lieut; C.L.W.HAFFENDEN went forward with the Infantry at 7-0 a.m. as F.O.O.	
	8-6-17		Counter Attacks reported at 12 noon, and 9-15 p.m. - apparently both false. 2/Lieut; R.G.JOHNSON acted as Liaison Officer. C/161 retrieved a Bosch Gun. 2/Lieut; C.H.MORTON (late of C/161) posted to 161st Bde.R.F.A. and attached B/161 from 32nd D.A.C.	
	9-6-17		Batteries of 161st Brigade R.F.A. went out of action and withdrew to wagon lines between 4 and 9 p.m. Liaison and F.O.O's recalled.	
	10-6-17.		161st Brigade R.F.A. Headquarters withdrew to wagon lines. 2/Lieut; A.W.DENNISTON & Monsieur L. MOULIN (Interpreter) proceeded to GODESWAERVELDE as Billeting party for Brigade Headquarters. First rain since Brigade left HAILLES.	
	11-6-17		161st Brigade R.F.A. complete marched to GODESWAERVELDE via BAILLEUL - FLETRE about 8-30 a.m. Weather cool and march pleasant, save for congestion along main roads. Batteries billeted in farms about 1 mile from village, Headquarters in Village itself.	

Army Form C. 2118.

WAR DIARY
~~INTELLIGENCE SUMMARY~~
(Erase heading not required.)

Instructions regarding War Diaries and Intelligence Summaries are contained in F.S. Regs., Part II. and the Staff Manual respectively. Title pages will be prepared in manuscript.

Place	Date	Hour	Summary of Events and Information	Remarks and references to Appendices
In the Field.	12-5-17		At GODESWAERVELDE general training carried out by the Brigade. Weather very hot. Thunder Storm in evening prevented Officers' ride.	
	13-6-17.		32nd Division transferred from XIVth Corps to XVth Corps, in DUNKERQUE area. Day spent in training. Officers' ride in evening. 2/Lt.A.W.DENNISTON and party went to WORMHOUDT to arrange billets for the Brigade, which was to march the following morning.	
	14th-6-17.		At 6-0 a.m. the Brigade left C/161's wagon line at GODESWAERVELDT and marched to WORMHOUDT - about 9 miles - very good roads. Weather very fine; route taken was via STENVORDE and was free from congestion of traffic.	
	15-6-17.	7-0 a.m.	Lieut-Col.A.S.COTTON, D.S.O. with two Officers from each Battery left Headquarters at in motor lorry to inspect Battery positions. Remounts arrived and were distributed to batteries. 2/Lieut: A.W.DENNISTON and party proceeded to CAPELLE to provide billets for Brigade.	
	16-6-17	11-15 a.m.	Brigade left WORMHOUDT for CAPELLE, marching via BERGUES, where it spent the night in billets. The day was very hot and several men fell out on the way. Lieuts.E.H.BINDLOSS and B.BAKEWELL proceeded to ZUYDCOOTE with Telephone Wagon and Headquarters' Signallers to arrange billets.	
	17-6-17	9-35 a.m.	Brigade marched out of CAPELLE at reaching ZUYDCOOTE 12-30 p.m. One section of A/161, B/161 and D/161 moved up into action on night 17/18th, coming under the orders of various French Groups of 29th French Divisional Artillery, in positions vacated by the French. One section A/161, B/161 and D/161 and 2 sections of C/161 moved up into action, C/161 being in the open. Brigade Headquarters established at OOST DUNKIRK BAINS.	
	18-6-17		Remaining Guns of Brigade went up into action. Battery wagon lines in vicinity of COXYDE.	
	19-6-17 20-6-17	9-0 a.m.	At Lieut-Colonel A.S.COTTON D.S.O. took over command of Brigade, covering 96th Infantry Brigade;(H.Q.161st Bde.R.F.A. - OOST DUNKIRK) taking over from Colonel GIVIERRE DSO. of 55th F.A.R.	
	23-6-17	12 midnight.	The enemy raided 16th Northumberland Fusiliers (Col; SCULLEY) and took 11 prisoners, at	
	24-6-17		96th Infantry Brigade was relieved by 1st Brigade, 1st Division. 161st Brigade R.F.A. moved their lines of fire so as to cover the front they were to remain on permanently, as 25th Brigade R.F.A. covered their own Infantry in NIEUPORT BAINS Sector. Lieut-Col. LEWIN (25th Brigade) took over command of NIEUPORT BAINS Sector and Lieut-Col. A.S.COTTON,D.S.C. LOMBARTZYDE Sector, covering 14th Infantry Brigade, commanded by Brig:Gen: TUIMSDEN V.C., D.S.O.) H.Q./161st Bde.R.F.A. moved up to farm in vicinity of Battery positions.	

(A7092) Wt W12639/M1293 75 c/o 1/17. D. D. & L., Ltd. Forms/C.2118/14.

Army Form C. 2118.

WAR DIARY
~~INTELLIGENCE~~ SUMMARY.

(Erase heading not required.)

Instructions regarding War Diaries and Intelligence Summaries are contained in F. S. Regs., Part II. and the Staff Manual respectively. Title pages will be prepared in manuscript.

Place	Date	Hour	Summary of Events and Information	Remarks and references to Appendices
In The Field.	25-6-17		161st Brigade R.F.A. Headquarters moved into BOIS TRIANGULAIRE.(¾ M.W.(NIEUPORT)	
	26-6-17		97th Infantry Brigade (Brig:Gen. BLACKLOCH) took over command from 14th Infantry Brigade. 2 Battalions in the line: (Headquarters NIEUPORT). 2/Lieut; A.S.DRYLAND joined Brigade on posting from Royal Military Academy, Woolwich, and attached to B/161.	
	27-6-17		Enemy Artillery shewed considerable activity, bombarding our front line system. 60-Pdr. Battery also heavily shelled.	
	29-6-17		Enemy again shelled 60-Pdr. Battery intermittently all day. Practically no shelling on our trenches. A/161 and D/161 positions almost completed.	

30-6-17.

O.L.C.......... Lieut-Colonel,
Commanding 161st (Yorks;) Brigade R. F. A.

161st (Yorks.) Brigade R.F.A.

War Diary

for period

1st to 31st July 1917.

Army Form C. 2118.

WAR DIARY
INTELLIGENCE SUMMARY.

(Erase heading not required.)

Instructions regarding War Diaries and Intelligence Summaries are contained in F. S. Regs., Part II. and the Staff Manual respectively. Title pages will be prepared in manuscript.

Place	Date	Hour	Summary of Events and Information	Remarks and references to Appendices
In the Field	2-7-17		2/Lieut; F.S.HARPER, B/161, wounded in head and side on his way back from inspecting forward gun at MAISON DU MARIN; admitted hospital 2-7-17.	
	3-7-17		2/Lieut; W.R.GOODMAN, C/161, slightly wounded in back but remained at duty. Enemy Artillery very active all day on roads in back areas; also on Bridge at HUITRIERE. O.P. at HUITRIERE hit several times. Headquarter wagon lines moved to proximity of C/161 wagon lines.	
	4-7-17		At 11-45 p.m. a raid was carried out by the 1/5 Border Regt. Bangalore torpedoes failed to explode until 12-15 a.m. during which time the enemy had manned his parapet and raiders were unable to get into enemy trenches. 2 Men killed 7 wounded. A/161 and D/161 fired on the point of entry after the raiders were back in our lines. At 1-45 a.m. 16th H.L.I. raided on the right, covered by fire from 161st Brigade R.F.A. XX Enemy trenches entered successfully and several dugouts bombed, but could only capture 1 prisoner. Raiders had one or two casualties. Enemy retaliated heavily at 3-30 a.m. 'S.O.S' sent up and was replied to by fire from the 161st Brigade R.F.A.	
	6-7-17		C/161 had 5 horses killed by shell whilst on the way up to LA TERREUR with ammunition. 2 Sappers of the R.E. who went to the assistance of the/Drivers were killed. wounded	
			Lieut-Colonel A.S.Cotton, D.S.O. proceeded on leave, leaving DUNKIRK by Torpedo Boat. Major E.H.P. Pease-Watkin D.S.O. took over command of the Brigade during the absence of Lieut-Colonel A.S.Cotton, D.S.O.	
	7-7-17		Enemy artillery became more active than usual.	
	9-7-17		Enemy artillery exceedingly active. A/161's O.P. at HUITRIERE was heavily shelled all day; 1 Signaller killed at this O.P. REDAN was also heavily shelled; also back areas.	
	10-7-17		After shelling the 1st and 32nd Divisional Fronts very heavily, the enemy attacked and forced back the Left Division (2nd Brigade). Our Right Battalion held its ground, but the Left Battalion (XI Border Regt.) gave way on the left and lost the front line system in M.22.b. The BOIS TRIANGULAIRE was very heavily shelled; also the Battery positions, Batteries having several casualties. L/12130 Bombardier L.PRESTON, H.Q./161 was killed in the O.P. in Farm whilst trying to pick up visual messages from REDAN. L/12072 Bdr. T.Jackson, who was in charge of Relay Post, was wounded whilst patrolling and repairing telephone lines. Situation became better after lunch and the enemy slackened off his fire somewhat. 16th Northumberland Fusiliers took over from Border Regiment. Capt; W.J.W.Richardson. A.V.C.,18/Veterinary Officer i/c 161st Bde.R.F.A. was wounded at B/161 wagon line by bomb dropped from hostile aeroplane.	

Army Form C. 2118.

WAR DIARY
~~INTELLIGENCE~~ SUMMARY.
(Erase heading not required.)

Instructions regarding War Diaries and Intelligence Summaries are contained in F.S. Regs., Part II. and the Staff Manual respectively. Title pages will be prepared in manuscript.

Place	Date	Hour	Summary of Events and Information	Remarks and references to Appendices
In the Field	11-7-17		Very much quieter all day except for desultory shelling of back areas. The 161st Brigade R.F.A. twice opened fire on 'S.O.S' Lines at request of Infantry. Left Battalion endeavoured to get back its old front line system, being supported by A/161, B/161 and C/161 R.F.A. No report received yet.	
	12-7-17		14th Infantry Brigade relieved 97th Infantry Brigade. Reinforcing Brigades of Artillery came into action on night of 11/12th July 1917. 72nd A.F.A.Brigade and 14th Bde.R.H.A. came under the orders of O.C. 'B' Artillery Group (Lieut-Colonel A.S.Cotton D.S.O.) they being allotted zones in the LOMBARTZYDE Sector. Much enemy artillery activity. All bridges shelled successfully cutting off all communications by Pontoon. 5 Canal Bridges still standing. 72nd A.F.A.Brigade registered, using C/161's O.P.	
	13-7-17		Night very quiet. 32nd Division holding the same line as after attack on 10th. Day very quiet. Our Heavy Artillery registered during the afternoon and our Aeroplanes were very active.	
	12-7-17		Lieut-Colonel A.S.Cotton D.S.O. rejoined 161st Brigade R.F.A. and resumed command of 'B' Artillery Group, Major E.H.P.Pease-Watkin D.S.O. returning to his Battery (D/161).	
	14-7-17		Enemy effected lodgment in NOSE TRENCH from its junction with NOSE AVENUE to its junction with NOSE LANE, in NOSE LANE SUPPORT from its junction with NOSE ALLEY to its junction with in NOSE LANE, and as far South as its junction with BACK WALK. Enemy Machine Gun in action about M.22.b.0.8. Enemy holds crossing of the GELEIDE Stream. 14th Infantry Brigade will endeavour to capture and consolidate the portion of NOSE TRENCH NOSE SUPPORT and NOSE LANE in the possession of the enemy, and form a defensive flank in NOSE LANE. 32nd Divisional Artillery will assist in the operations. Batteries fired a Creeping Barrage from 1-15 p.m. but the attempt failed. The 15th H.L.I. who attempted to establish posts failed on the left, but managed to get into the front line on the right. They had fairly heavy casualties.	
	16-7-17		Attempt was made to drive out enemy post during the afternoon, but failed, as the enemy put down a heavy barrage for about 15 minutes. This caused Division to order counter-preparations which commenced at 8-45 p.m. and went on until 9-15 p.m. Night became quiet afterwards.	
	17-7-17		148th Infantry Brigade (49th Division) relieved the Infantry in the line in LOMBARTZYDE Sector. Each Battery in 'B' Group fired for one hour in LAMBART WALK LAMBART TRENCH, LORRY WALK and LORRY TRENCH. This is to be done daily until further orders.	

Army Form C. 2118.

WAR DIARY

~~INTELLIGENCE SUMMARY~~

(Erase heading not required.)

Instructions regarding War Diaries and Intelligence Summaries are contained in F. S. Regs., Part II. and the Staff Manual respectively. Title pages will be prepared in manuscript.

Place	Date	Hour	Summary of Events and Information	Remarks and references to Appendices
In the Field.	18-7-17		The enemy tried to get into front line and into left part, but were driven out by Stokes Bombs and Lewis Guns, leaving a number of dead. 161st Bde.R.F.A. and 72nd AFA.Bde. fired on 'S.O.S' Lines at 2-40 a.m. and continued firing on and off until about 6-0 a.m.	
	19-7-17		A minor enterprise was carried out by the Left Battalion 4/5th K.O.Y.L.I. on the post occupied by the enemy at GELEIDE BROOK in M.22.a.4.7. They penetrated the post but lost their O.C. (killed) and came back. 8 Germans were seen to leave the post hurriedly during this operaton. D/161 fired on MAMELON VERT. C/161 covered the party at the GELEIDE BROOK. In the evening a patrol went out with the intention of occupying the post but the enemy put up a fairly heavy barrage, to which 161st Bde.R.F.A. and 72nd A.F.A.Brigade replied firing on their 'S.O.S' Lines.	
	20-7-17		Day very quiet all over the front. Night also very quiet.	
	21-7-17		Enemy very active, shelling the BOIS TRIANGULAIRE, B/168 Battery position and Back areas. Hostile aeroplanes very active during the afternoon, five being over our lines at the same time. Enemy shelled NIEUPORT with Gas Shell of a new type, causing many casualties. Enemy very active all night.	
	22-7-17		Hostile aeroplanes very active during morning, four being up flying very low over our lines. Enemy devoted his time to shelling back areas. Major T. Kay, A/161 and 2/Lieut; C.H.Morton sent to hospital (shell shock).	
	23-7-17		Day moderately quiet. At 11-7 p.m. 'S.O.S' rockets went up in Left Coy on Left Battalion front. 'B' Group fired on S.O.S.Lines, for one hour, as also did the Heavy Artillery. No attempt made by enemy to enter our line. At 3-15 a.m. S.O.S. was reported on Right Battalion front. 'B' Group fired on S.O.S. Lines for one hour at a slow rate. Appears to have been a false alarm. NIEUPORT again shelled with Gas Shell.	
	24-7-17		Enemy active on back areas, shelled the BOIS TRIANGULAIRE and B/161 position heavily from 3-30 p.m. to 8-0 p.m. One gun of B/161 put out of action. No casualties. NIEUPORT again shelled with Gas Shell. 66th Division relieved 49th Division in the line.	
	25-7-17		Day exceedingly quiet; night very quiet also. D/161 commenced cutting wire in front of LORRY AND BAMBURGH TRENCHES. No; L/12072 Bdr. T.Jackson died in hospital from wounds received in action 10-7-17.	
	26-7-17		Lieut-Colonel A.S.Cotton D.S.O. attended Conference at AMIRAL. NIEUPORT was shelled intermittently during the day and at night also. Otherwise the sector was quiet.	

Army Form C. 2118.

WAR DIARY
INTELLIGENCE SUMMARY.
(Erase heading not required.)

Instructions regarding War Diaries and Intelligence Summaries are contained in F. S. Regs., Part II. and the Staff Manual respectively. Title pages will be prepared in manuscript.

Place	Date	Hour	Summary of Events and Information	Remarks and references to Appendices
In the Field	27-7-17		NIEUPORT was shelled intermitently; otherwise, day fairly quiet.	
	28-7-17		161st Bde.R.F.A. and 72nd A.F.A.Bde. were detailed to cover a raid on German Post about M.22.b.8.3. by the 1/7th West Riding Regiment. Zero hour 12 midnight. Owing to an 'S.O.S' Signal being sent up the raid did not take place and the raiding party withdrew. Gas was ordered to be sent over but order cancelled. Enemy shelled our front pretty heavily; also NIEUPORT and BOIS TRIANGULAIRE were subjected to Gas Shell.	
	29-7-17		'B' Group 18-Pdr. Zero Barrage was tested by Lieut-Col. A.S.Cotton D.S.O. Raid which should have taken place last night took place to-day. Raiders failed to reach their objective, having three men killed. 'B' Group Headquarters shelled with Gas Shell.	
	30-7-17		Divisional Barrages tested at 8-0 p.m. Batteries firing for 12 minutes. The enemy reply was very weak. Night quiet.	
	31-7-17.		2/Lieut; Thomas Jones, D/161, killed at battery position by hostile artillery fire.	

Lieut-Colonel,
Commanding 161st (Yorks;) Brigade R.F.A.

All References - Trench Map NIEUPORT. Sheet 12 SW1. Edition 2a.

AWARDS:- Lieut; E.B.J.SHINER, B/161 - Awarded Military Cross (Authy. XV Corps A/372/199 d/- 9-7-17;
C.R.A. 32nd Division No; G.1022 d/- 15-7-17)
2/Lieut; E.COKE, A/161. Awarded Military Cross (Authy; 32nd Divisional Routine Order No; 2291 d/-31-7-17)
L/27657 Cpl. SPAVEN J., B/161 Awarded MILITARY MEDAL - (Authy. 36th Div.Arty.No; H.A.5/6/18
L/5779 Bdr. MASKREY I.M. B/161, G.1022 d/- 6-7-17; H.A.36th Div.Arty.D/N81.G/1022 d/- 6-7-17;
44759 Sgt.HISCOCK W.H., C/161, L/26619 Cpl. NIGHTINGALE A. B/161, L/12384 Bdr.GILL A.B/161
L/12184 a/Bdr.ELAND T., C/161, L/12386 Dvr HOWARD E., C/161, L/12131 Dvr TAYLOR.E.,C/161 all
awarded MILITARY MEDAL (Authy.C.R.A. XV. Corps No; A.C.7565/84/67-.; 29-7-17; C.R.A. 32nd Div.G.1022
d/- 30-7-17.

161st (Yorks;) Brigade R.F.A.

War Diary
для period
1st to 31st August 1917.

Army Form C. 2118.

WAR DIARY ~~INTELLIGENCE SUMMARY~~

Instructions regarding War Diaries and Intelligence Summaries are contained in F. S. Regs., Part II. and the Staff Manual respectively. Title pages will be prepared in manuscript.

(Erase heading not required.)

Place	Date	Hour	Summary of Events and Information	Remarks and references to Appendices
In the Field	1-8-17		Day and night very quiet. Rained.	
	2-8-17		At 9-0 a.m. under cover of Divisional Practice Barrage 199th Infantry Brigade raided enemy posts at M.22.b.85.21 and M.22.b.86.37; also, front line between M.23.a.25.26 and M.23.a.43.38. 'B','C' and 'A' Groups fired under instruction of Lieut-Colonel A.S.Cotton, D.S.O. Barrage continued for half an hour. Rain still continued.	
	3-8-17		Nothing to report. Rain still continuing. Some shelling of our front line system by 4.2's at 6-25 p.m. 5 minutes' fire by 'B' Group on 'S.O.S' Lines at 6-40 p.m. C.R.A. 32nd Division resumed tactical command. Adjutant returned from leave. 2/Lt.A.W.Denniston reported sick (Gas).	
	4-8-17		4th year of War. Weather improved; visibility better. 5 minutes 'S.O.S' fire at 6-5 p.m. and 20 minutes at 6-45 p.m. retaliation.	
	5-8-17.		Weather fair and bright. Artillery activity increased. Enemy shelled NIEUPORT and bridges in the evening. 2/Lieut. F.S.Harper, B/161, wounded by shell fire., in NIEUPORT; hit in the stomach. Most of Headquarters Staff have been admitted to hospital suffering from the effects of Gas Shell bombardment of the 29th ulto. Since 18th July 1917 161st and 72nd Brigades have been firing continuously 130 rounds per day per battery and 50 rounds per night; 320 BX and 40BX; on various tasks on enemy front lines in perpetual bombardment. Heavies continued bombardment.	
	6-8-17		Weather grey. Nothing to report.	
	7-8-17		'B' Group supported a successful raid carried out by 5th West Riding Regiment, 147th Infantry Brigade on enemy posts and trenches in front of LOMBARTZYDE. Raid took place at 1 a.m. under BOX Barrage. 5 Prisoners and 1 M.G. captured.	
	8-8-17		This night a Gas Attack was made at 1-30 a.m. on LOMBARTZYDE by 'K' Special Co.R.E. with projectors and Stokes' Mortar Gas Bombs, 'B' Group co-operating with artillery fire. 'C'/161 were shelled during the day losing one man wounded.	
	9-8-17		161st Brigade Headquarters were relieved by Headquarters 72nd A.F.A.Brigade; 161st Bde.Headquarters withdrew to their Wagon Line. Batteries still in action. Lieut-Col.A.S.Cotton, D.S.O. and Lieut.E.H.Bindloss admitted hospital suffering from gas ~~effects~~. ~~Adjutant went~~ Headquarters for Wagon Line.	
	~~10-8-17~~ 11-8-17		Headquarters 161st Bde.R.F.A moved to VILLA MARTHA LOUISA at COXYDE BAINS.	

Army Form C. 2118.

WAR DIARY (2)

INTELLIGENCE SUMMARY

(Erase heading not required.)

Instructions regarding War Diaries and Intelligence Summaries are contained in F. S. Regs., Part II. and the Staff Manual respectively. Title pages will be prepared in manuscript.

Place	Date	Hour	Summary of Events and Information	Remarks and references to Appendices
In the Field	12-8-17 Augt.		Headquarters 161st Bde.R.F.A. moved to COXYDE.	
	15/16th Augt.		Brigade came out to rest to Wagon Lines, D/161 leaving their guns in battery position.	
	17-8-17		Major E.H.P.Pease-Watkin D.S.O.; Major P.C.Hunt, Lieut. J.St.J.Hindmarsh and 2/Lieuts. E. H.W.Tilman M.C., T.Campbell and P.W.Bowles proceeded on leave.	
	18-8-17		Lieut-Col.A.S.Cotton D.S.O. and Lieut.E.H.Bindloss proceeded on leave. Major/A.Chisholm assumed command of Brigade.	
	25-8-17		Batteries went into action and came under the command of O.C.72nd A.F.A.Brigade. Signal Sub-Section attached to Headquarters returned to former Headquarters in BOIS TRIANGULAIRE. D/161 Wagon lines shelled. No casualties. During the 10 days spent at their Wagon lines Brigade had time for a thorough overhaul and a certain amount of training. Guns were inspected and repaired and in some cases calibrated at the special range. Ride for officers took place daily under 2/Lt.F.W.Hook, Two instructions were provided for Headquarters 97th Infantry Brigade Riding School. 32nd Division relieved 33rd Division on nights 27/28th and 28/29th Augt. 14th Infantry Brigade in LOMBARTZYDE Sector and 97th Infantry Brigade in St; GEORGE's Sector.	
	28-8-17		Major E.H.P.Pease-Watkin D.S.O., Major P.C.Hunt, Lt.J.St.J.Hindmarsh, 2/Lieuts.Tilman, Campbell and Bowles returned from leave. 3 Sgts. and 1 Gnr of C/161 wounded.	
	29-8-17		Capt. P.Crow.M.C. and 2/Lieut.G R.Cliff rejoined the Brigade from England. Capt.J.W. Buckley, 2/Lt.A.W.Denniston and 2/Lt.R.G.Johnson proceeded on leave. 2/Lt.Hon.T.F.J.I Massy rejoined from 32nd Div.T.M's. Bdr.Sutcliffe of C/161 wounded.	
	30-8-17		Headquarters 161st Bde.R.F.A. moved up to BOIS TRIANGULAIRE. Weather has been very stormy last few days and in the absence of our aeroplanes enemy artillery activity increased especially on back areas e.g. COXYDE etc. Front appears to be normally quiet. A number of our Heavy Batteries have moved out recently.	
	31-8-17		Lieut-Colonel A.S.Cotton, D.S.O. and Lieut.E.H.Bindloss returned from leave. The undermentioned awards were made during the month of August 1917:- MILITARY CROSS. BAR TO MILITARY CROSS. Capt:J.M.Richardson A.V.C. (late 161) 2/Lt. H.W.Tilman M.C., C/161. 2/Lieut.E.Coke, A/161 and 2/Lt.P.W.Bowles. (Continued)	

Army Form C. 2118.

WAR DIARY (3)
OF
INTELLIGENCE SUMMARY

(Erase heading not required.)

Instructions regarding War Diaries and Intelligence Summaries are contained in F.S. Regs., Part II. and the Staff Manual respectively. Title pages will be prepared in manuscript.

Place	Date	Hour	Summary of Events and Information	Remarks and references to Appendices
			DISTINGUISHED CONDUCT MEDAL. BAR TO MILITARY MEDAL.	
			L/19580 Sgt. Holmes H., C/161. L/26519 Cpl. Nightingale C., D/161	
			MILITARY MEDAL.	
			L/26519 Cpl. Nightingale C., D/161	
			L/57779 Bdr. Maskrey I.M., B/161	
			L/27657 Cpl. Spaven J., B/161	
			L/12184 Bdr. Eland T., C/161	
			L/12386 Dvr Howard E.S., B/161	
			L/12384 Bdr. Gill A., B/161	
			L/12131 Dvr Taylor E., C/161	
			44759 Sgt. Hiscock W.H., C/161	
			L/12253 Sgt. Boyes T.F., A/161	
			43412 Gnr Dopson P.A., A/161	
			L/19607 Sgt.Foord S., C/161	
			78278 Gnr Bwett S.C., C/161	
			31st August 1917.	

(signed) C. L. Cotton
Lieut-Colonel,
Commanding 161st (Yorks;) Brigade R.F.A.

161st (Yorks) Brigade R.F.A.

War Diary

1st September 1914

to

30th September 1914

Army Form C. 2118.

WAR DIARY
or
INTELLIGENCE SUMMARY.
(Erase heading not required.)

Instructions regarding War Diaries and Intelligence Summaries are contained in F. S. Regs., Part II. and the Staff Manual respectively. Title pages will be prepared in manuscript.

Place	Date	Hour	Summary of Events and Information	Remarks and references to Appendices
In the Field.	2-9-17		During the morning batteries fired a practice barrage on their S.O.S.lines for 8 minutes. 2/Lieut.R.T.PEACOP, C/161, killed at gun position.	
	3-9-17		Lieut-Colonel A.S.COTTON,D.S.O. took over command of 'B' Group from Lieut-Colonel RITCHIE (72nd A.F.A.Bde.). 'B' Group now consists of 161st Bde.alone - the following Groups also covering the front of LEFT Brigade, 32nd Div. - 'C' Group (Lieut-Colonel FURNIVALL), SYKES GROUP (2nd N.Z. A.F.A.Bde.), PHIPPS S.O.S.Group. O.C. 'B' Group in liaison with 14th Infantry Bde. (Brig.General LUMSDEN, V.C.,D.S.O.), and Batteries supplying liaison Officer with left Infantry Battalion.	
	4-9-17		C/161 moved their battery position to neighbourhood of BOIS TRIANGULAIRE into position recently vacated by a 6" How:battery. This position provides dug-out accommodation for personnel of battery. D/161 Wagon Lines were shelled by a 6" gun during the night, but no casualties were inflicted beyond 1 horse slightly wounded. Wagon Lines subsequently moved to LA PANNE.	
	5-9-17		D/161 spotted an enemy T.M. firing, and claim to have silenced it.	
	6-9-17		A/161 were engaged in wire cutting - For this sheet (and for the report which led to it) the Brigade received the thanks of the G.O.C. Division.	
	7-9-17		C.R.A., 32nd Division, resumed command of the Artillery covering 32nd Division. D/161 on wire cutting in front of enemy post at GELEIDE.	
	8-9-17		Night firing and day firing on special ordered tasks ceased ceased - an endeavour being made to break off the Artillery duel. A/161 on wire cutting in front of GELEIDE Post. The front has quietened down considerably, though back areas and wagon lines are still shelled. At 10 p.m.Special companies R.E. carried out a Gas projector and Stokes Mortar attack on enemy trenches. B/161 fired in co-operation.	
	9-9-17		D/161 on wire cutting in front of GELEIDE POST.	
	11-9-17		A raid was made by the 5/6ths Royal Scots on GROOTE BAMBURGH FARM. Raiding party left our trenches 9 p.m., and proceeded across the Polder; an entrance was made through the German wire (a machine-gun,with crew of 2, being disposed of en route) A dug-out was bombed and two men taken prisoners (unfortunately these latter had to be disposed of on the return journey). On the order to withdraw,a coloured rocket was fired and the Artillery barrage came down,under which the party succeeded in regaining our own lines.. Two men were killed and 13 wounded of the raiding party; of the enemy at least 8 were killed in dugouts, and more probably in the ensuing fighting. Lieut.R.L.ELLIS, B/161, to hospital -Jaundice.	

Army Form C. 2118.

WAR DIARY
or
INTELLIGENCE SUMMARY.
(Erase heading not required.)

Instructions regarding War Diaries and Intelligence Summaries are contained in F. S. Regs., Part II. and the Staff Manual respectively. Title pages will be prepared in manuscript.

Place	Date	Hour	Summary of Events and Information	Remarks and references to Appendices
	12-9-17		Lieut.A.W.DENNISTON, HQ/161, returned from leave. 2/Lieut.HAFFENDEN, D/161, awarded MILITARY CROSS, for work as F.O.C. at MESSINES. C/161 shelled with 21 cm. gun for 2½ hours - no casualties. 2/Lieut.R.G.JOHNSON and Capt.J.W.BUCKLEY returned from leave. 2/Lieut.W.R.GOODMAN, D/161, proceeded on leave. 2/Lieut.R.A.WYRLEY-BIRCH, returned from T.M's and was posted to C/161. At 10.45 p.m. Special Coy.R.E. discharged Gas on the Divisional Front. B/161 fired in connection with this.	
	13-9-17		Major P.CROW,M.C., A/161, to hospital - sick. 2/Lieut.T.S.CAMPBELL, C/161, to England - sick.	
	14-9-17		At 5.5 p.m. the enemy put up a practice barrage for 20 min. on our front system, NIEUPORT, REDAN and PRESQUILE. Our artillery retaliated. Otherwise all quiet.	
	15-9-17		Wagon Lines of HQ/161, A/161 and C/161 shelled out from 12 midnight to 2 a.m. No casualties. No.726511 Dvr.W.H.BLOODWORTH, and No.726359 Dvr.H.E.E.Deighton, both of D/161, awarded the MILITARY MEDAL for gallantry on Sept.4th,1917,when D/161 Wagon Lines were shelled.	
	17-9-17		Early this morning the enemy attempted to raid the trenches of the Right Battalion; the S.O.S. signal was sent up at 5.23 a.m., and our artillery barrage was in full swing by 5.27 a.m. The enemy appears to have entered our trenches,where one man was shot; the remainder turned tail and fled. There were no prisoners captured on either side.	
	19-9-17		The G.O.C. Division inspected A/161, B/161 and C/161 battery positions. 1 officer from 14th Infantry Bde. attached every two days to batteries:- Sept.19 - 21 Capt. PATERSON B/161 5/6ths Royal Scots. 21 - 24 Major UTTERSTONE C/161 1st Dorsets. 23 - 25 Lieut.EASTGATE-SMITH B/161 2nd Manchesters 25 - 27 Capt. W.T.DAVIES,M.C. C/161 15th H.L.I. 27 - 29 Lieut.G.B.DALLAS A/161 14th M.G.Coy. 29 - 1st Lieut.A.K.JAMES B/161 5/6ths Royal Scots.	
	19-9-17 to 22-9-17		Nothing of particular note occurred. Enemy T.M.activity increased and the following plan has been adopted to cope with them:- By day A/161 have guns laid out on known emplacements, by night D/161 or D/72. If T.M's are observed firing,but not spotted, retaliation is fired on known positions; if however they are spotted, the howitzers deal with them. No.12534 Dvr.W.Lockey and No. L/25499 Gnr.J.H.Brooksbank, both of C/161, awarded MILITARY MEDAL.	

Army Form C. 2118.

WAR DIARY
or
INTELLIGENCE SUMMARY.

(Erase heading not required.)

Instructions regarding War Diaries and Intelligence Summaries are contained in F. S. Regs., Part II. and the Staff Manual respectively. Title pages will be prepared in manuscript.

Place	Date	Hour	Summary of Events and Information	Remarks and references to Appendices
	23-9-17		T/Capt.&/Major E.A.CHISHOLM, C/161, awarded the MILITARY CROSS.	
	24-9-17		During the night 'B' Group H.Q. in BOIS TRIANGULAIRE was subjected to 20 min.gas shelling at a rapid rate. Four slight casualties resulted, which can be traced to contact with clothes, earth, or telephone wires (in one case the seat of a bicycle) exposed to the gas.	
	26-9-17		From 12 noon to 1.30 p.m. today for practise purposes, telephonic communications between Artillery units was "dis"; communication being maintained by runner, wireless, and visual - At 4 p.m. a practise "Counter-Preparation" was fired until 4.11 p.m. - from 4.11 p.m. to 4.14 p.m. a practise S.O.S. on the whole of the Divisional Front. The enemy did not disclose his artillery, contenting himself with retaliating for 6 min.at 4.30 p.m. on our trenches and NIEUPORT.	
	27-9-17		HQ/161, B and C Batteries were shelled by a 6" gun - from 8 to 10 a.m. - No casualties, but two dug-outs smashed in. At 6.15 a.m. an S.O.S. was reported on the LOMBARTZYDE Sector. Batteries opened fire until the situation was clearly shewn to be a false alarm. Infantry reported very favourably on this barrage. A practise LL call was a failure, owing to message from the air being jammed	
	28-9-17		Lieut. E. TURNBULL rejoined the Brigade from England and was posted to D/161, 2/Lieut. W.R.GOODMAN rejoining C/161. An LL call was received during the afternoon and target engaged. The 97th Infantry Bde. relieved the 96th Infantry Bde. in the LOMBARTZYDE Sector.	

MILITARY CROSS.
T/Capt.&/Major E.A.CHISHOLM. C/161
2/Lt C.W. HAFFENDEN D/161.

(Continued.)

Army Form C. 2118.

WAR DIARY
or
INTELLIGENCE SUMMARY.
(Erase heading not required.)

Instructions regarding War Diaries and Intelligence Summaries are contained in F. S. Regs., Part II. and the Staff Manual respectively. Title pages will be prepared in manuscript.

Place	Date	Hour	Summary of Events and Information	Remarks and references to Appendices
			MILITARY MEDAL. 726511 Dvr.Bloodworth W.H., D/161. 726359 Dvr.Deighton H.E.E., D/161. L/25499 Gnr.Brooksbank J.H., C/161. 12534 Dvr. Lockey W. C/161. CASUALTIES. Officers. O.R. Killed 1; Wounded,remained at Duty 1. Killed 1; Wounded,remaining at Duty 6 (including 3 GAS); Wounded,and admitted Hospital 7 (including 2 GAS).	
	30th September 1917.			

A. L. Otter
Lieut-Colonel,
Commanding 161st (Yorks;) Brigade R. F. A.

161st (Yorks.) Brigade R.F.A.

Vol 22

W. 15517—M. 141. 250,000. 1/16. L.S.&Co. Forms/W 3091/2.   Army Form W. 3091.

Cover for Documents.

Nature of Enclosures.

War Diary (A.F., C.2118)

for period

1st to 31st October 1917

Notes, or Letters written.

Army Form C. 2118.

WAR DIARY
~~INTELLIGENCE~~ SUMMARY.
(Erase heading not required.)

Instructions regarding War Diaries and Intelligence Summaries are contained in F.S. Regs., Part II. and the Staff Manual respectively. Title pages will be prepared in manuscript.

HDQRS. 161ST (YORKS.) BDE. R.F.A.
No. _____
OCT 31 1917

Place	Date	Hour	Summary of Events and Information	Remarks and references to Appendices
In the Field	1-10-17		During the afternoon the tide began to flood out parts of the Right Battalion front, and at one time it appeared it might be necessary to withdraw part of the garrison under cover of smoke barrage. This, however, proved unnecessary. Capt: W.A. SMELLIE, 1st Dorset Regt. attached to C/161 for instruction.	
	2ᵡ-10-17		The Corps Commander inspected wagon lines in neighbourhood of COXYDE, and expressed himself well satisfied.	
	3-10-17		Test of 'S.O.S' Rockets on Left Brigade front was held at 6 p.m. to 6-30 p.m. This was not a success. 2/Lieut. B. McSHERRY, 2nd Manchester Regt. attached to B/161 for instruction.	
	4-10-17		Weather broke in rain and wind, which continued during the 5th. Trenches are mostly flooded out. Major P.C. HUNT, Condg; B/161, went on a month's leave to England.	
	Night 5-10-17 / 6-10-17.		42nd Division (less Artillery) commenced relief of 32nd Division (less Artillery), the 125th Infantry Brigade (5th, 6th, 7th & 8th Lancashire Fusiliers) Brig; Gen. H. FARGUS, C.M.G., D.S.O. relieving the 97th Infantry Brigade in the LOMBARTZYDE Sector.	
	5-10-17		'S.O.S' Rocket Test repeated; Again a failure. 2/Lieut. J. MUIR, 15th Highland Light Infantry, attached C/161, for instruction.	
	6-10-17		Relief completed in St; GEORGE'S SECTOR. Summer time ceased at 1 a.m. night 6/7th. Weather extremely unfavourable to operations, high wind or rain prevailing.	
	7-10-17 ⎫ 8-10-17 ⎬ 10-10-17 ⎭		Hostile Artillery activity increased somewhat. 168th Brigade R.F.A. pulled out of action. Lieut-Colonel A.S. COTTON D.S.O. (D/161) taking over command of 161st Brigade R.F.A. and Capt; J.W. BUCKLEY taking over command of D/161.	
	11-10-17		E.H.F.PEASE-WATKIN D.S.O. (D/161) assumed command of 41st Divisional Artillery, Major 1 Section per Battery were relieved by sections of 211th Brigade R.F.A., 42nd Divisional Artillery; 161st (Yorks;) Brigade R.F.A withdrawing to wagon lines.	

Army Form C. 2118.

WAR DIARY
INTELLIGENCE SUMMARY

(Erase heading not required.)

Instructions regarding War Diaries and Intelligence Summaries are contained in F.S. Regs., Part II. and the Staff Manual respectively. Title pages will be prepared in manuscript.

HUDRS. 161ST (YORKS.) BDE. R.F.A.
OCT 31 1917

Place	Date	Hour	Summary of Events and Information	Remarks and references to Appendices
In the Field	12-10-17		Remaining Sections of 161st Brigade R.F.A. withdrew to wagon lines after dark on completion of relief.	
	13-10-17 14-10-17 15-10-17		161st Brigade R.F.A. marched to GHYVELDE after dark. Weather very wet. Brigade rested at GHYVELDE.	
	16-10-17		Brigade marched to WORMHOUDT via BERGUES, starting at 5-0 a.m. and being settled in by 12 noon. Weather was clear during the march with a cold wind. At 7-0 a.m. Battery Commanders and a small Staff left WORMHOUDT by motor lorry and proceeded to YPRES, reporting to 18th Divisional Artillery preparatory to relieving 255th Brigade R.F.A.	
	17-10-17		Brigade marched from WORMHOUDT to neighbourhood of POPERINGHE, starting at 9-0 a.m. and arriving at 3 p.m. Traffic was very heavy and march consequently disjointed and uncomfortable. Gun detachments travelled by motor lorry to YPRES area and relieved detachments of outgoing Brigade in neighbourhood of POELCAPPELLE. Guns were exchanged. Lieut-Colonel A.G.ARBUTHNOT C.M.G., D.S.O. took over command of the Brigade from Major E.H.F.PEASE-WATKIN D.S.O.	
	18-10-17		Wagon lines of 161st Brigade moved to lines vacated by 255th Brigade R.F.A. Headquarters 161st Bge. R.F.A. took over at 10 a.m. from Headquarters, 255th Bde.R.F.A. forming part of 'D' Group (Lieut-Col; PARRY D.S.O.; 34th A.F.A.Brigade) 18th Divisional Artillery Group. During the day the Brigade took part in the bombardment of enemy works N.E. of POELCAPPELLE, a defensive 18-Pounder Barrage being substituted for the Infantry, who withdrew into dugouts to enable the heavies to carry out close shooting. 9 other ranks wounded and 1 other rank slightly wounded remaining at duty during the day. Programme carried out on 18th was repeated. 'B' and 'C' Batteries lost two guns destroyed by enemy shell fire and two guns slightly damaged. Ammunition was taken up to Batteries by pack.	
	19-10-17		The Batteries were intermittently shelled during the day, rising to fairly heavy shelling from 12 noon to 2 p.m. Some Gas shell were fired during the night 'A' Battery being the chief sufferers. 4 O.R. wounded (including 2 who died of wounds), 2 O.R wounded (GAS) and 1 O.R. Shell Shock during the day.	
	30-10-17.		Brigade fired Barrage and Bombardment programme from 5-30 a.m. to 11 p.m. Major E.H.P.PEASE-WATKIN D.S.O., D/161, was wounded by artillery fire and evacuated.	

Army Form C. 2118.

WAR DIARY
INTELLIGENCE SUMMARY
(Erase heading not required.)

(3)

Instructions regarding War Diaries and Intelligence
Summaries are contained in F. S. Regs., Part II.
and the Staff Manual respectively. Title pages
will be prepared in manuscript.

Place	Date	Hour	Summary of Events and Information	Remarks and references to Appendices
In the Field	21-10-17		Bombardment programme continued. Enemy Batteries less active than usual. 2/Lieut. F.G.STEVENS, A/161, died of wounds received in action during the course of the day at Battery position. Major P. CROW, M.C., Comdg A/161, Captain C.W.WARD M.C., Comdg A/161, Lieut: J. ST: J. HINDMARSH, B/161, 2/Lieut; E. COKE M.C., A/161, 2/Lieut; C.H.MORTON, B/161, all suffering from result of Gas shelling., and despatched to wagon lines. Weather was fine but ground shewed little signs of drying. Practice Barrage was fired in the course of the afternoon to check lines and switches, under Brigade arrangements. 1 O.R. died of wounds received in action during the course of the day and 1 O.R. wounded (GAS).	
	22-10-17		At 5-35 a.m. an advance was made on the front of XIV and XVIII Corps to reduce the salient held by the enemy in the form of the northern houses of POELCAPPELLE. Attack on XVIII Corps front was carried out by the 8th NORFOLKS and 10th ESSEX of the 53rd Infantry Brigade, 18th Division. Under cover of a creeping Barrage all objectives were gained, the advance extending to a depth of 1000 yards. The 161st Brigade R.F.A. formed part of the Artillery supporting the attack. The barrage was intended to be in enfilade, but was only partly so, for the Batteries of the Brigade. This entailed greater difficulties from the gunners point of view and more accurate shooting. Considering the mud and general conditions under which the work had to be carried out, the success of our Infantry under the protection of the Field Artillery barrages is gratifying. During the course of the day 1 O.R. was killed, 1 O.R. wounded, 3 O.R. wounded (GAS) and 1 O.R. slightly wounded remaining at duty.	
	23-10-17		Day passed quietly and Batteries were able to get some rest and sleep. D/161 (Howitzers) withdrew their guns and parked them in neighbourhood of Canal Bank, preparatory to a further advance. The guns were successfully withdrawn in spite of considerable hostile shelling. Weather continued stormy with brighter intervals. Major P. CROW, M.C., Comdg; A/161, was admitted into hospital suffering from effects of Gas shell bombardment on 21st inst.	
	24-10-17		Bombardment of enemy front lines and rear positions re-commenced in conjunction with Heavy Artillery. Enemy shelled vicinity of Battery positions especially during the morning. Enemy bombing aeroplanes caused two casualties in D/161 in the early afternoon, 2/Lieut: C.L.W.HARFENDEN and 1 O.R. being wounded. In addition to above two Casualties 2/Lieut; P.W.BOWLES M.C.,A/161, 5 O.R. were	

WAR DIARY
INTELLIGENCE SUMMARY
(Erase heading not required.)

Place	Date	Hour	Summary of Events and Information	Remarks and references to Appendices
In the Field	24-10-17 continued.		wounded, 1 O.R. killed and 2 O.R. shell shock. Lieut; J. ST; J. HINDMARSH, B/161, was admitted into hospital suffering from effects of Gas shell bombardment on 21-10-17. Bombardment continued.	
	25-10-17		D/161 commenced work on new forward positions etc. An advanced Wagon Line of 6 teams per Battery was established on ground just East of Canal Bank, to save time in carting up ammunition to forward positions. 18th Divisional Artillery were relieved by 58th Divisional Artillery. During the course of the day 1 O.R. was killed.	
	26-10-17		An attack was made along the Divisional and Corps fronts; the 161st Brigade R.F.A. supporting the Left Battalion of 173rd Infantry Brigade. (58th Division). The situation still appears very obscure. The objectives appear to have been gained, and then lost under pressure of counter-attacks. The weather throughout the day was indescribably foul, rain falling continuously. Teams to withdraw guns preparatory to a further advance were ordered up, but the situation remained too obscure to enable any movement to be made. 2 Howitzers of D/161 moved up to new position, and a certain amount of ammunition was got up, in spite of enemy shelling of approaches. During the day 3 O.R. were wounded and 1 O.R. slightly wounded remained at duty.	
	27-10-17.		About 200 prisoners were taken in yesterday's operations, but no advance was made on the Divisional front, though some gain of ground was made to the North and on the South. 2 more Howitzers of D/161 went up into action. During the day 1 O.R. was killed 1 O.R. wounded and 1 O.R. slightly wounded remained at duty.	
	28-10-17.		A 48 hours bombardment commenced again at 6-30 a.m. Orders for same were not received until 4-45 a.m. Lieut-Colonel A.G. ARBUTHNOT C.M.G., D.S.O.; Comdg; Brigade took over command of 'D' Group on relief of 74th A.F.A. Brigade by 126th A.F.A. Brigade. Casualties during day were:- 2 O.R. wounded and 1 O.R. wounded (Gas). Major J.F.X. LOCKHART was temporarily attached to B/161 from 32nd D.A.C. Lieut; W. ELLIS was temporarily attached to B/161 from Z/32 T.M. Battery. 2/Lieut: Hon. T.F.J.T.MASSY, A/161 and 2/Lieut; R.G.JOHNSON returned on completion of course of Fourth Army Artillery School.	
	29-10-17		Bombardment continued. Batteries were shelled during the night by Gas Shell, causing	

Army Form C. 2118.

(5)

WAR DIARY
or
INTELLIGENCE SUMMARY.

(Erase heading not required.)

Place	Date	Hour	Summary of Events and Information	Remarks and references to Appendices
In the Field	29-10-17. (Contd:)		a number of casualties, as precautionary measures are difficult to take in the ground at present occupied. D/161 registered from new forward position. Casualties for the day were:- 9 O.R. wounded (GAS).	
	30-10-17.		An attack was launched at 5-50 a.m. on the Corps Front; the usual creeping and combing barrages were fired. The situation remained very obscure all day, and still is so. Affairs seem to have taken same course as on the last attack i.e. an advance successfully made and subsequent withdrawal, due probably to machine gun fire and loss of direction. F.O.O's were supplied by 161st Brigade R.F.A. and 126th A.F.A.Brigade, but information was not obtained so satisfactorily as before. Casualties for the day were:- 2 O.R. wounded (GAS) 3 O.R. wounded and 1 O.R. slightly wounded remained at duty.	
	31-10-17.		Day passed quietly. Batteries re-registered. C/161 continued work on forward position with a view to occupation very shortly. Casualties during the day:- 2/Lieut: F.W.HOOK, D/161 slightly wounded remaining at duty and 2 O.R. wounded.	

Connett

Lieut-Colonel,
Commanding 161st (Yorks:) Brigade R.F.A.

Officer Commanding,

/161st Brigade R.F.A.

On relinquishing the command of 161st (Yorks;) Brigade, R.F.A., Brig; General A. S. COTTON, D.S.O., desires to place on record his appreciation of the excellent work performed by all ranks since he has had the honour to command them.

It is particularly gratifying to hear the high opinion expressed by our comrades in the Infantry of the efficiency of the Brigade; an opinion which is expressed not only by 32nd Division Infantry but by all other Divisions the Brigade has had the privilege of covering, both during Active Operations and in the ordinary course of Trench Warfare.

Brig; General A.S. COTTON feels sure that in future the 161st (Yorks;) Brigade R.F.A. will maintain the high standard already reached and will still further add to its reputation; he will always follow its doings with the greatest interest, and wishes all ranks the best of luck.

11th October 1917.

Brig; General,
Commanding 161st (Yorks;) Brigade R.F.A.

161st (Works:) Brigade, R.F.A.

War Diary

1st to 30th November 1917.

Army Form C. 2118.

WAR DIARY
INTELLIGENCE SUMMARY
(Erase heading not required.)

Instructions regarding War Diaries and Intelligence
Summaries are contained in F. S. Regs., Part II.
and the Staff Manual respectively. Title pages
will be prepared in manuscript.

Place	Date	Hour	Summary of Events and Information	Remarks and references to Appendices
In the Field.	1-11-17.		During the night, D/161 pulled two more guns into action, and one was taken down to the Wagon line that had been damaged by shell fire. B/161 exchanged a gun from their position and C/161 took two guns out of action, preparatory to moving into advanced positions during the night. B/161 and C/161 moved into fresh Wagon Lines at BRIELEN. The day was marked by a certain amount of hostile artillery activity. Harassing fire was carried out on enemy Communications.	
	2-11-17		Day passed without incident; Enemy appeared to have attacked Division on our right during the night, and Batteries fired some minutes on 'S.O.S' Lines until the situation appeared cleared.	
	3-11-17		Day passed quietly. A bombardment was carried out by 'D' Group on Shell Holes and suspected enemy strong points in Group Zone. Headquarters, 161st Brigade R.F.A. moved into NISSEN HUTS near GOURNIER FARM. These were shelled during the night but no casualties. Casualties for the day - 1 O.R. wounded.	
	4-11-17		A Creeping Barrage was fired on 'S.O.S' front at 4-40 a.m. for half an hour; Batteries dropping after creeping forward to catch any enemy who might be expecting an Infantry Attack. Casualties for the Day - 1 O.R. wounded.	
	5-11-17		Barrage as above was repeated at 4-50 a.m. 'S.O.S' alarm at 5-30 p.m. Casualties for the day - NIL.	
	6-11-17		Barrage as above repeated at 6-0 a.m. in conjunction with an attack by the Canadian Corps on our right on PASCHENDAELE. All objectives were gained in this attack. Enemy action on our front confined to shelling of tracks, approaches etc., and some considerable use of longe range H.V. Guns against rear areas. Major P.G.HUNT, B/161, returned from leave, taking over command of B/161, from Major J.F.K. LOCKHART, who took over command of A/161. CASUALTIES FOR THE DAY:- 2 O.R. Killed; 5 O.R. wounded and 1 O.R. slightly wounded remained at duty.	
	7-11-17		A Barrage was fired at 5-30 a.m. At 1 p.m. a Practice Barrage was fired on area to the South of Group Zone on which enfilade fire could be brought to bear; barrage being creeping and in enfilade. CASUALTIES - Nil.	
	8-11-17		Preparatory Barrages were fired on the Group Front as on previous days at 4-15 a.m. and 5-0 a.m., with bursts of fire at 4 p.m. Harassing fire was also continued on enemy tracks and approaches. A/161 Commenced work on forward position near RETOUR CROSS ROADS. - CASUALTIES - Nil.	

Army Form C. 2118.

WAR DIARY
or
INTELLIGENCE SUMMARY.

(Erase heading not required.)

Instructions regarding War Diaries and Intelligence Summaries are contained in F. S. Regs., Part II. and the Staff Manual respectively. Title pages will be prepared in manuscript.

Place	Date	Hour	Summary of Events and Information	Remarks and references to Appendices
In the Field	9-11-17		Preparatory Barrages were fired again at 4-20 a.m. and 6-0 a.m. Work was continued on Forward positions. CASUALTIES - Nil.	
	10-11-17		In cooperation with the Artillery of 1st Division, the Brigade fired in support of an attack Northwards along the Ridge towards WESTROOSBEKE. The attack by the 1st Division and the 1st Canadian Corps appears to have reached its objectives, only to be compelled to withdraw under the heavy barrage put up by the enemy. Day wet and cold. CASUALTIES - 2 O.R. killed and 1 O.R. wounded.	
	11-11-17		Brigade fired preparatory Barrages at 6-0 a.m. and harassing fire by day on enemy tracks. Work was continued on new positions. CASUALTIES - Nil.	
	12-11-17		A fine clear day with frost. C/161 moved two more guns up to Forward position. Brigade fired a Preparatory Barrage at 4-45 a.m. CASUALTIES - Nil.	
	13-11-17		C/161 moved two guns into action in forward position and A/161 two guns. The C.R.A. inspected the positions and expressed his appreciation of the work done by this Brigade. Day was misty and work progressed. Enemy counter-attacked Canadian Division on right at PASCHENDAEL, but were repulsed. - 3 attacks being made during the day. CASUALTIES - 1 O.R. wounded (bomb splinter) and 1 O.R. slightly wounded remained at duty.	
	14-11-17		Preparatory Barrage fired at 5-15 a.m. A/161 moved 4 guns forward; C/161 occupied position with one section; also, A/161, remainder of these Batteries being withdrawn to Wagon Lines. B/161 remained in action as before. B/161 and D/161 only Batteries of Brigade in action, A/161 and C/161 being silent. CASUALTIES - 2 O.R. killed and 4 O.R. wounded.	
	15-11-17		A preparatory Barrage was fired at 6-15 a.m. and harassing fire continued. A/161 now have 6 guns in action at forward position, as well as C/161; one section of each Battery being in action in case of 'S.O.S'. B/161 were heavily shelled in the morning losing 1 gun and 4 men. CASUALTIES - 1 O.R. Killed, 1 O.R. Shell shock and 2 O.R. wounded.	
	16-11-17		Barrage at 7-15 a.m. fired. 1 gun of C/161 was damaged by shell-fire during the night. CASUALTIES - Nil.	
	17-11-17		At midnight 16/17th orders were received for personnel of the Brigade to relieve detachments of 36th Brigade, 2nd Divisional Artillery, on the Divisional front immediately on	

(A7092). Wt. W12899/M1293. 75,000. 1/17. D.D. & L., Ltd. Forms/C.2118/14.

Army Form C. 2118.

WAR DIARY
INTELLIGENCE SUMMARY.
(Erase heading not required.)

Instructions regarding War Diaries and Intelligence Summaries are contained in F. S. Regs, Part II. and the Staff Manual respectively. Title pages will be prepared in manuscript.

Place	Date	Hour	Summary of Events and Information	Remarks and references to Appendices
	18-11-17		our right. A/161, B/161 and C/161 withdrew detachments and took over positions of 15th, 64th and 71st Batteries during the day. They now form part of a Group under O.C. 168th Brigade R.F.A. near ST: JULIAN. D/161 withdrew detachments to wagon line. Guns were left in position under a guard. No change of wagon lines took place; Headquarters did not move. Forward positions were shelled fairly heavily at 9-15 a.m. causing casualties to other Batteries and Infantry working parties, 20 minutes after detachments and G.S. wagons of Brigade had cleared. Also, the forward Telephone Exchange handed over to 126th A.F.A. Brigade was blown in just after relief was completed. CASUALTIES - 5 O.R. wounded and 1 O.R. slightly wounded remained at duty.	
	19-11-17		Nothing of importance occurred. New positions seemed quieter than the old front, and ammunition supply easier as the roads are in better condition. Lieut; H.W.TILMAN, M.C., C/161, left to join R.H.A. of 1st Cavalry Division. CASUALTIES - 1 O.R. wounded.	
	20-11-17		Nothing of importance occurred. CASUALTIES - Nil. Headquarters, 161st Brigade R.F.A. withdrew to wagon lines near VIAMERTINGHE vacated by 36th Brigade. CASUALTIES - Nil.	
	21-11-17		Headquarters Wagon Line moved to new Billets. To-day the weather broke and everything once again is a sea of mud. 2/Lieut. W. E. WILSON (S.R) posted C/161 from 32nd D.A.C. CASUALTIES - Nil.	
	22-11-17		A/161 moved two guns forward to position near B/161. C/161 commenced to withdraw detached section to rejoin remainder of Battery. Belgian Interpreter MONS. JULES VAN STAPPEN joined. CASUALTIES - Nil.	
	23-11-17.		Weather fine and ground dry. The Lieut-Colonel Commanding inspected B/161 Wagon line. CASUALTIES - Nil.	
	24-11-17.		32nd Division - less Artillery - relieved 1st Division. 32nd Division less Artillery. Command of Divisional Artillery Group passed to C.R.A. 32nd Division at 10-0 a.m. A/161 moved remaining 4 guns into action at forward position. 2/Lieut. F.A.CLAXTON, attached A/161, posted to Z/32 T.M.Bty. CASUALTIES - 1 O.R. wounded.	
	25-11-17		Nothing unusual to report. CASUALTIES - Nil.	
	26-11-17			

1 O.R. wounded.

Army Form C. 2118.

WAR DIARY

INTELLIGENCE SUMMARY.

(Erase heading not required.)

Instructions regarding War Diaries and Intelligence Summaries are contained in F. S. Regs., Part II. and the Staff Manual respectively. Title pages will be prepared in manuscript.

Place	Date	Hour	Summary of Events and Information	Remarks and references to Appendices
In the Field	26-11-17		'S.O.S' alarm was raised at 7-14 p.m. and Batteries opened fire. No Infantry attack was reported. CASUALTIES - Nil.	
	27-11-17		Nothing unusual to report. CASUALTIES - Nil. 1 O.R. wounded.	
	28-11-17		A/168 relieved B/161 who withdrew to their wagon lines. 2/Lieut V.J.HORTON (S.R) reported for duty on posting from 32nd D.A.G. and was posted to D/161. CASUALTIES:- Nil.	
	29-11-17		Lieut- Colonel A.G.ARBUTHNOT C.M.G., D.S.O. wounded and admitted into hospital. Command of Brigade passed to T/Capt; &/Major E.A.CHISHOLM M.C., C/161. Enemy shewed considerable activity against back areas, shelling VLAMERTINGHE and POPERINGHE with long range H.V. Guns. CASUALTIES - 1 Officer and 3 O.R. wounded.	
	30-11-17		Enemy continued to shell back areas as on 29-11-17. CASUALTIES - Nil.	

In the Field,
30-11-17.

[signature]
Captain & Adjutant,
for Major,
Commanding 161st (Yorks;) Brigade R. F. A.

161ST (Works) Brigade R.F.A.

W. 15517—M. 141.   250,000.   1/16.   L.S.& Co.   Forms/W 3091/2.   Army Form W. 3091.

Cover for Documents.

Nature of Enclosures.

War Diary

for period

1st to 31st December 1917.

Notes, or Letters written.

Army Form C. 2118.

WAR DIARY
or
INTELLIGENCE SUMMARY.
(Erase heading not required.)

161st (Yorks;) Brigade R.F.A. (1)

Instructions regarding War Diaries and Intelligence
Summaries are contained in F. S. Regs., Part II.
and the Staff Manual respectively. Title pages
will be prepared in manuscript.

Place	Date	Hour	Summary of Events and Information	Remarks and references to Appendices
In the Field	2-12-17		At 3 a.m. 97th Infantry Brigade, plus 2 Battalions 98th Infantry Brigade, attacked. No artillery barrage was employed, but certain spots were shelled continuously, fire lifting as our Infantry advanced. The first rush was carried out with no artillery fire at all. Our Infantry captured all their objectives, but at 4-15 P.M. a strong enemy counter-attack developed, and we were compelled to withdraw to our original line. The Division on our right were similarly forced back. 51 Prisoners were captured on the Divisional front. 2/Lieut. W.G.LAUNDER, A/161, admitted hospital sick. CASUALTIES - Nil.	
	3-12-17		2/Lieut. V.J.HORTON, D/161, killed at Infantry Battalion Headquarters. other Casualties - Nil. Day passed quietly. Original intention of re-attacking abandoned.	
	4-12-17 to 6-12-17		Period passed quietly. On the 5th O's C., B/161, C/161, D/161 reconnoitred Battery positions of 1st Divisional Artillery on the STROMBEKE, preparatory to taking over on the 10/11th and 11/12th. CASUALTIES during this period - Nil.	
	7-12-17		Lieut-Colonel LORD WYNFORD D.S.O. posted to and assumed command of Brigade from 2nd D.A.G During the night the enemy crossed the PADERBEKE, which was frozen, and drove between our Left Battalion and the Division on our left. They were eventually repulsed with very few casualties to us, leaving 8 prisoners in our hands. Weather clear and frosty. CASUALTIES - Nil.	
	9-12-17		B/161, C/161 & D/161 relieved personnel of 114th, 46th and 40th Batteries respectively of 1st Divisional Artillery on the STROMBEKE, and form - with A/161 - No: 3 Group of 32nd Divisional Artillery Group. Lieut. E.H.BINDLOSS (Signal Officer) proceeded to H.q. 32nd Divisional Artillery, vice Capt: T.RANSFORD on leave; 2/Lieut. E. COKE M.C. A/161 to H.Q/161 vice Lieut. BINDLOSS; 2/Lieut. T.E.WILSON C/161 to A/161 vice 2/Lieut. COKE.	
	10-12-17		CASUALTIES - 2 O.R. wounded and 1 O.R. injured by collapse of dug-out caused by hostile fire. A/161 moved guns to new position close to former one. Relief completed.	
	11-12-17		Major E.A.CHISHOLM M.C., C/161, proceeded on leave to U.K. from this date until 25-12-17. Major J.F.K.LOCKHART - attached A/161 - rejoined 32nd D.A.G., Capt: M. KING-FRENCH assuming command of A/161.	
	12-12-17		CASUALTIES - 1 O.R. wounded (Gas) and died on 12-12-17.	
	13-12-17		Brigade Headquarters took over from No; 3 Group at CHEDDARVILLA, ST: JULIEN. Capt: C.M.WARD M.C. took over command of A/161.	

Army Form C. 2118.

WAR DIARY
or
INTELLIGENCE SUMMARY.
(Erase heading not required.)

(2.)   161st (Yorks:) Brigade R.F.A.

Instructions regarding War Diaries and Intelligence
Summaries are contained in F. S. Regs., Part II.
and the Staff Manual respectively. Title pages
will be prepared in manuscript.

Place	Date	Hour	Summary of Events and Information	Remarks and references to Appendices
In the Field.	14-12-17		B/161 and D/161 withdrew one section from positions in the STROMBEKE. CASUALTIES Nil.	
	15-12-17		C/161 were relieved by personnel of 32nd Battery. D/161 withdrew remaining Howitzers and B/161 one more section. CASUALTIES - Nil.	
	16-12-17		Brigade Headquarters moved to ALBERTA - a large concrete German Battalion command post - very comfortable. Personnel of C/161, B/161 (less 1 section) and D/161 relieved personnel of A/84, C/84 and D/84 A.F.A. Brigade at SPOT FARM. B/161 still retains forward section in STROMBEKE. CASUALTIES - Nil.	
	17-12-17		B/161 (2 sections) took over. C/161 position, C/161 moving 6 guns into their original position. CASUALTIES - Nil.	
	18-12-17		Weather clear and frosty. Brigade Headquarters moved back to CHEDDAR VILLA, as ALBERTA was taken over by Infantry Brigade Headquarters. CASUALTIES - 1 O.R. to hospital (Shell Shock).	
	19-12-17		Day hard and frosty. Harassing fire carried out continuously during the 24 hours, each Battery firing about 170 rounds in 24 hours of the 24. Salvage of ammunition, material etc; etc; being pressed on, and clearing of empty cartridge cases continued. 2/Lieutenants (S.R) R.L.BLAKE, J.H.G.WAY, F. ADDISON, posted from 32nd D.A.C. and attached to D/161, C/161 and A/161 respectively. Capt. C.H.WARD M.C. A/161 authorised to wear badges of rank of Major; Auth; 32nd Div. No. Lieut. B.C.TRAFFES-LOMAX M.C. C/161 ditto ditto (Capt;) A/100/201 d/- 19-12-17 CASUALTIES - Nil.	
	20-12-17		Brigade Headquarters moved back again from CHEDDAR VILLA to ALBERTA to be in close touch with the Infantry Brigade. Lieut. J. FILTNESS, D/161, granted leave to United Kingdom from 22-12-17 to 5-1-18. 2/Lieut. HON. T.F.J.I.MASSY , A/161, admitted hospital sick and evacuated to C.C.S. Other CASUALTIES, Nil.	
	22-12-17		An attempt was made to straighten our line by cutting across the reentrant by a series of Posts. This was not successful owing to enemy artillery and M.G. fire. CASUALTIES - Nil.	
	23-12-17		A prisoner captured bearing Orders for enemy reliefs. Batteries barraged approaches and tracks instead of their usual night firing. (Continued)	

Army Form C. 2118.

WAR DIARY

or

INTELLIGENCE SUMMARY.

(Erase heading not required.)

161st (Yorks.) Brigade R.F.A

Instructions regarding War Diaries and Intelligence
Summaries are contained in F. S. Regs., Part II.
and the Staff Manual respectively. Title pages
will be prepared in manuscript.

Place	Date	Hour	Summary of Events and Information	Remarks and references to Appendices
In the Field	23-12-17 (Contd.)		2/Lieut. E.H.WEILER (S.R) posted from 22nd D.A.C. and attached to B/161. CASUALTIES - Nil.	
	24-12-17		14th Infantry Brigade relieved the 97th Infantry Brigade. CASUALTIES - N.1 O.R. wounded (Gas).	
	25-12-17		CHRISTMAS DAY. Messages and good wishes were received from the Divisional Commander and from BRIG: GEN: A.S.COTTON D.S.O. late O.C. Brigade. CASUALTIES - Nil.	
	26-12-17		Snow fell prevented an attempt to rush an enemy Post - bright Moon. Enemy barraged our line from 6 a.m. to 6-45 a.m. and the Division on our right from 7-40 p.m. to 9-0 p.m. CASUALTIES - Nil.	
	27-12-17		Major E.A. CHISHOLM M.C., C/161, returned off leave. Lieut-Col. LORD WYNFORD D.S.O. attached to No; 5 Squadron R.F.C. until 31-12 -17. Major F.C. HUNT, B/161, assumed command of Brigade vice Lieut-Col. LORD WYNFORD D.S.O. Lieut. dearhem B.C. TRAFFES-LOMAX M.C., C/161, posted to and assumed command of B/161 vice Major HUNT. At 7-40 p.m. enemy barrage fire opened on front of Division on our right. Batteries fired on S.O.S. lines for 45 minutes in support of flanking Brigade. Infantry reported as follows:- "Density of barrage was good; well distributed and no noticeable Gaps. It gave a feeling of confidence to the troops in the line. Barrage could not have been better placed from a protective point of view". During the night a 4.2 Gas bombardment of B/161 took place between 1 and 2 a.m. CASUALTIES - Nil.	
	28-12-17		Snow still covers the ground and weather remains clear. B/161 were shelled out between 12 noon and 2 p.m., about 200 5.9's falling in vicinity of battery position, but no damage was done. CASUALTIES - 1 O.R. wounded.	
	29-12-17		A slight thaw, which continued to 30th inst. Casualties:- 1 O.R. wounded (Gas).	
	30-12-17		2/Lieut. R.E.T.BELL (S.R) posted from 32nd D.A.C. and attached to A/161. Casualties - 2 O.R. wounded (Gas).	
	31-12-17		2/Lieut. E.A.NEW (S.R) posted from 32nd D.A.C. and attached to C/161. 14th Infantry Brigade were relieved on night 30/31st by 117th Infantry Brigade (39th Division), the 32nd Division (less Artillery) going to back areas for rest and training. The enemy put down a 20 minutes "straffe" of all calibres on front line at 6 a.m., a few /rounds	

(A7092) Wt W14899/M1593 75.10.00. 1/17. D. D. & L., Ltd. Forms/C.2118/14.

WAR DIARY
INTELLIGENCE SUMMARY.
(Erase heading not required.)

Army Form C. 2118.

Place	Date	Hour	Summary of Events and Information	Remarks and references to Appendices
In the Field	31-12-17 (Contd.)		rounds falling on Battery position areas. The "S.O.S." was sent up and the Brigade fired accordingly. No hostile Infantry action developed. A/161 and B/161 moved their wagon lines on 30th and 31st to stables adjacent to D/161 and H.J./161 wagon lines EAST OF CANAL. Casualties:- 3 O.R. admitted hospital (Gas shell poisoning) The period from Decr. 12th to end of month has been marked by the resumption of peace warfare. Harassing fire on communications, strong points and tracks has been continued day and night, and a 'Sniping Gun' of B/161 has taken every opportunity of inflicting casualties on the enemy. A 'Close Defence' Gun has also been pushed forward. The work of salvage has been pushed on, some thousands of empty cartridge cases being returned, as well as ammunition, equipment, and miscellaneous. Construction of better shelter for detachments has been hindered by the snow and cold weather. Reserve positions for defence of the Corps Line have been marked out and now started. Throughout, work has been very seriously hampered by shortage of men - an average of 40 in hospital, 60 on command and 50 under strength, seriously depletes the strength of the Brigade. There is a shortage of N.C.O's, and the work of training Gunners never more urgent than at the present moment, is thereby rendered difficult. It is hoped that an opportunity of resting, training and overhauling may shortly be ours. In spite of the losses and hardships suffered in the past campaign, it is the sure confidence of victory, and with a set determination to uphold our reputation, that the 161st (Yorks) Brigade, R.F.A. enters upon another year of the war. HONOURS & AWARDS FOR THE MONTH OF DECEMBER 1917:- Major E.A.CHISHOLM M.C. C/161, awarded Bar to Military Cross. Capt. J.W.BUCKLEY, B/161 awarded MILITARY CROSS. 2/Lieut. A.S.BLACKMAN, D/161, awarded MILITARY CROSS L/26563 Bombardier J.FOX, D/161, awarded D.C.M. Brig: Gen. A.S.COTTON D.S.O. (late Comdg: 161st (Yorks) Bde. R.F.A.) and Capt: H.L.McCORMICK R.A.M.C. mentioned in despatches.	Authority.- 11 Corps No. 2/H.R/32/3-4.5 c/- 16-12-17, 32nd D.R.O. 2652 d/- 16-12-17. R.H.Hunt Major, Commanding 161st (Yorks) Brigade R.F.A.

31-10-17.

161st (Yorks.) Brigade R.F.A.

W. 15517—M. 141. 250,000. 1/16. L.S.&Co. Forms/W 3091/2. Army Form W. 3091.

Cover for Documents.

Nature of Enclosures.

— War Diary —

covering period

1st to 31st January 1918

Notes, or Letters written.

Army Form C. 2118.

WAR DIARY

161st (Yorks;) Brigade R.F.A.

INTELLIGENCE SUMMARY.

(Erase heading not required.)

Instructions regarding War Diaries and Intelligence Summaries are contained in F. S. Regs., Part II. and the Staff Manual respectively. Title pages will be prepared in manuscript.

Place	Date	Hour	Summary of Events and Information	Remarks and references to Appendices
In the Field	1-1-18		C/161 moved to new wagon lines with the rest of the Brigade EAST of the CANAL, by Bridge Four. Lieut-Colonel LORD WYNFORD D.S.O. resumed command on return from attachment to No: 5 Squadron R.F.C., Major P.C.HUNT resuming command of B/161.	
	2-1-18		Enemy shelled C/161 position lightly - a stray shell causing 4 casualties (2 killed and 2 slightly wounded remaining at duty) inside a dug-out. 1 O.R. of B/161 slightly wounded remained at duty. Prisoner was captured with orders for enemy relief. Approaches etc; were barraged accordingly. Casualties - Nil.	
	3-1-18		Weather continues hard and cold. Enemy aircraft active, 1 flying 200 ft above Brigade Headquarters having apparently lost its way in the fog.	
	4-1-18		a/Major C.W.WARD M.C. A/161, proceeded to attend Battery Commanders' Course at SHOEBURYNESS commencing 6-1-18, A/Capt. M. KING-FRENCH assuming command of A/161. a/Major C.W.WARD M.C. granted 14 days leave on completion of above Course. Casualties - Nil.	
	5-1-18		Day foggy and very quiet. No harassing fire carried out. Casualties - Nil.	
	6-1-18		Day passed quietly; nothing to report. Relief of 168th Brigade R.F.A. by 174th Brigade. (39th Div.Arty.) commenced. 2/Lieut. F.W.HOOK and 2/Lieut. J.H.G.WAY attended Course at Fourth Army Artillery School. Casualties - Nil.	
	7-1-18		Enemy shelled area of Battery positions - 2 guns of D/161 were knocked out;2/Lieut. A.S. BLACKLAWS M.C., D/161 and 1 O.R. slightly wounded. Relief of 168th Brigade R.F.A. completed. a/Capt; B.C.TRAPPES-LOMAX M.C., B/161 attached to No; 7 Squadron R.F.C. Lieut. B. BAKEWELL B/161 attached to 'R' Anti-Aircraft Battery. Lieut. C.R.CLIFF C/161 granted leave to England from 7-1-18 to 21-1-18.	
	8-1-18		Snow fell during the morning and weather turned hard again. 1 Section of A/161, C/161 and D/161 were relieved by sections of 186th Brigade R.F.A., (39th Div.Arty.) Command of Divisional Artillery passed to C.R.A. 39th Division. Casualties 1 O.R. wounded.	
	9-1-18		Remaining 2 Sections of A/161, C/161, and D/161 were relieved by sections of 186th Brigade R.F.A. and moved to wagon lines. Casualties 1 O.R. slightly wounded remained at duty.	

Army Form C. 2118.

WAR DIARY
or
INTELLIGENCE SUMMARY.

161st (Yorks;) Bde. R.F.A.

(Erase heading not required.)

Instructions regarding War Diaries and Intelligence Summaries are contained in F.S. Regs., Part II. and the Staff Manual respectively. Title pages will be prepared in manuscript.

Place	Date	Hour	Summary of Events and Information	Remarks and references to Appendices
In the Field	10-1-18		Lieut-Colonel LORD WYNFORD D.SO. assumed command of 32nd Divisional Artillery vice Brig; Gen. J.A.TYLER C.M.G., on leave, Major E.A.CHISHOLM M.C. C/161 assuming command of 161st Brigade R.F.A. and a/Capt; H. BARRETT command of C/161. Headquarters 161st Brigade R.F.A. moved from ALBERTA to wagon lines, having been relieved by 186th Brigade R.F.A.	
	12-1-18		a/Capt; B.C.TRAPPES-LOMAX M.C. rejoined B/161 from attached No; 7 Squadron R.F.C. 2/Lieut. T.F.J.I.MASSY, a/161 on leave from 12-1-18 to 26-1-18.	
	13-1-18		a/Capt; B.C.TRAPPES-LOMAX M.C., B/161 granted leave from 13-1-18 to 20-1-18.	
	16-1-18		Lieut-Col; LORD WYNFORD D.SO. relinquished command of 32nd Divisional Artillery.	
	18-1-18		Lieut-Col; LORD WYNFORD D.S.O. proceeded to attend Senior R.A.Officers' Course at SHOEBURYNESS commencing 20-1-18. aCapt. & Adjt. R.L.CREASY M.C. on leave from 17-1-18 to 31-1-18, a/Capt; J. FILTNESS D/161 assuming duties of Adjutant. Lieut.C.L.W.HAFFENDEN M.C. reposted to Brigade and posted to D/161.	
	15-1-18		Lieut.E.H.BINDLOSS M.C. (R.E) - attached H.W. 32nd Divisional Arty. - granted leave from 15-1-18 to 29-1-18.	
	16-1-18		2/Lieut. E.COKE M.C. on leave from 16-1-18 to 30-1-18.	
	20-1-18		a/Capt; B.C.TRAPPES-LOMAX M.C., B/161, attended Battery Commanders' Course at SHOEBURYNESS. Capt; H.L.McCORMICK R.A.M.C. on leave from 20-1-18 to 3-2-18, he having been relieved by Capt; J.T.HEFFERNAN R.A.M.C. 91st Field Ambulance, on 18-1-18. 2/Lieut.W.E.WILSON A/B61 attached to C/161. 2/Lieut. E.A.JEW C/161 attended Course at II Corps Anti-Gas School.	
	19-1-18		96th Infantry Brigade moved into HOSPITAL FARM area.	
	20-1-18		97th Infantry Brigade moved into LANGEMARCK No; 3 Area.	
	20/21-1-18		3 guns per Battery were taken up into action at positions near CHEDDAR VILLA, a guard being placed over the Guns. Batteries form part of II Corps Defence Line.	
	22-1-18		32nd Divisional Headquarters - less Artillery - moved from Camp X. to CANAL BANK C.25.d.0.0. 14th Infantry Brigade moved to HOSPITAL FARM area; 96th Infantry Brigade moved to area EAST of CANAL.	
	23-1-18		Lieut. B. BAKEWELL rejoined B/161 from 'R' Anti-Aircraft Battery.	
	24-1-18		Major E.H.P.PEASE-WATKIN D.S.O. reposted from Base and assumed command of Brigade, a/Major E.A.CHISHOLM M.C. resuming command of C/161.	

Army Form C. 2118.

WAR DIARY
or
INTELLIGENCE SUMMARY.
(Erase heading not required.)

161st Brigade R.F.A.

Instructions regarding War Diaries and Intelligence Summaries are contained in F. S. Regs., Part II. and the Staff Manual respectively. Title pages will be prepared in manuscript.

Place	Date	Hour	Summary of Events and Information	Remarks and references to Appendices
In the Field	25-1-19		a/Major E.A.CHISHOLM M.C., C/161, a/Major J.W.BUCKLEY M.C., D/161 and 2/Lieut; R.G.JOHNSON B/161 on leave in PARIS until 29-1-18 inclusive.	
	25-1-18		Major E.H.P.PEASE-WATKIN D.S.O. Commanding Brigade reconnoitred with Battery Commanders positions occupied by 82nd and 83rd Brigades R.F.A.	
	25-1-1		a/Capt; M. KING-FRENCH, A/161, on leave from 25-1-18 to 1-2-18.	
	26-1-18		a/Major P. CROW M.C. reposted to 161st Brigade R.F.A. from Base and assumed command of A/161 on this date.	
	27-1-18		2/Lieut. A.G.DRYLAND B/161 attended Course at Fourth Army Anti Gas School commencing on this date,	
	28-1-18		a/Capt; H. BARRETT, C/161, on leave from this date to 27-2-18.	
	27/29-1-18		32nd Division (less Artillery) relieved 18th and 1st Divisions (less Artillery).	
	29-1-18		Lieut. B. BAKEWELL, B/161, on leave from this date to 12-2-18.	
			2/Lieut. E.A.JEW rejoined C/161 on completion of course at II Corps Anti-Gas School.	
			Lieut. C.R.CLIFF C/161 rejoined on expiration of leave which had been extended by War Office from 21-1-18 until 28-1-18.	
	30/31-1-18		1 Section per Battery moved into new positions covering 32nd Divisional Infantry on the HOUTHULST FOREST sector, relieving sections of 82nd and 83rd Brigades R.F.A.	
	31-1-18		Lieut. F.J.PHILIPS T.F. posted from Hdqrs. 32nd Divisional Artillery to 161st Brigade R.F.A. and attached A/161.	
	31-1-18/1-2-18		Remaining sections of Batteries of 161st Brigade R.F.A. moved up into action, relieving remaining sections of 82nd and 83rd Brigades R.F.A. 161st Bde.R.F.A. forms part of Right Group, 32nd Divisional Artillery 65th Battery R.F.A. and 123rd Battery R.F.A.) came under the orders of O.C. Right Group 32nd Divisional Artillery (161st Brigade R.F.A.) at 11 a.m. 1-2-18.	
	10-1-18/30-1-18		This period was occupied in re-fitting, re-equipping and instructional and recreational Training of Batteries.	
			HONOURS & AWARDS. Lieut. E.H.BINDLOSS (R.E) Signal officer attached to 161st Brigade R.F.A. from 32nd Divisional Signal Co; R.E. awarded MILITARY CROSS in New Year's Honours List.	
	31-1-18.			

Jonathan Henry Major,
Commanding 161st (Yorks;) Brigade R.F.A.

161st (Works.) Brigade R.F.A.

War Diary

covering period

1st to 28th February 1918.

WAR DIARY or INTELLIGENCE SUMMARY

Army Form C. 2118.

151st (Yorks.) Brigade R.F.A.

(Erase heading not required.)

Instructions regarding War Diaries and Intelligence Summaries are contained in F.S. Regs., Part II. and the Staff Manual respectively. Title pages will be prepared in manuscript.

Place	Date	Hour	Summary of Events and Information	Remarks and references to Appendices
In the Field	1-2-18		Headquarters moved into action from wagon lines, Headquarters being established at IAFIN FARM. Command of Right Group, 32nd Divisional Artillery, passed from Major W.E.CONNOLLY - commanding Right Group (82nd Brigade R.F.A.) to Major E.H.P.PEASE-WATKIN D.S.O. Commanding 151st Brigade R.F.A. at 11 a.m. Capt: & Adjt. R.L.CREASE, M.C. returned off leave and proceeded to Headquarters, 32nd Divisional Artillery, to study the duties of Brigade Major vide G.H.Q. letter O.S./1911/3 dated 19-8-17. 2/Lieut; R.A.WARLEY-SIMON, C/151, assumed duties of Acting Adjutant on this date. Lieut; A.W.DENNISON - Adars - and 2/Lieut; F. ADDISON, A/151, proceeded to Fourth Army Artillery School on Course.	
1/2-2-18			14th Infantry Brigade relieved 97th Infantry Brigade in the HETSAS Sector, the 97th Infantry Brigade being in Divisional Reserve in BOESINGHE No: 2 Area with Headquarters at ZOMMERBLOOM	
3-2-18			Orders received that the Divisional Front would be re-adjusted so as to hold the front with all three Infantry Brigades in the line, each on a front of one Battalion. The 14th Infantry Brigade would be in the Right Brigade Sector, 95th Infantry Brigade in Centre Sector and 97th Infantry Brigade in Left Brigade Sector. 2/Lieut; T.H.G.WARD rejoined C/151 on completion of course at Fourth Army Artillery School. 2/Lieut; F.W.MUCK, D/151 on leave until 17-2-18. 2/Lieut. A.G.DRYLAND rejoined B/151 on completion of Course at Fourth Army Anti-Gas School Lt.a/Capt; R. KING-FREW, A/151, attended Battery Commander's Course at Shoeburyness commencing on this date.	
4-2-18			Raid carried out on GRAVEL FARM V.8.a.0.0. by 105th Infantry Brigade on our right at 7-0 p.m. B/151, C/151, D/151 and 123rd Battery fired in support. The raid was a complete success, the Farm and neighbouring posts were destroyed, also large shelter destroyed. 9 enemy killed in shelter by Bangalore torpedoes which was pushed through loop-hole, the occupants refusing to evacuate. 29 enemy actually killed by our Infantry and 1 O.R. wounded of 4th Company, 94th I.R. brought in for identifications. 1 M.G. destroyed by bombs. Our casualties were 3 O.R. slightly wounded. Message was received expressing excellence of the Artillery fire. Capt: H.L.McCORMICK R.A.M.C. returned off leave. Capt; J.F.HEWERMAN returning to 91st Field Ambulance.	
4/5-2-18			Lieut-Col. LORD MIFFORD D.S.O. proceeded on leave on completion of course at Shoeburyness. 2/Lieut; Hon F.F.J.L.MASSY, A/151 - leave extended to this date on Medical Certificate. 97th Infantry Brigade - less 17th M.L.I - relieved 14th Infantry Brigade in Left Brigade Sector.	

Army Form C. 2118.

WAR DIARY
or
INTELLIGENCE SUMMARY.

(2)   161st (Yorks,) Brigade RFA

(Erase heading not required.)

Instructions regarding War Diaries and Intelligence Summaries are contained in F. S. Regs., Part II. and the Staff Manual respectively. Title pages will be prepared in manuscript.

Place	Date	Hour	Summary of Events and Information	Remarks and references to Appendices
In the Field	5-2-18		Lieut: F.J.PHILLIPS, A/161 and a party of 1 N.C.O. and 10 men proceeded to CALAIS to draw remounts from No; 5 Base Remount Depot.	
	5/6-2-18		14th Infantry Brigade (less 2nd Manchester Regt;) relieved 96th Infantry Brigade in Right Brigade Sector.	
	6-2-18		2nd Manchester Regiment was transferred to 96th Infantry Brigade. Disbandment of 16th Northumberland Fusiliers commenced.	
	7/8-2-18		96th Infantry Brigade relieved 14th and 97th Infantry Brigades in Centre Brigade Sector.	
	8-4-18		Lieut: W. ELLIS, A/161, on leave from this date until 22-2-18.	
	9-2-18		Lieut: E. TURNBULL, D/161 proceeded to R.F.C. as Balloon Observer on probation and is struck off the strength of D/161.	
	10-2-18		14 Reinforcements received from 2nd D.A.C. 1 O.R. wounded.	
	11-2-18		At 10 a.m. A/161 and B/161 came under the orders of O.C.157th Brigade R.F.A. (35th Div.Arty;) and form part of left Brigade, 35th Divisional Artillery. A/28th RFA and B/168 came under the orders of O.C.161st Brigade RFA and along with C/161 and D/161 form Right Group, 32nd Divisional Artillery 2/Lieut: S. MURPHY posted from Second Army Artillery School and attached to D/161. 2/Lieut: A.J.FREAKES posted from Base and attached to D/161. 2/Lieut: F.A.CLAXTON posted from 2/32 T.M.Bty. and attached to C/161. 1 N.C.O. accidentally wounded when clearing a dug-out of refuse. Major E.A.CHISHOLM M.C., C/161, proceeded to attend Battery Commanders' Course at SHOEBURYNESS commencing 16-2-18. Lieut: C.R.CLIFF assuming command of C/161. 2/Lieut:Hon. T.F.J.MASSY's leave extended to this date.	
	12-2-18		7 Reinforcements arrived from 2nd D.A.C.	
	13-2-18		2/Lieut: R.L.BLAKE, D/161, admitted hospital sick.	
	14-2-18		Lieut-Col; LORD WYNFORD D.S.O. rejoined on expiration of leave and resumed command of the Brigade, Major E.H.F PEASE-WATKIN D.S.O. resuming command of D/161.	
	15-2-18		Major C.W.WARD M.C. rejoined and resumed command of A/161.	
	18-2-18		96th and 97th Infantry Brigades under cover of artillery barrage carried out raids on enemy Pill-Boxes etc; the object of the raids being to kill, take prisoners and obtain identifications. Batteries of 161st Brigade R.F.A. fired in support of raid by the 96th Infy.Bde.	
	18/19-2-18		During the operations 27 prisoners and 1 M.G. were brought in. Our casualties were slight. Severe losses were inflicted on the enemy in killed.	

Army Form C. 2118.

WAR DIARY
or
~~INTELLIGENCE SUMMARY~~

(3) 161st (Yorks:) Brigade R.F.A.

(Erase heading not required.)

Instructions regarding War Diaries and Intelligence Summaries are contained in F. S. Regs., Part II. and the Staff Manual respectively. Title pages will be prepared in manuscript.

Place	Date	Hour	Summary of Events and Information	Remarks and references to Appendices
In the Field	19-2-18		Lieut: B. BAKEWELL's leave extended to this date on Medical Certificate.	
	19/20-2-18		14th Infantry Brigade relieved 97th Infantry Brigade in left Sub-Sector.	
	20-2-18		2/Lieut: T.C. CREIGHTON posted from Base and was attached to C/161.	
	21-2-18		Lieut: C.V. THURSTON posted from 32nd D.A.C. to A/161.	
	21/22-2-18		Enemy raided Belgians on our left. Batteries of 161st Brigade R.F.A. opened slow rate of fire in accordance with Mutual Support Scheme.	
	22-2-18		Lieut: F.T. PHILIPS, A/161 and 1 N.C.O. from D/161 proceeded on 2 days course at Salvage and By-Products Depot, CALAIS.	
			2/Lieut: Hon. I.F.T.I. MASSI, A/161 struck off strength - Medical Board ordered by War Office.	
			2/Lieut: F.W. HOOK, D/161 admitted hospital sick.	
	23/24-2-18		16th Lancashire Fusiliers relieved 2nd Manchester Regt; in front system of forward zone, 2nd Manchesters moving to ABRI WOOD and becoming No: 3 Battalion. 15th Lancashire Fusiliers relieved 16th Lancashire Fusiliers in support system of forward zone and became No: 2 Battalion.	
	23-2-18		2/Lieut: R.G. JOHNSON, B/161, granted leave from 24-2-18 to 10-3-18.	
			2/Lieut: S. MURPHY, D/161, attended course commencing to-day at II Corps Anti-Gas School Capt: a/Major J.W. BUCKLEY M.C. on leave from to-day until 26-3-18.	
			1 O.R. wounded.	
	25-2-18		Lieut: a/Capt: F. CROW M.C., attached to No: 9 Squadron R.F.C. for instruction.	
	26-2-18		Raids were carried out on MARECHAL FARM and neighbourhood by 14th and 96th Infantry Brigades.	
	27-2-18		All objectives were captured and 12 prisoners and 2 M.G's taken. Large number of enemy killed. Batteries of 161st Brigade R.F.A. fired in support of raid.	
	28-2-18/1-3-18		Batteries of 161st Brigade R.F.A. fired in support of raid carried out by 35th Division on our right. Enemy retaliated during the night by shelling Battery positions and vicinity thereof with gas shell.	

During the month 21 Reinforcements arrived.

HONOURS and AWARDS during the month :-
27877 Sgt. M.H. GILBERT, A/161) Awarded the Belgian CROIX DE GUERRE.
L/28048 Sgt. C.H. ASHMORE C/161)
L/-3516 Sgt. R.G. GILES, C/161, awarded CHEVALIER DE L'ORDRE DE LEOPOLD II.
(Authy: for above awards - W.S./A/7591 d/-27-1-18; 32nd D.R.O. 2751 dated 3-2-18).

[signature] Lieut-Colonel,
Commanding 161st Brigade R.F.A.

32nd Divisional Artillery.

161st (Yorks) BRIGADE

ROYAL FIELD ARTILLERY

MARCH 1 9 1 8

161st (Yorks.) Brigade R.F.A.

War Diary

for period
1st to 31st March 1918.

WAR DIARY
~~INTELLIGENCE SUMMARY~~

(Erase heading not required.)

161st (Yorks.) Brigade R.F.A. Army Form C. 2118.

Instructions regarding War Diaries and Intelligence Summaries are contained in F. S. Regs., Part II. and the Staff Manual respectively. Title pages will be prepared in manuscript.

Place	Date	Hour	Summary of Events and Information	Remarks and references to Appendices
In the Field	1-3-18			
	2-3-18		14 Reinforcements arrived from 32nd D.A.C. Information received at 7.40 p.m. that enemy would raid COLOMBO HOUSE at 8.20 p.m. Batteries warned accordingly. No enemy action materialised.	
	3-3-18		2/Lieut. S.MURPHY, D/161 posted to 168th Brigade R.F.A. on completion of course at II Corps Anti-Gas School. Lieut.a/Capt. P.CROW,M.G. rejoined No.9 Squadron R.F.C. 2/Lieut. R.A.WYRLEY-BIRCH ceased to perform duties of Acting Adjutant and assumed duties of Orderly Officer.	
	3-3-18		97th Infantry Brigade relieved 96th Infantry Brigade in Right Brigade Sector.	
	4-3-18		Lieut. B.C.TRAPPES-LOMAX,M.G., B/161, attached H.Q./161, and assumed duties of Acting Adjutant.	
	5-3-18		At 3 a.m. Batteries of Brigade fired in support of raid carried out by 35th Division on our right. Results - We reached objectives, but found no enemy - Casualties slight.	
	6-3-18		Information received in the evening again that the enemy might raid COLOMBO HOUSE - Never came off.	
	7-3-18		At 4.15 a.m. C/161 and D/161 fired in support of a raid by the 35th Division on our right. Results - Nil. 4 Other ranks wounded.	
	8-3-18		5 Reinforcements arrived from 32nd D.A.C. Lieut. A.W.DENNISTON, H.Q./161, and 2/Lieut. F.ADDISON, A/161, rejoined on completion of Course at Fourth Army Artillery School. 2/Lieut. R.A.WYRLEY-BIRCH ceased to perform duties of Orderly Officer and was posted to D/161. At 4 a.m. the enemy raided our front and pushed back the 10th Argyll & Sutherland Highlanders, on a 500 yards front. The S.O.S. Signal did not go up. Flammenwerfer were employed. At 9.20 a.m. 161st and 168th Brigades R.F.A. assisted by 157th Bde.R.F.A., fired a barrage (creeping) for a counter-attack by the 2nd K.O.Y.L.I. (2 Coys.) on the right, and the 5th/6th Royal Scots on the left. The enemy was forced to retire, and in one place. the K.O.Y.L.I. advanced to 300 yds. beyond our lines. The barrage continued until 11.15 a.m. on the final objective	
	11-3-18.		2/Lieut. R.G.JOHNSON, B/161, returned off leave.	
	12-3-18		5 reinforcements arrived from D.A.C.	
	13-3-18.		At 7.25 p.m. the enemy opened a heavy bombardment (77 mm. 10.5 cm. 15 cm.,T.M's.and M.G's) on our front opposite COLOMBO HOUSE. About 20 of the enemy were seen advancing: the S.O.S. was put up and they were dispersed by rifle, M.G.fire,and our barrage. They did not reach our lines	
	14-3-18.		Lieut. C.L.W.HAFFENDEN,M.G.; D/161, wounded by Machine Gun Fire in leg. 6 reinforcements arrived.	
	15-3-18.		Lieut.C.L.W.HAFFENDEN, M.G., D/161, to C.C.S.	

Army Form C. 2118.

(2)

WAR DIARY
INTELLIGENCE SUMMARY

161st (Yorks.) Brigade R.F.A.

(Erase heading not required.)

Instructions regarding War Diaries and Intelligence Summaries are contained in F.S. Regs, Part II. and the Staff Manual respectively. Title pages will be prepared in manuscript.

Place	Date	Hour	Summary of Events and Information	Remarks and references to Appendices
In the Field.	16-3-18.		The enemy opened up a heavy M.G., T.M. and shell bombardment on our Left Battalion Front. The S.O.S. was sent up and the Brigade fired in support. The enemy did not reach our lines. This happened at 9 p.m.	
	17-3-18.		At 5 a.m. the enemy heavily shelled the Batteries and Headquarters with 'Mustard' Gas. No Infantry action followed.	
	18-3-18.		At 2 a.m. the Batteries and Headquarters were again subjected to a heavy Gas Shell bombardment. 5 O.R.wounded (GAS).	
	19-3-18.		Lieut. J.FITNESS, D/161, rejoined on completion of Course and Leave. 1 O.R.wounded (GAS).	
	20-3-18		A slight gas bombardment during night. Very misty. 1 O.R.wounded (GAS); 1 O.R.wounded, remained at duty.	
	21-3-18.		Heavy back area bombardment all day. 161st Brigade R.F.A.Wagon Lines shelled, also ELVERDINGHE, BOESINGHE, POPERINGHE, PROVEN, and PESELHOEK. No attack followed. (Enemey offensive South commenced). 1 O.R.killed.	
	22-3-18.		Lieut. J.FITNESS, D/161, assumed duties of Acting Adjutant; Capt.B.C.TRAPPES-LOMAX M.C., B/161, attached H.Q./161, ceased to perform duties of Acting Adjutant, and rejoined B/161. Lieut. C.V.THORNTON, A/161, attached D/161. 2/Lieut. F.ADDISON, A/161, attached H.Q./161, rejoined A/161. 10 reinforcements arrived from 32nd D.A.C. 2 O.R.wounded (GAS); 1 O.R.wounded.	
	23-3-18.		Lieut. C.L.W.HAFFENDEN,M.C., rejoined D/161 from hospital. 2/Lieut. T.G.CREIGHTON, C/161, attached R.A.,Fifth Army. Lieut. W. ELLIS rejoined A/161 on completion of Gas Course. 1 O.R.wounded.	
	24-3-18		1 O.R.wounded (GAS).	
	25-3-18.		Lieut. C.V.THORNTON, A/161 (attached D/161) rejoined A/161.	
	26-3-18.		Lieut. C.E.LEACH, 16th Northumberland Fusiliers, attached H.Q./161 for Course of Instruction. 1 O.R.killed; 4 O.R.wounded: 3 O.R.wounded (GAS). 10 reinforcements arrived from 32nd D.A.C.	
	27-3-18.		Belgians arrived with a view to taking over from the Brigade. Belgian Infantry took over line in evening. Capt.J.W.BUCKLEY,M.C., D/161, returned off leave.	

Army Form C. 2118.

WAR DIARY 161st (Yorks.) Brigade R.F.A.
or
INTELLIGENCE SUMMARY.
(Erase heading not required.)

Place	Date	Hour	Summary of Events and Information	Remarks and references to Appendices
In the Field.	27-3-18.		2/Lieut. W.R.GOODMAN, C/161, returned off leave.	
	28-3-18.		Very quiet. Belgians again visited Battery Positions. 1 O.R. wounded.	
	29-3-18	6 a.m.,	Belgian Artillery brought in a few guns; during the evening the Belgians had four guns in C/161 position and 4 guns in C/161 position.	
	30-3-18.		Relief by Belgian Artillery completed. Headquarters,161 Bde.R.F.A.moved down to Wagon Lines at SIEGE CAMP.	
	31-3-18		H.Q./161 and Batteries entrained at PROVEN and detrained at SAVY BERLETTE. Headquarters and Batteries then marched to HABARCQ.	

31-3-18.

Lieut;
for Lieut-Colonel,
Commanding 161st (Yorks.) Brigade R.F.A.

32nd Div.
VI.Corps.

Headquarters,

161st BRIGADE, R.F.A.

A P R I L

1 9 1 8

WB 28

War Diary

April 1915.

161st Brigade R.F.A.

WAR DIARY   161st (Yorks.) Brigade R.F.A.

INTELLIGENCE SUMMARY

(Erase heading not required.)

Instructions regarding War Diaries and Intelligence
Summaries are contained in F. S. Regs., Part II.
and the Staff Manual respectively. Title pages
will be prepared in manuscript.

Place	Date	Hour	Summary of Events and Information	Remarks and references to Appendices
In the Field	1-4-18.		Headquarters and Batteries detrained at SAVY and TINQUES; billeting for the night at HABARCQ.	
	2-4-18.		1 section per Battery relieved 1 section per battery of 152nd Brigade R.F.A.	
	3-4-18.		Headquarters,161st Brigade R.F.A. relieved headquarters,152nd Brigade R.F.A. at RANSART; remaining sections completed reliefs; Wagon Lines at GAUDIEMPRE.	
	4-4-18.		Forward positions reconnoitred by Battery Commanders and ammunition taken up. A/161 moved Anti-tank Gun to forward position.	
	5-4-18.		Capt.(& Adjutant) R.L.CREASY,M.C., returned from Course of attachment at R.A.H.Q., 32nd Div. Lieut. A.W.DENNISTON rejoined from leave. A/161 moved to new positions; one section per remainder moved forward. Day quiet. 3 O.R. wounded, 1 O.R.killed.	
	6-4-18.		Registration commenced. Remaining guns moved forward. 2/Lieut. R.ROTHWELL posted & joined Brigade from R.H.'& R.F.A. Base Depot. 2/Lieut. J.E.BEANLAND posted & joined Brigade from R.H. & R.F.A.Base Depot.	
	7-4-18.		Day passed quietly; forward O.P.chosen and registration completed. 1 O.R.wounded.	
	8-4-18.		Headquarters, 97th Infantry Brigade moved out of RANSART. Enemy quiet except for gas shelling of ADINFER WOOD. 1 Officer wounded (Gas) - 2/Lieut. F.A.CLAXTON, D/161 D/161 heavily gas shelled in ADINFER WOOD. 3 O.R.wounded (Gas).	
	9-4-18.		D/161 drew back to positions out of gas zone; all Officers and 19 O.R.effected and sent down to Wagon Lines - mostly in eyes. 8 O.R.wounded (Gas).	
	10-4-18.		45 Reinforcements arrived from 32nd D.A.C. Harassing fire has continued during this period between 7 p.m. and 6 a.m.; sniping and registration during the day. A concentration was fired during the day on hostile Batteries thought to be active.	
	11-4-18.		An enemy attack is thought possible at any moment; rear positions and routes have been reconnoitred and arrangements made for ammunition supply. O.Ps. are in depth; visual has been arranged, and close liaison with the Infantry.	

INTELLIGENCE SUMMARY

(Erase heading not required.)

Instructions regarding War Diaries and Intelligence Summaries are contained in F. S. Regs., Part II. and the Staff Manual respectively. Title pages will be prepared in manuscript.

Place	Date	Hour	Summary of Events and Information	Remarks and references to Appendices
In the Field	12-4-18.		Day passed quietly; very warm and fine; great E.A.activity. Enemy shelled back areas with long range guns with some pertinacity. 2/Lieut. E.H.WEIER, B/161, posted to 32nd D.A.C.	
	13-4-18.		72nd Army Brigade R.F.A. (Lieut-Colonel RICHEY) came into action as a Sub-group under O.C.,161st Brigade R.F.A. Lay quiet.	
	14-4-18.		28 Reinforcements arrived from 32nd D.A.C. Headquarters,161st Brigade R.F.A. moved to valley near 97th Infantry Brigade Headquarters. (Nearest enemy battery some 4,000 yds. away'.) A cold wind made tents rather chilly change.	
	15-4-18.		Day was quiet; 72nd Brigade registering. Continual reports of short shooting have lead to the discovery of some bad ammunition; this has caused a great deal of trouble. Day was quiet. 2/Lieut. A.J.FREAKS wounded at D/161 position.	
	16-4-18.		Lay quiet; nothing to report. A/161 made a silent battery, firing only "for S.O.S. and Counter Preparation".	
	17-4-18.) 18-4-18.)		Passed quietly. Under orders from C.R.A. B/161 became a silent Battery vice A/161. 12 reinforcements arrived from 32nd D.A.C. 17-4-18. 1 O.R.wounded 18-4-18.	
	19-4-18.		Gas bombardments by Howitzer Batteries of Divisional Artilleries during night have been carried out on an average of once every two nights. The enemy's gas shelling has died down. The front is in all respects normal except for no wiring on the enemy's front.	
	21-4-18.		B/161 was engaged by a 15 c.m. How. during early afternoon - Target appears to have been the old gun pits used by the Battery as a mess. 1 man slightly wounded; no casualties to equipment.	
	22-4-18.		D/161 assisted in a Gas Bombardment of suspected enemy Headquarters. 1 O.R. wounded (Gas). Lieut. G.DUNDAS,M.C., posted to the Brigade from 32nd D.A.C.	
	23-4-18.		**Enemy artillery rather more active, several area bombardments being put down,but none near the Batteries.** Several reportsof faulty ammunition received. 2/Lieut. T.CAMPBELL posted to Brigade from R.H. & R.F.A.Base Depot.	

Instructions regarding War Diaries and Intelligence
Summaries are contained in F. S. Regs., Part II.
and the Staff Manual respectively. Title pages
will be prepared in manuscript.

-3-

INTELLIGENCE SUMMARY

(Erase heading not required.)

Place	Date	Hour	Summary of Events and Information	Remarks and references to Appendices
In the Field	24-4-18		Day passed quietly.	
	25-4-18		A bright clear day. Enemy shelled ADINFER WOOD rather heavily, and enemy artillery was considerably more active. 1 O.R.wounded.	
	26-4-18		A dull day with some rain. General SHUTE relinquishes Command of 32nd Division on promotion to command of Corps.	
	27-4-18		Day passed quietly. One section per battery 161st Brigade and 168th Brigade relieved one section of 74th and 75th Brigades, Guards Division, during the night 27/28th. The left Group of the 2nd Division, who were on our left.	
	28-4-18		Headquarters 161st Bde.R.F.A.relieved the Headquarters of the Guards Artillery, taking over command at noon. Sections that went in on night 27/28th were registered. Remaining two sections of each battery took over during night 28/29th and were all in action by 10.30 p.m. There was some shelling furing the relief, but no casualties.	
	29-4-18.		A dull quiet day. Batteries registered during the day. Lieut. E.S.ROBINSON posted to Brigade from 32nd D.A.C.	

30-4-18.

(signature)

Lieut-Colonel,

Commanding 161st (Yorks.) Brigade R. F. A.

Vol 29

161st (Yorks.) BRIGADE, R.F.A.

WAR DIARY

COVERING PERIOD

1st MAY, 1918 ~ 31st MAY, '18

Army Form C. 2118.

WAR DIARY

161st (YORKS.) BRIGADE R.F.A.

INTELLIGENCE SUMMARY

(Erase heading not required.)

Instructions regarding War Diaries and Intelligence Summaries are contained in F. S. Regs., Part II. and the Staff Manual respectively. Title pages will be prepared in manuscript.

Place	Date	Hour	Summary of Events and Information	Remarks and references to Appendices
In the Field	1-5-18		Wagon Lines are now near BAILLEUMONT and BAILLEUVAL in open. Quantities of material are available from old huts, camps and wagon lines near battery positions, and they are getting shelters, etc. built. Some friction over exchange with Guards D.A.	
	2-5-18		Headquarters, 161st Brigade R.F.A. at BLAIREVILLE covering 6th Infantry Brigade, 2nd Divn. under 40th Divisional Artillery, forming with 168th Brigade R.F.A., the Left Artillery Group. Day passed quietly. At 2.30 a.m. Group fired in support of raid by 2nd Canadian Division on our left; 8 prisoners were captured with 5 Machine Guns and many of the enemy were otherwise accounted for. Artillery fire lasted for 35 minutes for 161st Bde.R.F.A., and for 15 minutes for 168th Bde.R.F.A., the latter carrying out a feint barrage.	
	3-5-18		Rather increased hostile artillery activity, neighbourhood of A/161 being engaged during most of the day by 5.9 Battery. Some harassing fire on BLAIREVILLE in the evening. 1 O.R. wounded.	
	4-5-18) 5-5-18)		Nothing of interest; some counter-battery work on A/161 and neighbouring batteries; a captured 8" Battery and 106 fuzes being used. 1 O.R.wounded & remained at duty, 4-5-18. 1 O.R.wounded, 5-5-18.	
	6-5-18		At 9.10 p.m. the S.O.S. was reported on the left of the Infantry Brigade on our right. The Group fired for 30 minutes in support of the Group on our right; no Infantry action was reported. 1 O.R.wounded.	
	7-5-18		Headquarters of 161st Bde.R.F.A. moved to quarry outside BLAIREVILLE, occupying two Nissen Huts and some dugouts. These have been constructed by 6th Infantry Bde. of 2nd Division for us.	
	8-5-18		A test of all means of communication other than telephone was carried out today, with, on the whole, satisfactory results. There was a good deal of artillery activity during the night. Captain (& Adjutant) R.L.CREASY,M.C., ceased to perform duties of Adjutant on posting to 41st Divisional Artillery; Lieut. G.V.THORNTON assumed duties of a/Adjutant vice Captain R.L.CREASY, M.C.	
	9-5-18		Nothing of interest. Some counter-battery work on B/161.	
	10-5-18		The day passed quietly. A/161 moved four of their guns to a new position, their old position having been shelled rather heavily during the last few days. D/161 carried out a bombardment with incendiary shell on a large dump of ammunition boxes, setting it well ablaze to the great joy of the Infantry. 0 w.R.wounded.	

Army Form C. 2118.

WAR DIARY
INTELLIGENCE SUMMARY
(Erase heading not required.)

161st (YORKS.) BRIGADE R.F.A.

Instructions regarding War Diaries and Intelligence Summaries are contained in F. S. Regs., Part II. and the Staff Manual respectively. Title pages will be prepared in manuscript.

Place	Date	Hour	Summary of Events and Information	Remarks and references to Appendices
In the Field.	11-5-18		Increase in activity of hostile artillery on back areas. Brig-General HART-SYMOT (Infantry Brigade) had both legs blown away and his Brigade Major WRIGHT killed by same shell whilst walking through BLAIREVILLE.	
	12-5-18.		A quiet, dull day. Our Divisional Infantry relieved the 2nd Division last night; but our Divisional R.A. H.Q. are not taking over yet.	
	13/14-5-18.		Nothing of interest.	
	15-5-18		'A' Battery's forward guns were shelled today and are moving. Hostile artillery carried out several area shoots today. 1 O.R.Wounded.	
	16-5-18.		'A' Battery's forward guns moved forward to a position on the railway, close to D/161 Battery position.	
	17-5-18.		Last night, in conjunction with the Canadian Right Group on our left, we fired a fishing-net barrage N.E. of BOYELLES. Hostile artillery is becoming considerably more active and has started on counter-battery work.	
	18-5-18.		Nothing of interest. Headquarters, 32nd Divisional Artillery relieved the 40th today.	
	19-5-18.		There has been considerable increase in enemy fire, especially as regards counter-battery work, both B/161 and D/161 receiving attention. 1 O.R.wounded.	
	20-5-18.		Enemy artillery activity continues. 1 O.R.wounded.	
	21-5-18.		Last night we assisted in two raids - one on the Right Brigade front, in co-operation with the Centre Group, the other by the Left Brigade covered by the Right Group Canadian Artillery and D/161. 2 O.R's wounded.	
	22-5-18.		Hostile artillery carried out an effective destructive shoot on D/161 this afternoon. Major E.H.P.PEASE-WATKIN,D.S.O.,was wounded and Lieut.J.FILNESS was badly wounded, and died in hospital in the evening. Four men were hit, and 2 guns put out of action.	
	23-5-18.		'D' Battery moved their position to the position on the railway of their forward section.	
	24-5-18) to) 26-5-18.)		Enemy artillery busy with counter-battery work throughout this period. A/161 and C/161 have each had a gun put out of action. On the 24th, 11 reinforcements were posted to the Brigade from 32nd D.A.C.	1 O.R. wounded on 25ᵈ
	27-5-18.		At 2.0 a.m. the enemy put down a very heavy barrage on our support lines and North of us, but no Infantry action developed. A direct hit on 'C' Battery's signal dug-out killed 5 signallers. (Contd)	

Army Form C. 2118.

WAR DIARY 161st (YORKS.) BRIGADE R.F.A.

INTELLIGENCE SUMMARY

(Erase heading not required.)

Instructions regarding War Diaries and Intelligence Summaries are contained in F.S. Regs., Part II. and the Staff Manual respectively. Title pages will be prepared in manuscript.

Place	Date	Hour	Summary of Events and Information	Remarks and references to Appendices
In the Field.	27-5-18. (Contd).		In the evening a direct hit on 'B' Battery's officers' mess wounded Major C.W.WARD, M.G., Lieut.B.BAKEWELL and 2/Lieut.T.CAMPBELL; Two of the servants were killed and another wounded. Major WARD was only slightly hit and did not have to go to the Dressing Station.	
	28-5-18. 29-5-18.		Enemy artillery activity has died down considerably. 23 reinforcements from D.A.C. 2 O.R's wounded. Batteries are registering for a raid to be carried out by the 17th Lancs; Fusrs. (This has since been cancelled).	
	30-5-18.		6 reinforcements arrived from 32nd D.A.C. The 155th Army Bde. R.F.A. were taken out of the line from the Group on our right. Left Group now consists of our own Batteries, the 16th Battery C.F.A., and D/166.	
	31-5-18.		A quiet day; very little shelling.	

[signature]

Lieut-Colonel,

Commanding 161st (Yorks.) Brigade R.F.A.

31st May 1918.

161ST (Yorks.) BRIGADE, R.F.A.

Vol 30

WAR DIARY

From :- 1st June, 1918
To :- 30th June, 1918.

Army Form C. 2118.

Instructions regarding War Diaries and Intelligence Summaries are contained in F. S. Regs., Part II. and the Staff Manual respectively. Title pages will be prepared in manuscript.

WAR DIARY   161st (YORKS.) BRIGADE R.F.A.

~~INTELLIGENCE SUMMARY~~

(Erase heading not required.)

Place	Date	Hour	Summary of Events and Information	Remarks and references to Appendices
In the Field	1-6-18.		C/161's Forward Section in BOISLEUX-au-MONT was shelled today, and Lieut.C.R.CLIFF wounded. One gun was badly damaged by shell-fire. They are moving to a new position in the COJEUL VALLEY. 2/Lieut.R.E.T.BELL, A/161, proceeded to Third Army Artillery School on Course.	
	2-6-18.		Gas concentrations were fired in the valley behind our Batteries. The detached section of D/161 had 2 men hit by H.E., and 3 men gassed by a shell that burst in the mouth of one of the dug-outs.	
	3-6-18.		The Canadian Division on our left carried out a raid. We put down a barrage for 10 minutes to divert attention. 1 O.R.wounded.	
	4-6-18.		Lieut. E.S.ROBINSON, D/161, wounded and admitted hospital. Lieut. T. COWAN joined Brigade and was posted D/161.	
	4/5-6-18.		The 72nd Army Brigade R.F.A. relieved the 186th Brigade R.F.A. in this sector. The 16th Bty C.F.A. are no longer in this Group. B/161 has been withdrawn to BRETENCOURT, becoming the Mobile Battery of the Group. Their position has been taken over by A/72.	
	5-6-18.		Lieut. W.ELLIS, A/161, returned from Leave. 1 O.R.wounded.	
	6-6-18.		A/161 Forward Section were shelled again today, and 2/Lieut. F. ADDISON wounded.	
	7-6-18.		The Divisional Commander and C.R.A. visited the O.P's and Battery Positions today. An aeroplane dropped a bomb close to C/161 Forward Section, wounding 1 O.R.who remained at duty. Lieut. P.R.HAMILTON,M.C., joined the Brigade and posted to A/161. 1 O.R.wounded.	
	8-6-18. 8/9 -6-18.		8 reinforcements were posted to the Brigade from 32nd D.A.C. Nothing of interest. The front is becoming much quieter.	
	9-6-18.		2/Lieut.J.H.G.WAY, C/161, transferred to England (Sick); 2/Lieut.T.S.CAMPBELL, B/161, transferred to England (Wounded).	
	10-6-18.		Major V.A.HILLMAN joined the Brigade as Horse Adviser. 2/Lieut.J.G.COONEY joined the Brigade and posted C/161.	
	11-6-18.		A quiet day. Lieut.C.R.CLIFF, C/161, transferred to England (Wounded). Lieut.G.O.d'IVRY,M.C., joined Brigade and posted B/161.	
	12-6-18.		Last night the 96th Inf.Brigade carried out a raid on enemy posts and secured 3 prisoners. We fired a protective box barrage, of which the Infantry spoke in high praise. 2/Lieut.A.H.FINDLAY and 2/Lieut.G.W.BRITTEN joined the Brigade and posted D/161 and B/161 respectively.	

(A7092) Wt. W12539/M1293. 75,000. 1/17. D.D. & L., Ltd. Forms/C.2118/14.

Army Form C. 2118.

2.

WAR DIARY 161st (YORKS.) BRIGADE R.F.A.

INTELLIGENCE SUMMARY

(Erase heading not required.)

Instructions regarding War Diaries and Intelligence Summaries are contained in F.S. Regs., Part II. and the Staff Manual respectively. Title pages will be prepared in manuscript.

Place	Date	Hour	Summary of Events and Information	Remarks and references to Appendices
In the Field.	12-6-18. (Contd).		Lieut.G.O.d'IVRY,M.C.,B/161, posted 168th Brigade R.F.A.	
	13-6-18.		Nothing of interest. 1 O.R.wounded.	
	14-6-18.		The Heavy Artillery carried out a concentration on Trench Mortars in BOYELLES this afternoon. Our Batteries also fired on the same targets.	
	15-6-18.) 16-6-18.)		Except for Trench Mortar firing on our front and support lines, there has been very little activity on our front. 17 reinforcements posted to Brigade from 32nd D.A.C.on 15-6-18.	
	17-6-18.		2/Lieut.W.S.KIRK and 2/Lieut.L.A.MOULD joined the Brigade and posted B/161 & C/161 respectively. 2/Lieut.R.E.T.BELL, A/161, rejoined on completion of Course at Third Army Artillery School.	
	18-6-18.		With a view to deceiving the enemy as to the position of our S.O.S.Lines, an S.O.S.was sent up at 4.0 a.m. this morning and we fired on our DEFEND S.24 Barrage Lines to the South of our S.O.S.Lines. 2/Lieut.P.W.ALLEN, D/161, proceeded on Course of Instruction in the "Forward Area Anti-Aircraft Sight" at VI Corps School. 2/Lieut.A.G.DRYLAND, B/161, proceeded on leave to England. Nothing of interest.	
	19-6-18 .. 20-6-18 ..		The 96th Inf.Brigade carried out a raid with 200 men on posts in and near BOYELLES. Very few of the posts were found occupied, but identification was obtained. 1 wounded prisoner was taken. We fired Creeping and Flank Barrages for the operation. 14 reinforcements were posted to the Brigade from 32nd D.A.C.	
	21-6-18.		The Canadians on our left carried out a raid last night. No prisoners were taken and but few of the enemy seen. We fired a flank barrage for the operation.	
	22-6-18.		Nothing of interest. 1 O.R.wounded.	
	23-6-18.		Slight shelling of Forward Sections. 2 O.R's wounded.	
	24-6-18.		A Quiet day. 2/Lieut.F.W.ALLEN, D/161, rejoined on completion of Course of instruction in the "Forward Area Anti-Aircraft Sight" at VI Corps School.	
	25-6-18.		The Canadians carried out a raid on a large scale on their right front. 22 prisoners were taken, 6 machine guns, and 1 trench mortar. We fired a flank barrage as a diversion. Lieut.G.JUDAS,M.C., C/161, proceeded to Third Army Gas School on Course.	

Army Form C. 2118.

WAR DIARY

161st (YORKS.) BRIGADE R.F.A.

~~INTELLIGENCE SUMMARY~~

(Erase heading not required.)

Instructions regarding War Diaries and Intelligence Summaries are contained in F. S. Regs., Part II. and the Staff Manual respectively. Title pages will be prepared in manuscript.

Place	Date	Hour	Summary of Events and Information	Remarks and references to Appendices
	26-6-18. 27-6-18. 28-6-18.		Our front is now held on a one Battalion frontage. Nothing of interest. A/72 Battery were heavily shelled today and two pits set on fire. Luckily there were no casualties. Lieut.G.DUNDAS,M.C., C/161, rejoined on completion of Course at Third Army Gas School.	
	29-6-18. 30-6-18.		2/Lieut.T.COWAN, D/161, proceeded to Third Army Artillery School on Course. Brigadier-General GIRDWOOD, 96th Infantry Bde. presented a cup to representatives of the Brigade as a mark of appreciation of good work done by the Brigade whilst on the HOUTHULST FOREST Front.	

HONOURS AND REWARDS DURING MONTH.

No.835445 Sergt.F.WILLIAMS, D/161, Awarded THE DISTINGUISHED CONDUCT MEDAL.
(VI Corps R.O.3366, dated 9-6-18.)

[signature]
Lieut-Colonel,
Commanding 161st (Yorks.) Brigade R.F.A.

30th June 1918.

161st (Yorks.) BRIGADE, R.F.A.

~ WAR ~
~ DIARY ~

COVERING PERIOD

1st. July, 1918,
to
31st. July, 1918.

35807. W16879/M1879 500,000 3/17 R.T. (1074) Forms/W3091/3   Army Form W.3091.

Cover for Documents.

Nature of Enclosures.

Notes, or Letters written.

Army Form C. 2118.

WAR DIARY
or
INTELLIGENCE SUMMARY

161st (Yorks.) Brigade R.F.A.

(Erase heading not required.)

Instructions regarding War Diaries and Intelligence Summaries are contained in F. S. Regs., Part II. and the Staff Manual respectively. Title pages will be prepared in manuscript.

Place	Date	Hour	Summary of Events and Information	Remarks and references to Appendices
In the Field.	1-7-18.) 2-7-18.)		Nothing of interest.	
	3-7-18.		Two sections per Battery were relieved by 74th Brigade, Guards Divisional Artillery this evening, and proceeded to HUMBERCOURT.	
	4-7-18.		Headquarters and the remaining section per Battery were relieved today, and marched to HUMBERCOURT. 2/Lieut. A.G.DRYLAND, B/161, rejoined from leave. 1 O.R.wounded.	
	5-7-18.		The Brigade is now at rest, but in readiness to move at 1 hour's notice from dawn to 9 a.m., and 4 hour's notice from 9 a.m. onwards. Major E.A.CHISHOLM, M.C., reconnoitred the positions we should have to occupy in case of attack.	
	6-7-18.		B/161's guns went to OCCOCHES today for calibration. Batteries are carrying out training in Driving Drill, Marching and Setting-up Drill, Gun Drill and Drill Orders.	
	7-7-18.		2/Lieut. R.ROTHWELL, A/161, proceeded to VI Corps Gas School on course.	
	8-7-18.		6 reinforcements posted to the Brigade from 32nd D.A.C. D/161's guns were calibrated today at the Calibration Range.	
	9-7-18.		Major-General HALDANE, the Corps Commander, inspected the Brigade, dismounted, in the courtyard at Brigade Headquarters, today. He afterwards went round the horse lines and gun parks. 'A' and 'C' Batteries guns were calibrated today.	
	10-7-18) 11-7-18) 12-7-18)		Batteries are continuing with their training.	
	12-7-18.		6 reinforcements posted to Brigade from 32nd D.A.C. 2/Lieut. L.A.MOULD C/161, proceeded to Third Army Artillery School on course.	
	13-7-18.		A test Emergency Turn-out was ordered by Divisional R.A. H.Q., and carried out successfully. 2/Lieut. R.ROTHWELL, A/161, rejoined on completion of course at VI Corps Gas School.	
	16-7-18.		The first half of the Brigade Sports was held this afternoon. 2/Lieut. F.A.POHL joined Brigade and posted A/161.	
	17-7-18.		There was a Brigade Skeleton Drill Order this morning, and in the afternoon the second half of the Brigade Sports were run off; the Divisional Band playing for the occasion. 2/Lieut. H.JONES (T.F.) joined Brigade and posted B/161.	
	18-7-18.		Orders received to entrain. 12 reinforcements posted to Brigade from 32nd D.A.C.	

Army Form C. 2118.

WAR DIARY
INTELLIGENCE SUMMARY
(Erase heading not required.)

161st (Yorks.) Bde. R.F.A.

Instructions regarding War Diaries and Intelligence Summaries are contained in F. S. Regs., Part II. and the Staff Manual respectively. Title pages will be prepared in manuscript.

Place	Date	Hour	Summary of Events and Information	Remarks and references to Appendices
In the Field.	19-7-18.		The Brigade entrained at DOULLENS, BOUQUEMAISON, and MONDICOURT.	
	20-7-18.		The Brigade detrained at WEVENBERG and PROVEN, and marched about 2 miles to good billets on the HARDINGE - WATOU Road. During the afternoon Batteries moved one section per Battery into reserve positions close to LA LOVIE Aerodrome to cover BLUE Line.	
	21-7-18.		A reconnaissance of the BLUE Line and O.P's was carried out.	
	22-7-18.		Batteries are continuing training of personnel under Battery arrangements.	
	23-7-18.		Two N.C.O's and 4 men are remaining with the sections in position.	
	23-7-18.		2/Lieut. R.A.WYRLEY-BIRCH, D/161, on leave until 6-8-18.	
	24-7-18.		Brigade and Battery Commanders proceeded by lorry to reconnoitre positions in the neighbourhood of RENINGHELST.	
	25-7-18.		General BUCKLE, R.A. inspected our horses this afternoon. Batteries sent working parties to XIX Corps area to prepare positions.	
	26-7-18)		Nothing of interest. 2/Lieut.W.E.WILSON proceeded on 26-7-18 to attend course at II Corps	
	27-7-18)		Signal School: 2/Lieut.A.G.DRYLAND, proceeded on 28-7-18 to attend course at Second Army	
	28-7-18)		Artillery School: 2/Lieut. L.A.MOULD, rejoined on 27-7-18 on compeltion of course at Third	
	29-7-18)		Army Artillert School: 2/Lieut.J.G.COONEY proceeded on leave to U.K. on 28-7-18.	
	30-7-18.		168th Brigade R.F.A. held their sports meeting.	

31st July 1918.

Commanding 161st (Yorks.) Brigade R.F.A.

Lieut.-Colonel,
R.F.A.

161st (Yorks.) Brigade, R.F.A.

–WAR DIARY–

COVERING PERIOD

FROM :- 1st Aug: 1918,

TO :- 31st Aug: 1918.

(6339) Wt. W160/M3016 1,500,000 10/17 McA & W Ltd (E 1898) Forms W3091.   Army Form W.3091.

Cover for Documents.

Nature of Enclosures.

Notes, or Letters written.

Cover for Documents.

Army Form C. 2118.

WAR DIARY
or
INTELLIGENCE SUMMARY

161st (YORKS.) BRIGADE R.F.A

(Erase heading not required.)

Instructions regarding War Diaries and Intelligence Summaries are contained in F.S. Regs., Part II. and the Staff Manual respectively. Title pages will be prepared in manuscript.

Place	Date	Hour	Summary of Events and Information	Remarks and references to Appendices
In the Field.	1-8-18 to 6-8-18.		Batteries reconnoitred positions to cover the EAST POPERINGHE Line, the WATOU Line, and WEST POPERINGHE Line, to cover the 32nd Division, 30th American Division, and Belgians respectively.	
	6-8-18.		2/Lieut. P.ENGLAND, B/161, granted leave to England until 19-8-18.	
	7-8-18.		5 reinforcements were posted to the Brigade from 52nd D.A.C. The Brigade left WATOU during the afternoon and evening, and entrained at WAAYENBERG. Major V.A.HILLMAN, D/161, granted leave to U.K. until 7-9-18.	
	8-8-18.		Headquarters and 'A' Battery detrained at VILLE-LE-MARCLET. Remaining Batteries received orders not to detrain and were taken on to AMIENS and SAULES. The Brigade marched to LONGEAU and billeted in the vicinity. Major E.A.CHISHOLM, M.C., C/161, rejoined from (PARIS) leave.	
	9-8-18.		The Brigade marched out during afternoon to DEMUIN, arriving late in the evening. Roads were blocked with traffic and progress was very slow. Whilst the Brigade was entering billeting area the road was bombed. 'A' Battery had one man killed and two horses killed and three men wounded.	
	10-8-18.		Orders received to march to LE QUESNEL at 3.0.a.m. Brigade halted just East of LE QUESNEL, and Battery Commanders and Staffs went forward to reconnoitre positions. Batteries moved up into action East and North East of BOUCHOIR in the early afternoon, covering the 96th Infantry Brigade, who relieved the 3rd Canadians. 1 O.R. wounded.	
	11-8-18.		The 32nd Division took the old front line West of PARVILLERS. The 32nd Division was relieved by the 3rd Canadian Division during the night 11th/12th. Major C.W.WARD, M.C., B/161, wounded by Machine Gun fire and admitted hospital. 1 O.R. wounded.	
	12-8-18.		The 7th Canadian Infantry Brigade, who are holding the front on our sector, advanced their line slightly today by means of peaceful penetration. Major R.EMMET, D.S.O., posted to command B/161 from 168th Brigade R.F.A. 1 O.R. wounded.	
	13-8-18.		The advance on DAMERY WOOD and PARVILLERS was held up by Machine-Gun fire. 2 O.R. wounded.	
	14-8-18.		Line was advanced a little today, but there is still heavy Machine-gun fire from PARVILLERS. The French on our right attacked DAMERY, but were forced to retire. 2/Lieut. E.A.JEW, C/161, admitted hospital (Injured). 3 O.R. wounded.	
	15-8-18.		The 9th Canadian Infantry Brigade went through the 7th Brigade, and, under a heavy barrage, (P.T.O.)	

Army Form C. 2118.

SHEET II

WAR DIARY

INTELLIGENCE SUMMARY

(Erase heading not required.)

Instructions regarding War Diaries and Intelligence
Summaries are contained in F. S. Regs, Part II.
and the Staff Manual respectively. Title pages
will be prepared in manuscript.

Place	Date	Hour	Summary of Events and Information	Remarks and references to Appendices
In the Field.	15-8-18. (Contd).		attacked and captured DAMERY and PARVILLERS. Enemy counter-attacked with two battalions, but were caught in our barrage and beaten off with very heavy casualties. 1 O.R.wounded.	
	16-8-18.		'A' Battery moved to a new position near BOIS-EN-EQUERE. Capt. M.KING -FRENCH, A/161, granted leave to PARIS until 26-8-18.	
	17-8-18.		'C' Battery moved to new position close to A/161. Infantry have advanced their line East of PARVILLERS. 2/Lieut.J.G.COONEY, C/161, rejoined from leave. 4 O.R.wounded.	
	18-8-18.		Brigade moved North, by road to the Australian Corps area. Batteries were to have taken over from 4th Australian F.A.Brigade; 1 section per battery to relieve tonight. Order was cancelled and Batteries remained for the night at Wagon Lines.	
	19-8-18.		Positions East of VAUVILLERS were reconnoitred and occupied, Batteries remaining silent.	
	21-8-18.		2/Lieut.P.ENGLAND, B/161, rejoined from leave. 1 O.R.wounded.	
	22-8-18.		8 reinforcements posted to Brigade from 32nd D.A.C. Australian Corps attacked on the front HERLEVILLE - CHUIGNES; 96th Infantry Brigade on the right, covered by the 161st Brigade R.F.A. and the 4th Australian Brigade R.F.A. All objectives gained and 2,500 prisoners taken on the Corps front. Our front only advanced slightly and straightened out. Captain H.L.McCORMICK, R.A.M.C., granted leave to U.K. until 5-9-18. 2/Lieut. A.G.DRYLAND, B/161, rejoined on completion of course at Second Army Art'y School.	
	23-8-18.		Enemy reported to be retiring and our Infantry sending out patrols to keep touch. French on our right have advanced to AILLETTE. 1 O.R.wounded, remained at duty.	
	24-8-18.		Our line advanced to VERMANDOVILLARS. Enemy has retired except for a few Machine-gun posts. 2/Lieut. R.E.T.BELL, A/161, granted leave to U.K. until 7-9-18. Lieut-Colonel LORD WYNFORD, D.S.O.,Commanding Brigade, was attached H.Q.,32nd Div'l.Artillery, vice Brigadier-General J.A.TYLER, C.M.G.,absent on duty. Major R.EMMET, D.S.O., B/161, assumed command of Brigade vice Lieut-Colonel LORD WYNFORD,DSO. Lieut-Colonel LORD WYNFORD,D.S.O., wounded by hostile aircraft bomb and admitted hospital.	
	25-8-18.		Enemy still retiring; our patrols failed to maintain touch. A heavy hostile gas barrage	

(A7092) Wt. W12839/M1293. 75,000. 1/17. D. D. & L., Ltd. Forms/C.2118/14.

SHEET III.
WAR DIARY or INTELLIGENCE SUMMARY

161st (YORKS.) BRIGADE R.F.A.

Army Form C. 2118.

Instructions regarding War Diaries and Intelligence Summaries are contained in F.S. Regs., Part II. and the Staff Manual respectively. Title pages will be prepared in manuscript.

(Erase heading not required.)

Place	Date	Hour	Summary of Events and Information	Remarks and references to Appendices
In the Field.	25-8-18.		during the evening in the neighbourhood of Battalion H.Q. caused severe casualties to our Infantry. Line strengthened by Pioneer Battalion of H.L.I. Lieut. W. ELLIS and Lieut. F.A. POHL, both of A/161, admitted hospital and diagnosed "Wounded, Gas". 4 O.R. admitted hospital and diagnosed "Wounded, Gas".	
	26-8-18.		Batteries moved up to support advance of Infantry; 'C' Battery on the right covering the Manchesters; 'A' Battery on the left covering the 1/5th Borders. Lieut-Colonel H.H.HULTON,D.S.O., posted to command Brigade from 5th Aust: Div'l Artillery. 2/Lieut. R.ROTHWELL, A/161, admitted hospital and diagnosed "Wounded, Gas". Capt.M.KING-FRENCH, A/161, rejoined from PARIS leave. Major R.EMMET,D.S.O. resumed command of B/161. 4 O.R. admitted hospital and diagnosed "Wounded, Gas".	
	27-8-18.		At 5.0 a.m. Infantry advanced under cover of an Artillery barrage. ABLAINCOURT occupied at 7.50 a.m. Batteries are moving up; 'A' and 'C' Batteries in close support of the two front line Battalions, 'B' and 'D' Batteries in reserve. 2/Lieut. E.H.WEILER, X/32 T.M.Bty., and 2/Lieut. E.H.WILSON, Y/32 T.M.Bty., attached A/161. 2/Lieut. P.ENGLAND, B/161, admitted hospital and diagnosed "Wounded, Gas". 96th Inf.Brigade advanced under a barrage at 5.0 a.m. By 7.30 a.m. Infantry had advanced to a line 1,000 yds. East of ABLAINCOURT; 'A' 'A' and 'C' Batteries, moving up in close support, encountered mines in the road at ABLAINCOURT. 'A' Battery had three men wounded and two horses killed, and one gun put out of action. 'C' Battery had the wheels blown off one gun, and 3 men wounded.	
	28-8-18.		Batteries are avoiding the village and using a very bad cross-country track. All Batteries in action by 4.0 p.m. French are reported to have reached the SOMME on our right.	
	29-8-18.		Batteries moved up again to positions to cover crossing of the SOMME. Infantry hold line within 500 yds. of SOMME. 97th Brigade relieved the 96th Inf.Bde. during night 29th/30th. Lieut-G.DUNDAS,M.C., C/161, wounded by artillery fire and admitted hospital.	
	30-8-18.		The whole front has now been taken over by the 97th Inf.Bde., the 2nd K.O.Y.L.I. holding the original 96th Inf.Bde.front, and the 1/5th Borders 2,000 yds.of the front to the North. We are covering the 2nd K.O.Y.L.I 'B' and 'D' Batteries have taken up positions to the North close to HORGNY. The Infantry now hold the West bank of the SOMME. 2 O.R.wounded. 25 reinforcements posted to the Brigade from 32nd D.A.C.	

Army Form C. 2118.

SHEET IV.
WAR DIARY
INTELLIGENCE SUMMARY.

161st (YORKS.) BRIGADE R.F.A.

(Erase heading not required)

Instructions regarding War Diaries and Intelligence Summaries are contained in F.S. Regs., Part II. and the Staff Manual respectively. Title pages will be prepared in manuscript.

Place	Date	Hour	Summary of Events and Information	Remarks and references to Appendices
In the Field.	31-8-18.		Australians on our left have crossed the SOMME and are advancing on PERONNE. Our Infantry attempted to cross the SOMME, but were held up by M.G.fire. 'A' and 'C' Batteries are sending sections forward.	

4th Sept.1918.

[signature]
Lieut-Colonel,
Commanding 161st (Yorks.) Brigade R.F.A.

Army Form C. 2118.

WAR DIARY 161st (YORKS.) BRIGADE R.F.A.

INTELLIGENCE SUMMARY

(Erase heading not required.)

Instructions regarding War Diaries and Intelligence Summaries are contained in F. S. Regs., Part II. and the Staff Manual respectively. Title pages will be prepared in manuscript.

Place	Date	Hour	Summary of Events and Information	Remarks and references to Appendices
In the Field	1-9-18.		Batteries remained in the same positions throughout the day, and carried out Harassing Fire on Machine-Gun emplacements in ST.CHRIST, and at V.9.d. and V.3.b.	
	2-9-18.		The 97th Inf.Bde. again attempted to cross the Canal this morning by the bridge at U.14.b.80.15. Batteries were prepared to assist with a barrage, but this was not asked for. The attempt was unsuccessful. Harassing Fire was continued through the day on roads in V.5. and 6. A 10 c.m.gun was engaged by D/161 on the Western edge of FOUR SHEAVES WOOD with good results. A/161 pushed one gun forward to Sunkenroad in U.8.c., which remained silent.	
	3-9-18		A/161 moved to a new position in T.18.a. last night. Their forward gun has been put out of action by hostile shell fire and is being withdrawn tonight. Other Batteries remained in their same positions.	
	4-9-18		D/161 moved one Howr. to U.1.a.4.5. and cut wire along the Brigade front. Gaps were cut as follows:- U.9.c.60.15., U.15.a.5.5. to U.15.b.0.3., U.15.b.0.1., U.15.c.85.75., U.21.b.2.5 to U.21.b.4.4., U.17.a.7.9., V.3.d.6.7., V.3.d.50.85., V.3.b.9.0., V.3.b.80.15. 350 rds. were fired. All Batteries were employed on firing at movement seen. The Germans were observed in trenches U.15.a.and c. German Artillery active at intervals on forward areas between 9.0 a.m. and 12 noon. 4.2" Hows. were fired by the enemy on V.9.c.5.9. Harassing fire was carried out by all Batteries during the night on suspected Machine Guns and centres of enemy activity.	
	5-9-18.		97th Infantry Brigade, after several attempts, crossed the River SOMME by BRIE & GIZANCOURT Bridges and cleared ST.CHRIST. Batteries sniped all movement during the day. D/161 silenced a 4.2" How. firing from U.16.b.4.5. In the evening 97th Infantry Brigade established the line U.24.b.5.0 - U.12.d.5.0 thence along ATHIES - PERONNE Road. Orders were issued to Batteries at 7.0 p.m. re advance on morning of 6th vide Appendix 1 attached. Major J.W.BUCKLEY, M.C., D/161, granted leave to PARIS until 12-9-18. 2/Lieut.E.H.WEILER, X/32 T.M.Bty.,(attached A/161), granted leave to U.K. until 19-9-18. Major E.A.CHISHOLM,M.C., C/161, and two Signallers wounded by mine explosion.	Vide Appendix 1 attached.
	6-9-18.		Bridge at ST.CHRIST was not completed until 6.30 a.m., delaying the Batteries. B/161 crossed the SOMME by BRIE Bridge and followed up in close support of the 1/5 Borders. HQ/161, A/161, C/161 and D/161 crossed by ST.CHRIST BRIDGE. Infantry reached final objective by 11.0 a.m. Final positions of Batteries: A/161, V.11.c.7.1.; B/161, V.5.c.5.5.; C/161, 4 guns V.18.c.8.5.; 2 guns V.22.a.4.7.; D/161, 4 Hows. V.9.c.8.7.; 2 Hows. V.16.a.3.3. Orders concerning advance on 7th issued to Batteries 7.0 p.m. vide Appendix 2 attached. B/161 took 3 prisoners; C/161 took 2 prisoners.	Vide Appendix 2 attached.

Army Form C. 2118.

WAR DIARY
or
INTELLIGENCE SUMMARY.

161st (YORKS.) BRIGADE R.F.A.

(Erase heading not required.)

Instructions regarding War Diaries and Intelligence Summaries are contained in F.S. Regs., Part II. and the Staff Manual respectively. Title pages will be prepared in manuscript.

Place	Date	Hour	Summary of Events and Information	Remarks and references to Appendices
In the Field.	7-9-18.		Advance continued this morning and all objectives reached by 10.0 a.m., B/161 and C/161 moved up in close support, taking up final positions at Q.35.c.6.6. and W.15.a.8.5.,respectively, with a section of C/161 forward at W.17.c.9.5. A/161 sent forward two sections in close support Right and Left Companies KOY.L.I., and did very useful work against Machine Guns that were holding up the Infantry advance, vide appendix 3 attached. Final positions occupied by A/161: 3 guns W.11.b.5.2., 1 gun W.12.a.2.0. D/161 came into action at W.14.a.8.8, and sniped movement, and moved in the evening to W.10.c.5.8. 2/Lieut.R.J.ALLEN, D/161, granted leave to U.K. until 21-9-18.	Vide Appendix 3 attached.
	8-9-18.		Line has not advanced today. Batteries are now located: A/161 - 3 guns - W.11.b.5.1. 1 gun - W.12.a.2.0. B/161 - 6 guns - Q.54.d.6.2. C/161 - 2 guns - W.22.b.3.5. 2 guns - W.22.b.8.6. D/161 - 4 Hows.- W.10.c.5.9. 2 Hows.- W.16.d.5.5. 6th Australian A.F.A.Bde. reconnoitred and occupied positions in W.6.a.4.5. and W.5.a.7.4., forming a sub-group to the Brigade. During the day, the Batteries fired 50 rds. per gun on Machine-Gun emplacements, vide Appendices 4 and 5 attached.	Vide Appendices 4 & 5 attd.
	9-9-18.		Batteries still occupy the same positions. Vigorous harassing fire has been carried out on DEAD WOODS, Sunken roads in vicinity of ATILLY, and Copse X.15.central. At the request of the French, high ground in X.16.c. was also harassed. Capt.H.L.McCORMICK, R.A.M.C., rejoined from leave. 2/Lieut.W.E.WILSON, A/161, rejoined on completion of course at II Corps Signal School. 2/Lieut.G.H.MAWER, 2/Lieut.H.S.NUNDY, 2/Lieut.M.J.MANNING, 2/Lieut.R.R.TAYLOR, were posted to the Brigade from 32nd D.A.C.	
	10-9-18.		96th Infantry Brigade relieved the 97th Infantry Brigade today. C/161 Batteries harassed the high ground in X.16.c. and fired on movement East of ATILLY. C/161 moved to a new position at W.12.d.5.5. For situation - vide appendix 6 attached.	Vide Appendix 6.
	11-9-18.		B/161 moved to new positions: 2 guns X.7.c.4.0, 2 guns X.7.a.5.4., and 2 guns X.13.a.9.8. C/161 moved to a new position at W.12.d.4.7. B/161 were shelled at the position they had originally selected and had two men slightly wounded, and moved to position above. Very little firing was done, as the situation was obscure throughout the day. Major E.A.CHISHOLM,M.C., C/161, rejoined from hospital. 2/Lieut.M.J.MANNING, A/161, posted X/32 T.M.Bty. 2/Lieut.E.A.WILSON, X/32 T.M.Bty., posted A/161.	

Army Form C. 2118.

WAR DIARY of 161st (YORKS.) BRIGADE R.F.A.

INTELLIGENCE SUMMARY.

(Erase heading not required.)

Instructions regarding War Diaries and Intelligence Summaries are contained in F. S. Regs., Part II. and the Staff Manual respectively. Title pages will be prepared in manuscript.

Place	Date	Hour	Summary of Events and Information	Remarks and references to Appendices
In the Field.	12-9-18.		An attack by the 96th Infantry Brigade, supported by the 6th Australian A.F.A.Bde., 23rd A.F.A.Bde., and 168th Bde.R.F.A., due to take place at 5.30 a.m., was cancelled at 3.0.a.m., as the Infantry had reached the final objective without opposition.	Vide Appendix 7
	13-9-18.		The 161st Bde.R.F.A. was relieved by the 23rd A.F.A.Bde., and withdrew to Wagon Lines during the afternoon and evening - vide Appendix 7 attached. Batteries rested at their Wagon Lines. It being contemplated to withdraw the Batteries to ATHIES for a period of rest and training, a reconnaissance of Wagon Lines was made, under the direction of the Adjutant, in the afternoon. Before the Batteries moved, instructions were received issued cancelling the move (vide Appendix 8). Major J.W.BUCKLEY,M.C., D/161, rejoined from (PARIS) leave.	Vide Appendix 8.
	14-9-18.		Batteries remained at their Wagon Lines, under orders to be ready to move into action at a moment's notice.	
	15-9-18.		2/Lieut.J.R.B.HERN and 2/Lieut.C.G.CHAPPELL were posted to the Brigade from 32nd D.A.C. An attack with the view of driving the enemy towards the main HINDENBURG LINE being contemplated, the Brigade received instructions to reconnoitre positions in X.4.a. and c. This reconnaissance was carried out by the C.O. and Battery Commanders in the afternoon, when positions were selected as follows:- A/161 - X.4.c.6.8. C/161 - X.4.c.30.85. B/161 - X.4.a.43.00. D/161 - X.4.a.92.15. In the evening, Batteries brought up ammunition to these positions to make up dumps of 400 rds. per gun and 300 per Howr.	
	16-9-18.		Batteries worked on their positions during the day, and at night they brought up their guns and hid them in ST.QUENTIN WOOD and adjacent copses, and got up the remainder of their ammunition. Lieut.P.R.HAMILTON,M.C., A/-61 admitted to hospital (Sick).	
	17-9-18.		Batteries worked on their positions and at night placed their guns in position, and received instructions for the barrage to be fired the following morning (Vide Appendices 9 and 11). H.Q./161 moved to X.3.a.4.1. 2/Lieut.W.E.WILSON, A/161, granted leave until 1-10-18.	Vide Appendices 9 and 11.
	18-9-18.		Attack by Infantry (16th Inf.Bde.), supported by Artillery, took place at 5.20 a.m. 161st Bde.R.F.A. (attached LEFT GROUP under command of Colonel WEBER,D.S.O.) supported 2/Y.& L.R. (a Battalion of 6th Division). O.Ps. were manned near KEEPER'S HOUSE and at about M.25.d., and a Forward Intelligence Officer with a roving commission with the object of gaining information of the progress of the Infantry, went forward (vide Appendix 10). The Infantry passed the GREEN LINE (their First Objective) after meeting with little opposition. In attacking the Final Objective, the opposition became more serious, and they were withdrawn with the object of (Continued).	Vide Appendix 10.

WAR DIARY
or
INTELLIGENCE SUMMARY.

161st (YORKS.) BRIGADE R.F.A.

Army Form C. 2118.

(Erase heading not required.)

Place	Date	Hour	Summary of Events and Information	Remarks and references to Appendices
In the Field.	18-9-18 (Contd.)		consolidating on the line CHAMPAGNE TRENCH - DOUAI TRENCH. The position on the right was obscure, the enemy being reported to be in HOLNON Village. It had been arranged that our Batteries should fire the barrage as far as the GREEN LINE, and that the two hours during which the barrage remained on this line, should be utilised in moving forward the Batteries to positions in R.36.a., where they were to take up the barrage again, and continue up to the final objective. Before the two hours had elapsed, all Batteries were in position and all were in telephonic communication with Brigade Hdqrs. At night, owing to the change in the situation, C/161 and D/161 were withdrawn to the positions they had occupied earlier in the day (Vide Appendix 12). 2/Lieut.J.R.B.HERN, and 2/Lieut.G.H.MAWER, both of C/161, were wounded by artillery fire and admitted hospital.	Vide Appendix 12.
	19-9-18.		Captain H.BARRETT, C/161, proceeded to attend Battery Commanders' Course at SHOEBURYNESS commencing 22-9-18. Lieut.P.R.HAMILTON,M.C., A/161, rejoined from Hospital. Instructions were issued at about 2.0 a.m. by Group Hdqrs., to prepare for a barrage in support of the Infantry, who were to make another attempt to reach the Final Objective of the previous day. The Infantry attacked at 5.30 a.m., but Machine-Guns held them up and the line remained stationary. Orders were issued to A/161 and B/161 to withdraw to the positions they had occupied at dawn the previous day. (Vide Appendix 13). All Batteries harassed the enemy during the night.	Vide Appendix 13.
	20-9-18.		The Infantry spent the day consolidating on the line M.21.c.3.2 along road in M.27.a. and c. to the old communication trench about M.27.d.1.3, then to the T of CHAMPAGNE TRENCH to the junction of DOUAI TRENCH and AMERICAN ALLEY. Orders were issued regarding the action of Battery Commanders in the case of a successful counter-attack by the enemy (Vide Appendix 14).	Vide Appendix 14.
	21-9-18.		Quiet day. At the request of the Infantry, who reported that the enemy were in the trench junction at M.28.c.05.85, this point and the surrounding trenches were engaged by B/161's forward section. The 6th Division "side-slipped" to the right and the lanes of Batteries had consequently to be altered (Vide Appendix 15).	Appendix 15.
	22-9-18.		The enemy put down a heavy fire on the Batteries and in the vicinity of Brigade Hdqrs. between 3.30 a.m., and 5.15 a.m. In the evening, Batteries brought up 1500 rds. of ammunition to new forward positions to be occupied before the next attack as follows:- A/161 - R.36.a.84.80. C/161 - R.36.a.92.14. B/161 - R.3 O.c.44.13 D/161 - R.36.a.15.50.	

Army Form C. 2118.

WAR DIARY
of
161st (YORKS.) BRIGADE R.F.A.
INTELLIGENCE SUMMARY.
(Erase heading not required.)

Instructions regarding War Diaries and Intelligence Summaries are contained in F. S. Regs., Part II. and the Staff Manual respectively. Title pages will be prepared in manuscript.

Place	Date	Hour	Summary of Events and Information	Remarks and references to Appendices
In the Field.	22-9-18. (Contd.)		Each Battery brought one gun up to these new positions at night. A reconnaissance of Wagon Lines at MONCHY LA GACHE was made during the afternoon. Harassing Fire during the day and night on the QUADRILATERAL in S.3. and 4. Instructions were issued to Batteries regarding the action to be taken in the event of Counter-preparation being ordered. 2/Lieut.R.J.ALLEN, D/161, rejoined from leave.	Vide Appendix 16.
	23-9-18.		Batteries moved their Wagon lines to RONCHY LA GACHE. Instructions were issued by Group for the barrage to be fired in support of an attack by the Infantry the following morning. Batteries moved up to their forward positions in R.36., and did Harassing Fire at night Capt.C.I.W.HAFFENDEN,M.C., D/161, granted leave until 7-10-18.	Vide Appendices 17 and 18.
	24-9-18.		At 5.0 a.m. the attack by the Infantry commenced. The Final Objective of the IX Corps and the French was the high ground MANCHESTER HILL - FRANCILLY - SELENCY - QUADRILATERAL - M.34.b.&.d. - M.28.b.and d. - M.16.b.and d. Our barrage was in support of the 16th Inf.Bde., whose first objective was S.4.a.4.5.8 (NORTH ALLEY), along RIDGE TRENCH to M.28.c.65.00; and the second objective was the junction of BRETON ALLEY with the new trench at S.4.b.30.65, along the new trench, and thence ARGONNE TRENCH and PERONNE TRENCH to trench junction M.28.d.35.15. The dividing line between 1/K.S.L.I. on right and 2/Y.& L. (which 161st Bde.R.F.A. supported) on left, was AMERICAN ALLEY. The attack met with success at first, the objectives being gained on the left. Strong opposition was encountered at the QUADRILATERAL, which the Infantry failed to take with a frontal attack. The French were in possession of FRANCILLY SELENCY and the high ground to the South of it. The Infantry bring in possession of DOUAI TRENCH as far South as S.4.a.0.8, made an attempt to take the QUADRILATERAL by bombing down the trench, but it met with little success. They established a post on the HOLNON - ST.QUENTIN Road at S.8.d.95.95, but had to withdraw it later on. SELENCY at this time was in the hands of the enemy. In the evening and during the early hours of the following morning, a further attempt was made on the QUADRILATERAL, when we gained possession of it. A.F.I.O. and a.F.O.O were sent forward and were given a free hand in gathering information of the progress of the attack. It was difficult to keep the lines going and information was slow in coming through. At 10.0 p.m., instructions were issued for the withdrawal of the Brigade to Wagon Lines. Batteries reached their Lines at an early hour the following morning. 2/Lieut.W.R.WILSON, A/161, rejoined from leave.	Vide Appendix 19.

Army Form C. 2118.

WAR DIARY of 161st (YORKS.) BRIGADE R.F.A.

INTELLIGENCE SUMMARY.

(Erase heading not required.)

Place	Date	Hour	Summary of Events and Information	Remarks and references to Appendices
In the Field.	25-9-18.		Instructions were issued for Brigade and Battery Commanders to be at VRAIGNES at 11.0 a.m., to receive orders about going into action in support of the 46th Division. Positions were reconnoitred as follows:- A/161 ... L.35.a.70.65. B/161 ... L.35.b.3.2. C/161 ... L.35.d.4.5. D/161 ... L.35.d.1.4. At night, Batteries brought up ammunition with the assistance of the D.A.C. to these positions 400 rds. per gun and 300 rds. per Howr. 2/Lieut. H.JONES, B/161, admitted hospital sick.	
	26-9-18.		Batteries worked on these positions during the day and at night brought their guns into action. For the first time, 18-Pdrs. fired Gas Shell (designated 'B.B'), 1800 rounds of Gas Shell were fired by A/161, B/161, and C/161; D/161 firing H.E. Enemy was obviously surprised, as he immediately put up rockets, bursting into single REDS and single GREENS (his 'S.O.S' signal. The firing of the Gas Shell was a source of much delight to the Gunners of the Brigade.	
	27-9-18.		Instructions were issued regarding the part which the Brigade would have to take in the forthcoming attempt to break through the HINDENBURG Line. The Scheme was, that the 46th Divn. should attack, cross the CANAL, and push forward as far as the GREEN Line which ran through H.20.central to N.2.central; and that the 32nd Division should take up the attack there and go through to the final objective, which ran as follows: H.11.c.0.0.,-H.23.c.0.0 - East of LEVERGIES - N.9.central, which was the line of exploitation. Reconnaissances were carried out by Battery Commanders of positions in the vicinity of G.26., 32., or 34., which would be occupied in the move forward, and also of the routes to be taken. Batteries were instructed to collectively provide personnel for the manning of an enemy gun in case of capture. (See Appendix 21). Batteries harassed the enemy to the extent of 600 rounds per Battery during the day and night. Major P.CROW,M.C., A/161, granted leave to U.K. until 11-10-18.	
	28-9-18.		Batteries worked on their positions during the day and were allotted zones for Harassing Fire. D/161 spent the day making gaps in the enemy wire West of the CANAL at G.28.d.9.3. & G.34.b.8.8.3; A/161, B/161, and C/161 fired on these gaps during the night (See appendix 22). Instructions were issued that the intermediate positions to be occupied the following day were to be in G.21. and not as previously ordered. 2/Lieut. E.A.WILSON, A/161, proceeded to attend Course at Fourth Army Artillery School commencing 29-9-18.	
	29-9-18.		The 46th Division, on a two Brigade front, attacked the HINDENBURG Line at 5.50 a.m. At the time, and until 11.0 a.m., there was a thick mist, so dense that it was not possible to see an object even 5 yds. away. The attack met with great success, the CANAL being crossed at an early hour,	

Army Form C. 2118.

WAR DIARY
or
INTELLIGENCE SUMMARY.

(Erase heading not required.)

161st (YORKS.) BRIGADE R.F.A.

Place	Date	Hour	Summary of Events and Information	Remarks and references to Appendices
In the Field.	29-9-18. (Contd)		hour, and the objective of the 46th Division being reached in good time. Our Batteries took part in the first part of the Barrage from positions in L.35, firing their guns with great difficulty owing to the mist. About 11.0 a.m. they received orders to take up positions in G.21, and the following were occupied: A/161 .... G.21.d.4.0. B/161 .... G.21.d.6.2. C/161 .... G.21.d.3.9. D/161 .... G.27.b.6.8. The enemy shelled the approaches to these positions when Batteries moved up and A/161 had one Driver killed and C/161 two wounded; while several horses were killed and wounded. C/161 were ordered to cross the CANAL and keep in close support of the BORDERS; A/161 to follow shortly afterwards in support of the K.O.Y.L.I., and B/161 to go across later in support of the A.& S.H. (The Battalion in support), while D/161 were to come on afterwards. All Batteries had crossed the CANAL by 4.0 p.m., and the following positions were taken up: A/161 .... G.30.a.8.8. B/161 .... G.30.a.8.6. C/161 .... G.30.a.9.4. D/161 .... G.29.d.8.8. The 32nd Division were late in getting into position and partly as a consequence of this, the success of the 46th Division could not be exploited to the fullest extent. They remained for the night roughly on the line which the 46th Division had captured. This was not wholly caused by the lateness of their arrival, but largely on account of their flank being "in the air", the enemy still being in JONCOURT. Batteries brought up ammunition throughout the night, as they were frequently called upon to fire, by the Infantry; and the condition of the horses was very bad, caused by the amount of work which they had lately been called upon to do, and the wretched state of the roads & tracks. Batteries had Liaison Officers with the Battalions which they supported. 2/Lieut.R.R.TAYLOR, C/161, wounded by Artillery fire and admitted hospital.	
	30-9-18.		Batteries fired during the day and night on frequent calls from the Infantry. The 96th Inf. Bde. were brought into the line to fill the gap between the 97th Inf.Bde. and the Australians, who were on our left. They attempted with the A.& S.H. (of the 97th Inf.Bde.) to take JONCOURT from the South, but the undertaking failed, the A.& S.H. having two officers and about 40 O.R. who had gone too far forward, captured. An attempt to take LEVERGIES also failed. South of the CANAL, 1st Division took TALANA HILL and the high ground East of THORIGNY. Major R.EMMET, D.S.O., B/161, and Lieut.E.COKE,M.C., H/161, granted leave to U.K. until 14-10-18. (Continued).	

Army Form C. 2118

WAR DIARY
or
INTELLIGENCE SUMMARY

(*Erase heading not required.*)

8. 161st (YORKS.) BRIGADE R.F.A.

Instructions regarding War Diaries and Intelligence Summaries are contained in F. S. Regs., Part II. and the Staff Manual respectively. Title Pages will be prepared in manuscript.

Place	Date	Hour	Summary of Events and Information	Remarks and references to Appendices
			CASUALTIES DURING MONTH of SEPTEMBER 1918.	
			Killed. Wounded. Gas. Evacuated Sick.	
			OFFICERS. - 4 - 2.	
			O.R's. 7 52 4 38.	
			2nd October 1918. [signature] Lieut-Colonel,	
			Commanding 161st (Yorks.) Brigade R.F.A.	

Headquarters, 32nd D.A.
Headquarters, 97th Inf. Bde.
O.C., A/161st Bde. R.F.A.
O.C., B/161st Bde. R.F.A.
O.C., C/161st Bde. R.F.A.
O.C., D/161st Bde. R.F.A.

1. It is not expected that the Infantry will advance their line today.

2. Batteries will harass possible machine-gun nests during the day with observed fire where possible.

3. Lanes are allotted to Batteries for Harassing Fire as follows:-

    A/161 - Lane bounded by an East and West line through X.7.c.0.0 and X.1.c.0.0. paying particular attention to sunken roads in vicinity of ATTILLY.

    B/161 - Lane bounded by an East and West line through X.1.a.0.0. and X.1.c.0.0. paying particular attention to BEAD WOODS.

    C/161) Lane bounded by an East and West line
      &   ) through X.7.c.0.0 and X.13.c.4.0.
    D/161) paying particular attention to road junction and wood X.15.central and trench system in X.15.a.

4. Not less than 50 rounds per gun and Howr. will be fired.

8-9-18.

Lieut-Colonel,
Commanding 161st (Yorks.) Bde. R. F. A.

URGENT.

O.C., A/161st Bde.R.F.A.
O.C., B/161st Bde.R.F.A.
O.C., C/161st Bde.R.F.A.
O.C., D/161st Bde.R.F.A.

5
War Diary

1. The French are advancing on ETREILLERS today.

2. To cover their flanks, Artillery support is required on squares X.15 and X.16., paying particular attention to wood at X.15.central.

3. Reference this office No.G.202 of to-day's date; Lanes for B/161, C/161 and D/161 still hold good. A/161 will harass the South-East edge of HOLNON WOOD instead of sunken roads in vicinity of ATTILLY.

8-9-18.

Captain,
Adjutant, 161st (Yorks.) Brigade R.F.A.

SECRET.

H.Q., 32nd Divisional Artillery.
H.Q., 96th Inf.Bde.
H.Q., 97th Inf.Bde.
O.C., 6th Aust.F.A.Bde.
O.C., A/161st Bde.R.F.A.
O.C., B/161st Bde.R.F.A.
O.C., C/161st Bde.R.F.A.
O.C., D/161st Bde.R.F.A.

161st (YORKS.) BRIGADE R.F.A. OPERATION ORDER No.8.

1. The Northern Divisional Boundary is now the MONS – VERMAND Road East and West through R.25.d.0.5.
   The Southern Divisional Boundary is a line East and West through X.22.central.

2. The Brigade front is held by two Battalions in the front Line:
   15th Lancs.Fusrs. on right; the 16th Lancs.Fusrs. on left.
   Inter-Battalion Boundary: East and West along grid line between X.2. and X.8.
   Present Front Line is reported to run: X.2.c.5.5. along Sunken Road to X.8.b.2.4., X.8.b.8.0. to Cross Roads X.9.d.2.8. down track to X.9.d.5.4. due East X.10.c.0.4., X.10.c.4.9., X.10.c.8.0., X.16.a.2.0., X.16.c.1.0.

   161st Brigade R.F.A. will cover Right Battalion; the 6th A.F.A. Brigade the Left Battalion.

3. Lanes are allotted to 161st Brigade R.F.A. as follows:-

   B/161 --- (N.Boundary E. and W. along grid line from X.2.d.0.0.
             (S.Boundary E. and W. along grid line through X.8.d.0.0.

   A/161 --- (N.Boundary E. and W. along grid line through X.8.d.0.0.
             (S.Boundary E. and W. along grid line through X.14.b.0.0.

   C/161 --- (N.Boundary E. and W. along grid line X.14.b.0.0.
             (S.Boundary E. and W. along grid line through X.20.b.0.0.

   D/161 --- Superimposed on Right Battalion Front.

4. LIAISON OFFICERS will be found by the 161st Brigade R.F.A. as follows:-

   9.0 a.m. 11-9-18 to 9.0 a.m. 12-9-18 - D/161.
   9.0 a.m. 12-9-18 to 9.0 a.m. 13-9-18 - A/161.
              a n d   s o   o n.

   6th A.F.A.Bde. will work in liaison with Left Battalion and arrange S.O.S.Line direct, reporting line selected, to this office.

5. S.O.S.LINE covered by 208th Brigade will be taken over by 6th A.F.A.Brigade from 10.0 p.m. tonight. Line runs as follows:- R.31.b.00.50 to R.25.d.05.50.

6. H.Q.,161st Brigade R.F.A. will close at W.8.a.8.8. at 10.0 a.m., 11th instant, and re-open at W.11.a.7.7. at the same hour.

(Continued).

-2-

7. All Batteries will be prepared to turn their fire on any area asked for by Battalion Commanders through Liaison Officers as soon as possible.

8. C/161 will move to position at W.12.d.5.5. on the night 10th/11th.

9. ACKNOWLEDGE.

for Lieut-Colonel,

10-9-18.   Commanding 161st (Yorks.) Brigade R. F. A.

Issued at 9.45 p.m.

SECRET.

H.Q., 33nd Divisional Artillery.
H.Q., 66th Inf. Brigade.
O.C., 6th (Army Aust.)Bde.F.A.
O.C., A/161st Bde. R.F.A.
O.C., B/161st Bde. R.F.A.
O.C., C/161st Bde. R.F.A.
O.C., D/161st Bde. R.F.A.

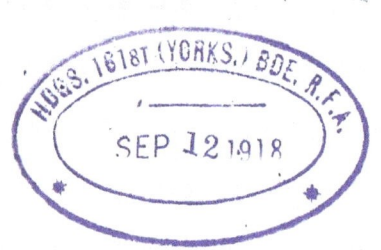

161st (YORKS.) BRIGADE OPERATION ORDER No.11.

1. The 23rd A.F.A. Brigade is taking over the front at present covered by the 161st Brigade R.F.A., today.

2. Batteries of 161st Brigade R.F.A. will withdraw to their Wagon Lines as soon as the Batteries of the 23rd A.F.A. Brigade are in position.
   Hdqrs., 23rd A.F.A. Brigade from 5.0 p.m. - W.11.a.7.3.

3. All ammunition surplus to Echelon will be left at Battery positions and should be protected from damp as far as possible.

4. Hdqrs., 161st Brigade R.F.A. will close at W.11.a.7.3. at 5.0 p.m. and open at position to be notified later, at the same hour.

5. ACKNOWLEDGE.

12th Sept.1918.

Captain,
Adjutant, 161st Brigade R.F.A.

Issued at   p.m.

SECRET.

Copy No... 7...

161st (YORKS.) BRIGADE R.F.A. OPERATION ORDER No.12.

1. The 161st Brigade R.F.A. will move to an area South of ATHIES tomorrow, 14th instant.

2. Batteries will march in the following order:

   A/161.
   B/161.
   C/161.
   D/161.

   Route: MONCHY-LAGACHE - ESTRES - ATHIES.

3. Starting Point: Cross Roads, ESTRES. U.8.d.00.88.

   Head of column of A/161 will pass the Starting Point at 9.0 a.m.; B/161 at 9.15 a.m.; C/161 at 9.30 a.m.; D/161 at 9.45 a.m.

4. Attention is drawn to S.S.724 "March Discipline and Traffic Control" issued to Batteries 14-8-18.
   35 yds. distance will be maintained between Sections.

5. Guides should be placed on the ST.CHRIST - ATHIES Road to direct Supply Wagons to Batteries.

6. Present Wagon Lines will be left in a clean and sanitary condition.

7. ACKNOWLEDGE.

13th September 1918.

Captain,
Adjutant, 161st Brigade R.F.A.

Issued at   p.m.

Distribution: Copy No.1 = C.R.A.
                       2 = O.C., A/161.
                       3 = O.C., B/161.
                       4 = O.C., C/161.
                       5 = O.C., D/161.
                       6 = War Diary.
                       7 = File.

SECRET.  Copy No......8......

161st (YORKS.) BRIGADE R.F.A. OPERATION ORDER No.13.

1. Fourth Army are attacking the enemy outpost line at an early date, probably 18th instant, with a view to driving the enemy back towards the main HINDENBURG Line.

2. OBJECTIVES: as shown on tracing attached (To 161/Batteries only).

3. The 6th Divisional Boundary is as follows:-

    (a) Southern.
    N.30.b.5.0 - S.3.c.60.20 - S.8.b.80.30 - S.8.c.30.00 - X.18.a.80.00 - X.18.c.00.40 - X.21.d.70.90 - W.30.a.00.70 - W.28.b.70.60 - W.27.a.00.80 - V.23.d.60.00 - V.27.b.8.8 - V.26.a.6.8 - V.25.a.4.7 - U.22.c.00.90 - T.24.b.2.8.

    (b). Northern.
    N.17.central - M.22.a.central - M.21.c.0.0 - M.20.central - M.26.c.0.0 - R.35.d.6.4 - Corner of Wood at X.5.a.35.70 - X.4.b.7.5 - thence along track to level crossing at X.10.a.6.7 - thence through to X.9.central - X.8.central - X.7.central - X.7.a.0.0 - to OMIGNON River at W.12.b.65.40 - thence Westward along OMIGNON River.

4. The 6th Division are pushing up to jumping off line shown on attached tracing.(To Batteries of 161st Bde.only).

5. The following Field Artillery are taking part in the operation:-

    RIGHT GROUP: 24th Bde.R.F.A.
    Lt.-Col.J.A.C.FORSYTH,D.S.O.   23rd A.F.A.Bde.

    LEFT GROUP: 2nd Bde.R.F.A.
    Lt.-Col.W.F.H.WEBER,D.S.O.   161st Bde.R.F.A.
                                     14th A.F.A.Bde.

6. The following positions have been selected for 161st Bde.R.F.A. to cover the attack up to and inclusive of the GREEN LINE.

    HQ/161 - X.3.a.2.3.
    A/161 -
    B/161 - X.4.a.43.00.
    C/161 - X.4.c.30.85.
    D/161 - X.4.a.92.15.

    Batteries will move up all guns on the night 16th/17th Sept. and conceal them in the N.W.corner of HOLNON WOOD, or any other suitable locality East of a North and South line through X.15.central.
    Necessary horses and limbers will be kept East of this line to move guns into action on Y/Z night.

7. There will be a pause of two hours in the attack on reaching the GREEN LINE. During this interval, 161st Bde.R.F.A. will move up to and occupy positions in vicinity of R.36.a., and take their place in the Creeping and Final Barrage according to the time at which Batteries come into action.

8. Batteries may move up by any route.
    Tracks being prepared by R.E.:-
    (a). Track X.4.a.0.6 - X.4.b.2.3.
    (b). Road X.4.b.3.3 - X.6.a.0.8.
    (c). Track X.5.b.5.7 - KEEPERS HOUSE.
    (d). Track X.4.a.9.3 - X.4.b.3.7.

9. An Officer and party will be sent forward at ZERO HOUR to reconnoitre position in vicinity of R.36.a. This party should be in possession of wire cutters to prepare approaches to position, special attention being paid to the wire in R.35.b.

(Continued).

10. The following dumps of ammunition will be established at
positions in X.d.a.and c. by dawn 17th instant:-

	A.	AM.	AS.
18-Pounder	300 rds. per gun.	225 rds. per gun.	75 rds. per gun.

    4.5" Howr; ...... 400 rds. per gun BX.; as much 106 fuze as possible.

11. Every Battery will have a portable trench bridge, and wire cutters should be easily accessible.

12. Batteries will establish O.P's for the positions in R.36.a. in the vicinity of KEEPERS HOUSE (C/161 and D/161); M.23.d.(A/161 and B/161).
    O.P.Parties should be sent forward at ZERO Hour to run telephone lines from O.Ps. to Battery areas.

13. Every precaution should be taken to conceal positions, dumps, guns, etc. Personnel should not be allowed to walk about near the positions, etc. during daylight.

14. ACKNOWLEDGE.

                                                                                                     WThomson Capt

16th Sept.1918.   for Lieut-Colonel,
                   Commanding 161st (Yorks.) Brigade R.F.A.

Issued at 6.30 p.m.

        Distribution: Copy No.1 - H.Q.,32nd D.A.
                          2 - H.Q.,6th D.A.
                          3 - O.C.,Left Group.
                          4 - O.C.,A/161.
                          5 - O.C.,B/161.
                          6 - O.C.,C/161.
                          7 - O.C.,D/161.
                          8 - War Diary.
                          9 - File.

Copy 10

151st Bde.R.F.A.   S e c r e t.

Instructions No.2.

1. 15th Inf.Bde.Hdqrs. will probably be in N.d.d. in first
instance.

2. The I.B.plan is understood to go as follows —
   (a). The advance to the Green Line will be carried out
   by the 2/ York & Lancaster R. alone. Their right
   will follow the barrage, but their left will probably
   stop short of PRESNOY which will be entered from the
   South.
   The 151st Bde.R.F.A. will find liaison with 2/Y.& L.R.
   (b). The advance to the Red Line will be carried out by the
   1/DUKES on the right and the K.S.L.I. (1st Bn:) on
   the left. Dividing line GARDEN COPSE & BERNARD ALLEY.
   Similar action will be taken at UNICORN as at PRESNOY.
   The 2nd Bde.R.F.A. will find liaison with the DUKES.
   2/Lieut. JAMES will perform this duty.
   The 14th A.F.A.Bde. will find liaison with the KING'S
   SHROPSHIRE LIGHT INFANTRY.

3. Battalion Hdrs. will be notified later.

                              (Sgd) W.S.GEBER, Lieut-Colonel R.A.
Copy Group 88. D.A: Commanding.

— 2 —

O.C., A/151.
O.C., B/151.
O.C., C/151.
O.C., D/151.

[Stamp: HEAD. 151st (YORKS) BDE. R.F.A. C.171. SEP 16 1918]

   Reference above; O.C.,D/151 will detail an experienced officer
to be in liaison with 2/Y.& L.R. This officer will take two
Signallers, 1 runner, and 2 miles of wire with him and should
report to Battalion Hdqrs. tomorrow, and remain with them until
the completion of the operations. (Name of officer selected to
be reported to this office.) He should be thoroughly acquainted
with the intended action of Artillery and should ascertain from
the Brigade Signal Officer the proposed communications.

                                        W D Lambton
                                        Captain,
15-9-18.   Adjutant, 151st Brigade R.F.A.

SECRET.  Copy No...8......

161ST (YORKS.) BRIGADE R.F.A. OPERATION ORDER No.14.

1. In continuation of 161st (Yorks.) Brigade R.F.A. Operation Order No.13 ;
   Barrage diagrams giving Zones and Lifts have been issued to Battery Commanders.
   4.5" How. Targets as detailed in 6th D.A. Operation Order No.151.

2. Rates of Fire and Ammunition: As laid down in 6th D.A. Operation Order No.151.

3. Zero Hour: 5.30 a.m., 18th September 1918.

4. Synchronisation: An Officer from Brigade Hdrs. will bring a watch with synchronised time to batteries about 8.30 p.m., 17th Instant.

5. A Line (D/W .181) has been laid by Brigade to a dug out in bank at L.14.a.5.7. F.O.Os. and F.L.Os. can tap into this line to establish communication with Brigade Hdqrs.

6. ACKNOWLEDGE.

                                    C W Thornton
                                    Captain,
17th September 1918.   Adjutant, 161st (Yorks.) Bde.R.F.A.

Issued at 7...

        Copy No.1 - H.Q., 32nd D.A.
              2 - H.Q., 6th D.A.
              3 - O.C., Left Group.
              4 - O.C., A/161.
              5 - O.C., B/161.
              6 - O.C., C/161.
              7 - O.C., D/161.
              8 - War Diary.
              9 - File.

SECRET.   Copy No. 9

161st (YORKS.) BRIGADE R.F.A. ARTILLERY INSTRUCTIONS No.33.

1.   Line now runs:

        1st Division – BERTINCOURT – LEBUC Trench – EASLING Trench –
     N.22.b., with post about N.21.d.1.3.

        Our line runs – W. of FRENOY, down CHAMPAGNE Trench, and
     joins 71st Infantry Brigade at DOUAI Trench, N.33.d.8.1.

        Enemy believed to hold HOLNON, and French JAVY Wood.

2.   S.O.S. LINES are as follows:-

             C/161   ---- N.83.d.9.6. to N.35.a.0.5.
             A/161   ---- N.35.a.0.5. to N.35.c.0.5.
             B/161   ---- N.35.c.0.5. to O.5.a.0.5.
             D/161   ---- N.35.a.5.7.
                           N.35.a.9.7.
                           N.35.d.0.8.
                           N.35.d.0.0.
                           N.35.c.4.0.
                           S.5.a.5.75.

     S.O.S. RATES ARE AS FOLLOWS:-

             First 5 minutes ---- INTENSE.
             Followed by 5 minutes RAPID.

3.   C/161 and D/161 will withdraw from present positions after dusk
     and re-occupy former positions.
        During the period C/161 is out of action, Northern half of the
     zone allotted to C/161 will be covered by two guns of B/161; Southern
     half by two guns of A/161.

4.   The following dumps of ammunition will be established:-

             18-Pdrs. 400 rds. per gun, and 50 rds. Smoke per gun.
             4.5" Hows: 300 rds. per Howitzer.

        Ammunition at present at C/161 position will be taken over by A/161
     and B/161.

5.   LIAISON OFFICERS with K.S.L.I. (Colonel SCRUTTON) will be found
     by Batteries as follows:-
             D/161 – Up to 10.0.a.m. 19.9.18.
             A/161 – From 10.0.a.m. 19th to 10.0.a.m. 20th.
             B/161 – From 10.0.a.m. 20th to 10.0.a.m. 21st.
             C/161 – From 10.0.a.m. 21st to 10.0.a.m. 22nd.
        Location of Battalion Headquarters: Sunken Road W. of BADGER Copse.

6.   NIGHT O.P. will be manned by Batteries in rotation as follows:-
             B/161 – Night 18th/19th September.
             C/161 – Night 19th/20th September.
             A/161 – Night 20th/21st September.
             D/161 – Night 21st/22nd September.
        All Batteries will man an O.P. from dawn to dusk.

18th Sept.1918.   C.W.Thompson Captain,
Issued at 8 p.m.   Adjutant, 161st Brigade R.F.A.

        Copy No.1 – H.Q.,32nd D.A.   5 – O.C.,B/161.   9 – File.
               2 – H.Q., 6th D.A.   6 – O.C.,C/161.
               3 – O.C.,Lert Gp.   7 – O.C.,D/161.
               4 – O.C.,A/161.   8 – War Diary.

SECRET.   Copy No...8...

151st (YORKS.) BRIGADE R.F.A.
ARTILLERY INSTRUCTIONS No.39.

1. The line held by the Infantry is not at present definitely known. Attack this morning was unsuccessful.

2. S O S.LINES until further orders will be as follows:-

   C/151 ...M.28.c.4.5 to M.34.a.70.75.
   B/151 ...M.34.a.70.75 to M.34.a.85.00.
   A/151 ...M.34.a.85.00 to M.34.c.80.80.
   D/151 ..Trench Junctions: M.34.d.8.4; M.35.a.0.8; M.28.d.85.10.
          and 3 Hows. Sunken Road,M.34.d.60.75.

3. A/151 and B/151 will each withdraw two sections to positions occupied on night 17th/18th Sept.

4. Instructions reference Liaison, O.Ps. and Ammunition, detailed in 151st Bde.R.F.A. Artillery Instructions No.38, hold good.

5. ACKNOWLEDGE.
                                              CD London
19-9-18.   Captain,
Issued at 11.15 a.m.   Adjutant, 151st Brigade R.F.A.

   Copy No.1 - H.Q.,32nd D.A.   4 - O.C.,A/151.   7 - O.C.,D/151.
            2 - H.Q., 9th D.A. 5 - O.C.,B/151.   8 - War Diary.
            3 - O.C.,Bart (?)   6 - O.C.,C/151.   9 - File.

SECRET.   Copy No. 8

161st (YORKS.) BRIGADE R.F.A.
ARTILLERY INSTRUCTION NO. 40.

1. Taking up for the moment a defensive policy, the LEFT GROUP is distributed in depth as follows:-

   2 Sections 161st Bde. RFA. in R.36;
       approx. range to S.O.S.LINES, 3,800.

   Remainder 161st Bde. RFA. in X.4;
       approx. range to S.O.S.LINES, 5,000.

   21st Battery, R.34.c.9.6;
       approx. range to S.O.S.LINES, 4,400.

   1 Section 42nd Battery, R.35.central;
       approx. range to S.O.S.LINES, 3,500.

   Remainder 42nd Battery, R.34.a.7.8;
       approx. range to S.O.S.LINES, 4,900.

   53rd Battery, R.35.a.3.8;
       approx.range to S.O.S.LINES, 3,800.

   1 Section 87th Battery N.E.Corner of Copse about R.35.central;
       approx. range to S.O.S.LINES, 3,500.

   Remainder 87th Battery, R.34.d.5.8;
       approx. range to S.O.S.LINES, 4,500.

2. The intention is that the four forward sections shall pursue an active sniping policy, relying on visibility and maintaining local observation and close touch with the Infantry.
   Teams to be within easy reach and 200 rds. per gun to be dumped on the position.

3. Pending developments, no policy of silent positions can be laid down.

4. In the event of a counter-attack by the enemy being successful, forward sections will withdraw to positions in R.35; and rear sections will withdraw to positions in X.2 as soon as the intervening crests prevent further fire being brought to bear on the enemy.

5. All positions, other than forward positions, will maintain dumps as follows:-

   18-Pdrs. 400 rds. per gun, and 50 rds. Smoke per gun.
   4.5" Hows. 300 rds. per hour.

6. Forward Wagon Lines will be maintained.

7. There will be two Battalions in the line, BUGEAUD ALLEY being the dividing line. The line being consolidated runs: M.21.c.3.2. along road in M.27.a. and c., to the old Communication Trench about M.27.d.1.3, then to the T of CHAMPAGNE TRENCH - junction of DOUAI TRENCH and AMERICAN ALLEY.
   On the left, the line of the 1st Inf.Bde. runs: M.9.c.45.30 - M.9.c.6.0 - M.15.a.7.6 - M.15.a.50.25 - M.15.a.4.0 - M.15.c.3.6 - M.15.c.5.3 - M.15.c.55.00 - M.21.a.25.60 - M.21.a.25.40 - M.21.a.4.0 - M.21.c.4.7 - M.21.c.05.00.

8. LIAISON OFFICERS. Tour of duty with Battalions will be 48 hours, as follows:-
       C/161 ... From 10.0 a.m. 21-9-18 to 10.0 a.m. 23-9-18.
       D/161 ... From 10.0 a.m. 23-9-18 to 10.0 a.m. 25-9-18.
       A/161 ... From 10.0 a.m. 25-9-18 to 10.0 a.m. 27-9-18.
       B/161 ... From 10.0 a.m. 27-9-18 to 10.0 a.m. 29-9-18.

   Location of Battalion H.Q.: Quarry X.5.b.9.9.

-2-

9. HEADQUARTERS: Group H.Q is at R.34.c.4.5.
161st Bde.RFA. H.Q. is at X.3.a.4.1.

10. S.O.S.LINES will be as follows:-

    C/161 ... M.28.c.15.70 - M.28.c.40.50 - M.28.c.30.11.
    B/161 ... M.28.c.30.15 - M.34.a.30.55.
    A/161 ... M.34.a.35.65 - M.34.c.30.90.
    D/161 ... Trench Junctions: M.34.d.8.4; M.35.a.0.0; M.28.d.35.10.
             3 Mors. Sunken Road M.34.d.60.75.

11. LANES are allotted to Batteries for Harassing Fire as follows:-

    C/161 ... Northern Boundary: From M.27.d.0.0 - N.20.b.30.05.
              Southern Boundary: From M.33.b.20.47 - N.20.d.20.30.

    B/161 ... Northern Boundary: From M.33.b.30.47 - N.20.d.20.30.
              Southern Boundary: From M.33.b.35.00 - N.26.b.00.60.

    A/161 ... Northern Boundary: From M.33.b.35.00 - N.26.b.00.60.
              Southern Boundary: From M.33.d.30.60 - N.26.b.70.00.

    D/161 ... Northern Boundary: From M.27.d.0.0 - N.20.b.30.05.
              Southern Boundary: From M.33.d.30.60 - N.26.b.70.00

12. ACKNOWLEDGE.

                                        Act/Captain,
20-9-18.   Adjutant, 161st Brigade R.F.A.

Issued at 7.30 p.m.

            Copy No. 1 H.Q.,32nd D.A.
                     2 - H.Q.,6th D.A.
                     3 - O.C. Left Group.
                     4 - O.C.,A/161.
                     5 - O.C.,B/161.
                     6 - O.C.,C/161.
                     7 - O.C.,D/161.
                     8 - War Diary.
                     9 - File.

SECRET.

War Diary 15

H.Q., 32nd Divisional Artillery
H.Q., 6th Divisional Artillery.
O.C., Left Group.
O.C., A/161.
O.C., B/161.
O.C., C/161.
O.C., D/161.

1. On the night of 21st/22nd Sept. the 6th Division will hand over to the 1st Division that part of its front line between the present Inter-Divisional Boundary and the grid line between squares M.27. and M.33.

2. On the same night, the 16th Infantry Brigade will relieve the 71st Infantry Brigade in that part of its front between the present Inter-Brigade Boundary and the grid line between squares M.36 and S.3.

3. Boundaries after completion of this relief will be as under:-

    Between 1st and 6th Divisions.
East and West grid lines between M.27. and 33 - M.25 and 31 as far as R.29.c.0.0. thence R.33.c.9.5 - R.32.c.8.5 and thence along OMIGNON River.

    Between Infantry Brigades.
East and West grid lines between squares M.3 3 and S.3 to where it cuts the present Boundary and thence as at present.

    Boundary between 6th Division and French.
M.26.central - S.5.b.5.0 - S.3.d.5.0 thence Westward as before.

4. S.O.S. LINES from 10.0 p.m., 21st Sept. are allotted to Batteries as follows:-

    A/161 ... M.34.c.50.09 - M.34.a.35.11.
    B/161 ... M.34.a.35.05 - M.34.a.35.90.
    C/161 ... M.34.a.3 5.85 - M.28.c.40.50 - M.28.c.20.65.

5. LIAISON will be from night 21st/22nd Sept. be found with 1/BUFFS instead of with Y.& L.R.

6. ACKNOWLEDGE by wire.

                                        Captain,
21st Sept.1918.   Adjutant, 161st Brigade R.F.A.

SECRET.

H.Q., 32nd Divisional Artillery.
H.Q., 6th Divisional Artillery.
O.C., Left Group.
O.C., A/161.
O.C., B/161.
O.C., C/161.
O.C., D/161.

1. On the night of 21st/22nd Sept. the 6th Division will hand over to the 1st Division that part of its front lying between the present Inter-Divisional Boundary and the grid line between squares M.27. and M.33.

2. On the same night, the 16th Infantry Brigade will relieve the 71st Infantry Brigade in that part of its front between the present Inter-Brigade Boundary and the grid line between squares M.33 and S.3.

3. Boundaries after completion of this relief will be as under:-

    Between 1st and 6th Divisions.
East and West grid lines between M.27. and 33 - M.25 and 31 as far as R.29.c.0.0. thence R.33.c.9.5 - R.32.c.8.5 and thence along OMIGNON River.

    Between Infantry Brigades.
East and West grid lines between squares M.33 and S.3 to where it cuts the present Boundary and thence as at present.

    Boundary between 6th Division and French.
N.26.central - S.5.b.5.0 - S.8.d.0.0 thence Westward as before.

4. S.O.S. LINES from 10.0 p.m., 21st Sept. are allotted to Batteries as follows:-

    A/161 ... M.34.c.50.09 - M.34.a.35.11.
    B/161 ... M.34.a.35.05 - M.34.a.35.90.
    C/161 ... M.34.a.35.85 - M.28.c.40.50 - M.28.c.20.65.

5. LIAISON will be from night 21st/22nd Sept. be found with 1/BUFFS instead of with Y.& L.R.

6. ACKNOWLEDGE by wire.

21st Sept.1918.

Adjutant, 161st Brigade R.F.A.
Captain,

SECRET.   Copy No...9....

161st (YORKS.) BRIGADE R.F.A.
BATTERY INSTRUCTIONS No.21.

1. S.O.S.LINES are allotted as follows:-

   A/161 ... M.34.a.00.90 - M.34.a.35.11.
   B/161 ... M.34.a.35.05 - M.34.a.85.00.
   C/161 ... M.34.a.85.00 - M.28.c.40.50 - M.28.c.80.05.
   D/161 ... M.28.c.00.11; M.28.d.35.11;
             M.34.b.10.80; M.34.d.20.85;
             M.34.d.70.70; M.34.d.20.40.

2. COUNTER-PREPARATION.

   (a). ONE/A will have a methodical searching of the area between
        S.O.S.Lines and vertical grid line dividing 34 and 35,
        opening on S.O.S.Lines and lifting back by 100 yds. every
        three minutes and repeating the process, rate NORMAL, except
        when on S.O.S.Lines, then rate will be INTENSE.

   (b). ONE/B will have periods of fire of 5 minutes followed by
        pauses of 5 minutes; each period of fire two minutes INTENSE
        three minutes NORMAL; fire will be searching and sweeping.
        Fire will be switched about on the following targets:-

           New trench M.28.b. and d.   34.b. and d.
           ARGONNE and PUNCHER Trenches.
           Valleys N. of PAXLE.
           Area M.34.c. and d.

   (c). A Zero hour will be given and time limit.

   (d). Lanes for Counter-Preparation are allotted to Batteries
        as follows:-

        A/161 ... Lane bounded by East and West lines through
                  M.34.c.0.0 and M.34.c.00.65.
        B/161 ... Lane bounded by East and West lines through
                  M.34.c.00.65 and M.34.a.00.35.
        C/161 ... Lane bounded by East and West lines through
                  M.34.a.00.35 and M.28.c.00.65.
        D/161 ... Superimposed on Brigade front.

3. Should it become necessary to withdraw, positions will be
   available as follows:-

        X.3.d., X.2.d., X.8.a., X.7.c.(Southern half) and L.13.a.

4. ACKNOWLEDGE.

                                              AB Compton
22nd Sept.1918.   Captain,
                                   Adjutant, 161st (Yorks.) Brigade R.F.A.
Issued at   p.m.

                Copy No.1 - H.Q., 62nd D.A.
                     2 - H.Q., 6th D.A.
                     3 - O.C., Left Group.
                     4 - O.C., A/161.
                     5 - O.C., B/161.
                     6 - O.C., C/161.
                     7 - O.C., D/161.
                     8 - War Diary.
                     9 - File.

War Diary

ORDER.

1. The next barrage will last about 30 minutes probably.

2. It will probably be over and slightly S. of our present zone ~~as shown in~~

3. 161 will take the right, 2nd Brigade the left.
   Two 18-Pdr. Batteries in the barrage, one superimposed.
   One section of each Battery in the barrage using smoke.
   4.5" Hows. will fire smoke in the later stages (probably one section per Battery).
   The barrage does not seem complicated.

4. If one Battalion only of 16th I.B. attacks, 2nd Brigade will find liaison. If two Battalions attack, 161 will liaise with right Battalion, 2nd Bde. with the left.

5. Unless other orders are received, each Brigade will run one Brigade O.P. and one moving O.P. which will move forward. The moving O.P. will include two Officers (one being a F.O.O.) Its objective is to get observation E. of GRECOURT and SAVY, over the trench system in N.30. and 36 and, if possible, into the hollow behind that system. The most careful arrangements must be made to get this information back to Group Headquarters. The Group Commander intends this time to remain at Group Hdqrs. with Major NICHOLS at 16th Inf. Bde Hqrs.

6. In recent operations further North, the enemy appears to have counter-attacked in some force from "The HINDENBURG LINE". Batteries must be able to get their teams up quickly, as well as ensure a powerful protective barrage for a considerable time after the completion of the operation.

7. X X X X X X X X X X X

                                   (sgd) R.E.SMITH, 2/Lieut.R.F.A.,
25-9-18.   For Adjutant, 2nd Brigade R.F.A.

-2-

O.C., Left Group.
O.C., A/161.
O.C., B/161.
O.C., C/161.
O.C., D/161.

With reference to above order. Liaison Officers, if necessary will be found by B/161. C/161 will man their present O.P. throughout operation, moving O.P. with two Officers will be furnished by A/161 and D/161. Names of officers selected for above today to be forwarded to this office as soon as possible.

The F.O.O. and F.I.O. found by A/161 and D/161 will consult Signalling Officer, 161st Bde. R.F.A. forthwith, and make the necessary arrangements to carry out their tasks. These officers will personally communicate their plans to Brigade Commander as early as possible.

                                              Captain,
25-9-18.   Adjutant, 161st Brigade R.F.A.

SECRET.  Copy No. 8

161st (YORKS.) BRIGADE R.F.A. OPERATION ORDER No.15.

Reference 1/20,000 Sheet 62.B. S.W.

1. On the 24th September, at an hour, Zero, to be communicated later, the IX Corps is attacking to secure high ground MANCHESTER HILL - FRANCILLY - SELENCY - QUADRILATERAL - M.34.d.and b. - M.28.d.and b.- M.16.d.and b.

2. 16th Infantry Brigade - FIRST OBJECTIVE.- S.4.a.5.8.(NORTH ALLEY) along Ridge trench to M.28.c.65.00.
　　　　　　　　　　SECOND OBJECTIVE.- Junction of BRETON ALLEY with new trench at S.4.b.30.65, along the new trench and thence along ARGONNE Trench & PERONNE Trench to Trench Junction M.28.d.35.15.
　Dividing line between 1/K.S.L.I. on right and 2/Y.& L. on left, will be AMERICAN ALLEY.
　Four tanks assist 16th Inf.Bde., but will not lead them.
　Headquarters of both attacking Battalions: in TROUT Copse.
　16th Inf.Bde.Hdqrs.: in Quarry X.5.b.9.9.

3. The Left Group supports the 16th Inf.Bde. attack; 161st Bde.RFA on right, 2nd Brigade R.F.A. on left.
　Barrage Maps have been issued separately to Batteries.

4. For Rates of Fire and Ammunition - vide 6th Divisional Artillery Instructions No.1.

5. Liaison Officer with the 16th Inf.Bde. will be found by 2nd Bde.RFA.

6. It is not improbable that the enemy will counter-attack. The S.O.S.Signal is RED over RED over RED.
　Warning by aeroplane of impending attack will be:
　　Aeroplane flies towards counter-attacking troops and fires a WHITE parachute as close to them as possible.
　Such a warning will be answered by the Brigade on whose Zone it occurs, without reference to Group Headquarters.

7. Answering of "G.F" and "L.L" Calls - vide 6th Divisional Artillery Instructions No.1.

8. Batteries move to forward positions tonight 23rd Sept. at the following times:-
　　　　　　C/161.　7.30 p.m.
　　　　　　A/161.　8.15 p.m.
　　　　　　B/161.　9.0 p.m.
　During the move, responsibility for covering the front in the event of S.O.S. is allotted as follows:-
　　At 7.30 p.m.　A/161 right half of present Bde.S.O.S.Lines.
　　　　　　　　　B/161 left half.
　　　8.15 p.m.　B/161 left half.　C/161 right.
　　　9.0 p.m.　A/161 left half.　C/161 right.
　At 10.0 p.m., Brigade S.O.S.front is reduced to Barrage frontage. B/161 is allotted the right half, A/161 the left half, with C/161 superimposed on the Brigade front. D/161 as before.

9. Each Battery will leave one section in old position to carry out the following 3 minute (INTENSE) concentrations:-
　　10.22 p.m.　Sunken Road from FAYET to MONT NEEDLE.
　　11.17 p.m.　N. and S.Road in M.36.c.
　　12.40 a.m.　Trench M.35.a.87.68 - M.35.d.05.80.
　　1.28 a.m.　Valley in M.35.d.

10. On completion of the Operation, B/161 and C/161 will be prepared to advance Sections to the area M.32.c.
A/161 and one Section D/161 will be prepared to withdraw to re-occupy positions in X.4.

11. Watches will be synchronized at 161st Bde.R.F.A. Hdqrs. at 7.30 p.m., 23rd instant.

12. Attention is drawn to 6th Divisional Artillery Instructions No.1, para.2.

13. Zero Hour will be notified later.

14. A c k n o w l e d g e.

Captain,
Adjutant, 161st Brigade R.F.A.

23-9-18.

Issued at 7.0 p.m.

Copy No. 1 - H.Q., 32nd D.A.
2 - H.Q., 6th D.A
3 - O.C., Left Group.
4 - O.C., A/161.
5 - O.C., B/161.
6 - O.C., C/161.
7 - O.C., D/161.
8 - War Diary.
9 - File.

161st (Yorks.) Brigade. R.F.A.

WK 34

WAR DIARY

COVERING PERIOD

From :- 1st October. 1918.

To :- 31st October. 1918.

Army Form C. 2118.

Instructions regarding War Diaries and Intelligence
Summaries are contained in F. S. Regs., Part II.
and the Staff Manual respectively. Title pages
will be prepared in manuscript.

WAR DIARY
or
INTELLIGENCE SUMMARY.

(Erase heading not required.)

151st (York's.) Brigade R.F.A.

Place	Date	Hour	Summary of Events and Information	Remarks and references to Appendices
In the Field	1-10-18.		The Australians attacked TONCOURT from the North, and at 8.30 a.m. they reported that they were in possession of it. The 97th Inf. Bty Brigade also reported that they had ENTWARDIS. At 4.0 p.m. Batteries fired a barrage in support of an attack by the MANCHESTERS on the Torgane Line between N.10.d. and N.17.a. The attack was entirely successful and all objectives were gained. The enemy heavily barraged this line after they had lost it, the bulk of the shelling coming from the N.E. of R.17.c. The Helvies caused this area and silenced two heavy Batteries. The enemy was reported at 6.0 p.m. to be preparing for a counter-attack. B/151 and D/151 and two Batteries of the 14th Bde. R.F.A. were put on to all the suspect and attempt was stopped. 2/Lieut. H. JONES, D/151, rejoined from hospital.	
	2-10-18.		The enemy heavily attacked our new positions on the BEAUCAMP Line during the night and drove the MANCHESTERS out. The MANCHESTERS heavily afterwards regained the trenches, but the enemy counter-attacked again and was once more in possession of them. A further attack by the MANCHESTERS was successful and was at daylight, in full possession of the line. At 6.50 a.m. we put down a barrage in support of the Infantry, and the line was pushed forward slightly. The 13th Lancs. Fusiliers had very heavy casualties in the operation, Colonel STONE, the C.O., being amongst the killed. Batteries increased the enemy during the night (See appendices 23 and 24). The 99th Infantry Brigade was relieved during the night by the 199th Infantry Brigade. Batteries fired a barrage at 6.5 a.m. in support of an attack by the 199th Inf.Bde. on BEAUCAMP. The attack was very successful at first and the objectives were reached. Later on it was feared that the enemy would counter-attack, and our troops were brought back some distance. The Cavalry were ordered up when it was seen that the success of the morning could be exploited, but they did not arrive up until the afternoon, when it was too late, the enemy having then re-organized his forces. Batteries all moved forward to positions as follows :-	
			A/151 ... N.20.c.90.15.	
			B/151 ... N.26.b.00.80.	
			C/151 ... N.21.a.50.30.	
			D/151 ... N.20.d.45.80.	
	3-10-18.		Batteries harassed the enemy during the night on points selected by the Infantry. During the day Batteries fired on several calls from the Infantry. 2/Lieut. E. DEAN, D/151, admitted hospital (gassed).	

Army Form C. 2118.

WAR DIARY
or
INTELLIGENCE SUMMARY.

161st (Yorks.) Brigade R.F.A.

(Erase heading not required.)

Instructions regarding War Diaries and Intelligence Summaries are contained in F.S. Regs., Part II. and the Staff Manual respectively. Title pages will be prepared in manuscript.

Place	Date	Hour	Summary of Events and Information	Remarks and references to Appendices
In the Field	4-10-18.		Batteries fired on several targets at the request of the Infantry, and on movement and Hostile Batteries. The enemy was especially observed during the day, immediately wiping on any movement seen. The day passed off quietly. At night Batteries harassed the enemy on their lanes, and at midnight received instructions for a barrage the following morning.	
	5-10-18.		At 6.5 a.m. the Infantry of the 153rd Bde. attacked INNIQUIN HILL, A/161 and B/161 firing a creeping barrage, and C/161 putting down a protective flank barrage. The attack was only partly successful, the enemy retaining possession of the Eastern slope of the Hill, and the Infantry incurred heavy casualties from Machine-gun and shell fire. Batteries received preliminary instructions for moving forward in preparation for the contemplated attack by the Infantry of the 6th Division. They were allotted the squares H.22., 23., 28., and 29 for Battery positions. Battery Commanders reconnoitred positions during the afternoon as follows:- A/161 ... H.28.b.70.65. C/161 ... H.22.d.5.1. D/161 ... H.28.b.59.44 D/161 ... H.28.c.0.9. 200 rounds of ammunition per gun were brought up to these positions at night. Batteries were given instructions to bring their guns up the following day.	see Appendix 25.
	6-10-18.		At night, the 179th Inf.Bde. took over the line from the 14th and 97th Inf.Bdes. Lieut.F.W.HOOK, D/161. Granted leave to U.K. until 19-10-18. At 11.0 a.m., Batteries received instructions to postpone bringing their guns forward for 24 hours. The day passed off quietly. Batteries were instructed to increase the dumps at forward positions to 450 rounds per gun. At night, Batteries harassed the enemy.	
	7-10-18.		During the day, Batteries brought their guns forward, one Battery at a time being on the road. Batteries received final instructions for the barrage to be fired the following morning. The day was very quiet, enemy doing little shelling. Batteries fired on targets in their lanes at night, in their new positions. The 6th Division, as part of the IX Corps, attacked at 5.10 a.m., the objective being a line running East of BRAUNCOURT and BEAUREGARD.	Appendices 26 & 27.
	8-10-18.		The 161st Brigade R.F.A. were part of the R.A. of Group, which consisted of the 168th (Group Commander), 161st and 14th Brigades R.F.A. There was no attack immediately South of the 6th Division, but the Americans attacked on our left. At 6.0 a.m. it was reported that the objectives being obtained in good time, and that no rockets had gone up. At 7.55 a.m. the 71st Infantry Brigade reported that they and D Coch Corps and 300 prisoners, and word was received about the same time that the Americans were meeting with	

(A7093). Wt. W12859/M1293. 75,000. 1/17. D.D. & L., Ltd. Forms/C.2118/14.

Army Form C. 2118.

151st (Yorks.) Brigade R.F.A.

WAR DIARY
or
INTELLIGENCE SUMMARY.
(Erase heading not required.)

Instructions regarding War Diaries and Intelligence Summaries are contained in F. S. Regs., Part II. and the Staff Manual respectively. Title pages will be prepared in manuscript.

Place	Date	Hour	Summary of Events and Information	Remarks and references to Appendices
In the Field.	8-10-18. (Contd).		resistance and that 71st Inf.Bde. had sent a Battalion to their assistance. At 7.55 a.m. a message was received that the French were held up on the right. At 10.0 a.m. we received orders to fire on the Protective Barrage for one hour. At 10.45 a.m., D/151 fired on a machine-gun at H.30.d.9.5, which was holding up the WEST YORKS. Later on the latter, with three tanks, attacked MANNEQUIN WOOD at 11.55 At 11.55 a.m. the Americans were 1000 yds. West of BANCOURT. At 12.45 p.m. the enemy was observed in the trenches in I.25.c and I.31.a and B/151 had an observed shoot on them. In the afternoon it was reported that MANNEQUIN WOOD was in our hands, and that the enemy was retreating hurriedly. The Cavalry, however, were unable to afford much assistance. At night fires were observed burning in MARCOURT, which was free from the enemy although not yet in our possession.	Appendix 28.
	9-10-18.		Battery Commanders reconnoitred positions to cover the Railway East of FRESNOY. At night the Brigade moved to WAGON Lines under Battery arrangements	Appendix 29.
	10-10-18.		The Brigade moved to the neighbourhood of VAUXCOURT, being located as follows:- HQ/151 ... R.9.b.8.3. A/151 ... R.4.d.9.6. B/151 ... R.4.d.5.4. C/151 ... R.16.b.5.9. D/151 ... R.17.b.2.0. Captain (Adjutant) C.W.THORNTON, granted leave to U.K. until 24-10-18. Lieut. R.J. JOHNSON, B/151, assumed duties of Acting Adjutant vice Captain C.W. THORNTON on leave.	
	11-10-18.		Lieut. T.A. CLAXTON posted to Brigade from R.2.d R.F.A. Base Depot and attached C/151. At 10.0 a.m. the Brigade was inspected by the G.O.C. Division, in a field near 'C' Battery's Wagon Line. Major-General LAMBERT was accompanied by Brig.-General TYLER and members of his Staff. He expressed his appreciation of the work of the Brigade during the recent strenuous period of open fighting when the Brigade had been engaged for two months almost continuously in advanced guard fighting. Three cheers for General LAMBERT, led by the Colonel, were very heartily given.	
	12-10-18. 13-10-18.		Batteries carried out their own programmes of training. Batteries continued their training. Battery Wagon Lines were visited by the Corps Horse Adviser.	
	14-10-18.		Orders were received at 12.30 a.m. for the Brigade to move up in support of the 6th Divn. In the morning, the Brigade and Battery Commanders went forward and positions were selected as follows:- A/151 ... V.24.c.25.30. C/151 ... V.24.a.05.45 B/151 ... V.24.d.25.30. D/151 ... V.25.b.95.40.	

Army Form C. 2118.

WAR DIARY
or
INTELLIGENCE SUMMARY.

161st (Norths.) Brigade R.F.A.

(Erase heading not required.)

Instructions regarding War Diaries and Intelligence Summaries are contained in F. S. Regs., Part II. and the Staff Manual respectively. Title pages will be prepared in manuscript.

Place	Date	Hour	Summary of Events and Information	Remarks and references to Appendices
In the Field.	14-10-18.		The Batteries moved up to BRANCOURT in the morning and were located as follows:- A/161 ... C.29.a.5.7. C/161 ... C.23.a.7.3. B/161 ... C.28.a.0.0. D/161 ... C.28.a.45.30. HQ/161 ... C.28.a.5.5.	
	15-10-18.		Ammunition was brought up by B/161 and D/161 at night. 2/Lieut. P.M.ALLEN, D/161, granted leave to U.K. until 28-10-18. Further instructions were issued by 6th D.A.	Appendices 30,31 & 32
	16-10-18.		Batteries brought up ammunition during the night.	Appendices 33,34 & 35
			Batteries moved their guns into action during the afternoon and received further instructions for the Barrage. HQ/161 moved to V.23.c.45.00. Captain L.KING-TRENCH, A/161, and Capt.B.C.TRAPPES-LOMAX,M.C., B/161, granted leave to U.K. until 1-11-18.	
			Lieut-Colonel N.H.HUTTON,D.S.O., granted leave to U.K. until 25-10-18. Major E.A.CHISHOLM,M.C., C/161, assumed command of Brigade vice Lieut-Colonel N.H.HUTTON,D.S.O. on leave.	
NIZZKM FARM	17-10-18.		The Infantry of 6th Division attacked at 5.20 a.m. They met with a fair amount of success at first and secured the RED DOTTED Line in good time. The 1st Division in going through them met with considerable opposition and were slow in making progress. In the afternoon it was reported that they had reached the RED Line, which was their first objective. The enemy made several counter-attacks during the day and contested the ground hotly. A large number of prisoners and several machine-guns were taken. The 161st Brigade R.F.A. were included in the RIGHT GROUP (2nd, 5th, 161st and 298th Bdes.) The 161st Brigade R.F.A. fired the barrage up to the RED Line from their present positions, and at Zero plus 270, moved forward to positions from which they could fire the barrage for the GREEN Line (the final objective of the 1st Division), as follows:- A/161 ... W.21.c.4.7. C/161 ... W.22.a.5.7. B/161 ... W.28.a.7.3. D/161 ... W.28.c.4.6. When these positions were occupied the enemy were less than a thousand yards East, as the Infantry had not made the progress expected. The barrage for the GREEN Line was fired in time, but the Infantry were not in position at the appointed time, and consequently were unable to take advantage of the Barrage. At night, our line roughly ran:- ANDIGNY - BLANCS FOSSES - MALASSISE FARM. Major R.LEWETT,D.S.O., B/161, rejoined from leave and assumed command of Brigade. Major E.A.CHISHOLM,M.C., C/161, resumed command of C/161.	

Army Form C. 2118.

WAR DIARY
INTELLIGENCE SUMMARY.

161st (Works.) Brigade, R.F.A.

(Erase heading not required.)

Instructions regarding War Diaries and Intelligence Summaries are contained in F. S. Regs., Part II. and the Staff Manual respectively. Title pages will be prepared in manuscript.

Place	Date	Hour	Summary of Events and Information	Remarks and references to Appendices
In the Field.	18-10-18.		Orders were issued for a barrage to be fired in support of the 1st Division Infantry who were attacking at 11.30 a.m. The Start Line was from F.4.c.0.5. - X.19.a.0.C., and the objective from F.4.c.0.5. - X.22.c.0.0. - X.21.b.5.0. A/161 took the right two-thirds of zone, and B/161 the left one-third, C/161 being superimposed until A/161 became out of range, when C/161 took over their task. B/161 fired 200 yards East of 18-Pounder lines. The attack was very successful. At 12.45 p.m. it was reported that the CAMERONS were in touch with WELSH at Railway in K.19.c., and that BLACK WATCH were beyond Railway in K.25.b., and that not much opposition had been encountered. In places our Infantry pushed beyond their objective as far as the Canal, the line at night running roughly through WASSIGNY and RIBEAUVILLE.	
	19-10-18.		At 9.0.a.m. it was reported that 1st Division held line ETOCUS D'EN HAUT, where they were in touch with French, thence road WASSIGNY Cemetery and along road to RIBEAUVILLE where they were in touch with Americans. Patrols went out in X.23. and all along the front. 161st Brigade, R.F.A. were warned to be prepared to advance to positions to cover the Canal between S.1.b.7.0. to L.21.d.0.0. At 9.50.a.m. 2nd and 5th Brigade, R.F.A. were ordered to reconnoitre positions, and 161st Brigade, R.F.A. to remain for the present in a position in READINESS. At night Brigades were re-grouped under 1st Divisional Artillery as follows:- Right Group ... 25th and 39th Brigades, R.F.A ... 161st, 163rd, 5th and 298th Brigades, R.F.A. Left Group ... under command of C.R.A. 32nd Division.	
	20-10-18.		EMMET, D.S.O.) to get Brigade into action as soon as possible, as Left Group were responsible for covering Left Infantry Brigade front from 2.0.p.m. 161st and 5th Brigades, R.F.A. were allotted left half, and 163rd and 298th Brigades, R.F.A. the right half of Group zone. O.C. Brigade met Battery Commanders at L'ARBRE DE GUISE, and ordered Batteries to assemble at once at Rendezvous in W.13.a. Positions for 161st Brigade, R.F.A. were selected as follows:- A/161 .... R.31.c.9.0. C/161 .... X.1.b.2.8. B/161 .... X.1.b. central, D/161 .... X.1.a.70.95. H./161 was located for the night at W.10.b.05.95. Major EMMET spent the night with 2nd Infantry Brigade at X.13.a.1.0. At night front line ran X.21.a.9.6. along MAZINGHIEN road to X.4.c.2.5., thence X.4.d.2.0. - X.4.d.3.5. - X.5.b.7.8. - R.53.b.7.0. - R.33.b.85.20. - R.27.c.25.50. Batteries fired 150 rounds per Battery on LA HAIE TONNOILE Farm and communications at the request of O.C. 2nd Infantry Brigade.	

Army Form C. 2118.

WAR DIARY

161st (Yorks.) Brigade R.F.A.

INTELLIGENCE SUMMARY.

(Erase heading not required.)

Instructions regarding War Diaries and Intelligence Summaries are contained in F. S. Regs, Part II. and the Staff Manual respectively. Title pages will be prepared in manuscript.

Place	Date	Hour	Summary of Events and Information	Remarks and references to Appendices
In the Field.	21-10-18.		HQ/161 moved to X.13.a.1.6. (The F.O. of the 1st Inf.Bde.) Batteries carried out harassing fire at night on LA HAIE TONNOILLE Farm and the outskirts of CATILLON at the request of G.O.C.,1st Inf.Bde Batteries received preliminary instructions for the barrage to be fired on the morning of the 23rd instant. (See Appendices 36 and 37.	Appendix 38. Appendices 36 & 37.
	22-10-18.		Instructions were issued for the barrage to be fired the following morning in support of the 1st Infantry Brigade. At the request of G.O.C., Batteries fired before the barrage on LA HAIE TONNOILLE FARM. Lieut.A.W.DENNISTON, H./161, reported leave to U.K. until 5-11-18.	
	23-10-18.		The Infantry attacked at 1.20 a.m. (by moonlight), the objective being the high round in R.23.a. and c., R.29.a., R.30, and R.35. The attack was successful and the objectives were reached in good time. Few enemy were met with, but a heavy barrage was put down shortly after the attack opened, and our casualties were somewhat heavy. The enemy gassed the Battery areas previous to the barrage, which had to be fired in gas masks. Patrols pushed out beyond the objective and reached the Canal at CATILLON, where they found the bridge in good order. They temporarily withdrew to obtain assistance, but in the meantime the enemy had re-entered CATILLON and has posted Machine-guns at the Western and Southern entrances to the village. Subsequently the enemy blew up the bridge over the Canal. At night, the Field Artillery was re-grouped, 5th Brigade going out of the line. The Left Group now consists of 161st and 168th Brigades R.F.A., under the orders of 161st Bde.R.F.A. At night the 1st and 3rd Infantry Brigades were relieved by the 2nd Infantry Brigade, the Division l'Front being held by the two Battalions. Lieut.H.F.SCOVAN,M.C.,C/161, granted leave to U.K. until 6-11-18. Lieut.F.R.LAMPTON.M.C.,A/161 granted leave to U.K. until 6-11-18.	
	24-10-18.		Quiet day. Artillery again re-grouped, Left Group now being taken over by 59th Bde. (1st Div.Art'y). Batteries moved to their Wagon Lines at night. Lieut-Colonel H.H.SUTTON,D.S.O., returned from two days special leave, and resumed command of the Brigade.	Appendix 39.

Instructions regarding War Diaries and Intelligence
Summaries are contained in F. S. Regs, Part II.
and the Staff Manual respectively. Title pages
will be prepared in manuscript.

WAR DIARY
or
INTELLIGENCE SUMMARY.
(Erase heading not required.)

161st (Yorks.)Brigade, R.F.A. Army Form C. 2118.

Place	Date	Hour	Summary of Events and Information	Remarks and references to Appendices
In the Field	25-10-18.		Batteries occupied in cleaning up, rest and recreation. 2/Lieut. T.CONLIN, A/161 granted leave to U.K. till 8-11-18. Major R.EMDEN,D.S.O. resumed command of D/161.	
	26-10-18.		C/161 shelled by H.V. and moved to W.9.c.8.9.- two casualties. Capt.(& Adjutant) C.Y THORNTON rejoined from leave and resumed duties of Adjutant. Lieut.R.C.JOHNSON, B/161 (Attchd) HQ/161) ceased to perform duties of Acting Adjutant.	
	27-10-18.		Nothing of interest.	
	28-10-18		2/Lieut. W.S.KIRK B/161 proceeded to attend Course at IX Corps Anti-Gas School. Major T.H.BUCKLEY, D/161 granted leave to U.K. till 10.11.18. G.H.A. inspected Gun Parks and Horse lines. Lieut.R.G.JOHNSON, B/161 attached Hq.32nd Divisional Artillery. 2/Lieut.E.H.WELLER, RFA.(A/52 T.M.Btt.) attached A/161) rejoined 32nd T.M.Btty.	
	29-10-18 to 31-10-18.		Batteries remained at their Wagon Lines. No news and Awards during month.	Appendix "A"

Casualties during Month of October.

	Killed.		Wounded.		Gassed.		Evacuated (sick).	
	Offrs.	O.R.	Offrs.	O.R.	Offrs.	O.R.	Offrs.	O.R.
A/161 ...	-	1	-	6	-	12	-	5
B/161 ...	-	1	-	8	-	2	-	5
C/161 ...	-	1	-	30	-	2	-	3
D/161 ...	-	1	-	8	1	4	-	12
TOTAL. ...	-	4	-	52	1	20	-	25.

Wholm
Lieut-Colonel.
Commanding 161st (Yorks.) Brigade, R.F.A.

31st October, 1918.

Copy No. 8

151st (YORKS.) BRIGADE R.F.A.
OPERATION ORDER NO. 27.

1. The 120th Infantry Brigade are taking over the line on night of the 5th/6th October from the 14th and the 97th Infantry Brigades.

2. The 151st Bde.R.F.A. will cover that part of the 120th Brigade front formerly held by the 97th Infantry Brigade, and the 165th Brigade R.F.A. will cover that part formerly held by the 14th Infantry Brigade.

3. S.O.S.Lines of the 151st Brigade R.F.A. will remain as at present.

4. Each Battery will expend 100 rounds during the night on Harassing Fire on targets to be selected by Battery Commanders.

5th Oct.1918.

Captain,
Adjutant, 151st Brigade R.F.A.

Issued at 20.45 hours.

Copy No. 1 — Bde., 23rd D.A.
2 — O.C.,165th Bde.R.F.A.
3 — O.C., A/151.
4 — O.C., B/151.
5 — O.C., C/151.
6 — O.C., D/151.
7 — War Diary.
8 — File.

SECRET. 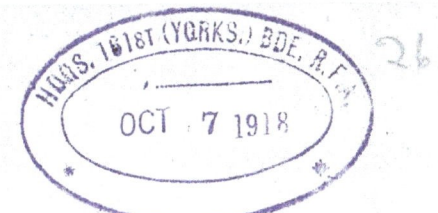 Copy No. 9

161st (YORKS.) BRIGADE R.F.A. OPERATION ORDER No.18.

1. On the 8th October, 1918, at an hour Zero to be notified later, the 6th Division, as part of the IX Corps, is attacking to secure the objective marked on the attached Barrage Map.

2. The 161st Brigade R.F.A. fire on the Southern portion, and the 168th Brigade R.F.A. on the Northern portion of the RIGHT Group Zone, as shown on the attached Barrage Map.

3. Of the 161st Brigade R.F.A. Zone, B/161 take the Southern portion, and C/161 the Northern portion, as shown on attached Barrage Map. A/161 are superimposed over the whole 161st Brigade R.F.A. Zone.
   D/161 are superimposed over the whole RIGHT Group Zone, firing 100 yds. East of the lines marked for 18-Pounder Batteries.

4. Orders regarding Rates of Fire, Ammunition, Liaison with Infantry, Synchronization of Watches, &c., will be issued later.

5. ACKNOWLEDGE (Batteries only).

                                                    Lieut;

7th Oct.1918.   for Adjutant, 161st Brigade R.F.A.

Issued at 16.00 hours.

              Copy No. 1 - H.Q., 32nd D.A.
                      2 - H.Q., 6th DA.
                      3 - O.C., 168th Bde.R.F.A.
                      4 - O.C., A/161.
                      5 - O.C., B/161.
                      6 - O.C., C/161.
                      7 - O.C., D/161.
                      8 - Artillery Liaison Officer.
                      9 - War Diary.
                    10 - File.

SECRET.   Copy No. 4

[Stamp: HQRS. 161ST (YORKS.) BDE. R.F.A. OCT 7 1918]

161st (YORKS.) BRIGADE R.F.A. Operation Order No.19.

1. D/161 will be superimposed over the whole of the RIGHT GROUP Zone, firing 200 yds. East of the lines for 18-Pdr. Batteries.

2. RATES OF FIRE.- for 18-Pdrs. and 4.5" Hows.

Zero to Zero plus 24:	3 rds. per gun per min.
Zero plus 24 to Zero plus 64:	2 rds. ,, ,, ,,
Zero plus 64 to Zero plus 84:	3 rds. ,, ,, ,,
Zero plus 84 to Objective Line:	2 rds. ,, ,, ,,
Objective Line to Protective Line:	1 rd. ,, ,, ,,
Protective Line:	1 rd. ,, ,, ,,

3. AMMUNITION.

    18-Pdrs.   Up to 4,500: Shrapnel.
               Over 4,500: H.E.

    Hows.   H.E., 106 Fuze.

    1 Gun in each 18-Pdr. Battery will fire Smoke.

4. SIGNALS.
    The 'S.O.S' Signal is RED over RED over RED.
    WHITE parachute changing into RED, means "Our advanced Infantry are here".

5. AEROPLANE CALLS.

    During Barrage: "L.L" and "G.F" Calls will be answered by 1 Section of A/161 and 1 Section of D/161.
    After Barrage: "L.L" and "G.F" Calls will be answered by all Batteries.

    Rate and length of fire in all cases: 3 minutes INTENSE.

6. S.O.S. LINES.
    S.O.S. Lines will be the same as those mentioned in 161st Brigade R.F.A. Artillery Instructions No.49, dated 6-10-18, until Zero Hour. After the completion of the Barrage, they will be on the Protective Barrage Line.

7. ZERO HOUR.
    Zero Hour will be notified later.

8. ACKNOWLEDGE (Batteries only).

                                                R. Johnson
                                                              Lieut;
7th Oct.1918.   for Adjutant, 161st Brigade R.F.A.

Issued at 1830 hours.

            Copy No.1 - H.Q., 32nd D.A.
                 2 - H.Q., 6th D.A.
                 3 - O.C., 168th Bde. RFA
                 4 - O.C., A/161.
                 5 - O.C., B/161.
                 6 - O.C., C/161.
                 7 - O.C., D/161.
                 8 - Artillery Liaison Officer.
                 9 - War Diary. ✓
                10 - File.

SECRET.   Copy No. 5

161st (YORKS.) BRIGADE R.F.A.
ARTILLERY INSTRUCTIONS No.49.

S.O.S.LINES from 19.00 hours, 8th Oct.1918, will be as follows:-

```
A/161 ... I.17.a.0.0. - I.23.a.0.0.
B/161 ... I.17.c.0.0. - I.23.a.0.0.
C/161 ... I.17.a.0.0. - I.17.c.0.0.
D/161 ... 1 Howr. I.17.c.4.6.
          1 Howr. I.17.c.2.2.
```

                                         Lieut;
8th Oct.1918.   for Adjutant, 161st Bde.R.F.A.

Issued at 19.00 hours.

            Copy No. 1 - O.C., A/161.
                     2 - O.C., B/161.
                     3 - O.C., C/161.
                     4 - O.C., D/161.
                     5 - War Diary.
                     6 - File.

SECRET.   Copy No. 6

161st (YORKS.) BRIGADE R.F.A.

O.O. No. 29.

Reference Maps 1/40,000, 57.B. and 57.C.

1. Batteries will withdraw to their Wagon Lines on the night Oct.9th/10th, under Battery arrangements.

2. Batteries before leaving their present positions will wire to this office the amount of Ammunition, by kinds, left dumped at the positions they are vacating.

3. The 161st Brigade R.F.A. will march to the VADENCOURT area on October 10th in accordance with attached March Table.

4. Billeting parties of one Officer and 1 N.C.O. per battery will meet the Adjutant at Cross Roads LA BARAQUE, G.35.a.9.9. at 8.0 a.m. October 10th, 1918.

5. The march will be carried out in accordance with S.S.724.

6. Present wagon lines will be left in a clean and sanitary condition.

7. ACKNOWLEDGE (Batteries only).

                                                        Lieut;
9th Oct.1918.   a/Adjutant., 161st Brigade R.F.A.

Issued at 15.00 hours (by orderly).

            Copy No. 1 - O.C., A/161.
                    2 - O.C., B/161.
                    3 - O.C., C/161.
                    4 - O.C., D/161.
                    5 - R.S.M.
                    6 - War Diary.
                    7 - H.Q., 32nd D.A.
                    8 - H.Q., 46th D.A.
                    9 - File.

101st (TORON.) BRIGADE R.F.A.

K A R U B   T A B L E.

Unit.	Starting Point.	Time of passing Starting Point.	Route.	Destination.
A/101.	Ford Junction O.27.b.7.8.	9.30 a.m.	O.27.b.3.2., N.1.b., R.6., R.11	VAUXMOUNT AREA.
B/101.	ditto.	9.50 a.m.	ditto.	ditto.
BM/101.	ditto.	10.10 a.m.	ditto.	ditto.
C/101.	ditto.	10.30 a.m.	ditto.	ditto.
D/101	ditto.	10.50 a.m.	ditto.	ditto.

Adjutant, 101st Brigade R.F.A.
Lieut.

9th October 1918.

SECRET. Copy No. 5

HQRS. 161ST (YORKS.) BDE. R.F.A.
OCT 14 1918

161st (YORKS.) BRIGADE R.F.A. ARTILLERY INSTRUCTIONS No. 59.

Reference map 1/20,000 Sheet 57.b.S.E., Edition 2.a.

1. The 6th Division will attack the enemy on a date to be notified later.

2. The Artillery to support the attack will be in two Groups as under:-

   RIGHT GROUP: 2nd Bde.R.F.A.
   5th Army Bde.R.F.A.   ) Under the command of
   161st Bde.R.F.A.   ) Lieut-Col. W.F.WEBER,D.S.O.,
   108th Bde.R.F.A.   ) R.F.A.

   LEFT GROUP: 24th Bde.R.F.A.
   38th Bde.R.F.A.   ) Under the command of
   39th Bde.R.F.A.   ) Brig-General   LEWIS,
   298th Army Bde.R.F.A.   ) C.M.G.,D.S.O.

   The 161st Brigade R.F.A. will form a Sub-Group under 108th Brigade R.F.A.

3. Positions for the 161st Brigade R.F.A. have been selected as follows:-

   A/161 ... V.24.c.5.3.
   B/161 ... V.24.b.85.00.
   C/161 ... V.24.a.85.45.
   D/161 ... V.23.b.95.40.

4. The following Ammunition will be at gun pits by 10.0 p.m. October 16th, 1918:-

   18-Pdrs.   400 rds. per gun; 45% H.E., 45% A.X., 10% A.S.

   4.5" How. 300 rds. per How; 10% B.Smoke, 90% B.E.

5. A new enemy trench line is reported as follows:-

   N.14.central, N.14.d.9.0., N.20.b.9.0., N.21.c.0.0., N.20.d.8.8., V.25.b.9.0., V.26.d.3.0., S.1.d.0.8.; and an unfinished trench from S.1.d.7.9. - S.1.d.3.5.

6. Lieut-Colonel WEBER'S Headquarters are at O.16.a.8.4.

   Battle Headquarters of 161st Bde.R.F.A. will be notified later.

7. The 161st Brigade R.F.A. will probably fire for barrage purposes as follows:-

   Start Line About V.20.d.60.30 - V.26.b.50.50

   Protective Barrage Line: N.24.d.30.50 - V.30.a.70.10.

   R.B.F.Muir
   Lieut;
   a/Adjutant, 161st Brigade R.F.A.

14th Oct.1918.
Issued at 20.15 hours.

   Copy No. 1 - O.C.,A/161.   6 - War Diary.
            2 - O.C.,B/161.   7 - H.Q.,6th D.A.
            3 - O.C.,C/161.   8 - H.Q.,23rd D.A.
            4 - O.C.,D/161.   9 - O.C.,108th Bde.R.F.A.
            5 - File.   10 - O.C.,2nd Bde.R.F.A.

SECRET.  Copy No. 6

31

161st (YORKS.) BRIGADE R.F.A. ARTILLERY INSTRUCTIONS No.51.

1. Brigades of Artillery will be grouped as follows for the Creeper Barrage on to RED LINE:-

   LEFT GROUP. (Brig-General LEWIN, C.M.G., D.S.O.)
   25th Bde.R.F.A.
   39th Bde.R.F.A.
   94th Bde.R.F.A.
   168th Bde.R.F.A.

   RIGHT GROUP. (Lieut-Colonel W.H.F.WEBER, D.S.O., R.F.A.)
   2nd Bde.R.F.A.
   5th Bde.R.F.A.
   161st Bde.R.F.A.
   298th Bde.R.F.A.

   The dividing line between the Groups will be a line through STATION VAUX and ANDIGNY W.20.d.3.5., - ANCIN FARM W.22.c.6.0.

2. The field Artillery detailed to move forward in close support of the advance of the 1st Division will be the two Brigades of the 1st Divisional Artillery and 298th Bde.R.F.A.
   The 298th Bde.R.F.A. will be superimposed on Right Group Zone.

3. When the 1st Division passes through the 6th Division on the capture of the BLUE LINE, C.R.A., 1st Division will assume command of the Artillery covering their front.

4. On the capture of the RED LINE, C.R.A., 1st Division, will issue all necessary orders for the move forward of the following Artillery to cover the advance of the 1st Division from the RED LINE to the GREEN LINE:-

   6th Divisional Artillery.
   32nd Divisional Artillery.
   5th Army Bde.R.F.A.

5. AMMUNITION. Ammunition to the following amounts will be dumped at gun positions:-

   18-Pdr.   500 rds. per gun (200 A.S. per Battery).
   4.5" Hows. 300 rds. per How.

   All Echelons will be kept full.

   A.S. is difficult to obtain. Each 18-Pdr. Battery will draw 145 rds. from C.22.d.1.4. and the balance will be made up at the earliest moment.

6. Main A.R.P. is at C.22.d.1.4. An Advanced Re-filling Point is at D.14.b.2.4., but the bulk of the Ammunition is at present at C.22.d.1.4. This latter dump will be depleted as quickly as possible, and all fresh ammunition will be sent up to D.14.b.2.4.

7. Batteries will, on moving to new positions, re-fill at their old positions if ammunition is left behind, before drawing on A.R.P.

8. The following Returns will reach this office at 1.0 p.m. daily:-

   (1). Amount of Ammunition at Guns at 12 noon, amount in Echelons, and amount expended 12 noon to 12 noon.
   (2). Number of Guns and Hows. in action, and number out of action, and number at I.O.M.

-2-

9. It is proposed that each Brigade will have two Batteries on each Brigade front and one superimposed; and that the superimposed Battery shall move forward on capture of the First Objective, so as to get some effective range fire on the First Protective Barrage Line.
A/161 will be superimposed on the 161st Bde.R.F.A. front.

10. A C K N O W L E D G E (Batteries only).

[signature]
Lieut;
15th Oct.1918.   a/Adjutant, 161st Brigade R.F.A.

Issued at 23.00 hours.

```
Copy No. 1 - O.C.,A/161.
         2 - O.C.,B/161.
         3 - O.C.,C/161.
         4 - O.C.,D/161.
         5 - File
         6 - War Diary.
         7 - H.Q.,6th D.A.
         8 - H.Q.,32nd D.A.
         9 - O.C.,168th Bde.R.F.A.
        10 - O.C.,2nd Bde.R.F.A.
```

SECRET.

6th DIVISIONAL ARTILLERY INSTRUCTIONS No.5.

16th Oct.1918.

1. Barrage Maps are issued at Battery Scale and Group Lanes allotted. The Inter-Group Boundary is as shown on Barrage Map.

2. In addition to the superimposed Brigades of 1st Divl.Artillery on the whole front, one 18-Pdr. Battery in each Brigade will be superimposed on the Bde.front.
   One section 18-Pdrs. Right Group will enfilade trenches in E.13.b.9.7. to E.13.b.6.1. from Zero to Zero plus 70 after that be employed in the Creeping Barrage.

3. Lifts will be 100 yds. First lift at Zero plus 3.
   4.5" Howr.Barrage will be 200 yds. beyond 18-Pdr Creeping Barrage.

4. Rates of fire.

   (a). 18-Pounders.

Zero to Zero plus 3	...	Intense Rate.
Zero plus 3 to plus 9	...	Rapid rate.
Zero plus 9 to plus 112	...	Normal rate.
Zero plus 112 to plus 129	...	½ rd. a minute.
Zero plus 129 to plus 132	...	Intense rate. This will be the Signal to the Infantry that the barrage is about to move on.
Zero plus 132 to plus 180	...	Normal rate.
Zero plus 180 to plus 195	...	Slow, Then it will cease.

   (b). Above rates will be maintained by Howitzer Batteries on the Creeping Barrage.

5. Ammunition for Creeping Barrage.

   18-Pdrs.
   LEFT GROUP - Shrapnel up to 5,000 yds. - after 5,000 yds. H.E. with 106 fuze will be used.
   RIGHT GROUP - Shrapnel up to 4,000 yds. - after 4,000 yds. H.E. with 106 fuze will be used.

   4.5" Howitzers.
      H.E. 106 fuzes as far as possible.

   18-Pdrs. - SMOKE.
      1 gun in each 18-Pdr. Battery in the Creeping Barrage will fire 50% SMOKE throughout the Creeper.

6. "C.F" and "L.L" Calls.
   (a). "C.F" Calls will be answered by the 18-Pdr. Batteries referred to in para.2 and by sections of Howr.Batteries.
   (b). "L.L" Calls.
      When engaged on barrage work as in 6 (a).
      When not engaged on barrage work "L.L" calls will be answered by every battery which can bring fire to bear.
      Rates of fire in all cases - 3 minutes Intense.

7. There will be a 3 hours pause on the capture of the RED LINE to enable the following Artillery Dispositions to be made:-
   (a). At Zero plus 180 1st Divl.Artillery (25th and 39th Bde.RFA) will move forward under the orders of C.R.A.,1st Division.
   (b). At Zero plus 180 Right Group Commander will detail 2nd and 293th Bdes. at once to move forward to positions about the area N.25 to fire a Creeping Barrage in support of the 1st Division, with objective approximately the line X.19.d.0.0. - F.1.b.0.0.

-2-

The Start Line of Barrage will be the line of the Protector on the Southern portion of the RED LINE.
The two Brigades detailed will be in position ready to open fire 2 hours after the RED LINE has been reached.

(c). On completion of this task the two Brigades will move forward to the area W.22.c.and d. to assist in the barrage from the RED LINE to GREEN LINE.

(d). At Zero plus 180 Left Group Commander will detail 168th Brigade to advance to about area W.22.a.and d. to positions to assist in the barrage from RED LINE to GREEN LINE covering the advance of 1st Division to GREEN LINE.
As soon as the Brigade has arrived at its new position, it will at once prepare to assume its Protective Barrage on RED LINE Protector, and the fourth or last Brigade of Left Group will move up to same area to assist in this Barrage.

(e). As soon as the two Brigades of Right Group have arrived at their new positions for the barrage mentioned in para.7(b). the 5th and 161st Bdes.R.F.A. of Right Group will in turn be detailed to move forward to the area Square W.22 to positions to take part in the barrage from RED LINE to GREEN LINE.

(f) Barrage maps for tasks in para.7(b) and 7(d) with times and rates of fire indicated are being issued to all concerned.

(g). Every endeavour must be made to mark the position and to note the amount of ammunition left behind at positions when batteries advance so that it can be collected at the earliest opportunity.

8. S.O.S.Barrage Line.
During the three hours pause on the RED LINE, S.O.S.Line will be the Protector Barrage Line for RED LINE.

9. Orders as to S.O.S.Signal and Success Signal will be issued later.

10. Synchronization of Watches.
Left and Right Groups will send one representative with two watches each to Headquarters, 6th Divisional Artillery to synchronize watches today at 12.15 hours and 18.15 hours.
Groups will then arrange synchronization with their Brigades.

11. Zero hour will be notified later.

12. ACKNOWLEDGE.

(Sgd) .... Major R.A.
Issued at 11.00 hour Brigade Major, R.A.,6th Division.

O.C.,A/161.
O.C.,B/161.
O.C.,C/161.
O.C.,D/161.

Forwarded.

16-10-18.
a/Adjutant, 161st Brigade R.F.A.
Lieut;

SECRET.   ADDENDUM   TO

6th Divisional Artillery Instructions No.5.

1. (a). Right Group Commander will detail six 18-Pdr. Batteries
       from the Creeping Barrage to lift on to the area N.20.a.5.0 -
       N.26.b.5.3 - N.27.a.6.3 - N.21.c.5.0 at Zero and to remain
       there until Zero plus 24 minutes when the whole Group will
       move forward together on the Creeping Barrage.
   (b). One Howitzer Battery of Right Group will "smoke" this
       area from Zero to Zero plus 24 minutes when it will resume
       its task in the Howitzer Creeping Barrage.

       Rates of fire.
       Six Batteries 18-Pounders.
           Zero to Zero plus 5 mins.   ...   Intense Rate.
           Plus 5 to plus 9 mins.   ...   Rapid Rate.
           Plus 9 to plus 24 mins.   ...   Normal.
       One Battery Howitzers 4.5in.
           At Zero 2 salvoes - then Battery fire 10 seconds to
           plus 24 minutes. If wind is favourable, C.G. shell
           will be mixed with the Smoke.

2. Rates of Fire for the Barrages to be fired by Brigades when
    advanced to new positions will be at normal rate throughout,
    except Zero plus 363 to Zero plus 368 when it will be rapid.

4. Right Group Commander will order the 2nd and 298th Bdes. on
    completion of their task in Barrage at Zero plus 371 to carry
    on at Zero plus 371 to limit of their range.

5. Right Group Commander will allot Brigades boundaries for
    the 161st and 5th Bdes. on Barrage Map for 1st Division advance.
    The Boundary between Right and Left Groups is the grid line
    running East and West through X.19 - X.20 and X.21 central.
    This barrage for 161st and 5th Brigades will commence at
    Zero plus 368 minutes.

                                    (Sgd) .. Major RA.
16th Oct.1918.   Brigade Major, R.A., 6th Division.

O.C., A/161.
O.C., B/161.
O.C., C/161.
O.C., D/161.

                Forwarded.

16-10-18.   a/Adjutant, 161st Bde.RFA.
                                                Lieut;

161st Brigade R.F.A.   16th Oct.1918.

INSTRUCTIONS No.2.

1. 6th Division is to capture the BLUE LINE.
   1st Division will capture the RED and GREEN LINES.
   As regards 6th Division, 18th I.B. on right, 16th on left.
   Barrage opens at Zero, first lift Zero plus 3.
   No preliminary bombardment.
   Half an hour's pause in BLUE LINE.
   Three hours pause on the RED LINE will include No.2. Barrage.
   At the end of the three hours the attack on the GREEN LINE
   will take place under Barrage 3.
   A few tanks will be employed.

2. Boundary between Left and Right Group is a line through
   VAUX ANDIGNY Station and ANGIN FARM.
   Right Group consists of 2nd., 5th., 161st., and 293th Bdes.,
   R.F.A.
   Available to support the 1st Division in their advance to
   the GREEN LINE (under Barrage No.3) will be two Bdes. of
   each Group., while the 1st Divisional Artillery will be in
   readiness.

3. From Zero till Zero plus 70 the 21st Battery of the 2nd Bde.RFA.
   will detail a section to enfilade a trench opposite 46th Divn.

4. The General Plan of the Right Group Barrage will be:-
   Right half 2nd and 5th Bdes.R.F.A. superimposed on
   one another.
   Left half 161st and 293th Bdes.R.F.A. superimposed on
   one another.
   Each Bde. will keep one battery ready to leave the barrage
   and to answer zone calls engage fleeting targets,etc.
   This will be the 21st Battery in the case of the 2nd Bde.RFA.

5. On the capture of the first objective (BLUE LINE) the 2nd and
   293th Bdes.R.F.A. will each send a battery forward. The task
   of these Batteries will be (a) to render more effective the
   Protective Barrage on the RED LINE on their own fronts
   (b) to fire Barrage No.2 (through the Wood in N.30. and X.25).
   As they later will be reinforced by the remainder of the
   Batteries of their respective Bdes. the advancing batteries
   will be accompanied by Reconnoitring Officers of those
   other Batteries, who will mark positions, lay out lines,etc.
        Position allotted 2nd Bde.   N.26.b. and d.
        Position allotted 293th Bde. E.2.b.and d.
        21st Battery will advance in case of 2nd Bde.

6. Immediately the RED LINE is captured, the remainder of the
   2nd and 293th Bdes. will advance to areas allotted in N.26
   and E.2. Their task will be to fire Barrage No.3.
   Details of Barrage No.3 later.

7. Immediately the 2nd and 293th Bdes. are in action the
   5th and 161st Bdes. will advance to areas as follows:-
        161st Army Bde.   N.28 or 29.
        5th Army Bde.   E.4. or 5.
   Their task will be to fire barrage No.3.
   The O.s.C., 5th and 161st Bdes. are made responsible for
   ascertaining when the 2nd and 293th Bdes. are in action.

8. Group H.Q. will be from 15.00 OCTOBER 16th at BECQUIGNY
   (probably V.22.d.05.15) On Zero Day it will move according
   to the movements of the Right Bde. of the 1st Div.
   Communication will be entirely by mounted orderly after Group
   has left BECQUIGNY. The 5th and 161st and 293th Bdes. will
   maintain two mounted orderlies each with Right Group Hdqrs.from
   16.00, 16th instant.
        Hdqrs. will be in the first instance:-

(Contd)

2.

    2nd Bde. with 42nd Battery   V.29.d.30.35.
    5th Bde.   D.4.d.3.5.
  161st Bde.   V.25.c.45.00.
  293th Bde.   V.29.a.20.30.

9. Each Bde. will maintain throughout the operation one O.P. suitably to its task and position.
The Right Group O.P. will be manned by Capt. LANSDALE in the first instance at the Quarry N.19.a.8.8. Capt. LANSDALE will in the later stage of the operation communicate with the Right Group at Hdqrs. Right Bde. 1st Div. Early information will be of the utmost value in the operation as it effects the movements of Batteries.

10. 2nd Bde. will maintain liaison with the left Battalion, 15th I.B. from 17.00 16th instant (Lt.BOURNE).
293th Bde. with Right Battalion 15th I.B.
Hdqrs. will be notified later.
161st Brigade will obtain liaison at a later period with the left Battalion of the new I.B. (1st Division), and 5th Bde. with the Right Battalion.

11. The scheme of Artillery support in the later stages will be elucidated in the course of tomorrow.

12. A.R.P. is at C.29.d.1.8.
Advanced A.R.P. D.14.b.2.4.
It is understood that lorries will bring up ammunition during the battle to near VAUX ANDIGNY on the BOHAIN-VAUXANDIGNY Road. No.2 and 3 Barrages will not use up more than the echelon and empty wagons will have to refill from the "Advanced" Advanced A.R.P.

RIGHT GROUP.   (sgd) D.F. WEBER, Lt-Col;
    Commanding 2nd Bde. R.F.A.

O.C. A/16.
O.C. B/16. } Forwarded.
O.C. C/16.
O.C. D/16.

16 10/78

SECRET.  Copy No. 5

161st (YORKS.) BRIGADE R.F.A. OPERATION ORDER No.21.

1. Reference 6th D.A. Instructions No.5 and Addendum to same, and Right Group Instructions Nos. 2 and 3 attached (To Batteries only).

2. For No.1 Barrage, 161st Brigade R.F.A. and 298th Bde.R.F.A. are superimposed on one another and fire on the left half of the Right Group Zone.
   A/161 will be on the right, C/161 in the centre, and B/161 will be on the left. D/161 will fire on the whole of the 161st Brigade Zone.
   There will be no superimposed Battery in the Brigade Zone as mentioned in para.2 of 6th D.A. Instructions No.5.

   For No.3 Barrage, the 161st Bde.R.F.A. will fire on the left half of the Right Group Zone.
   B/161 will be on the right, and C/161 on the left, and A/161 and D/161 will be superimposed on the 161st Bde.R.F.A. Zone. D/161 will fire 200 yds. East of 18-Pdr. Lines.

3. B/161 will find a Liaison Officer with the Left Battalion of the Right Brigade of the 1st Division.

4. C/161 will maintain throughout the Operation an O.P. suitable to its task and position.

5. S.O.S. LINES for 161st Bde.R.F.A. are superimposed on S.O.S. Lines of 5th Bde.R.F.A. They are allotted as follows:-

    A/161 ... E.2.a.5.5 - W.26.b.70.15.
    B/161 ... W.26.b.70.15 - W.20.d.7.5.
    C/161 ... W.20.d.7.5 - W.14.d.7.0.
    D/161 ... Selected points East of 18-Pdr.S.O.S. Lines.

6. When in action, Batteries will send by wire to this office the Code Words "TWENTY-FOUR".

7. Each Battery will send to this H.Q. by 4.0 p.m. today one mounted orderly.

8. Each Battery will send to this H.Q. by 9.30 p.m. today one orderly with a watch to obtain the correct time.

9. Attention is drawn to para.4 of Right Group Instructions No.3.

10. Medical Arrangements.
    Car Stand: BUSIGNY V.16.b.
    Bearer Post: LE ROND POINT V.24.a.1.8.

11. Zero Hour will be notified later.

12. Acknowledge (Batteries only).

16-10-18.   Lieut;
Issued at 17.30 hours.   a/Adjutant, 161st Bde.RFA.

        Copy No.1 - O.C., A/161.   6 - File.
             2 - O.C., B/161.   7 - O.C., 2nd Bde.RFA.
             3 - O.C., C/161.   8 - O.C., 186th Bde RFA.
             4 - O.C., D/161.   9 - H.Q., 6th D.A.
             5 - War Diary.   10 - H.Q., 38nd D.A.

O.C., 161st Bde. R.F.A.　　　　　　　　　　VERY URGENT.

RIGHT GROUP INSTRUCTIONS No.3.

1. 6th Divisional Artillery Instructions No.5 contains certain certain modifications to Right Group Instructions No.2. Copies of 6th D.A. Instructions No.5 have been issued to all Sub-Groups.

2. The section of the 21st Battery detailed to fire on 46th Div. front will engage trench E.13.b.9.7 - E.13.b.6.1. from Zero till Zero plus 70.

3. From Zero to Zero plus 24
   (a). 298th Bde. will put its 3 18-Pdr. Batteries on the area W.26.b.5.3 - W.26.b.5.3 - W.27.a.6.3.
   (b). 5th Bde. will put its 3 18-Pdr. Batteries on the area W.20.d.5.0 - W.26.b.5.7 - W.27.a.6.3 - W.21.c.5.0.
   (c). 87th Battery will smoke area W.20.d.5.3 - W.26.b.5.5 - W.27.a.6.3 - W.21.c.5.0 (See para.1 (b) of Addendum to 6th D.A. Instructions No.5).

4. As regards moving, it will be noticed that the moves are to be made at definite times, except the move of the 5th and 161st Bdes. This exception has been cancelled. The 5th and 161st Bdes. will move to area W.22. at Z. plus 270.
   All Batteries must use patrols for the purpose of security especially the Batteries of the 2nd and 298th Bdes.
   The 2nd and 298th Bdes. R.F.A will move forward to area W.22.a. and d. (or, if necessary, W.28.a. and b.) when they have reached the limit of their range from W.26.

5. From Z. plus 99 till Z. plus 102 all Howitzer Batteries will fire Smoke. Orders have been given (presumably by 6th D.A.) for every Howitzer Battery to draw 115 rounds of Smoke.

6. As regards period Z. plus 317 till Z. minus 371, the Right Group will not be asked to fire North of the railway. Therefore the dividing line between the 2nd and 298th Bdes. (during Barrage No.2) will be due East and West through F.1.a.0.6.

7. Attention is directed to para.7 (g) of 6th D.A. Instructions No.5. Every Battery will flag a position where it leaves ammunition.

8. It is absolutely essential to report by mounted orderly when a new position has been occupied, giving map location.

9. Acknowledge.

　　　　　　　　　　　　　(Sgd) F.G. RAYNER, Capt; RFA.
Issued 14.50　　　　　　　Adjutant, 2nd Bde. R.F.A.
　　hours.

SECRET.   Copy No. 5

161st (YORKS.) BRIGADE R.F.A.
OPERATION ORDER NO.22.

1. The 2nd Infantry Brigade will attack on the night of 22nd/23rd October, 1918, during the hours of moonlight.

2. Right Battalion will be 1st Northants, and Left Battalion will be 2nd Royal Sussex. 2nd K.R.R. will be in reserve.

3. TASKS.
   Left Battalion. To capture LA HAIE TONNOILE and secure high ground in R.23.a and c. and R.29.a. This Battalion will also push forward posts to maintain touch with the right of the 5th Division (Division on left of 1st Divn.) on their reaching the HAIE in R.17.c.8.0.
   Right Battalion. To secure high ground in R.30 and R.36. with its right resting throughout on the ground on the ground leading from X.4.d.central through LA LOUVIERE.

4. No smoke will be used in the Creeping Barrage. Batteries will fire about 10 rounds per gun to mark the Protective Barrage.

5. B/161st Bde.R.F.A. will provide a Forward Observation Officer, who will go forward with the Left Battalion. The most careful arrangements must be made to get information back to this Headquarters, as it is essential that news of the progress of the Infantry should reach Headquarters quickly. He will report to Left Battalion at 6.0 p.m. this evening and will be accompanied by two Signallers and two Runners, who should have an ample supply of German wire.
   2/Lieut.H.S.BUNDY, B/161, will be F.O.O.

6. C/161 will man an O.P. from dawn on 23-10-18.

7. Each Battery will send an Orderly with two Watches to this Office at 7.30 p.m. today to have watches synchronized.
8. Hdqrs. 161st Bde.R.F.A. is now at X.13.a.1.6.
9. ACKNOWLEDGE.

22-10-18.   Lieut;
                                    a/Adjutant, 161st Brigade R.F.A.

Issued at 16.15 hours.

                Copy No.1 - O.C.,A/161.
                     2 - O.C.,B/161.
                     3 - O.C.,C/161.
                     4 - O.C.,D/161.
                     5 - War Diary.
                     6 - File.
                     7 - H.Q.,32nd D.A.

War Diary 37

O.C., A/161.
O.C., B/161.
O.C., C/161.
O.C., D/161.

1. As there is to be no firing West of the Canal after the Barrage, Batteries will not be required to fire unless special retaliation is called for by the Infantry.

2. No forward move of the Brigade is at present contemplated after the attack.

3. Zero Hour is 01.20 hours, 23-10-18.

4. B/161 will take the right half, and C/161 the left half, and A/161 will be superimposed on the 161st Bde.R.F.A.zone.
D/161 will fire on the whole of the 161st Bde.R.F.A. zone, firing 200 yds. ahead of 18-Pdr. Batteries.

5. ACKNOWLEDGE.

22-10-18.

Lieut;
a/Adjutant, 161st Brigade R.F.A.

O.C., A/161.
O.C., B/161.
O.C., C/161.
O.C., D/161.

Between 5.30 a.m. and 5.45 a.m., 23-10-18, Batteries will fire on targets set out below.

Each Battery will fire two guns which will search or sweep from the Westerly exits of GATILLON to Protective Barrage.

At 5.30 a.m. they will fire 2 rounds gun fire and from then to 5.45 a.m., 2 rounds per gun per minute.

A/161 (2 guns) = R.23.d.0.7 - R.23.d.55.60.
B/161 (1 gun) = R.23.d.95.90 - R.23.b.93.05.
      (1 gun) = R.23.d.90.55 - R.23.b.93.90.
C/161 (2 guns) = R.24.a.05.50 - R.23.b.93.60.
D/161 (1 How.) = R.24.c.15.50 - R.23.d.90.55.
      (1 How.) = R.23.d.92.92 - R.23.b.93.05.

                                    Lieut;
22-10-18.   a/Adjutant, 161st Brigade R.F.A.

O.C., A/161.
O.C., B/161.
O.C., C/161.
O.C., D/161.

WARNING ORDER.

Batteries may be moving to their Wagon Lines tomorrow morning.

In the event of a move, Signallers should be left behind to salve as much wire as possible, unless Battery Positions are being handed over to another Brigade.

Lieut;
a/Adjutant, 161st Brigade

23-10-18.

Appendix "A".

Extract from 32nd Divnl. Routine Orders dated 18.10.18.

BAR TO MILITARY CROSS.

Lieutenant   P.R.HAMILTON, M.C.   A/161st Bde. R.F.A.

THE MILITARY CROSS.

Lieutenant   W.R.GOODMAN,   C/161st Bde. R.F.A.

Extract from 32nd Divnl. Routine Orders dated 29.10.18.

MILITARY MEDAL.

No.171   Bombr.   W.DOWNIE,   161st Bde. R.F.A.

(6339) Wt. W160/M3016 1,500,000 10/17 McA & W Ltd (E 1898) Forms W3091. Army Form W.3091.

Cover for Documents.

Nature of Enclosures.

Notes, or Letters written.

161st (Yorks.) Brigade, R.F.A.

Vol 35

WAR DIARY

· COVERING · PERIOD ·

From :— 1st NOVEMBER, '18.
To :— 30th NOVEMBER, '18.

WAR DIARY 161st (Yorks.) Brigade, RFA.

INTELLIGENCE SUMMARY.

(Erase heading not required.)

Army Form C. 2118.

Place	Date	Hour	Summary of Events and Information	Remarks and references to Appendices
In the Field.	1.11.18.		Batteries reconnoitred positions in Squares R.10. a and c., and R.9.b and d, Sheet 57 B. The following positions were selected:- A/161 ... R.9.d.80.65. C/161 ... R.10.a.10.30. B/161 ... R.9.a.70.60. D/161 ... R.9.d.40.00. Batteries dumped six wagons of ammunition each on the positions selected. Brigade Commander attended a Divisional Conference at 6.0.p.m., and a conference at 97th Infantry Brigade Headquarters at 8.30.p.m.	Appces. 40 & 41
	2.11.18.		Ammunition at positions made up to 150 rounds per gun, and final instructions given to Battery Commanders.	
	3.11.18.		Batteries moved to new wagon lines in vicinity of ST.BENIN in the morning, and moved up into action during the afternoon. Headquarters established at R.8.d.8.5.	
	4.11.18.		96th and 14th Infantry Brigades attacked the SAMBRE A L'OISE Canal defences at 5.45 a.m. B/161 and C/161 fired bursts of fire at irregular intervals from Zero to Zero plus 50 on road M.1.b.0.0. - M.2.a.3.6., and from Zero plus 50 to Zero plus 110 on RUE D'EN HAUT from M.1.d.55.70 - M.2.c.55.40. A/161 and D/161 fired a creeping barrage across LE DONJON in R.11.b. from NORTH to SOUTH. Owing to the Infantry not getting on as well as expected, a standing barrage at a slow rate of fire was put down by A/161 and B/161 on the line R.12.c.5.9. to M.7.b.2.6. at 8.5.a.m. At 9.5.a.m. this was altered to M.7.d.2.6 - M.7.b.0.3. - R.12.c.5.9. This was continued until 9.40.a.m., but was re-opened at 9.45.a.m. at a slow rate and continued until 11.30.a.m. C/161 and D/161 re-opened fire on RUE D'EN HAUT at 8.5.a.m. and continued until 8.35.a.m. Batteries moved off from positions between 1.0.p.m. and 2.0.p.m., crossed by the bridge at ORS, and took up positions as follows:- A/161 ... R.6.c.6.0. C/161 ... R.6.c.7.7. B/161 ... M.7.b.10.15. D/161 ... R.12.a.2.7. Major E.A.CHISHOLM, M.C. captured 10 prisoners and 1 field gun. Conference of Infantry and Artillery Brigade Commanders, and Battalion, Battery and Company Commanders at Brigade Headquarters at 8.30.p.m. 2/Lieut.E.A.WILSON (A/161) rejoined on completion of Course at Fourth Army Artillery School, and proceeded on leave. 2/Lieut.W.S.KIRK (B/161) rejoined on completion of Course at IX Corps Gas School. 2/Lieut.P.W.ALLEN (D/161) and Capt.M.KING-FRENCH (A/161) rejoined from leave in U.K.	
	5.11.18.		B/161 and C/161 moved off in close support of the ARGYLLS & SUTHERLANDS, and BORDERS, who crossed the RED Line in G.29 & 35 at 7.30.a.m. A/161 and D/161 moved up shortly afterwards. About 100 rounds were fired during the day at machine-gun posts. A/161 also	

WAR DIARY 161st (Yorks.) Brigade, R.F.A. Army Form C. 2118.

INTELLIGENCE SUMMARY.

(Erase heading not required.)

Place	Date	Hour	Summary of Events and Information	Remarks and references to Appendices
In the Field.	5.11.18. (Continued)		pushed forward a gun and engaged a machine-gun post in I.35. The 2nd Brigade, R.F.A. were affiliated to 161st Brigade, RFA., and moved up into action in vicinity of FAVRIL. Locations of batteries on evening of the 5th:- A/161 ... H.33.c.4.2. C/161 ... N.2.b.5.2. B/161 ... H.33.d.2.5. D/161 ... N.2.a.9.1. These positions were 800 to 1500 yards from the front line, and were under rifle and machine-gun fire.	
	6.11.18.		2/Lieut.G.W.BRITTEN (B/161) granted leave to U.K. until 19.11.18. The advance continued today, the same Batteries being told off to support the leading Infantry. Single guns were pushed forward by C/161 often in front of the Infantry, to deal with hostile machine guns. Lieut.J.G.COONEY (C/161) took a gun several hundred yards in front of the Infantry, and silenced three machine guns that were holding up the advance of the Infantry from the other side of the River RIVERLETTE in I.32. Final positions occupied by the Batteries are as follows:- A/161 ... N.5.a.2.1. C/161 ... H.35.c.0.0. B/161 ... I.20.b.6.4. D/161 ... H.34.d.9.0.	
	7.11.18.		K.O.Y.L.I. advanced through the BORDERS, and A.& S. HIGHLANDERS at 8.30.a.m. this morning. A/161 moved in close support. B/161 and C/161 received orders to move up into positions to cover the objective or line established, with a range of approximately 3000 yards. A/161, B/161 and D/161 moved by the road through MAROILLES, and MARBAIX. C/161 moved through LE GRAND FAYT, and was delayed until a bridge was constructed, crossing about 11.0 a.m. A/161 engaged hostile machine guns through-out the day. Major E.A.CHISHOLM (C/161) accompanied by B.S.M. LAY, endeavoured to work round a hostile machine gun to capture the crew. Major CHISHOLM was killed by a machine-gun bullet. Harassing fire was carried out by the Batteries on the roads in J.18.d., K.13.c and d., K.19.c and d., K.25.a. b. and c. Final locations of Batteries as follows:- A/161 ... J.25.b.2.0. C/161 ... J.19.d.6.2. B/161 ... J.19.b.6.0. D/161 ... J.25.d.2.8.	Appdx 42.
	8.11.18.		The advance continued at 8.0.a.m., A/161 moving in close support of the K.O.Y.L.I., B/161 covering the left half of the Brigade front. C/161 covering the right half. B/161, at the request of the Infantry, fired from 8.30 a.m. to 9.30 a.m. on road in J.29 b.	

Army Form C. 2118.

WAR DIARY
INTELLIGENCE SUMMARY

161st (Yorks.) Brigade, R.F.A.

Instructions regarding War Diaries and Intelligence Summaries are contained in F. S. Regs., Part II. and the Staff Manual respectively. Title pages will be prepared in manuscript.

(Erase heading not required.)

Place	Date	Hour	Summary of Events and Information	Remarks and references to Appendices
In the Field.	8.11.18. (Continued).		and d., at machine-gun in Church Tower of AVESNES from 10.30 a.m. to 11.15 a.m., also on machine-guns at J.28.b.9.6. and J.29.a.2.4. A/161 brought up a gun to within 300 yards of a machine-gun nest just West of AVESNES, and with an O.P. in a house on the right flank, engaged and silenced the machine-guns. Two Germans were found killed in two of the pits, and blood found at two others. Locations of Batteries as follows:- A/161 ... J.29.a.5.5. C/161 ... J.27.d.2.8. B/161 ... J.24.d.2.2. D/161 ... J.29.a.5.7.	
	9.11.18.		Capt.M.KING-FRENCH (A/161) temporarily assumed command of C/161 vice Major E.A. CHISHOLM, M.C. Killed. Lieut. F.A.CLAXTON (C/161) temporarily attached to A/161. The advance continued a further 1500 yards; B/161 was detailed to move in close support. No opposition was met with. B/161 advanced a forward section to *Aveswelles*. The other Batteries did not change their positions. The Brigade came out of action at 5.0.p.m., being relieved by the 2nd Brigade, A.F.A. 2/Lieut.W.R.GOODMAN M.C. (C/161) and Lieut. A.W.DENNISTON (HQ/161) rejoined from leave.	APPDX 43
	10.11.18.		Batteries settled down in their wagon lines, locations as follows:- A/161 ... J.28.b.4.4. C/161 ... J.27.c.6.4. B/161 ... J.32.c.8.9. D/161 ... J.27.d.9.7.	
	11.11.18.		Lieut.P.R.HAMILTON, M.C. (A/161) and 2/Lieut.T.COWAN (A/161) rejoined from leave. 2/Lieut. J.H.G.WAY joined the Brigade from 32nd D.A.C. and posted to C/161.	
	12.11.18. to (12th)...		Orders received at 10.0.a.m. that hostilities were to cease at 11.0.a.m. Batteries remained at wagon lines, resting, cleaning-up, and refitting. Major J.W.BUCKLEY, M.C. (D/161) rejoined from leave. Capt.H.BARRETT (C/161) rejoined on completion of B.C's Course at SHOEBURYNESS.	
	(14th)...		Lieut.R.G.JOHNSON (B/161) granted leave to U.K. until 28.11.18.	
	15.11.18. (15th)...		Capt.B.C.TRAPPES-LOMAX, M.C. (B/161) rejoined from leave. Lieut.F.A.CLAXTON (C/161) admitted Hospital (sick).	
	16.11.18.		Batteries reduced to a four-gun Battery Establishment. Surplus section, under Capt.B.C.TRAPPES-LOMAX, M.C. (B/161) marched to BOHAIN.	
	17/18.11.18.		Batteries remained at Wagon lines.	
	19.11.18.		The Brigade marched eight miles to LIESSIES. Route. GUERZIGNIES - WAUDRECHIES - FLAUMONT - SEMERIES - RAMOUSIES, starting at 12.00 hours and arriving at 15.00 hours.	

Army Form C. 2118.

WAR DIARY 161st (Yorks.) Brigade, R.F.A.

INTELLIGENCE SUMMARY.

(Erase heading not required.)

Instructions regarding War Diaries and Intelligence Summaries are contained in F. S. Regs., Part II. and the Staff Manual respectively. Title pages will be prepared in manuscript.

Place	Date	Hour	Summary of Events and Information	Remarks and references to Appendices
In the Field.	19.11.18. (Continued). 20.11.18.		Batteries were billeted on the Eastern edge of the Village and Headquarters on the Western edge. The Brigade marched to RANCE, a distance of ten miles. Route - SIVRY - TRIEU - BOUCHAUX, and settled down in billets South of RANCE at about 14.00 hours. 2/Lieut. W.S.KIRK (B/161) granted leave to U.K. until 4.12.18. Lieut. T.KAY posted from R.H.& R.F.A. Base Depot at attached C/161.	
	21/23.11.18. 24.11.18.		The Brigade remained at RANCE, and occupied the time in cleaning, football, concerts &c. March continued to FOURBECHIES. Owing to the frozen state of the roads, and lack of frost cogs, the roads became congested, and the Brigade took three hours to cover the 3 miles.	
	25/26.11.18.		The Brigade remained in their Wagon lines. A thaw set it in the 25th. The Batteries moved to an area South of FROIDCHAPELLE, C/161 close to the Station, A/161 and D/161 in farm houses two miles South of FROIDCHAPELLE, and B/161 in GRATIERE. (25th). 2/Lieut. L.A.MOULD (A/161) granted leave to U.K. until 9.12.18. Lieut. P.R.HAMILTON, M.C. (A/161) proceeded to attend B.C's Course at SHOEBURYNESS. (26th). Lieut. E.COKE, M.C. (HQ/161) attached to Headquarters, 32nd Division. 2/Lieut. E.A.WILSON (A/161) rejoined from leave.	
	27.11.18. 28/30.11.18.		HQ/161 moved into billets close to FROIDCHAPELLE Station. The Brigade remained at FROIDCHAPELLE.	

Honours and Awards during month.

MILITARY MEDAL.

25798	Sergt. W.WORMALD,	...	A/161 Bde. RFA.
112497	Gunner C.H.RAMSEY,	...	-do-
L/5784	Driver J.TURNER,	...	-do-
171	Bombr. W.DOWNIE,	...	-do-

Casualties during month. ...

Appdx. "A"

30th November, 1918.

[signature]
Lieut-Colonel.
Commanding 161st (Yorks.) Brigade, R.FA.

APPENDIX "A".

CASUALTIES DURING MONTH OF NOVEMBER, 1918.

	Killed.		Wounded.		Gassed.		Evacuated.		Total.	
	Offrs.	O.R.	Offrs.	O.R.	Offrs.	O.R.	Offrs.	O.R.	Offrs.	O.R.
A/161 ...	-	2	-	6	-	-	-	6.	-	14.
B/161 ...	-	-	-	-	-	-	-	7.	-	7.
C/161 ...	1	-	-	-	-	-	1	10.	2	10.
D/161 ...	-	-	-	1 ∅	-	4	-	5.	-	10.
Totals...	1	2	-	7	-	4	1	28.	2	41.

∅ Accidental.

40   SECRET.   Copy 4

161st (HOW.) BRIGADE, R.F.A.
ARTILLERY INSTRUCTIONS No.1.

Reference Map 1/40,000 Sheet 57 'A' & 'B'.

1.   For General Instructions see 32nd Divisional Artillery Instructions No.15 previously issued.

2.   Action of 161st Brigade, R.F.A. during the Barrage:-

   (a) A/161, B/161 and C/161 will fire bursts of 2 rounds Gun fire on the road K.1.b.0.0. - L.2.a.7.0. at the following times:-

                Zero
                Zero plus 2.   Zero plus 30.
                Zero plus 5.   Zero plus 35.
                Zero plus 14.   Zero plus 38.
                Zero plus 21.   Zero plus 44.
                Zero plus 24.   Zero plus 48.

   (b) A/161, B/161 and C/161 will fire bursts of 2 rounds Gun fire on RUE d'en HAUT from L.1.d.58.70 to K.2.c.45.40. at the following times:-

                Zero plus 52.   Zero plus 84.
                Zero plus 58.   Zero plus 92.
                Zero plus 60.   Zero plus 96.
                Zero plus 64.   Zero plus 99.
                Zero plus 70.   Zero plus 105.
                Zero plus 78.   Zero plus 115.
                Zero plus 81.

   (c) A/161 will harass the banks of the Canal from R.11.b.4.5. - ONNAING from Zero plus 30 to Zero plus 60. Rate of fire ... 2 rounds per gun per minute.

        B/161 and C/161 must be prepared to turn on to this target if required.

3.   "C.1." and "C.2." targets will be engaged at once with bursts of 2 minutes gun fire.

4.   A/161 will establish telephonic communication with 14th Infantry Brigade.

5.   Reconnaissance of positions for 'Z' night should be carried out as soon as feasible and reports rendered to this office. Batteries will not move without orders from this office.

        Teams should be brought up to positions of readiness close to Battery positions at 12.30 hours.

6.   Location of Brigade Headquarters from 14.00 hours 3rd inst., D.13.d.8.5.

7.   ZERO HOUR and Instructions for BOMBARDMENT will be notified later.

8.   ACKNOWLEDGE.

                                          A.W. Thornton
                                               Captain.
2nd November, 1918.   Adjutant, 161st Brigade, R.F.A.

        Copy No.1... H.Q. 32nd D.A.   Copy No.5... O.C. A/161.
             2... H.Q. 14th Inf.Bde.   6... O.C. B/161.
             3... War Diary.   7... O.C. C/161.
             4... File.   8... O.C. D/161.

41

Copy No. 4.

161st (YORKS.) BRIGADE, R.F.A.
ARTILLERY INSTRUCTIONS No.

1. Exploitation on Zero plus Z one day.

   The 97th Infantry Brigade will advance on a two-battalion front, ARGYLES & SUTHERLANDS on the left, BORDERS on the right.

2. The 161st Brigade, R.F.A. will support the advance; B/161 moving in support of the ARGYLES & SUTHERLANDS, and C/161 in support of the BORDERS, each with a forward section in close liaison with the forward Company.
   A/161 and D/161 will be retained in Brigade Reserve, and will move under instructions from this office.

3. It is important that Echelons shall be full on Zero plus one morning.

4. The 32nd D.A.C. will supply ammunition to Battery Wagon Lines, and every effort must be made to keep the D.A.C. informed of location of these.

5. The advance commences at 05.30 hours.

6. Ammunition.

                                    W S Lowndon
                                    Captain.
                                    for Lieut-Colonel,
                                    Commanding 161st (Yorks.) Brigade, R.F.A.

3rd November, 1918.

Copy No. 1 ... H.Q. 32nd D.A.
         2 ... H.Q. 141st Inf.Bde.
         3 ... War Diary.
         4 ... File.
         5 ... O.C. A/161.
         6 ... O.C. B/161.
         7 ... O.C. C/161.
         8 ... O.C. D/161.

SECRET.   Copy No. 4

161st (Yorks.) BRIGADE, R.F.A. ARTILLERY
INSTRUCTIONS No. 3.

Reference Map 57.A. 1/40,000.

1. The IV Army has reached the GREEN line today with little opposition.

2. On the 97th Infantry Brigade front the K.O.Y.L.I. will continue the advance on the morning of the 7th inst. at 08.30 hours.
   Objective, approximate line K.14.a K.14 central, K 20 central, K.26.central.

3. 97th Infantry Brigade Boundaries:-

   Northern Boundary - N.and S. grid line through J.13 central.
   Southern Boundary - N.and S. grid line through J.35.a.5.5.

4. One Battalion of 97th Infantry Brigade will move up and billet in the area EAST of AVESNES. The remaining Battalions will billet in Squares J.29 and 35.
   14th Infantry Brigade are moving to Squares I.34 and 35, and will probably relieve the 97th Infantry Brigade on the evening of the 7th.

5. A/161 will move at dawn in close support of the K.O.Y.L.I.
   B/161 will take up a position in the area J.16.c.0.0., J.13.a.0.0., J.24.d.0.0., J.22.d.0.0.to cover Northern half of front K.14.c. to grid N/S line between K.20 and K.26.
   C/161 will move to a position in the area J.24.d.0.0., J.36.a.0.5., J.34.a.0.5., J.22.d.0.0., to cover the Southern half of the Brigade front.
   D/161 will select a position to cover the whole front at a range of approximately 3,500 yards.

6. In the event of the final objective not being gained, B/161 and C/161 will select positions at a range of approximately 3,000 yards from the line as established.

7. H.Q.161st Brigade, RFA. will close at H.35.c.0.6. at 07.00 hours, and open at J.25 central at the same hour.

8. ACKNOWLEDGE.

                                                                    Captain.
                                              Adjutant ,161st (Yorks.) Brigade, RFA.

6th Novr.1918.
  Issued at
  23.55.

        Copy No.1 - H.Q.32nd D.A.   No.6 - O.C. C/161.
              2 - H.Q.97th Inf:Bde.   7 - O.C. D/161.
              3 - O.C.2nd A.F.A.Bde.   8 - War Diary.
              4 - O.C. A/161   9.- File.
              5.- O.C. B/161.

REPORT OF OPERATIONS OF 161st (YORKS.) BRIGADE R.F.A.
from NOVEMBER 4th 1918 to NOVEMBER 10th 1918.

The 161st (Yorks.) Brigade, R.F.A. was given the task of moving forward with the 97th Infantry Brigade, and closely supporting it.

On the night of November 3rd/4th 1918 positions were occupied about R.9.b. and d, and during the attack on the morning of November 4th by the 14th and 96th Infantry Brigades, the 161st (Yorks.) Brigade, R.F.A. was employed on shooting at targets selected by Divisional Artillery.

18-Pounder Batteries were affiliated as follows:-

A/161 to the K.O.Y.L.I.
B/161 to the ARGYLLS,
and C/161 to the BORDERS.

Whenever any of these Battalions advanced, they were closely supported by their affiliated Battery.

About 2.0.p.m. on November 4th orders were received from Divisional Headquarters to advance across the Canal at ORS, and to clear the bridge by 3.30.pm. to avoid blocking the 97th Infantry Brigade, who were following up. On crossing the bridge it was found impossible to move towards the RUE d'en HAUT owing to hostile machine-gun fire. Batteries were accordingly moved South, and positions taken up in Squares R.6.c. and R.12a. and c.

Infantry Brigade Headquarters were also located in the RUE VERT, (R.12.)

As the Left flank situation was obscure, and the RUE VERT was under hostile machine-gun fire, application was made to the G.O.C., 97th Infantry Brigade for a platoon. A platoon of the ARGYLLS was supplied to cover the Left flank of C/161 in Square M.1.d.

The G.O.C., 97th Infantry Brigade held a conference on the night of November 4th/5th at which all Battalion Commanders, as well as Brigade and Battery Commanders of 161st Brigade, R.F.A., were present. Plans were made for the advance next day, with the ARGYLLS on left, BORDERS on right. The two supporting Batteries were ordered to move forward at dawn in close support, C/161 moving by the road M.7., M.14.a., M.8.d. B/161 was ordered to advance by the road G.32 and 33; as opportunity occurred A/161 and D/161 were moved forward, and at about 2.0.p.m. were ordered to take up positions East of FAVRIL in Squares H.32., N.2.

At night-fall it was found that the Infantry line was not nearly as far forward as had been previously reported, with the result that Batteries were from 500 to 700 yards from the front line.

B/161 and D/161 were in the area H.33., N.2. also.

Brigade Headquarters near 97th Infantry Brigade Headquarters in FAVRIL.

During this night, November 5th/6th the enemy withdrew, and the advance was continued next day, B/161 and C/161 again moving forward in close support; A/161 and D/161 were ordered to move forward to take up positions in N.4.

Full details of Battery moves are shown in attached reports.

On November 7th 1918 the K.O.Y.L.I. passed through the ARGYLLS and BORDERS, A/161 moving up in close support.

The advance continued at 8.0.a.m. November 8th 1918, A/161 moving up in close support of the K.O.Y.L.I; B/161 covering the left half of the Brigade front, C/161 covering the right half.

B/161, at the request of the Infantry, fired from 8.30.a.m. to 9.30.a.m. on road in J.29.b. and d., at machine gun in Church tower of AVESNES from 10.30a.m. to 11.15.a.m., also on machine guns at J.28.b.9.6. and J.29.a.2.4.

A/161 brought up a gun to within 300 yards of a machine-gun nest just West of AVESNES, and with an O.P. in a house on the right flank, engaged and silenced the machine guns. Two Germans were

PAGE 2 OF REPORT ON ADVANCE.
-o-o-o-o-o-o-o-o-o-o-o-o-

found killed in two of the pits, and blood found at two others.

Locations of Batteries as follows:-

   A/161 ... J.29.c.5.5.
   B/161 ... J.26.d.2.2.
   C/161 ... J.27.a.6..
   D/161 ... J.29.a.5.7.

9.11.18. The advance continued a further 1500 yards. D/161 was detailed to move in close support. No opposition was met with.
A\/161 advanced a forward section to Semeries; the other batteries did not change their positions.
The Brigade came out of action at 5.0.p.m., being relieved by the 62nd Brigade, R.F.A.

10.11.18. Batteries settled down in their wagon lines. Locations as follows:-

   A/161 ... J.23.b.4.4.
   B/161 ... J.32.c.0.0.
   C/161 ... J.27.c.6.4.
   D/161 ... J.27.d.9.7.

DIARY OF ADVANCE OF A/161 Brigade, R.F.A. from ST. OBS
to SEMERIES 4th Novr.1918 to 10th Novr.1918.
-o-o-o-o-o-o-o-o-o-o-o-o-o-o-o-o-o-o-

Ref: Sheets 57B;57A; 1/40,000.

4.11.18.   Lawn.   Battery in Action N.9.d.7.7.   Wagon Line W.6.a.
   Battery told off to support the attack on LE DONJON from the North with an enfilade Barrage, then to reconnoitre positions East of the Canal, and advance in support of the Divisional front.
   Barrage on LE DONJON effective, and place captured without difficulty. Position in N.6.c. reconnoitred and occupied in the afternoon, all men under cover; Wagon line returned to W.6.a.

5.11.18.   Battery in support of Divisional Front.   At 7.30.a.m. came into position in readiness at PARK VERSAILLE (G.33.d.3.0.). Finding that no opposition was being encountered, advanced to CROIX HAINAUT East of TAISNE, one gun going forward to N.4.c.3.3. to engage machine gun at road junction N.5.c.0.3.   Battery remained in action that night at CROIX HAINAUT, Wagon line in W.8.b.   Both heavily shelled 8.P.- 9.3.p.m.- direct hits on Mens'.billet and Horse lines- two men killed, five wounded, eleven horses and mules killed.
   Wagon line removed to West of TAISNE.

6.11.18.   Battery in support of Divisional front.   Did not advance till afternoon.   Came into action in N.5.c. at.dusk, Wagon line in N.4.b.

7.11.18.   Battery under orders to move in close support of K.O.Y.L.I. Enforced to march North in order to cross river at MARCILLES.
   One section under 2/Lieut.W.S.WILSON ordered to support Left Company and move along main MARCILLES-MARBAIX-AVESNES Road.
   This section had to turn South at I.24.b.7.3. to avoid crater and took up position J.26.b.6.9 to support Left Company held up on N.E S. line through J.21.central.
   Remainder of Battery (3 guns) under 2/Lieut. L.A.MOULD ordered to rendezvous at I.35.c.6.3.
   B.C. with staff swam river at MARC PAPP in order to get in early touch with the situation on front of K.O.Y.L.I.
   Word was sent back to 2/Lieut.L.A.MOULD to advance East along roads through I.35.a. and b., I.30.c. and d., J.25.c. and d., J.26.c. and d., J.27.c. and d., J.23.c.a and b.   Two guns were brought into action at J.27.d.4.3., and one was pushed forward under 2/Lieut. L.A.MOULD to J.28.a.8.3., the move effectually to engage machine guns on main MARBAIX-AVESNES Road at J.22.d.3.0.
   Machine-gun fire at this point was silenced, and enemy retired Eastwards down Main Road.
   Communication by telephone was then established through the forward gun to an O.P. at Farm J.28.b.4.4., to enable observed fire to be brought on cross-roads J.22.b.1.7; this farm was also Right Company Headquarters., which simplified the matter of keeping touch.
   At dusk the scattered Battery was collected and withdrew into position J.29.c.9.3.   Wagon Line at I.35.a.8.0.

8.11.18.   Battery in close support of K.O.Y.L.I.
   Difficulty expected in getting going, as horses were tired and guns were in action in a soft field, so one gun sent off in advance under 2/Lieut. W.S.WILSON to support Left Company, and one gun under Sergeant TAPLIN to support Right Company, remainder to follow as early as possible.
   2/Lieut. W.S.WILSON brought his gun into action at J.21.b.6.2. and fired on machine guns along main road J.29.a.
   Sergeant TAPLIN brought his gun into action J.28.b.43.
   Remainder of Battery brought into action J.28.a.7.4., with telephone communication to J.28.b.4.4. where an O.P. was established and targets located for lone gun and for Battery.   Very effective shooting was done by Lone gun firing at house J.28.b 9.5, and at a line of resistance along a hedge just N.E. of this.
   Advance continued in the afternoon, and Battery came into action J.29.b.2.7.   Wagon Line J.28.b.3.3.

9.11.18.   Battery in close support of K.O.Y.L.I., who reached objective without opposition; bridges all blown up and impossible to move Battery, but one gun advanced as far as SEMERIES and then returned.

REPORT OF ADVANCE OF B/161 IN OPERATION FROM
November 4th to 10th 1918.
-o-o-o-o-o-o-o-o-o-o-o-o-o-o-o-

Major R.EMMET. D.S.O. Comndg.

4.11.18.   Assisted in barrage covering crossing of SAMBRE Canal. At
15.00, I reconnoitred M.2.a. for waiting position for next day's
operations: Found enemy in C.31 and 32 as well as in front: was
repeatedly sniped. Reported situation to Brigade as situation was
not known then.
     Battery crossed Canal at ORS at 18.00, took up waiting position
just west of M.7.b. for night.

5.11.18.   Battery was ordered to closely support ARGYLE & S.H. Batt,
who were to jump off from N.& S. road in G.23, 29 and 35. Under
arrangements made with Lieut-Colonel SOUTHERBY, one section was to
follow road on the North Battalion Boundary viz. LANDRECIES-MARCILLES
road to N.26.c.0.5., thence to N.28.c and d., to N.36.b.80.95 thence
to GRAND FAYT. Section to keep in close touch with left
Company Commander. Detached Section in charge of 2/Lieut.A.C.
LEYLAND.
     Battery, less one Section, under B.C. was to follow on Right
flank of Battalion from N.35.a.0.0. to FAVRIL, thence to N.34.b.35.01.,
thence to GRAND FAYT, keeping in touch with C.O. Infantry Battalion,
and advanced Infantry line.
     Moving to rendezvous by different routes, both detached Section
and Battery had each to obtain a way around three road mine-craters.

     (a) 2/Lieut.A.C.LEYLAND carried out his programme as planned,
keeping with 300 to 400 yards behind front Infantry wave. At 12.20
Infantry were held up by machine-gun fire from N.22.d.0.7. Target
taken on by section at 1150 yards range. Machine gun neutralised or
destroyed, as Infantry advanced under Artillery fire.
     A little further on, Infantry were met by machine-gun fire
from all directions, and unable to advance. Visability was very bad,
and location of machine guns unobtainable. Infantry held that line
for the rest of the day and night. Section in action at N.21.c.6.5.
about 600 yards from our front line.

     (b) Battery, less one section, closely followed BORDER Battalion
through FAVRIL. Being out of A.& S.H. Battalion area for a time,
got out of touch with that Battalion. Battery reached N.33.d.0.0 at
10.15, half-an-hour ahead of A.& S.H.Battalion. At this time road
N.33.c.0.1 to N.33 central held only by two small Cavalry patrols.
     At 09.45 enemy 7.7 cm. Battery fired its last round from N.33.d.05.90.
     A 10.5 cm. H.V. was found over-turned at N.33.d.00.95 and abandoned.
     Battery waited here till A.& S.H. Battalion passed, and
Battalion Headquarters established at N.33.d.05.90. B.C. attached
himself to Battalion H.Q. for rest of day.
     Infantry held up by machine gun fire close in front of this
point, but none of the machine guns could be located. No advance made
till next morning. Day very wet; visibility bad. Battery in action
at N.33.d.4.6. for night within 600 to 700 yards of our front line,
and under sniping fire all night. Night very dark; vicinity very
heavily shelled for 1½ hours at 16.00 and for about ¾ of an hour at
20.30.

6.11.18.   Advance resumed. Both detached section and Battery followed
Infantry very closely. Some difficulty passing a road mine-crater
was experienced by Battery at N.34.b.9.1.
     During carrying and clearing up of GRAND FAYT from 11.00
Battery in action at N.36.b.7.5.
     Learning from 2/Lieut.H.S.BUNDY (Acting Liaison Officer) with
A.& S.H. Battalion H.Q. that river was impassible at GRAND FAYT, Battery
was counter-marched (after A.&S.H. Battalion H.Q. had been notified
of route) to MARCILLES, crossed river and advanced by MARCILLES -
MARBAIX road to I.13 and 17, thence into action for the night with
detached section at I.20.b.5.5. Section took up this position at 15.00
and Battery at 17.30. K.O.Y.L.I. advancing during night, so no S.O.S.
lines. Day wet, and visibility bad.

(Continued).

Page 2 of REPORT by B/161.

Throughout these two days inter-communication was kept up at frequent intervals between section and Battery, and both were in close touch with Infantry.

7.11.18.   Battery was in reserve behind K.O.Y.L.I., and moved by MAROILLES - MARBAIX road immediately behind the K.O.Y.L.I. Battalion to J.19.d.80.95, where road was completely destroyed by mine. Road through J.19, 25, 26 and 21 reconnoitred; a shorter way made by bridging stream at J.19.d.3.7. Battery took latter route, and anticipating shelling of only road around the crater. The road was heavily shelled as anticipated during P.M. and night.

Infantry unable to advance, so Battery went into action at J.19.b.7.3. notifying K.O.Y.L.I. and A.& S.H. Headquarters of location.   Range to our front line 600 to 700 yards.

8.11.18.   As soon as advance of Infantry permitted, Battery moved forward to J.21.a.3.7. at 08.00, notifying A.& S.H. Battalion H.Q., and sending an Officer to K.O.Y.L.I. Battalion H.Q. to act as temporary Liaison Officer for Battery.

Infantry immediately called for fire on road in J.29.b and d. Fire kept up for about one hour, until stopped by Infantry

At 10.37 fire ordered by Infantry on machine-gun in Church tower of AVESNES, and taken on with T.S. over open sights at irregular intervals for three-quarters of an hour. Nothing more heard of this machine gun.

Fire ordered by Infantry on machine guns at J.28.b.9.3.and J.29.a.2.4, which were holding up Infantry. These engaged with 106 fuze, and several direct hits obtained. Infantry later said these houses were rushed after Artillery fire, and five machine-gun teams were all found dead or wounded.

On report that Infantry were entering AVESNES, E.O. reconnoitred road into AVESNES through J.28., 23 c and a, b. and d. AVESNES reached 14.15. Civilians reported that enemy troops left at 13.30.

All exits EAST and NORTH examined and found impassable. Battery brought into action about 1800 at J.24.d.7.5. K.O.Y.L.I. and A.& S.H. Headquarters notified.

Battery was rather badly sniped while laying out lines of fire in dark.

At 21.30 A.& S.H. called for shoot on machine gun at K.30a.15.90. Reporting Infantry had been obliged to withdraw 100 yards at that point.   Battery responded with 106 fuze, range 1250 yards.   Lieut-Colonel LE MOTTE later told the B.C. he had feared a local counter-attack at that point, and that the Artillery fire had completely silenced the machine-gun fire.   The Battery was heavily, but inaccurately, sniped by machine-gun during the shoot, and immediately before it.   Sniping by rifle of the Battery continued for about an hour after the shoot.

9.11.18.   Came out of action in evening.

During the whole of the advance communication between Battery and Infantry was intimate and complete.   The Infantry were constantly pressed for targets, but they were unable to give them.   All Artillery enterprise to obtain targets was defeated by bad visibility, high hedges, and the extremely close nature of the country.

2/Lieut.W.H. BUSBY in liaison with A.& S.H. Battalion, kept Battery well informed with speedy, timely and accurate information throughout, thereby assisting the co-operation of the Battery.

2/Lieut. T. SMITH handled his section admirably with skill and dash, keeping communication with Infantry and Battery most successfully throughout.

REPORT OF C/161 ON ADVANCE
4th Novr. to 10th Novr.1918.
-o-o-o-o-o-o-o-o-o-o-o-o-

Reference 1/40,000 - 57.B; 57.A.

4.11.18.   On the morning of the 4th, the Battery was in position at R.10.a.5.2., with Wagon Lines at C.5.b.9.7.
During the Barrage we fired on selected points, including MILL at N.27. At about 09.30, Major E.A.CHISHOLM,M.C. with B.S.M. LAY, went forward to obtain information. He returned at noon, and again went forward in the afternoon, working with the Infantry, and capturing, with the assistance of B.S.M. LAY, 10 prisoners in a house at M.1.b.9.6., and subsequently a field gun at M.5.c.5.0. At 15.00 Battery crossed the Canal at M.6.a.0.4., and came into action at M.6.c.0.3. This is the First battery across.
At 15.30 about six rounds were fired for registration.
Wagon Lines moved up to R.9.a.9.5.

5.11.18.   At 05.30 the forward section, under Lieut.J.G.COONEY, advanced to M.6.b.9.9., and halted to await the Infantry. The Battery followed ten minutes later.
At 05.30 Lieut.J.G.COONEY and B.S.M. LAY rode forward to second objective, and found no enemy, so returned to forward section, meeting the advancing Infantry on their way back.
The forward section, working in close support of the Infantry (1st/5th L.N.LAN.) met machine-gun fire coming from H.35.c.0.0., and the wood in H.5.a. and b., which was successfully engaged from H.35.central.
The Infantry then took their second objective. At dusk the forward section was withdrawn to H.2.c.99.99, where the Battery was in action. At 15.00 the Battery, at the request of Infantry, fired on Eastern exits of GRAND FAYT. At 15.00, Major E.A.CHISHOLM, M.C. took a gun forward from H.2.c.99.99, and went into action at H.2.B.8.1, and engaged machine guns over open sights, which were firing from GRAND FAYT, H.9.c.1.9. This gun was withdrawn at 16.00. The Battery remained in action for the night at H.2.c.99.99. Wagon lines at C.30.d.9.1.

6.11.18.   On the morning of the 6th, Lieut. J.G.COONEY again went on with the forward section, and advanced in close support of the Infantry, and came into action at I.31.c.6.9.firing nine rounds at machine gun at I.25.c.8.2. This was ineffective, so B.S.M.LAY went forward with a Cavalry Officer to ascertain position. A gun was then run forward to I.26.c.5.7. and fired two rounds at houses about I.25.c.95.75. The machine gun then departed, and our Infantry advanced across the River. The forward section being unable to cross, came into action at I.26.c.9.6. From information received from a civilian who had escaped from the enemy lines, the forward section fired fifty rounds at a hostile battery in action at J.31. The rest of the Battery moved up at noon, and came into action at H.35.c.05.11, and remained there for the night. The forward section was withdrawn to I.31.a.5.9. Battery wagon lines were at H.2.b.9.2.

7.11.18.   At 09.30 the Battery moved up to the forward section, and the whole crossed the River at I.26.c.9.7., coming into action at J.19.d.25.50 at 12.00, and fired fifty rounds harassing fire on the road from J.20.a.9.6. to J.29.b.9.7., and during the evening another fifty rounds at the same target. Wagon lines were at I.16.d.4.1.
Major E.A.CHISHOLM, M.C. went forward at 07.30 with B.S.M.LAY and was killed at 11.00 endeavouring to rush a house containing machine guns at J.28.b.9.4.

8.11.18.   Captain A.KING-FRENCH arrived and took over command of the Battery. At 11.15, 325 rounds were fired at target J.29.a.0.5. to J.29.b.1.8. and J.29.a.0.9. to J.29.b.7.7. At 13.00 Battery moved forward to J.27.b.3.1. and wagon lines to J.27.c.0.5.

9.11.18.   At 08.30 forward section under 2/Lieut.C.G.CHAPPELL advanced through AVESNES, and came into action at J.30.d.99.20 in support of 1/5th BORDERS. No rounds were fired.
Major E.A.CHISHOLM, M.C. was buried at GRAND FAYT.
At 18.00 whole Battery withdrawn to Wagon Lines at J.27.c

10.11.18.   Remained at Wagon lines.

REPORT OF B/161 ON ADVANCE
4th Novr. to 10th Novr.1918.
-:-o-o-o-o-o-o-o-o-o-

4.11.18.   On the morning of 4.11.18, the Battery was in action just East of BAZUEL and fired the preliminary barrage for the crossing of the Canal near ORS at 5.45 a.m.
   A reconnaissance at about 10.0.a.m. showed that our Infantry held roughly the line, C.38, c.7.2., RUE d'on HAUT M.7.d.1.9.
   By mid-day the line was sufficiently advanced to permit of Batteries crossing the Canal, which we did about 5.30.p.m. coming into action in M.12.b.6.3. We were lucky in getting no casualties from machine guns and hostile Artillery fire.

5.11.18.   The next morning, the enemy having retired, we advanced in close support of the Infantry, meeting no opposition until we reached FAVRIL. Just East of FAVRIL, on the high ground in F.4., 13, and F.24, there were scattered machine guns, which owing to mist, and the coming dusk, were difficult to locate. Areas thought to be approximately the position were shelled as soon as the Battery got into action in F.2.a.95.00. This was a very tiring day for men and horses, owing to incessant rain, and bad roads, and the craters made by enemy mines.

6.11.18.   Next morning at 8.30.a.m. reconnaissance showed that the Infantry were approaching GRAND FAYT, and orders were received from brigade that we might move forward at 1.0.p.m. Roads were again a considerable obstacle, and the Battery got into action in E.3.a.3.8. at about 4.0.p.m. Reconnaissance at this time by 2/Lieut.F.A.ALLEN showed that the Infantry were approaching the line MARBAIX - CARTIGNIES, but no bridge existed at GRAND FAYT, and no opposition was being met with, so orders were received from brigade not to move forward again in the dark.

7.11.18.   On the morning of the 7th, Battery marched via MAROILLES and MARBAIX to I.34.b.7.2. in close support of the Infantry. A reconnaissance from this point by 2/Lieut.A.J.ALLEN showed that the enemy had machine guns on the high ground in J.22.c and d., and J.23, roads of approach being persistently swept. These were engaged by M/161 successfully, as the Battery moved to COUTANT CHATEAU, and took up a position of readiness there. Again mists and the close country made observation impossible, but as the enemy opposition was determined, machine guns were searched for. As enemy transport could be heard in DOMPIL, the exits from the town were shelled between 6.0. and 6.30.p.m.

8.11.18.   Next morning, the 8th, small bursts on approximate locations of machine guns were fired in support of our Infantry, but failed to dislodge him. Accordingly at 11.0.a.m. a barrage was fired in which the Battery fired 250 rounds.
   At 12.15 a request from the K.O.Y.L.I. was received for a few rounds to be fired on the hedge in J.19.a.4.7., as they proposed to try and rush the machine guns there. This was done and machine gun posts were successfully dealt with, leaving two Boche machine-gunners dead.
   At about 1.0.p.m. reports from reconnaissance and Headquarters K.O.Y.L.I. with whom Lieut.R.A. KELSEY-BIRCH was doing liaison at this time, showed that the enemy had been pushed back, and our Infantry were entering DVESNES. The Battery at once moved forward and as soon as the Infantry entered the town, took up a position in J.20.a.4.7. Before dark, reconnaissance showed that the Infantry had reached approximately their objective, and the Battery was withdrawn from action, the next day 9th Novr.1918.

L E S S O N S   L E A R N T.
-o-o-o-o-o-o-o-o-o-o-o-o-

1. The salving of wire for an Advanced Guard Brigade is a most serious drag on the operations, in fact, an impossible task.

2. Lack of support on the part of the Signal Company was keenly felt, no officer of this unit ever came forward to ask what help he could give.

3. The only telephone line back to Divisional Artillery was that laid by the Infantry Brigade Section, which intermittently serves both 97th Infantry Brigade, and 161st Brigade, RFA, obviously the more urgent the call, the more congestion on the line, and the greater the difficulty of getting through to Divisional Artillery.

4. Artillery line must be separate to Infantry line..

5. Close liaison between Artillery and Infantry Units was responsible for the success.

6. A supporting Brigade of Artillery should be at the call of the Brigade Commander of the Artillery supporting the Infantry without reference to Division.   This, and appreciation of situation is of paramount importance, "Action taken" reported to Division should be normal method.

7. Final decisions as to positions must be made by Artillery Brigade Commanders by 2.0.p.m. to enable batteries to get into position before dark at this time of the year.

8. The two-orderly system per unit on the whole worked well, but as was obvious from the start, when two units moved at once, this system broke down.

9. Working on the principle of Para 7, three batteries could be kept in telephonic communication each night.

10. It is desirable to lay plans so that each night the Artillery Brigade is collected under a centralised control.

11 Decentralisation during daylight in close support of Infantry Bdys.

12. In pursuit, the greater the daring, the bigger the result is true, and the less the risk.

14. It requires five weeks practice of mobile warfare to instill into Field Artillery Batteries that they are not Siege Artillery, due to the trench warfare

15. Half a week of fact is of more value than two months of theory.

16. Immediate preparation of roads forward is of great importance - also specialists to determine mines - lack of these preparations was acutely felt.

17. Artillery Brigade Headquarters should be moved with Infantry Brigade Headquarters, and all Batteries notified of a ==== move at the earliest opportunity once a move is decided on and circulated.
  It should not be changed except for the most dire reasons at this time of year. Final moves of ==== Headquarters should be decided on by 1.0.pm. , and at once circulated to all Batteries.

(6339) Wt. W160/M3016 1,500,000 10/17 McA & W Ltd (E 1898) Forms W3091.   Army Form W.3091.

Cover for Documents.

Nature of Enclosures.

Notes, or Letters written.

35807. W16879/M1879 500,000 3/17 R.T. (1074) Forms/W3091/3   Army Form W.3091.

Cover for Documents.

Nature of Enclosures.

161st (Yorks) Brigade R.F.A.

~~ War Diary ~~

Covering period

1st December 1918

– to –

31st December 1918.

Notes, or Letters written.

Army Form C. 2118.

Sh.3.

WAR DIARY

161st (YORKS.) BRIGADE R.F.A.

~~INTELLIGENCE~~ SUMMARY.

(Erase heading not required.)

Instructions regarding War Diaries and Intelligence Summaries are contained in F. S. Regs., Part II. and the Staff Manual respectively. Title pages will be prepared in manuscript.

Place	Date	Hour	Summary of Events and Information	Remarks and references to Appendices
			HONOURS & AWARDS (Continued).	
			THE DISTINGUISHED CONDUCT MEDAL.	
			49533 Sergt. TAPLIN, T.R. A/161.	

Army Form C. 2118.

Sh.1.

WAR DIARY

INTELLIGENCE SUMMARY.

161st (YORKS.) BRIGADE R.F.A.

(Erase heading not required.)

Instructions regarding War Diaries and Intelligence Summaries are contained in F. S. Regs., Part II. and the Staff Manual respectively. Title pages will be prepared in manuscript.

Place	Date	Hour	Summary of Events and Information	Remarks and references to Appendices
In the Field.	1-12-18 to 11-12-18.		The Brigade remained at FROIDCHAPELLE; attention being devoted to Sports and Recreational Training.	
	1-12-18.		Major P.CROW,D.S.O., A/161, attached HQ/161, and assumed duties of Education Officer and Sports Officer.	
	2-12-18.		Lieut.A.W.DENNISTON, HQ/-61, injured 2-12-18 and admitted hospital 3-12-18.	
	4-12-18.		Lieut-Colonel H.H.HULTON, D.S.O., admitted hospital for Dental Treatment. Major R.EMMET, D.S.O., B/-61, assumed command of Brigade vice Lieut-Colonel H.H.HULTON,D.S.O. Lieut.P.R.HAMILTON,M.C. rejoined from Shoeburyness.	
	5-12-18.		Lieut-Colonel H.H.HULTON, D.S.O., rejoined from hospital.	
	7-12-18.		Lieut.R.A.WYRLEY-BIRCH, M.C., D/161, posted to join 14th (Army) Brigade R.H.A.	
			Lieut.A.W.DENNISTON, HQ/161, rejoined from hospital.	
	9-12-18.		Lieut.E.COKE, M.C., rejoined from attached 32nd Division Hdqrs.	
	11-12-18.		2/Lieut.R.J.ALLEN, D/161, admitted hospital sick. Lieut-Colonel H.H.HULTON, D.S.O., granted 30 days leave to U.K., under A.G's No.D/2950. Major R.EMMET, D.S.O., B/161, assumed command of Brigade vice Lieut-Colonel H.H.HULTON, D.S.O. 2/Lieut.H.JONES, B/161, attached Fourth Army R.A.Reinforcement Camp.	
	12-12-18.		The Brigade marched to FRAIRE and FAIROUL, passing the starting point in FROIDCHAPELLE at 10.00 hours, and marching via FOURBECHIES, ERPION and WALCOURT, and settled into billets about 16.00 hours. HQ/161, B/161, and D/161, were billeted in FRAIRE; A/161 and C/161 in FAIROUL. Roads were good, but hilly. Rain throughout the day made marching very unpleasant.	Appendix 43.
	13-12-18.		March was continued to ST.GERARD. Leaving FRAIRE at 09.00 hours, the Brigade marched via DONVEAU and CRATE Station, arriving in billets about 15.00 hours. HQ/161 billeted at BOSSIERE, B/161 and D/161 at ST.GERARD, A/161 and C/161 at GRAUX. Roads were good and not hilly. Rain again made marching unpleasant.	Appendix 44.
	14-12-18.		March to NAMUR area completed. The Brigade passed the starting point in ST.GERARD at 08.45 hours, and marching via WEPION and thence along the MEUSE to SAMSON, arrived in billets about 16.00 hours. HQ/161 billeted at SUR-LES-FORGES; A/161, C/161 and D/161 at SAMSON; and B/161 at GOYET.	Appendix 45.
	15-12-18.		2/Lieut.W.S.KIRK rejoined from leave. Batteries settled down in their billeting areas. All men are in comfortable billets, but somewhat scattered, and in some cases, rather far from the Horse Lines. Only 50% of the horses are under cover, but stabling is being proceeded with.	
	16-12-18.		2/Lieut.H.JONES, B/161, rejoined from attached Fourth Army R.A.Reinforcement Camp.	

Sh.2.
Army Form C. 2118.

WAR DIARY

~~INTELLIGENCE~~ SUMMARY.
(Erase heading not required.)

161st (YORKS.) BRIGADE R.F.A.

Instructions regarding War Diaries and Intelligence Summaries are contained in F. S. Regs., Part II. and the Staff Manual respectively. Title pages will be prepared in manuscript.

Place	Date	Hour	Summary of Events and Information	Remarks and references to Appendices
In the Field.	13-12-18 to 20-12-18.		Batteries were occupied with cleaning up and settling down in billets.	
	18-12-18.		Major J.W.BUCKLEY, M.C. D/161, admitted hospital sick.	
	19-12-18.		2/Lieut.H.S.MUNDY, B/161, posted D/161.	
	20-12-18.		2/Lieut.L.A.MOULD, A/161, struck off strength - "Medical Board ordered".	
	21-12-18.		C.R.A., inspected Gun Parks and Horse Lines of all Batteries this morning.	
	22-12-18.		2/Lieut.H.S.MUNDY, D/161, proceeded to X Corps Concentration Camp i/c draft of Coalminers proceeding to England for demobilization.	
	22-12-18 to 24-12-18.		Time devoted to Sports and Recreational Training.	
	25-12-18.		Christmas Day.	
	26-12-18 to 31-12-18		Lectures in French, Agriculture, Typewriting, Shorthand, and Book-keeping, are now in full swing. Attention is also being paid to Sports and Recreational Training.	

R. Quinet,
Major R.F.A.
Commanding 161st (Yorks.) Brigade R.F.A.

HONOURS & AWARDS during month of DECEMBER 1918:

DISTINGUISHED SERVICE ORDER.
Major P.CROW, M.C. A/161.

2nd BAR TO MILITARY CROSS.
Major E.A.CHISHOLM, M.C., late C/161.

THE MILITARY CROSS.
Lieut.R.A.WYRLEY-BIRCH,   D/161.
Lieut.J.G.COONEY,   C/161.
2/Lieut.W.E.WILSON,   A/161.
2/Lieut.A.G.DRYLAND,   B/161.
87058 B.S.M. LAY,F.C.   C/161.

(Continued).

43   Copy No...6...

161st (YORKS.) BRIGADE R.F.A.

MARCH ORDER No.4.

1. The 161st Brigade R.F.A. will march to NAMUR area starting on December 12th, 1918.

2. Billeting parties, composed of 1 Officer and 3 Other Ranks will meet the Adjutant at FROIDCHAPELLE Station at 09.00 hours, 12th instant.

3. ROUTE: FROIDCHAPELLE - FOURBECHIES - ERPION - WALCOURT.

4. WATER & FEED: SILENRIEUX.

5. The Brigade will billet on the night 12th/13th Decr. in FRAIRE and FAIROUL.

6.   MARCH TABLE.

Unit.	Starting Point.	Time.
HQ/161	2nd E in FROIDCHAPELLE.	10.00 hours.
A/161		10.02 hours.
D/161		10.07 hours.
C/161		10.12 hours.
B/161		10.17 hours.

7. ACKNOWLEDGE by waiting orderly (Batteries only).

                                             Captain R.F.A.
11th Dec.1918.   Adjutant, 161st (Yorks.) Brigade R. F. A.

Issued at   hours.

         Copy No.1 - H.Q.,96th Inf.Bde.   6 - War Diary.
              2 - O.C.,A/161.   7 - File.
              3 - O.C.,B/161.   8 -
              4 - O.C.,C/161.
              5 - O.C.,D/161.

44

Copy No...8......

161st (YORKS.) BRIGADE R.F.A.

MARCH ORDER No.5.

1. The 161st (Yorks.) Brigade R.F.A. will continue the march to NAMUR area tomorrow, December 13th.

2. Billeting Parties, as before, will meet the Adjutant at FRAIRE at 08.30 hours.

3. <u>ROUTE</u>: FRAIRE - DONVEAU - CRATE Station - 10 Kilo.Stone GRAUX.

4. <u>WATER & FEED</u>: Between 15 and 18 Kilo. stone, if possible.

5. Batteries will each detail a reliable N.C.O. to proceed with the Billeting parties, to select place for the mid-day halt.

6. The Brigade will billet on the night 13/14th December in ST.GERARD, BOSSIERE - GRAUX.

7. M A R C H   T A B L E.

Unit.	Starting Point.	Time.
HQ/161.	Road Junction, 27 Kilo. stone.	09.00 hours.
B/161.		09.02 hours.
A/161.		09.07 hours.
D/161.		09.12 hours.
C/161.		09.17 hours.

8. ACKNOWLEDGE by waiting orderly (Batteries only).

12th Dec.1918.   Captain R.F.A.
                  Adjutant, 161st (Yorks.) Brigade R.F.A.

Issued at   hours.

        Copy No.1 - H.Q.,32nd D.A   6 - O.C.,C/161.
             2 - H.Q. 96th Inf.Bde.   7 - O.C.,D/161.
             3 - D.A.P.M.   8 - War Diary.
             4 - O.C.,A/161.   9 - File.
             5 - O.C.,B/161.   10 - R.S.M.

45   Copy No......8..

161st(YORKS.) BRIGADE R.F.A.

MARCH ORDER No.6.

1. The 161st Brigade R.F.A. will complete the march to NAMUR area tomorrow, December 14th, 1918.

2. Billeting parties, as before, will meet the Adjutant at Cross Roads at <u>D</u> of ST.GERARD, at 08.30 hours.

3. <u>ROUTE</u>:   ST.GERARD - XXXX WEPION - along MEUSE - SAMSON.

4.   M A R C H   T A B L E.

Unit.	Starting Point.	Time.
HQ/161.	Cross Roads at <u>D</u> in ST.GERARD.	08.45.
C/161.		08.47.
B/161.		08.52.
A/161.		08.57.
D/161.		09.02.

5. ACKNOWLEDGE by waiting orderly (Batteries only).

                                              Captain R.F.A.
13th December 1918.   Adjutant, 161st Brigade R.F.A.

Issued at   hours.

        Copy No.1 - H.Q.,32nd D.A.   6 - O.C.,C/161.
             2 - H.Q.,96th Inf.Bde. 7 - O.C.,D/161.
             3 - D.A.P.M.   8 - War Diary.
             4 - O.C.,A/161.   9 - File.
             5 - O.C.,B/161.   10 - R.S.M.

LANCASHIRE DIVISION
(LATE 32ND DIVN)

161ST BRIGADE R.F.A
JAN - OCT 1919

161st (Yorks.) BRIGADE, R.F.A.

WAR DIARY

FOR PERIOD :—

FROM :— 1st January, 1919.

To :— 31st January, 1919.

Army Form C. 2118.

161st (Yorks.) Brigade R.F.A.

WAR DIARY / INTELLIGENCE SUMMARY

(Erase heading not required.)

Instructions regarding War Diaries and Intelligence Summaries are contained in F. S. Regs., Part II. and the Staff Manual respectively. Title pages will be prepared in manuscript.

Place	Date	Hour	Summary of Events and Information	Remarks and references to Appendices
In the field.	3-1-19.		2/Lieut. A.C.ORYLAND, M.C., B/161, rejoined from leave.	
	4-1-19.		2/Lieut. W.E.WILSON, M.C., A/161, admitted hospital sick.	
NAMECHE AREA	5-1-19.		Major J.W.BUCKLEY, M.C., D/161, granted leave to U.K. until 19-1-19.	
	6-1-19.		Lieut. R.G.JOHNSON, B/161, proceeded to attend second Course at Education School, Trinity College, OXFORD.	
	9-1-19.		2/Lieut. H. JONES, B/161, granted leave to U.K. until 23-1-19.	
	10-1-19.		The following officers proceeded to Xth Corps Concentration Camp for despatch to England for demobilization under Industrial Group 43:- Major P.CROW, D.S.O., M.C., A/161. (attached# HQ/161) 2/Lieut. E.A.WILSON, A/161. 2/Lieut. J.H.G.WAY, C/161.	
			Captain C.T.W.HAFFENDEN, M.C., D/161, proceeded to attend B.C's Course at SHOEBURYNESS commencing 12-1-19. Captain H.BARRETT, C/161, assumed command of D/161 vice Capt. C.L.W.HAFFENDEN, M.C. The Brigade paraded in Marching Order for inspection by the C.R.A.	
	15-1-19.		The Divisional Commander presented Medal Ribands to 4 officers and 14 N.C.O's and men of the Brigade.	
	16-1-19.		Lieut-Colonel H.H.HUTTON, D.S.O., rejoined from leave and resumed command of Brigade. Major R.EMMET, D.S.O., resumed command of B/161.	
	17-1-19.		2/Lieut. T.COZAN, A/161, proceeded to Xth Corps Concentration Camp for despatched to England for Demobilization under Industrial Group 35.	
	18-1-19.		2/Lieut. H.S.NURDY, D/161, rejoined from leave.	
	22-1-19.		Major A.C.L.THEOBALD, posted A/161 from 498th Siege Battery R.G.A.	
	23-1-19.		Major J.W.BUCKLEY, M.C., D/161, rejoined from leave and hospital, and resumed command of D/161.	
	27-1-19.		Lieut. J.G.CLONEY, M.C., C/161 granted leave to U.K. until 10-2-19.	
	29-1-19.		Major J.W.BICKLE, M.C., D/161, attached HQ/161, and assumed duties of Educational and Recreational Officer. Lieut. R.G.JOHNSON, B/161, struck off strength. (Authy: Fourth Army No.G.10 (E).	

Army Form C. 2118.

WAR DIARY 161st (Yorks.) Brigade R.F.A.

INTELLIGENCE SUMMARY.

(Erase heading not required.)

Place	Date	Hour	Summary of Events and Information	Remarks and references to Appendices
In the Field.	30-1-19.		A Route March was held, and inspected by the G.O.C.	
			HONOURS & AWARDS during month of JANUARY 1919:	
			THE DISTINGUISHED CONDUCT MEDAL.	
			19872 Sergeant S. ROWE, D/161.	
			THE MERITORIOUS SERVICE MEDAL.	
			L/19400 Sergeant W. FAULDING, B/161.	
			DEMOBILIZATION.	
			During the month of January 1919, 2 Officers and 88 O.R's proceeded to England for demobilization.	
	2-1-19.			

Moylin
Lieut-Colonel,
Commanding 161st (Yorks.) Brigade R.F.A.

35807. W15879/M1879 500,000 3/17 R.T. (1074) Forms/W3091/3   Army Form W.3091.

Cover for Documents.

Nature of Enclosures.

Notes, or Letters written.

Army Form C. 2118.

Instructions regarding War Diaries and Intelligence Summaries are contained in F. S. Regs., Part II. and the Staff Manual respectively. Title pages will be prepared in manuscript.

WAR DIARY 161st (Yorks) BRIGADE, R.F.A.

or

INTELLIGENCE SUMMARY.

(Erase heading not required.)

Place	Date	Hour	Summary of Events and Information	Remarks and references to Appendices
NAMUR, Belgium.	3-2-1919.		HQ/161 and C/161 entrained at NAMUR, and B/161 at NAMECHE en route for GERMANY.	
	4-2-1919		HQ/161, A/161 and B/161 detrained at BEUEL at about 11.00 hours, and marched to billets near the BEUEL End of BONN Bridge, A/161 at BERLINGHOVEN, and B/161 at VILICH MULDORF.	
GERMANY.	5-2-1919.		C/161 entrained at NAMECHE, and D/161 at NAMUR en route for GERMANY.	
			C/161 and D/161 detrained at BEUEL and marched to billets, C/161 near BEUEL Station, and D/161 at RAUSCHENDORF.	
	6-2-1919		Major J.W.BUCKLEY, M.C. (D/161 attchd. Hdqrs.) proceeded to U.K. independently for Demobilization under Industrial Group 43.	
	10-2-1919.		Capt.A.DARVELL (R.A.C. Chaplain) joined Brigade from 32nd Divnl.Headquarters, and attached to B/161.	
	15-2-1919.		Lieut.R.G. JOHNSON rejoined on completion of Course at Education School, OXFORD, was attached HQ/161, and assumed duties of Education and Sports Officer of the Brigade.	
	15-2-1919.		C/161 provided Gun Carriage, team, and Drivers at the Military Funeral of a R.A.S.C. Driver who was accidentally killed.	
	17-2-1919		Capt.H.L.McCORMICK (R.A.M.C.) proceeded to U.K. on leave until 3-3-19.	
	19-2-1919.		Inspection of the Brigade by the G.O.C., R.A., Second Army. Instructions were received to the effect that during the Inspection the men were to carry on with their ordinary duties.	
			2/Lieut.C.W.BRITTEN (B/161) proceeded to attend Course in Agriculture at G.H.Q. Farms, CORBIE. Lieut.E.COKE, I.C. (HQ/161) proceeded to U.K. on leave until 5-3-19.	
	25-2-1919.		2/Lieut.C.G. CHAPPELL (C/161) proceeded to U.K. (via Nth Corps Concentration Camp) on Draft Conducting duties.	
	26-2-1919		Major A.C.L.THEOBALD (D/161) proceeded to U.K. on leave until 12-3-19	

[signature] Lieut-Colonel.

Commanding 161st (Yorks) Brigade, R.F.A.

WAR DIARY
or
INTELLIGENCE SUMMARY.

(Erase heading not required.)

Army Form C. 2118.

168 Bde R.F.A. Army Vol 31

Instructions regarding War Diaries and Intelligence Summaries are contained in F. S. Regs., Part II. and the Staff Manual respectively. Title pages will be prepared in manuscript.

Place	Date	Hour	Summary of Events and Information	Remarks and references to Appendices
NAMUR.	2/2/19		The Brigade Headquarters and "B" Battery, 168th Brigade, R.F.A. entrained at NAMUR at 4-25 p.m. and proceeded to BONN, GERMANY, at which place they arrived early on the morning of the 3rd. Feb. The Brigade, Headquarters were billeted in the CASTLE KOMMENDE, RAMESDORF. B/168 in RAMESDORF A/168 Brigade, RFA., entrained at NAMECHE at 2 p.m. and "C" Battery at 6 p.m., both Batteries proceeded to BONN, GERMANY, where they arrived early on the 3rd inst. "A" Battery were billeted in KUDINGSHOVEN and "C" Battery in BEUEL.	
RAMESDORF, GERMANY.	3/2/19		"D" Battery, 168th Brigade, RFA., entrained at NAMECHE at 2 p.m. and proceeded to BONN, GERMANY, where they arrived early on the morning of 4th. The Battery was billeted in LIMPERICH.	
	25/2/19		Much work was done to make billets and horse lines comfortable, gun parks were covered where necessary. Reconnaissance of defensive positions for Batteries was carried out. Lectures and sports were arranged.	
	26/2/19		The Brigade was inspected by Major-General BUCKLE, M.G.,R.A., Second Army, who reported satisfactorily on the Brigade.	
	27/2/19 & 28/2/19		The usual Routine work. Recreational Training was carried out.	
	3/3/19			

Commanding, 168th Brigade, Royal Field Artillery.

Lieutenant-Colonel,

(6392) Wt. W6192/P875 1,500,000 4/18 McA & W Ltd (E 2815) Forms W3091/4.   Army Form W.3091.

Cover for Documents.

Nature of Enclosures.

WAR DIARY.

161st (YORKS) Brigade R.F.A.

from.

1/3/19.   to   31/3/19.

Notes, or Letters written.

WAR DIARY

INTELLIGENCE SUMMARY

161st (YORKS.) BRIGADE R.F.A.   Army Form C. 2118.

(Erase heading not required.)

Instructions regarding War Diaries and Intelligence Summaries are contained in F. S. Regs., Part II. and the Staff Manual respectively. Title pages will be prepared in manuscript.

Place	Date	Hour	Summary of Events and Information	Remarks and references to Appendices
Germany.	1-3-19.		Lieut.J.G.GOJNEY, M.C., C/161, rejoined from leave.	
	4-3-19.		Captain C.J.T.HAFFENDEN, M.C., D/161, rejoined on completion of battery Commanders' Course at Shoeburyness	
	5-3-19.		Major R.EMET, D.S.O., B/161, proceeded to England for demobilization.	
	7-3-19.		2/Lieut. L.W.EYKYN posted to Brigade and attached D/161.	
	8-3-19.		Lieut.E.COKE, M.C., B0/161, rejoined from leave.	
			Lieut.F.W.HOOK, D/161, granted leave to U.K until 22-3-19.	
	9-3-19.		48 reinforcements posted to Brigade from 32nd D.A.C.	
	10-3-19.		Major A.C.L.THEOBALD, D/161, struck off strength whilst on leave in U.K. (A.10300.(O).	
	11-3-19.		Lieut.A.JONES, 93rd (Army) Brigade R.F.A. posted A/161 and attached Xth Corps for Educational duties.	
	9-3-19.		Capt. B.C.TRAPPES-LOMAX, M.C., B/161, on leave in U.K. until 2-4-19.	
			2/Lieut.P.W.ALLEN, D/161, proceeded to Xth Corps Concentration Camp on Draft Conducting duties.	
	20-3-19.		Major E.SHERLOCK, M.C., 110th Bde.R.F.A., posted to Bde. and attached A/161.	
	22-3-19.		Lieut-Colonel (Brevet-Colonel) R.G.KEYWORTH, D.S.O., posted to, and assumed command of, Brigade.	
	23-3-19.		2/Lieut.C.G.CHAPPELL, C/161, rejoined from leave.	
	25-3-19.		Lieut-Colonel H.H.HULTON, D.S.O., granted leave to U.K. until 8-4-19.	
	30-3-19.		2/Lieut.F.H.TRINDER, attached D/161 from 315th (Army) Bde.R.F.A.	

DEMOBILIZATION: 7 O.R's proceeded to England for demobilization during the month of March 1919.

O.Heyworth
Colonel,
Commanding 161st (Yorks.) Brigade R.F.A

161st (Yorks.) BRIGADE, R.F.A.

WAR DIARY

COVERING PERIOD

From :- 1st April, 1919.
To :- 30th April, 1919.

Army Form C. 2118.

Instructions regarding War Diaries and Intelligence Summaries are contained in F. S. Regs., Part II. and the Staff Manual respectively. Title pages will be prepared in manuscript.

WAR DIARY 161st (Yorks) Brigade, R.F.A.
or
INTELLIGENCE SUMMARY.
(Erase heading not required.)

Place	Date	Hour	Summary of Events and Information	Remarks and references to Appendices
BEUEL. Germany.	1-4-19.		Lieut.W.R.GOODMAN, MC. (C/161) rejoined from attached 5th Squadron R.A.F.	
	4-4-19.		Capt.T.TAY, (A/161) proceeded on leave to U.K.	
	6-4-19.		Capt.B.C.TRAPPES-LOMAX, MC (B/161) rejoined from leave in U.K.	
	8-4-19.		Capt.A.DARVELL (R.C. Chaplain attchd.B/161) rejoined from leave in France. Capt.A.DARVELL, proceeded to England for Demobilization. Lieut.R.G.JOHNSON (B/161) rejoined from attached HQ/161. Lieut.A.G.DRYLAND, MC (B/161) attached HQ/161.	
	9-4-19.		2/Lieut.F.W.ALLEN (D/161) rejoined from leave to U.K. Lieut.W.R.GOODMAN, MC.(C/161) proceeded on leave to U.K.	
	10-4-19.		2/Lieut.A.J.A.STUBBS, (93rd Bde. RFA) joined 161st Bde. RFA. and posted A/161.	
	12-4-19.		Capt.H.T.McCORMICK, RAMC. (attached HQ/161) proceeded to England. 2/Lieut.H.S.MUNDY (A/161) proceeded on leave to U.K.	
	13-4-19.		Major M.KING-FRENCH (C/161) proceeded to CONCENT, COLOGNE for purpose of Demobilization. Lieut.P.R.HAMILTON, MC. (A/161) proceeded to CONCENT, COLOGNE for purpose of Demobilization. Lieut.S.GRACE (A/108th Bde. RFA) joined 161st Bde.RFA. and posted A/161.	
	14-4-19.		2/Lieut.H.B.RISHWORTH, MC.(Lancs.Divnl.Signal Coy.R.E.) attached HQ/161. Lieut.M.G.BARNETT (joined 161st Bde. RFA. from 2nd Army Reinforcement Camp, and posted B/161. 2/Lieut.L.W.LYNN (D/161) from rejoined from leave in U.K.	
	16-4-19.		Lieut.E.COKE, MC. (HQ/161) proceeded to CONCENT, COLOGNE for purpose of Demobilization. Major R.B WARLON, DSO. (HQ/55th D.A.) joined 161st Bde. RFA. and assumed command of A/161. 2/Lieut.H.B.RISHWORTH, MC. (R.Es) assumed command of Lancs.Divnl.Signal Coy.Sub-section attached to the Brigade, vice Lieut.E.COKE, MC.	
	17-4-19.		Lieut.O.H.HACKFORTH-JONES, MC. (HQ/125 Bde.) joined 161st Bde. RFA. and posted B/161. 2/Lieut.E.D.DREW, (HQ/124 Bde.RFA) joined 161st Bde. RFA. and posted C/161. 2/Lieut.R.P.DUTTON (C/124 Bde.) joined 161st Bde. RFA. and posted C/161.	
	18-4-19.		Capt.T.MAY (A/161) rejoined from Leave in U.K.	
	19-4-19.		Lieut.A.G.DRYLAND (B/161) rejoined B/161 from attached HQ/161. Lieut.O.H.HACKFORTH-JONES, MC.(B/161) attached HQ/161. 2/Lieut.A.J.KINGS.(53rd Bde.RFA) joined 161st Bde.RFA. and posted B/161. Lieut.C.STUART (45th Bde. RFA) joined 161st Bde. RFA. and posted D/161. Capt.C.L.W.HATTENDEN, MC. (D/161) proceeded to CONCENT, COLOGNE for purpose of Demobilization.	
	20-4-19.		2/Lieut.R.HICKS (37th DAC) joined 161st Bde. RFA. and posted B/161.	

Sheet 2 of

WAR DIARY

INTELLIGENCE SUMMARY.

161st (Yorks) Brigade, R.F.A.

Army Form C. 2118.

(Erase heading not required.)

Instructions regarding War Diaries and Intelligence Summaries are contained in F. S. Regs. Part II. and the Staff Manual respectively. Title pages will be prepared in manuscript.

Place	Date	Hour	Summary of Events and Information	Remarks and references to Appendices
Beuel, Germany.	22-4-19.		2/Lieut.E.GILSON (93rd Army Bde.) joined 161st Bde. RFA. and posted D/161.	
	25-4-19.		2/Lieut.C.G.CHAPPELL (C/161) attached HQ/161.	
	25-4-19.		Lieut.A.W.DENNISTON (HQ/161) proceeded on one month's leave to U.K.	
	26-4-19.		Capt.K.V.HAMITSCH, (74th D.A.) joined 161st Bde. RFA. and posted C/161.	
			Lieut.A.G.DRYLAND,MC (B/161) proceeded on Leave to U.K. Lieut.W.R.GOODMAN,MC (C/161) rejoined from Leave in U.K.	
			Capt.& Adjutant C.V.THORNTON (HQ/161) proceeded to CONGENT,COLOGNE for purpose of Demobilization. Lieut.J.G.COOMEY, MC/(C/161) also proceeded to CONGENT,COLOGNE for purpose of Demobilization.	
			Lieut.O.H.HACKFORTH-JONES, MC. assumed duties of Acting Adjutant vice Capt.C.V.THORNTON, and posted to Headquarters, 161st Bde. RFA.	
	27-4-19.		2/Lieut.W.A.PYKE (B/48th Bde.RFA) joined 161st Bde.RFA. and posted C/161.	
			Lieut.E.HARVIE (119th Army Bde) joined 161st Bde. RFA. and posted B/161.	
	28-4-19.		The Brigade was inspected (along with other Divisional Troops) at HANGELAR by G.O.C. Division, as a preliminary to inspection by the Commander-in-Chief, British Army of the Rhine, in the near future.	
	30-4-19.		2/Lieut.F.H.TRINDER (attached A/161) proceeded on Leave to U.K.	
			2/Lieut.A.J.KINGS (B/161) proceeded on leave to U.K.	
			2/Lieut.A.L.WHITE (93rd Army Bde) joined 161st Bde. RFA. and posted D/161.	
			2/Lieut.H.B.RISHWORTH, MC.(R.Es) posted II Corps Signal Coy.R.E.	
			2/Lieut.G.W.BRITTEN (B/161) proceeded to CONGENT, COLOGNE for purpose of Demobilization.	

Personnel proceeded for Demobilization during APRIL 1919:-

Officers....9   Other Ranks.... 333.

Colonel.
Commanding 161st (Yorks) Brigade, R.F.A.

(6392) Wt. W6192/P875 1,500,000 4/18 McA & W Ltd (E 2815) Forms W3091/4.   Army Form W.3091.

Cover for Documents.

Nature of Enclosures.

Notes, or Letters written.

161st (Yorks) Brigade. R.F.A.

WAR
DIARY

COVERING PERIOD :-

From :- 1st May 1919.
To :- 31st May 1919.

Army Form C. 2118.

WAR DIARY
INTELLIGENCE SUMMARY.
(Erase heading not required.)

161st (Yorks) Brigade, R.F.A.

Instructions regarding War Diaries and Intelligence Summaries are contained in F.S. Regs., Part II. and the Staff Manual respectively. Title pages will be prepared in manuscript.

Place	Date	Hour	Summary of Events and Information	Remarks and references to Appendices
BEUEL, Germany.	2-5-19.		A/Capt.H.Barrett, (C/161) proceeded to U.K. on leave.	
	5-5-19.		Colonel R.G.KEYWORTH, DSO. attached Hdqrs. Lancs. Divnl.Artillery, and assumed duties of A/C.R.A. vice Brig-Genl.J.A.TYLER, CMG. to U.K. on Leave.	
	7-5-19.		T/Capt.W.M.MATHESON, DSO. joined 161st Brigade, RFA. and posted to command B/161.	
	11-5-19.		Lieut.F.W.HOOK (D/161) proceeded to England on transfer to Home Establishment. Lieut.N.R.P.HIGHMAN joined Brigade and posted to A/161. A/Major G.L.K.WISELY, MC. joined Brigade and posted to command C/161.	
	12-5-19.		Lieut.A.G.DRYLAND, MC. (B/161) rejoined from Leave to U.K.	
	13-5-19.		2/Lieut.H.S.NUNDY (A/161) rejoined from Leave to U.K. Batteries of this Brigade (along with Divisional Troops) were inspected by Commander-in-Chief of British Army of the Rhine - Genl.Sir W.R.ROBERTSON, GCB.,KCVO.,DSO.,ADC) at HANGELAR Aerodrome.	
	14-5-19.		A/Capt.T.HOGAN joined the Brigade and posted D/161. Major R.B.WARTON, DSO. (A/161) proceeded to U.K. on Leave. 2/Lieut.A.C.HARPER, MC. joined the Brigade and posted to A/161.	
	15-5-19.		Lieut.R.D.RUSSELL, MC. joined the Brigade and posted to C/161. Lieut.E.J.LAWSON joined the Brigade and posted to B/161. 2/Lieut.F.J.VINCENT FERNIE joined the Brigade and posted to C/161. Lieut.M.R.M.JONES joined the Brigade and posted to B/161. Lieut.J.M.TAYLOR joined the Brigade and posted to D/161.	
	16-5-19.		Lieut.J.M.TAYLOR (D/161) admitted Hospital (sick). Lieut.J.T.MACKENZIE joined the Brigade and posted to D/161. 2/Lieut.F.H.TRINDER (A/161) rejoined from Leave to U.K. 2/Lieut.A.J.KINGS (B/161) also rejoined from Leave.	
	17-5-19.		Capt.H.BARRETT (C/161) rejoined from Leave to U.K.	
	18-5-19.		Informal Inspection of Brigade by General BUCKLE, Lancs.Division. M G R A Army of the Rhine	
	20-5-19.		Lieut.E.G.SINNOTT R.E. attached Brigade from Lancs.Divnl.Signal Coy.R.E. as Signal officer.	
	21-5-19.		2/Lieut.W.A.PYKE (C/161) proceeded to U.K. on Leave.	
	22-5-19.		2/Lieut.W.A.PYKE (C/161), Lieut.C.STUART (D/161) and Lieut.M.R.M.JONES (B/161) posted to Lancs.D.A.C.	
	23-5-19.		Major R.B.WARTON DSO. (A/161) rejoined from Leave to U.K. Colonel R.G.KEYWORTH, DSO. rejoined from attached Hdqrs. Lancs.Divnl.Artillery.	
	24-5-19.		Lieut.J.E.GOODE (Ox.& Bucks.L.I.) attached to the Brigade as Educational Instructor.	
	26-5-19.		Lieut.A.B.DYKE joined the Brigade and posted to A/161.	
	27-5-19.		2/Lieut.F.J.VINCENT FERNIE (C/161) proceeded to U.K. on Leave.	
			(Continued)	

Army Form C. 2118.

WAR DIARY 161st (Yorks) Brigade, R.F.A.
INTELLIGENCE SUMMARY.
(Erase heading not required.)

Instructions regarding War Diaries and Intelligence Summaries are contained in F. S. Regs., Part II. and the Staff Manual respectively. Title pages will be prepared in manuscript.

Place	Date	Hour	Summary of Events and Information	Remarks and references to Appendices
BEUEL. Germany.	28-5-19.		Lieut.B.B.WATCHORN,MC. joined the Brigade and posted to C/161.	
	29-5-19.		Lieut.K.P.SAWYER joined the Brigade and posted to A/161.	
	30-5-19.		A/Capt.K.V.HANITSCH (C/161) proceeded to U.K. on Leave. Lieut.S.GRACE (A/161) proceeded to	
	31-5-19.		Lieut.E.HARVIE (B/161) proceeded to U.K. on Leave. CONCENT, COLOGNE for Demobilization.	

M Harper Lt
for
Colonel.
Commanding 161st (Yorks) Brigade, R.F.A.

(6392) Wt. W6192/P875 1,500,000 4/18 McA & W Ltd (E 2815) Forms W3091/4. Army Form W.3091

Cover for Documents.

Nature of Enclosures.

Notes, or Letters written.

Army Form C. 2118.

WAR DIARY
INTELLIGENCE SUMMARY
(Erase heading not required.)

161st (Yorks) BRIGADE, R.F.A.

Instructions regarding War Diaries and Intelligence Summaries are contained in F.S. Regs., Part II. and the Staff Manual respectively. Title pages will be prepared in manuscript.

Place	Date	Hour	Summary of Events and Information	Remarks and references to Appendices
BEUEL Germany.	1-6-19.		Lieut.(A/Capt) H.C.TERRY posted and joined D/161 from 57th Btty.RFA.	
	2-6-19.		2/Lieut.E.D.DREW (C/161) proceeded on leave to U.K.	
	3-6-19.		2/Lieut.A.J.A.STUBBS (A/161) proceeded on leave to U.K.	
	4-6-19.		Lieut.K.P.SAWYER (A/161) awarded Military Cross in Peace Honours List.	
	6-6-19.		2/Lieut.C.G.CHAPPELL (C/161 att: HQ/161) proceeded on leave to U.K.	
	6-6-19.		2/Lieut.F.H.TRINDER (A/161) attached R.A.Reception Camp. Lieut.A.W.DENNISTON (HQ/161) rejoined from leave.	
	7-6-19		2/Lieut.C.G.CHAPPELL (C/161) posted HQ/161 as Orderly Officer. Lieut.A.W.DENNISTON (HQ/161) posted B/161 and ceased to perform duties of Orderly Officer.	
	9-6-19.		Major C.E.F.GAITSKELL joined Brigade from 4.A. Reserve Brigade RFA. and attached HQ/161.	
	12-6-19.		2/Lieut.F.J.VINCENT FERNIE (C/161) rejoined from leave. 2/Lieut.F.H.TRINDER (A/161 attached R.A.R.Camp Cologne) attached "Cologne Post" 2/Lieut.L.W.EKKYN (D/161) admitted Hospital, sick.	
	13-6-19.		Lieut.(A/Capt) H.C.TERRY (D/161) attached HQ/Lancs.Divnl.Artillery as A/Staff Captain. Lieut.N.R.P.HIGHMAN (A/161) attached R.A.Reception Camp, Cologne.	
	15-6-19.		Lieut.E.HARVIE (B/161) rejoined from leave. Lieut.J.E.GOODE (11th Ox.& Bucks.L.I. att: HQ/161 as Brigade Educational Instructor) proceeded on leave to U.K. Lieut.(A/Capt) K.V.HANITSCH (C/161) rejoined from leave.	
	16-6-19.		Lieut.M.G.BARNETT (B/161) proceeded on leave to U.K. 2/Lieut.F.H.TRINDER (A/161 att: "Cologne Post") admitted Hospital, sick.	
	17-6-19.		Lieut.(A/Capt) T.KAY (A/161); Lieut.(A/Capt) B.C.TRAPPES-LOMAX, MC. (B/161); Lieut. (A/Capt) H.BARRETT, MC. (C/161); Lieut.A.G.DRYLAND, MC. (B/161); Lieut.W.R.GOODMAN,MC (C/161); and 2/Lieut.H.S.NUNDY (B/161) proceeded to England, in accordance with British Army of the Rhine Letter No.A.305/2055(O2) dated 6-6-19. 2/Lieut.E.D.DREW (C/161) rejoined from leave.	
	18-6-19.		rejoined from leave. The 161st (Yorks) Brigade, R.F.A. concentrated at NIEDER PLEIS in accordance with instructions received from 3rd Manchester Infantry Brigade, in order to be prepared to advance in the event of the Germans not signing the Peace Terms.	
NIEDER PLEIS	20-6-19.		2/Lieut.C.G.CHAPPELL (H/161) rejoined from leave.	
	21-6-19 to		HQ/161 and Batteries still at NIEDER PLEIS. Much rain during this time.	
	23-6-19.			
	24-6-19.		Lieut.B.B.WATCHORN, MC. (C/161) posted and joined A/161.	
	25-6-19.		The Brigade was inspected by Major-Genl.H.L.REED, VC.,CB.,CMG (G.R.A. Xth Corps), Major-Genl.Sir H.S.JEUDWINE, KCB.(Commanding Lancashire Division) and Brig-Genl.J.A.TYLER,CMG. 2/Lieut.F.H.TRINDER rejoined "Cologne Post" from hospital.	

Army Form C. 2118.

WAR DIARY
or
INTELLIGENCE SUMMARY.
(Erase heading not required.)

Instructions regarding War Diaries and Intelligence Summaries are contained in F. S. Rgs., Part II. and the Staff Manual respectively. Title pages will be prepared in manuscript.

Place	Date	Hour	Summary of Events and Information	Remarks and references to Appendices
NIEDER PLEIS. Germany.	27-6-19.		B/161 and C/161 left NIEDER PLEIS and returned to BILICH MULLDORF and BEUEL respectively and occupied billets vacated by them on 'J' minus 1 day. Lieut.R.D.RUSSELL,MC. (C/161) proceeded on short leave to U.K. Lieut.E.J.LAWSON (B/161) proceeded on leave to U.K. Major C.E.F.GAITSKELL posted and joined HIGHLAND Divisional Artillery.	
	28-6-19. 29-6-19.		News that Peace Terms had been satisfactorily signed at 16.00 hours, received. HQ/161 returned to BEUEL and occupied billets vacated on 'J' minus 1 day. Lieut.O.H. HACKFORTH JONES, MC. (A/Adjutant) proceeded on leave to U.K. 2/Lieut.C.G.CHAPPELL (HQ/161) assumed duties as A/Adjutant. Lieut.B.B.WATCHORN, MC. (A/161) attached HQ/161 and assumed duties as Brigade Orderly Officer.	
BEUEL.	30-6-19.		A/161 and D/161 returned to SIEGBURG MULLDORF and occupied billets vacated by them on 'J' minus 1 day.	

B.C.Chinne
2/Lieut.
for Colonel.
Commanding 161st (Yorks) Brigade, R.F.A.

Army Form C. 2118.

WAR DIARY 161st (Yorks) BRIGADE, R.F.A.

INTELLIGENCE SUMMARY.

(Erase heading not required.)

Instructions regarding War Diaries and Intelligence Summaries are contained in F.S. Regs., Part II. and the Staff Manual respectively. Title pages will be prepared in manuscript.

Place	Date	Hour	Summary of Events and Information	Remarks and references to Appendices
BEUEL. Germany.	1-7-19.		2/Lieut.PIRIE (219th Coy.R.E.) attached A/161 for Course of Instruction. Lieut.M.G. BARNETT (B/161) rejoined from leave in U.K.	
	3-7-19.		Major E.SHERLOCK,MC (D/161) proceeded to U.K. on leave. Lieut.R.D.RUSSELL,MC. (C/161) rejoined from leave in U.K.	
	4-7-19.		2/Lieut.A.L.WHITE (D/161) attached R.A. Reception Camp, COLOGNE for duty.	
	5-7-19.		2/Lieut.R.HICKS (B/161) proceeded on leave to U.K. Lieut.M.G.BARNETT (B/161) proceeded to England under Rhine Army Letter No.A.563/4 (O2) dated 10-6-19.	
	7-7-19.		Colonel R.G.KEYWORTH, DSO. (Cmdg. Bde.) proceeded to PARIS in command of Rhine Army R.A. Detachment in Peace March. Lieut.J.M.TAYLOR (D/161) evacuated to England (sick) and struck off strength.	
	8-7-19.		Lieut.K.P.SAWYER, MC. (A/161) proceeded to U.K. on leave.	
	10-7-19.		Lieut.P.W.ALLEN (D/161) proceeded to U.K. on leave.	
	12-7-19.		2/Lieut.L.W.FLYNN (D/161) proceeded to U.K. on leave. Capt.(A/Major) G.L.K.WISELY,MC. (C/161) proceeded to PARIS on leave until 16-7-19; also Lieut.B.B.WATCHORN,MC. (A/161), Lieut.E.G.SINNOTT, R.E.(att:HQ./161) and Lieut.J.E.GOODE (Cx.& Bucks) L.I.Att.HQ/161) to PARIS on leave until 15-7-19.	
	15-7-19.		Lieut.E.J.LAWSON (B/161) rejoined from leave in U.K.	
	16-7-19.		Lieut.(A/Capt) H.C.TERRY (D/161) rejoined from leave in U.K. and attached HQ/Lancs.D.A. as A/Brigade Major.	
	17-7-19.		Capt.(A/Major) G.L.K.WISELY, MC. (C/161) rejoined from leave in PARIS. Lieut.(A/Capt) & Adjutant O.H.BACKFORTH-JONES, MC.rejoined from leave in U.K.	
	18-7-19.		Lieut.B.B.WATCHORN, MC. rejoined A/161 from attached HQ/161. Colonel R.G.KEYWORTH. DSO. rejoined from PARIS (Peach March).	
	21-7-19.		Major E.SHERLOCK, MC. (D/161) rejoined from leave in U.K.	
	22-7-19.		2/Lieut.R.HICKS (B/161) rejoined from leave in U.K.	
	23-7-19.		Lieut.K.P.SAWYER, MC. (A/161) rejoined from leave in U.K.	
	25-7-19.		Lieut.R.D.RUSSELL, MC. (A/161) re-posted and joined C/161. Lieut.PIRIE (219 Coy.R.E.att: A/161) rejoined Unit.	
	26-7-19.		Lieut.P.W.ALLEN (D/161) rejoined from leave in U.K.	
	27-7-19.		Lieut.B.B.WATCHORN, MC. (A/161) proceeded to attend B.C's Course at SHOEBURYNESS. A/Capt. T.HOGAN (D/161) proceeded on leave to U.K.	
	28-7-19.		2/Lieut.F.J.VINCENT FERNIE (C/161) rejoined from leave in BELGIUM.	
	29-7-19.		2/Lieut.L.W.FLYNN (D/161) proceeded on leave to U.K. Major E.SHERLOCK,MC (D/161) on leave to U.K. prior to proceeding to CONSTANTINOPLE for service with Russian Force.	
	30-7-19.		Lieut.J.T.MACKENZIE (D/161) proceeded on leave to U.K.	

[signature] Captain.
for Colonel.
Commanding 161st (Yorks) Brigade, R.F.A.

Army Form C. 2118.

WAR DIARY
of
161st (Yorks) BRIGADE, R.F.A.
INTELLIGENCE SUMMARY.

(Erase heading not required.)

Instructions regarding War Diaries and Intelligence Summaries are contained in F. S. Regs., Part II. and the Staff Manual respectively. Title pages will be prepared in manuscript.

Place	Date	Hour	Summary of Events and Information	Remarks and references to Appendices
BEUEL. Germany.	15-8-19.		Nothing of interest to report for AUGUST, except:-	
			A successful Impromptu Race Meeting was held at HANGELAR.	

M'dewolfur
for Major.
Commanding 161st (Yorks) Brigade, R.F.A.

Army Form C. 2118.

WAR DIARY
~~of~~
INTELLIGENCE SUMMARY.

161st (Yorks) BRIGADE, R.F.A.

(Erase heading not required.)

Instructions regarding War Diaries and Intelligence Summaries are contained in F. S. Regs., Part II. and the Staff Manual respectively. Title pages will be prepared in manuscript.

Place	Date	Hour	Summary of Events and Information	Remarks and references to Appendices
BEUSI, Germany.			Nothing of interest to report for month of SEPTEMBER, 1919. *[signature]* Captain. for Colonel. Commanding 161st (Yorks) Brigade, R.F.A.	

Army Form C. 2118.

WAR DIARY 161st (Yorks) Brigade, R.F.A.

~~INTELLIGENCE SUMMARY~~

(Erase heading not required.)

Instructions regarding War Diaries and Intelligence Summaries are contained in F. S. Regs., Part II. and the Staff Manual respectively. Title pages will be prepared in manuscript.

Place	Date	Hour	Summary of Events and Information	Remarks and references to Appendices
Beuel, Germany.	28-10-19,		Nothing of interest to report during month of OCTOBER 1919 except:- All remaining personnel due for demobilization were sent to Concentration Camp by 28-10-19. Retainable personnel and Volunteers posted to 187th Brigade, R.F.A., 50th and 51st Brigades, R.F.A. on disbandment of 161st (Yorks) Brigade, R.F.A. Colonel R.G.KEYWORTH, DSO, proceeded to command of 187th Brigade, R.F.A. A/Major W.M.MATHESON, DSO, MC., (B/161) posted to 197th Brigade, R.F.A. A/Captain T.HOGAN (D/161) posted to 50th Brigade, R.F.A. Lieut.E.HARVIE (B/261) posted to 50th Brigade, R.F.A. All other Officers are being demobilized with exception of four who are remaining in charge of stores etc. at Lancs,Divnl,Railhead Dump.	

[signature]

Captain.
for Major,
Commanding 161st (Yorks) Brigade, R.F.A.

WAR DIARY
281st Brigade RFA
25 Sept 1918 – 13 Aug 1919

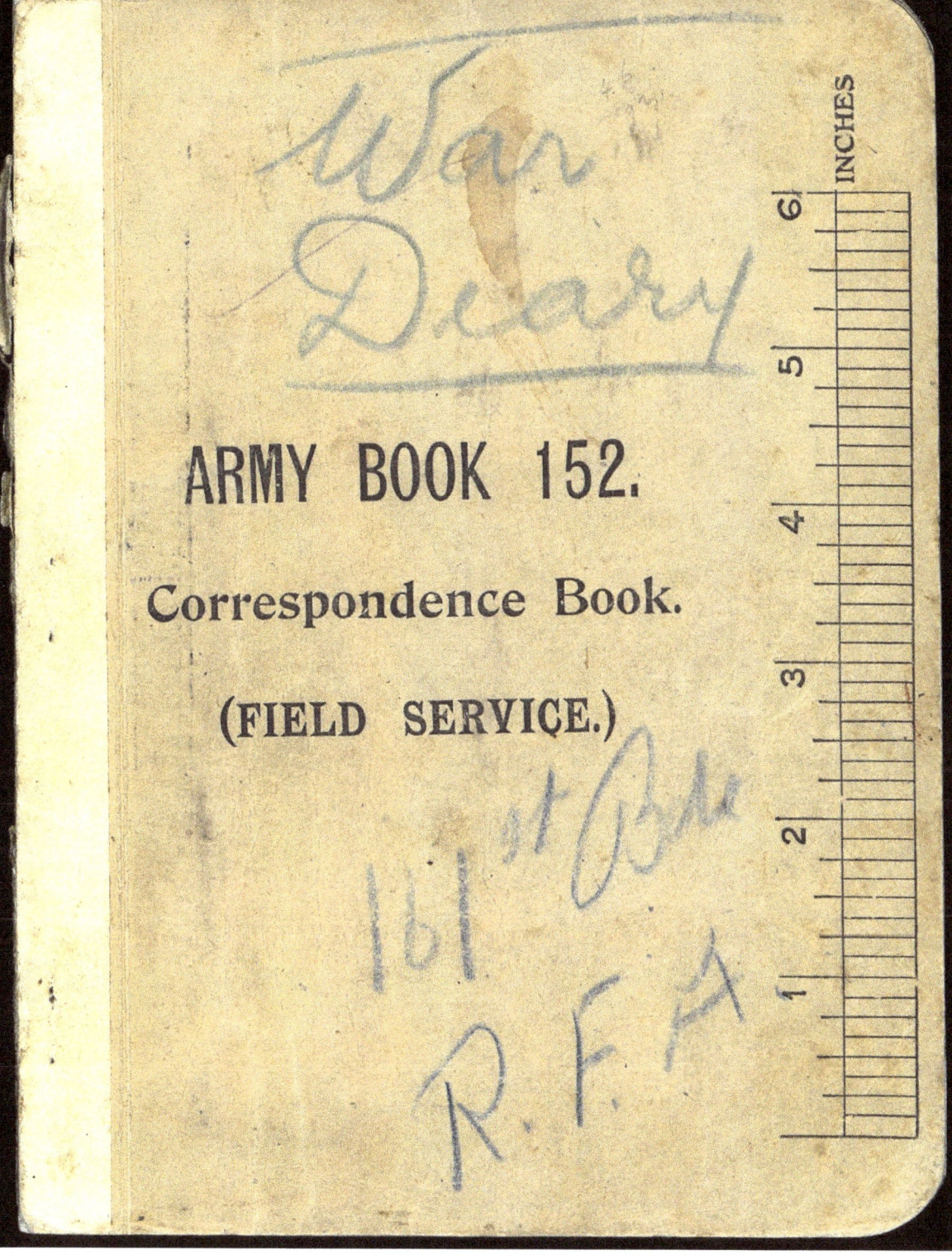

additional instructions which were for Coys. for attack at RAISINS of Coy Commanders to be at BRIGADE H.Q. at mean & to meet own advd gps into action in support of the 46th Div. Personnel were as follows — Coy fitters
A/161 — L.35 & 70 & 67
B/161 — L.35 - 6 & 32
C/161 — L.35 & 45
D/161 — L.35 & 14

At 4:45 p.m. letter (copy) at Annexure "E" was received from the D.A.E. as their positions & so far as its (the worm) & the position during the day as at page —
Tonight Men not up HQ AREA
For the Kings link 13 rue
3rd Ech Rue Louis (designated 33)
AOO at Bon Dieu
HQ Coy & D & G Secs
4 Staff & WMTC the Lorries was obviously supposed to be improved
End up under heavy shell and in considerable & rough...
not shelled. Some future
of the Gap was made...
much delayed that the observed of the Est.Ed...
working till last

27th Major R. Grant R.E. 21/9/61
(Granted leave to UK until)

28th 4th E.R. Watson 21/9/61
proceeded to attend General
at South Army City, course
commencing 29-9-17

28th - Also worked on new positions
during the day & were attacked
again for S barbarous from 'D' Co.
spent the day preparing gaps in
the enemy wire west of the CANAL
at G28 & 93 + G34 & 88 , & A ,
B & C Coys on these gaps
during the night (see appendix 22)
Instructions were issued that
the intermediate positions to be
occupied the following day were
to be in G21 & not as previously
ordered.

29th The 46th Div on a bus rate
first attacked the HINDENBURG LINE
at 5.50 am at the time &
until 11 am. there was a thick
mist so dense that it was
not possible to see an object
even 5 yards away.
The attack met with great
success the CANAL being crossed
at an 'early down & the Brigade
of the 46 & being assembled in good
time.
Non 18th Div. took part in the
great push off the Bavarian from
the positions in L35. first
their guns rule great difficulty
owing to the mist about the...

They received orders to take up
positions in G 21 & the following
were occupied

A/161 G 21 d 4 0
B/161 G 21 d 6 2
C/161 G 21 d 3 9
D/161 G 27 b 6 8

The enemy shewn the approach
to these positions when Battns
moved up, & A had one plateon
killed & C two wounded while
several horses were killed &
wounded.

"C" Bh were ordered up.
The CANAL & kept in close support
of the BORDERS. A & forward
Coys & Batt (paltforms) were supported
the R. D. F. of 3 Div to go across
Canal in support of 86 A & S. H.
(the 1st) in support) while "D"
was H Coy. in afternoon
All Battns had orders the
CANAL by the & & the following
positions were taken up

A/161 G 29 b 9 1
B/161 G 30 a 5 5
C/161 G 30 a 4 5
D/161 G 29 b 9 3
HQ/161 G 29 d 3 9
Bn 33 a Dw were ord

getting but broken + hardly
for a convergence of the
enemy to the 4th SC Dun
could not live exposed to
the future extent of the enemy
for the right roughes in the
place where the 16th Ind had
captured. She was not wholly
carried by the Catherine of
their assault but lambed in
the account of there flank being
"in the air" the extreme left
being in or incorrect
position prompted accumulate
throughout the night as the
was frequently called up on
to find her the hospital if an
the emergency of the horses he
drew (see above) for the
accounts of were while they
had lived here called upon
to do + the wounded when of
the Jowers and hearing Officers
with that hired mail they
supported
30 °
Also my army the day +
night be frequent call from
the Infanty to go to help
the now presente lost

have to put a gap between
the 27th Inf Bgd & the
Australians, who were on our
left. They attacked with
the A. & S. H. (of the 97th Inf Bgd)
& 6 new VICKERS from the South,
but the individual parties
of the A & S H bring 2 officers
+ about 40 ORs who they say
too far forward captured an
attempt to take LEVERGIE area
failed. South of the Canal
the 1st Sur. Inn. took TALANA
HILL & the high ground East
of THORIGNY.

6/10/18 1st The Australians attacked
JONCOURT from the North, and at
6.30 am they reported that they
in possession of it. The 97th
Infantry Bde. Also reported that
they had LEVERGIES.
At 4.0 pm Bahams fired
a barrage in support of an
attack by the 2/MANCHESTERS on
the FONSOMME LINE between H.19 d
+ H.19 a. The attack was entirely
successful and all objectives
were gained
The enemy hardly barraged
this line after they had lost it

the house of the shelling coming from the Catr of RAMECOURT. The Manc engage this awn & silenced the enemy batteries. The enemy was repulsed at 8.0 [am] trying to push again a Counter attacks of 2 [Lieut] + D Coy and 2 [platoons] of 1 + 17 Rif Bde were put in + the attempt was stopped.

2.0 The enemy heavily attacked our new positions in the FONSOMME Line during the night + drove the MANCHESTERS back. The MANCHESTERS shortly afterwards regained the Trenches but the Enemy Counter attacked again + drove them in possession of them. A further attack by the MANCHESTERS was Successful and at dawn my Bn [Battalion] was in possession of the Line at 8.30 am we put down a barrage in support of the dept [departure?] and the Line was pushed forward slightly. The 16th L.F. Reg [Regiment] was heavy Casualties in the operation and Litn [Lieut?] the C.O being amongst the Killed.

Battries [Batteries] knocked the [unclear]

during the night (see appendices 23} she 96th infantry Bn +24) relieved during the night by the 139th Infantry Bde.

3rd Btn fired a barrage in (15 am) support of an attack by the 139th Bde on FRAMECOURT. The attack was very successful at first and the Fusiliers were really later on it was found that the enemy were counter attacking and our troops were brought back some distance. The Artillery were called up when it was seen that the success of the morning could be exploited but they did not arrive until late afternoon when it was too late the enemy having then reorganised his force.

Batteries all moved forward to positions as follows:—
A/61. H 20 c 96.15
B/61. H 26 b 40 5.80
C/61. H 21 a 50 0.30
D/61. H 20 d 45.60

Btn. harassed the enemy during the night on points selected by the Infantry. During the day Btn fired

on arrival came from the Signal Station fires lit several times at the request of the Infantry and on movements, and reports batteries. The enemy was equally observant during the day. Immediately firing on any movement seen. The day passed off quietly. At night fires lit along the line of the advanced troops and at Shalangot received instructions for a barrage to morrow.

4 H.

On S.6.5 and 8 of the Advanced Trenches attacked MANEQUIN HILL A, B, C, put down a creeping barrage & fired down a protective barrage. The attack was only partly successful, the enemy working forward on the Shalangot of the White I and the Shalangot through heavy cascades from M.G. + aimed fire

6 H.

Also received fresh man instructions for moving forward in preparation for the centipede attack by the Infantry of the 6th Division. They were all open the x graves H 27, 23, 28 & 29 SW

6/10/16
Lieut E.W. Clark 38th promoted Leave to UK until 12 of October

the positions. B Co. reinforced
B positions during the afternoon as
follows —
A/161 H 28.6 70.65
B/161 H 28.6 39.44
C/161 H 2.d 54
D/161 H 2 & C 6.9

200 rounds of ammunition per gun
were brought up to these positions
at night. Bties were given
instructions to bring their guns
up the following day to the position
at light over the 139th Infantry
Ide. [ooR] near the line from the
14th to 97th Infantry Ides (see
appendix ??)

6th At 11 a.m. Bties received
instructions to postpone bringing
their guns forward for 24 hour.
The day passed off quietly.
Bties wheel instructed to withdraw
the dumps at forward positions
to 4.50 per gun.
At night Bties harnessed the
enemy.

7th During the day Bties brought
their guns forward, we Bty at
a trot, being in road at
Bties arrived finds instructions
for the barrage to be fired

the following morning (see appendices 26
& 27). The day was very quiet
every thing without shelling.
Rhins fell in large in the
dawn at night, no other new
features.
8th. The 6th Division as part of the
IX Corps attacked at 5.10 am
The objective being a line running
East of BRANCOURT & BEAUREGARD.
The 16th & 18th RBs were part of
the RIGHT group which consisted of
the 16th & 18th (first commands) 16th & 2nd
KRRC Rifle Bgde. There was no
attack immediately South of the
6th Div. but the Americans
attacked on our left.
The attack was successful
the objective being obtained,
in good time. At 6 am it
was apparent that there was little
enemy shelling or M.G. fire
& that no counter had gone up.
At 7.55 am the 71st Bgde. the
reported that they had soon
Capt. & 300 prisoners and were
who received about the same
time that the Americans were
meeting with resistance and
that 6 1st Bgde. Bn. had sent

a Battn. to whom acceptance at 7ᵗʰ Div. message was received that the Front line had pushed up the ridge. At 10 a.m. we received orders to fire on the position. Arrange for me to have at 10.45 D. fire on a M.G. at H.30.d.95. which was holding up the WEST YORKS. Later on the latter with 3 Coys. attacked MANNEQUIN WOOD at 11.55 am the advance was 10.00ᵗ west of BRANCOURT at 12.35 p.m. the line was observed in the Trenches in 4.3.c & 13.6. "B" Bot. am observed shot on them in the afternoon it was reported that MANNEQUIN WOOD was in our hands & that the enemy was retreating hurriedly. Few casualties however were known to afford kind assistance at night. As we advanced being in MEDICOURT which was far from the enemy although but yet in our possession (the appendix 28)

9ᵗʰ Bn. Commander reminded his division to cover the Railway East of FRESNOY, at night the Adv. moved to the hedges lines under it's/line arrangement

10.- The Brigade moved to the neighbourhood of LADENCOURT. Bridge parties so far as now:—

P.H.Q — R 9 & 83
A/161 R 7 & 96
B/161 R 4d 54
C/161 R 16 & 39
D/161 R 17 & 20

11" at 10 a.y. the Brigade was inspected by the G.O.C. Div in a field near C H.Q. It's begat some huge for Saulat his accompanied by for for for Taylor and review of the Staff. He expressed his appreciation of the work of the Bde during the recent strenuous period of fighting when the Bde had been engaged for two months almost continuously in advanced guard fighting. Some chival for front & rearguard dies by that Column were very heavily given.

13.A. Pilots carried out their own programme of training.

13.B. All his civilised. Pilot training Bty to gain live work rested by H. Corps Horse army

14/10/16

14h Orders were received at 12.30 am for the Bde to move up in support of the 6th Bde. In the morning the Brigade & Battery Commanders went forward and positions were arrived as follows:-

A/161 - V24c Q5.30.
B/161 - V24d Q5.90
C/161 - V24a Q5.45
D/161 - V23b Q5.40

The Batteries moved up to BRANCOURT in the morning and were located as follows:-

H.Q./161 - C28a 6.5
A/161 - C28a 5.7.
B/161 - C28a 0.0.
C/161 - C28a 7.3.
D/161 - C28a 45-80.

Ammunition was brought up by B & D Btys at night

15th Btys brought up ammunition during the night. Further instructions were issued by 6th DA (see Appendix 33/31/3)

16th Btys moved their guns into action during the afternoon and receiving further instructions for the barrage after attack by 33rd & 37th Divs attacked H.Q. moved to V23 c 45.00.

17th The Infantry of 6th Divsion

18/10/16

Lieut Robertson 2/7/11 leave to UK until 26/10/16

19/10/16

L/Cpl Megroyan from leave.

19/10/16 Lt R Cole Megroyan from leave. Left for King Corps.
Capt de Jephson Lomax granted leave to UK until 29/11/16
Lt Col LB Joll MC Lt fieldrs D30 granted leave to UK until 28/10/16

Major GA Afghalow R.E. assumed command of Bde etc.

14/9/16 Major R. Barnet D.S.O returned from leave and assumed command of 2nd Poser. 2d Bhotpal resumed command of B Coy.

attacked at 5.20 am. They met but a few remnants of Germans at first and arrived the RED DOTTED line in good time. The 1st Dur in going through them met with enormous opposition and were slow in moving up. In the afternoon it was reported that they had reached the RED line which was their first objective. The enemy made several counter-attacks during the day and contested the ground hotly. A large number of prisoners & several M.G. were taken.

The 161st Bde were included in the RIGHT GROUP (2nd & 5th, 161st & 298th Bdes)

The 164 & Bde fired the barrage up to the RED line from their present positions and at 0+270 moved forward to positions from which they cried fire the barrage for the GREEN line (the final objective of the 1st Div) as follows:-

A/161 - W 21 d 4.7
B/161 - W 28 a 7.8
C/161 - W 22 a 5-7
D/161 - W 28 a 4.6

When these positions were occupied the division were less than 1000ᵡ East of the Infantry had not made the progress expected. The barrage for the GREEN line was fired in time, but the Infantry were not in touch at the appointed time and consequently were unable to take advantage of the barrage. At night our line roughly ran –

ANDIGNY – BLANCS FOSSES – MALASSISE Farm.

18th. Orders were issued for a barrage to be fired in support of the 1st Div. Infantry who were attacking at 11.30 am. The start line was from F4C 05 – X19a 00 & the objective from F4C 05 – X22 c 00 – X21 b 50 A/161 took the right ½ of line & B/161 left ½. 4/161 was superimposed upon A/161 & came out of range when c/161 took up the task. B/161 fired 200ᵡ short of 18 pr line. The attack was very successful. At 12.45 pm it was reported that the CAMERONS were in touch with WELSH at Caulnay in X.19.c and that BLACK WATCH were being relieved in X.25.b and that part moved

opposition had their communications of plans our infantry moved beyond the objective as far as the Canal the line at night running through WASSIGNY and RIBEAUVILLE

19th At 9am it was reported that 1st Rns Huss had BLOCUS D'EN HAUT where in touch with Scouts. There was WASSIGNY cemetery & along road to RIBEAUVILLE where in touch with Americans Patrols went out in X23 & all along the front 16 ½ Bde were warned to be prepared to advance to positions to cover the Canal between S1630 to M3100. at 9.60 am 2nd & 5th Bdes were ordered to reconnoitre positions and 16 ½ Bde to remain for the present in a position in READINESS. At night Brigades were as follows:- Right front 1st DA. as follows:- Right front 25 & 39. 19 the REA. left front 16 & 168, 5th & 98 Bdes under command of CRA 32nd Div.

20th Orders were issued verbally by CRA 32nd DA to O.C. Brigades that hurried to get Bde in position as soon as possible to left group

were responsible for covering left
Infantry Bde front from 2 pm
1630. 2nd Bdes were allowed left
half + 168ª + 298ª Ratio the right
half of front zone. Bt. Bde.
and B C[?] at L'ARBRE DE GUISE
and ordered Batteries to assemble
at base at Remaigne in X13a.
(Rations for 1645 Bde were deliver
as follows
    A/161. - R31C 90
    B/161. - X.1 & Central
    C/161. - X.1 & 28.
    D/161. - X1a 70.75.
Night Hrs located for the right
at W10.6.05.95. My himself
spent the night with 2nd half
Bde at X13a16.
at night front line ran —
S21a06 along MAZINGHIEN road
to X4C25 thence X4a20 - X4a35 -
X3b78 - R33b70 - R33b85 20 -
R=70.95.50.
Bdes found 150 n.b. for Ptz w
LA HAIE TONNOILE Farm + Communication
at the request of GOC 2nd
Inf. Bde.
21ˢᵗ MQ moved to X13a16, the MQ
of the 1ˢᵗ Infantry Bde. This
(anvil) out harassing fire at "

on LA HAIE TONNOILE Fm & the attack of CATILLON regiment of GOC 1st Infanty Bde. (the Battn. receiving preparatory orders 38) instructions for the barrage to be fired on as shown & of the 2nd Bn (see appendices 36 & 37)

20/10/18 Instructions were issued for the barrage to be fired in support of following morning in support of the 1st Inf Bde at the assault of GOC 1st Bn from before the barrage on LA HAIE TONNOILE Farm.

23rd Infantry attack at 1.20 am (by moonlight) the objective being the high ground inc R 23 a v c, R 29 a, R 30 & R 35. The attack was successful and the objective was reached in good time. Our enemy were met with but a heavy barrage was put down shortly after the attack opened, & the Chenette were somewhat heavy. The enemy gained the Railway and French to the barrage, which had to be fired in gas. Their Catala made out Bizardi objective and reached the Canal at CATILLON where they found the bridge in good order. They

20/10/18 At Aus Semeters granted Leaves extended 5/11/18

23/10/18 At 10th Ordnance W/S Railed Issue to Trench dated 6/11/18
Cpl 10R Hamilton M.C. + others

temporarily withdrew to obtain
Ascendant, but in the meantime
the enemy had reoccupied CATILLON
and had posted M.G. at the
Western & Northern Entrances
to the village. Subsequently the
enemy blew up the bridge over
the Canal
    At night the Div. Artillery
was disposed S.E. of the spring line
of the line. The left front
two Coys of 16th & 6th
Divs under the order of Lt
Col. Rhe. At night the 1st &
3rd Bns of Rhe were relieved
by the 2nd of Rhe on the Divisional
front being held by two
Battalions.

24th Quiet day. Artillery again
     regrouped. Left group June
     ... taken over by 39th
     Bde (1st D.A.) Rlys moved to
     their wagon lines (See Appendix 30)
     Lt. Col. Keith relinquished
     7 days special leave & assumed
     Command of the Brigade.
25th Battalions engaged in cleaning up
     rest & recreation
26th C Battery shelled by H.V. and moved
     to W 9 a 8.9. Two casualties

25/10/18 O/C & Lieuts & gun parties
leave to UK ended 5/11/18
Lieut
Major R Emmett DSO
assumed command of Bty.

26/10/18 Capt & A/Maj EJ Roberts
rejoined from leave & resumed
duties of A/Adjt.
Lieut R.G. Johnson Bfoh. att.
H.Q. A/Adj. ceased to perform duties of
A/Adj.

27/10/18 Lt Kirk proceeded to attend
a course at IX Corps Bn. [?] Gas
School.

Lieut SW Burton [?] joined
leave to UK 27/10/18 to 10/11/18

28/10/18 Lieut RC Johnson attached
H.Q. 32 D.A
2/Lts [?] joining the Battery:
2/Lt Grace att. Battery
2/Lt Wheeler (×/14MB) rejoined
(32 T.M Bty)

27 # Nothing of interest
28 " CRA inspected gun parks & horse
    lines.
29-31 " Batteries renewed at their
    wagon lines.

NOVEMBER

1st Batteries reconnoitred positions in
to in squares R10 A & C v R 9 B & d
about 57 B. The following positions
were selected.

A/161	R 9 d 80 65
B/161	R 9 a 70 60
C/161	R 10 a 10.30
D/161	R 9 d 40 00

Batteries dumped six wagons of ammunition
each on the positions selected.
Brigade Commander attended a Divisional
Conference at 6.0 p.m. v a conference at
91" Inf Bde HQ at 8.3 p.m.

2nd Ammunition at position made up to
150 rds per gun, and fired an addition
given to Battery ammunition. (APPᵃ 40 & 41)

3rd Batteries moved to new wagon lines in
vicinity of Sᵗ Benin in the morning, and
moved off into action during the afternoon.
Headquarters established at R 8 d 8 5
9b & 14 & IB, attacked the SAMBRE A
L'OISE canal defences at 5.45 a.m. B & C

4th Batteries fired lively fire at irregular
intervals from zero to 2 ero plus 50 on
west M16 00 - M2 a 36 and from zero plus
50 to 2 ero plus 110 on RUE D'EN HAUT
from M1 d 55 70 - M 2 c 55 40. A & D batteries
fired a creeping barrage across Le DONJON

NOVEMBER

4/17 in R.I.T. from North to south, owing to the infantry not getting on as well as expected in advancing barrage at a slow rate of from ¾ [fast] down to A + B batteries on the line R12c59 do M7b36 at 8.5 a.m. at 9.5 a.m. this was altered to M7d26 - M7b03 do R12c59. This was continued until 9.40 a.m., but was received at 9.45 a.m. at a slower rate and continued until 11.20 a.m. C & D. Batteries relaxed fire on RUG DEN HAUT at 8.35 a.m. and continued until 8.35 a.m.

B batteries moved off from position between 10 + 20 p.m. crossed by the bridge at ORS, and took up positions as follows

A/161   R 6 c 60
B/161   M7b.10.15
C/161   R 6 c 77
D/161   R 12 a 27

Major Chisholm captured 10 prisoners and 1 field gun.

Conference of Inf. + Artillery Bde. commanders ov Battalion, Battery and company commanders at Bde. HQ at 8.30 p.m.

NOVEMBER

5

B/161 & C/161 moved off in close support of the Argyll & Sutherland Highlanders, and B ordn, who crossed the Red line in G 29 & 35 at 7.30 a.m. A/161 & D/161 moved up shortly afterwards. About 100 who were fired during the day at mg posts. A/161 also pushed forward a gun & engaged a machine gun post at L 35.

The 2nd Bde AFA were affiliated to 161 Bde and moved up into action in vicinity of FAVRIL.

Locations of batteries in evening of the 5th:

A/161 H 33 c 42
B/161 H 33 d 25
C/161 N 2 b 52
D/161 N 2 a 91

These positions were 800 to 1500 yds from the front line, and were under rifle & machine gun fire.

6

The advance continued to-day, the same batteries being told off to support the leading Infantry. Single guns were pushed forward by C/161, often in front of the Infantry, to deal with

November

6th hostile machine gun. Lt Cooray
shot with a gun several hundred
yds in front of the infantry
and silenced 3 m.g's that were
holding up the advance of the
Infantry from the other side
of the main RIVERLETTE or
T 32. Final positions occupied
by the Batteries are as follows

A/161   N 3 a 2 1
B/161   I 20 b 64
C/161   H 35 c 00
D/161   H 34 d 90

7th KOYLI advanced through the Borders
and A & S Ham at 8.30 a.m. this
morning. A/161 moving in close
support. B/161 & C/161 received orders
to move at once into positions to
cover the objective or line
established with a range of about
3000 yds. Aphedin 42
A, B and D Batteries moved
by the road through MAROILLES
& MARBAIX. C Battery moved
through LE GRAND FAYT, and
was delayed until the bridge
was constructed, crossing about 11.0.0
a.m. A/161 engaged hostile machine

guns throughout the day. Major Chisholm accompanied by B.S.M. Tay endeavoured to work round a hostile machine gun to capture the crew. Major Chisholm was killed by a machine gun bullet.

Harassing fire was carried out by the batteries on the roads in J18d K13c&d, K19c&d, K25a&c. Final locations of batteries as follows

A/161   J 25 b 20
B/161   J 19 b 60
C/161   J 19 d 62
D/161   J 25 d 98

8th The advance recommenced at 8.0 a.m.
A/161 moving in close support of the KOYLI. B/161 covering the left flank of the 8th Bn. C/161 covering the right half. B/161 at the request of the infantry fired from 8.30 a.m. to 9.30 a.m. on ravine in J 29 b & d, at M.G. in church tower of AVESNES from 10.30 to 11.15. also at MG's at J 28 b 96 & J 29 Q 24.

A/161 brought up a gun to within 300 yds of a machine gun nest just west of AVESNES, and under an O.P. in a house on the 1st flank engaged and B silenced the MG's. Two

Germans were found killed in two of the huts & blood found at two others.

Location of batteries as follows

A/101   J 29 a 55
B/161   J 26 x 22
C/161   J 27 d 98
D/161   J 29 a 57

9# The advance continued a further 1500 yds. B/161 was detailed to move in close support. @ No opposition was met with. B/161 received a forward order to cover the other batteries that were laying their positions. The Brigade came into action at 50 ft in long valley by the 2nd Bde.

10# Batteries settled down to fire upon their locations as follows

A/101   J 28 b 44
B/161   J 32 c 89
C/161   J 27 c 64
D/161   J 27 d 97

11# Orders received at 10 a.m. that batteries were to cease at 11 a.m.

9/11 A/R Bradway W.E. F(c) reported from leave. 111 (   )
     A.W. Denniston F (No)

10/11 1 June P.R. Slaughter reported from Leave. O (   )
      McFeigh P.R. T.G. Cumming
      + posts Cyrich   J.W.C. J.H.E. may together from B.O.C.

NOVEMBER

12-15 Batteries remained at Wagnon
Horse-shoeing, cleaning up and
refitting.

16 Battery reduced to 2 four gun
batteries so disbanded surplus sections
under Capt. Traffos-Lennox marched
to Bohan.

17 & 18 Batteries remained at Wagnon
lines.

19 The Brigade marched 8 miles to
Leuzes route GUERZIGNIES-
WAUDRECHIES-FLAUMONT-SEMERIES-
RAMOUSIES starting at 12.00 hours
and arriving at 15.00. Batteries
were billetted on the eastern
edge of the village and HQ on
the western edge.

20 The Brigade marched to TRANCE a
distance of 10 miles route SIVRY-
TRIEU-BOUCHAUX and settled
down in billets south of TRANCE
about 14.00 hours.

21-23 The Brigade remained at TRANCE
and carried out horse cleaning
football concerts etc.

24 Marched continued to FOURBECH-
IES. Owing to the frozen state
of the roads and lack of frost

NOVEMBER

Coys the masses Brewers wagons had and
has the Brigade book 31 Rosters. However
with the whole order. Boy & however

25-26 The Bn remained in their wagon
       lines at Maurwasch on No. 3L 25
27   The battline moved to an area
       south of FROIDCHAPELLE. O. Battery
       close to the station, A & D Batteries
       in a farm house 2 miles south of
       FROIDCHAPELLE & B battery in
       GRATIERE
27   H.Q. moved into billets close to
       FROIDCHAPELLE station
28-30 The Bn remained at
       FROIDCHAPELLE

DECEMBER

1-11 The Brigade remained at FROIDCHAPELLE attention being devoted to Sports and Recreation al training.

12th The Brigade marched to FRAIRE and FAIROUL, passing the starting point in FROIDCHAPELLE at 10.00 hours, and marching via FOURBECHIES, ERPION, WALCOURT and settled into billets about 16.00 hours. HQ, D & B Batteries were billeted in FRAIRE, A & C Batteries in FAIROUL. Roads were good but heavy rain throughout the day made marching very unpleasant. Batteries

43.

13th March was continued to St GERARD. Leaving FRAIRE at 0900 hours, the Brigade marched via DONVEAU, CRATE STATION arriving in billets about 15.00 hours. HQ billeted at BOSSIERE. B & D Batteries at St GERARD, A & C Batteries at GRAUX. Roads were good & not hilly. Rain again made marching unpleasant.

14th Attended 44 Army Book.
March to NAMUR area was cancelled. The Brigade faced about & the standing point in St Gerard at 06.45, and marching via WEPION, and thence

---

H4. Lt-Col. H.H. HULTON, D.S.O. adm. hosp. for Dental treatment.
Major R. EMMET, D.S.O. B/161 assumed Command of Bde vice Lt Col H.H. HULTON. D.S.O.
H4. Lieut. P.R. HAMILTON, M.C. rejoined from Shrewsbury.
5th Lt-Col. H.H. HULTON. D.S.O rejoined from hosp.
16.00 hours.

+ 2nd Lt. O.W. Dennison HB/161 injured on adm. hospital 2.12.18
1st Major P. CROW, D.S.T. stockch HB/161 and assumed duties of Education Off. at Hqrs Office.
5th Lieut. RA Wyrley Birch late posted to join 1st Bty (Army) RHA RHA

7th 2nd Lt. O.W. Dennison rejoined from hosp.
Lt. G. Cocks M.C. rejoined from attached dty. H.Q.
9th 2nd/Lt. R.J. Allen D/161 adm. hosp. sick
11th Lt. Col. H.H. HULTON. D.S.O. granted 30 days leave to U.K. under i/os K.
D/29/60 Major R. Emmet, D.S.O. assumed command of Bde. vice Lt Col HULTON
HQ H. JONES. B/161 attached Hq Army R.A.

Reinforcement Camp

14th 2/Lt WS Kirk 13/101 rejoined from leave

16th 2/Lt H. Fores 13/101 rejoined from attached South Armyf RA Reinforcement Camp

18th Maj. JWS Buckley 1516 adm to hosp. sick

19th 2/Lt HS Hundy 13/101 posted D/101

20th 2/Lt LA Mould A/101 struck off strength - "Medical Board ordered".

22nd 2/Lt. J. S Hundy 2/101 proceeded to X corps Concentration camp. A draft of Coalminers proceeding to England for demobilization

DECEMBER

along the MEUSE to SAMSON, arrived in billets about 16.00 hours. HQ billeted at SUR-LES-FORGES. A, C&D batteries at SAMSON and B battery at GOVET. afternoon 15.

15th Batteries settled down in their billeting areas. All men are in comfortable billets, but scattered, and in some cases so rather far from the horse lines. Only billets for east of the horses are under cover, but, billeting is being improved with

16-20th Batteries were occupied with clearing up and settling down in billets.

21st CRA inspected gun parks and horse lines of all Batteries, the morning.

22-24 Time devoted to sports and recreational training

25 Christmas day

26-31 Lectures in Front. A Gradation of gunnery), shorthand and bookkeeping are now in full swing. Attention is also being paid to sports and recreational training

January, 1919

3rd   2/Lieut. A.G. Dryland 15/1/1 rejoined from leave.

4th   2/Lt. W.E. Wilson. M.C. 2/1/1 admitted hospital sick.

5th   Major G.W. Buckley. M.C. D/1/1 granted leave to UK until 19-1-19

6th   Lieut. R.G. Johnson 15/1/1 proceeded to attend second course at Education School, Trinity College, Oxford.

9th 2/Lieut H. Jones 10/101 granted leave to UK until 23.1.19

10th Capt. P. Grow, D.S.O., M.C. C/101 proceeded to X Corps Con. Camp for transfer to England for Demobilization under 2nd. Group +3
2/Lieut. E.A. Wilson C/101 — do —
2/Lieut. J.H. Tipper C/101 — do —
Capt. C.L.W. Haffenden M.C. D/101 proceeded to attend 10 B.A. course at Sheerness commencing 12.1.19
Capt. H. Barrett C/101 assumed command of D/101 vice Capt. C.L.W. Haffenden. M.C.

Brigade paraded in marching order for inspection by BRA

15th. Divl. Commander presented Medal Ribbons to 4 Officers and 17 N.C.O's and men of the Batn.

16th. Lt. Col. H. H. Hulton, D.S.O. rejoined from leave and resumed Command of Batn.
Major R Bennet D.S.O. resumed command of B/16.

14th Lieut. J. Cowan A/Or proceeded to X Corps Con. Centre for despatch to England for demobilization under Ord. Group 25.

16th Lieut. H.S. Sunday B/Or rejoined from leave

22nd Major A.O.L. Theobald posted A/Or Hq 8 Bde R.G.A. and OC

23rd Major J.W. Buckley, M.C. rejoined from leave & hosp; and resumed command A/D/167

27th Lieut. L.G. Gooney, M.C. O/14 Granted leave to U.K. until 10-2-19.

28th Major J.W. Buckley, M.C. D/167 attached H.Q./167 and assumed duties of Educational & Recreational Officer
Lieut. R.G. Johnson B/167 struck off strength (Auth. Fourth Army No. G.9109E (E)

30th Route March

Honours & Awards

D.C.M.
19542 Sgt. S. ROWE D/M

M.S.M.
4197 —

B/M
L/9440 Sgt FAULDING. W.

3   During the month of Jan. 1919
4 Officers and 88 ORs proceeded
    to England for demobilization

February 1919

3rd. HQ/161 and A/161 entrained at NAMUR en route for Germany. B/161 entraining at NAMECHE.

4th. HQ/A & B. detrained at BEUEL at about 11.00 hrs and marched to billets. HQ near the BEUEL end of BONN Bridge, A/161 at BERLINGHOVEN and B/161 at VILICH MULDORF. C/161 entrained at NAMECHE and D/16t at NAMUR en route for Germany.

5th. C/161 + D/161 detrained at BEUEL and marched to billets. C/161 at BEUEL and D/161 at RAUSCHENDORF

6th Major J.W. Buckley M.C. (D/161 att: HQ/161) proceeded to U.K. independently for Demobilization under Group 173.

10th Capt. A. Darnell (R.C. Chaplain) joined Bde from 32nd Div: HQ and attached B/161

13th. Lieut R.G. Johnson reported on completion of Course at Education School, OXFORD, was attached H.Q./161 and assumed duties of Education & Sports Officer of the Brigade.

15th. C/161 provided Gun Carriage, team and drivers at the Military Funeral of a Driver of the R.h.S.C. who was accidently killed.

17th. Capt. H.L. M°Cormick (R.A.M.C. H.Q./161) proceeded to U.K. on leave until 13-3-19.

19th. Inspection of the Brigade by G.O.C. R.A. Second Army. Instructions were received that during the Inspection the men were to carry on with their ordinary duties.
2/Lt. G.W. Britten (B/161) proceeded to attend Agricultural Course at G.H.Q. Farm, CORBIE.
Lieut. B. Coke. M.C. proceeded to U.K. on leave until 5-3-19.

23rd 2/Lieut. B.G. Chappell (C/161) proceeded to X.th Corps Concent- rants to P on Draft Conducting duties.

26th Major A.C.L. Theobald 7/6/ proceeded to U.K. on leave until 12 3/7/9

Honours and Awards.

March 1919

1st. Lieut. P.E. Toomey. M.C. G/m rejoined from leave.

1st. Capt. C.L.W. Haffenden. M.C. D/17 rejoined, on completion of 16D/c course at Shorbusyness

5d. Major B Emmet, D.S.O. B/14 proceeded to England for demobilization

7th. 2/Lieut. L.W. Bykyr posted to 16D/c attached 4/D/14

8th. Lieut. E. COKE. M.C. HQ.14 rejoined from leave
Lieut. F.W. HOOK D/14 granted leave to U.K. until 22-5-19.

9th. 48 reinforcements posted to 16D/c from 32nd D a/c

10th Major A.C.L. Shewbald D/67 struck off strength (A.4.1073 or 10)

11th Lieut. A. Jones 93rd (Army) Bde RFA posted A/67 and attached X Corps for Educational duties

10th Lieut. 10 C. Shaffes Grian. M.C. 8/67 on leave in U.K. until 2.7.19
2/Lieut. 16. W Allen D/67 proceeded to Frévent concentration camp on 2nd conducting duties

20th Major E. Sherlock M.C. 110th Hodle. Posn. posted to Hodle and attached C/for

22nd Lt.Col. (Brevet. Col.) R.G. Kenworth D.S.O posted to and assumed command of 110de.

23rd 2/Lt. C.G. Chappell. C/for rejoined from leave

25th Lt. Col. H.H. Hulton D.S.O. granted leave to U.K. until 8.4.19.

30d 2/Lt. F.H. TRINDER attached 2/Lt. from 315t (Army) Bde RFA

4 ORs proceeded to England for demobilization during the month of March 1919

April 1919

1-4-19. Lt. W/S Goodman (C/16) rejoined from att; 5th Sqd RAF. Capt. J. Tay (a/16) proceeded on leave to U.K.

4-4-19. Capt. B.C. Treppers-Lomax M.C. rejd from leave.

6-4-19. Capt. A Darvell (R.C. Chaplain) rejd from leave in France.

8-4-19. Capt. A Darvell proceeded to England by Dunk.b.
Lt. R.S. Johnson (B/16)
2/Lt. P/16. from att. HQ/16
Lt. A.E. Duffield M.C. att. HQ/16
2/Lt. F.H. Townley (31st Army Bure Posn) att; A/16.
P. W. Allen (B/16) Rejne from leave.

9-4-19. 2/Lt. P.W.S. Goodman proceeded on leave to U.K.

10-4-19. 2/Lt. A.J. A. Stubbs (93 Battery) jd 161 Bde & posted a/16.

12-4-19. Capt. H. L. McCormick (Ram.C att HQ/16) proceeded to England.

2/4. P.S. Hunter to UK on leave

13-4-19 Major Smithing attach
C/161 to Concent for Demob
2/Lt R. Hamilton M.C. a/161
to Concent for Demob.
2/Lt S. Grace (a/a6) of 161 posted
2/161. 2/Lt L. B. Richardson M.C.
R.E. (Lanc Div Sig) att HQ/161
Lt M. G. Barned Ja 161 + att
B/161

14-4-19.
2/Lt L. W. Eyhayes S/161 rejd from
leave.

16-4-19 Lt. E. Coly MC (348/61) to
Concent Demob
Major R. B. Hanbow D.S.O. (348/53
Det) ja 161 wounded + assumed
command a/161.

17-4-19 2/Lt L. B. Richardson M.C.
assumes Com'd of Lancs. Divs.
Signal Co Rail section at 161 Bde
Lt O.H. Frankford Jones MC (348/123
Ja 161 + posting B/161.
2/Lt 2DReans (HQ/124) ja 161 +
posted C/161.
2/Lt R. P. Dutton (C/124) do.
+ posted C/161.

16-4-19 Capt T. Gay rejd from leave
(a/161)

19-4-19 Lt. A. G. Dryland MC rejd B/161 from att. HQ/161.
Lt. O.H. Stockfosth. James MC (B/161) att HQ/161.
2/Lt A.J. Inigo (33rd Bde) jd 161 + posted B/161.
2/Lt C. Stuart (48 Bde) jd 161 + posted D/161.

20-4-19 Capt. O.L.K. Hyssenden MC (B/161) to Concert for Demoth.
2/Lt R. Merko (37 Dec) jd 161 + posted B/161.

22-4-19 2/Lt E. Gibson (93 Army Bde) jd 161 + posted D/161.
2/Lt C.E. Chappell (C/161) att. HQ/161.

23-4-19 Lt A.W Dennistoun (D/G/161) on 1 months leave to U.K.

25-4-19 Capt R. Maitland (1 u Bn) jd 161 + posted C/161.
26-4-19 Lt A. G. Dryland MC (B/161) on leave to U.K.
Lt H.R. Gootman MC (C/161)

28-4-19 left from leave
Lt/Lt R.V.J. Jump. Capt R. dye C.Y. Thornton to Concert for demot.

26-4-19 Lt J.E. Carey MC (C/161) to Concert Depot.
Lt O.H. Hackforth Jones MC assumed duties of Adjt/Adjt & posted HQ/161.

27-4-19 2/Lt W.A. Ryke (3/48 Army Res) ft 161 & posted CHQ
G. 8. Hawne (119th Army Res) ft 161 & posted 8/161.

28-4-19 Brigade inspected by G.O.C Division & at preliminary to inspection by C-in-Chief in the near future.
2/Lt J.D. Trindle (att/161) leave to U.K.

30-4-19 2/Lt A.J. Kniga (13/161) on leave to U.K
2/Lt A.L. White (93rd A Res) ft 161 & posted 8/161.
2/Lt H.B. Richmond M.C. R8 (att. HQ) posted I Corps Signal Co R8
2/Lt G.W. Bulkin (13/161) to Concert to Demob;

Demob: during month – 9 Officers &

MAY. 1919.

2-5-19 Capt. X.T Sargent (C/161) on leave to U.K.
5-5-19 Lt Col R.G.KEYWORTH DSO. (Indg. Bde.) attached SD/Lanc Rd + resumed duties of of RA.

7-5-19 T/Capt W.M.Rathbone DSO joined 161. Bde. RFA + posted to command B/161

11-5-19 Lieut L.W.Hooks (A/161) proceeded to England on transfer to Home Estab: (Authority 7th D.R. R. Brightman joined + posted C/161
Major G.C.K.Wisely MC joined + posted to command C/161.
Lieut A.G.Dryland MC (B/161) rejoined from leave to U.K.

12-5-19. 2/Lt I.S.Rundy (A/161) rejoined from leave to U.K.

14-5-19 Capt. X.T.Sargent joined + posted to H.Q.

13-5-19 Units of this Brigade (along with Divisional troops) were inspected by C-in-C British Army of the Rhine (Genl. Sir

W.R.Robertson, G.CB, KCVO, DSO, ADC) at Hargeisa Aerodrome

14.5.19. 2/Capt. J. Hogan joined & posted D/161.
Major R.B. Wreford on leave to UK
2/Lt. A.C. Harper M.C. joined & posted A/161.

15.5.19. Lieut. R.D. Russell M.C. joined & posted C/161.
Lieut. E.J. Gordon joined & posted B/161.
2/Lt. G. Vincent Jennie joined & posted C/161.
2/Lt. M.R.G. Jones joined & posted B/161.
2/Lt. M. Taylor Jones & posted D/161.

16.5.19. Lt. J.M. Taylor admitted Hospital (sick)
Lt. J.J. Mackenzie joined & posted D/161.
2/Lt. J.H. Tremlen (A/161) rejoined from leave
2/Lt. A.J. Kings (B/161) rejd from leave

17.5.19. Capt. K Barret (C/161) rejoined from leave.

18.5.19 Batteries inspected by Genl. Buckle.

20-5-19. Lieut. E. E. Linnett (RO) at 96/161 as Signal Officer.

21-5-19 2/Lt M.A. Pyke (/161) on leave to UK.

22-5-19 2/Lieut W.A. Pyke (C/16), Lieut. C. Stuart (A/16) and Lieut M R M Jones (B/161) posted Jambo D.A.C

23-5-19 Major C B Wharton DSO. (A/16) rejoined from leave. Lt-Col R A Reybrough DSO resigned command of 9th Lancashire Bgde. Lieut. G Goode (Ox. Bucks LI) of 9 Lanc Bgde Signals joined. Lieut A B Pyke posted A/161.

24-5-19
26-5-19

27-5-19 2/Lt J Leuard Fernie (9/16) on leave to UK.

28-5-19. Lieut B R Watchorn joined & posted C/161.

29-5-19. Lieut ST P Khurger joined posted O-/161

30-5-19. Capt K V Jamidah (0/16) on leave to UK

31-5-19. Lieut. E Harvie (B/161) on leave to UK
Lieut S Grace (A/161) to Cormeen Cologne for demobilization.

JUNE 1919

1-6-19. 2/Lt (A/Capt) H.C. TERRY posted & joined B/161 from 5Y Bde RFA.
2/Lt E.B. DOE'H (C/16) proceeded on leave to U.K.

2-6-19. 2/Lt A.G. STUBBS (A/161) proceeded on leave to U.K.

3-6-19. Lt K.P. SAWYER (A/161) awdd M.C. (Peace Honours List)

4-6-19. 2/Lt C.G. CHAPPELL (C/161) at HQ/4 proceeded on leave to U.K.

6-6-19. 2/Lt F.H. TRINDER (A/161) att. RA Reinforcement Camp.
Lt A.W. DENNISTON (HQ/161) rejd from leave.

7-6-19. 2/Lt C.G. CHAPPELL (C/161) posted B&Q/161 & assumed duties of Bde Orderly Officer.
Lieut A.W. DENNISTON (AQ/161) posted B/161 & ceased to perform duties of Bde Adjt Offr.

9-6-19. Major C.E.F. GAITSKELL M, from HA Res Bde & att SHQ/161.

12-6-19. 2/Lt F.J. VINCENT-FERNIE (C/16) rejoined from leave.

12.6.19
2Lt. F.H.TRINDER (D/16, att. RRC Cologne) at: "Cologne Post".
2Lt. L.W. EYKYN (D/16) adm. P (Sick).

13-6-19
Lt. (A/Capt) H.C. TERRY (D/16) att: HQ/Blanco Dn. as A/Staff Capt.
Lt. N.R.P. HIGHMAN (A/16) att: R.A. Reinforcement Camp.

15-6-19.
Lt. E.G. HARVIE (B/16) rejoined from leave.
Lt. J.E. GOODE (Ox-Bucks L.I.) att HQ/16, proceeded on leave to U.K.
Lt.(A/Capt) K.V. HANITSCH (C/16) rejoined from leave.

16.6.19
Lt. M.B. BARNETT (B/16) proceeded on leave to UK.
2/Lt. F.H. TRINDER (D/16, att "Cologne Post") adm: PP sick.

17.6.19
2Lt (A/Capt) T. KAY (A/16)
Lt (A/Capt) B.C. TRAPPES-LOMAX (B/16) MC
Lt (A/Capt) H. BARRETT MC
Lt. A.S. DRYLAND MC (B/16)

14-6-19 (Cont'd) Lt. W. R. GOODMAN MC (C/161)
2/Lt M.S. NUNDY (C/161)
proceeded to England in
accordance with Rhine Army
Letter No. A 305/2035(03) of
6-6-19.
2/Lt E.D. DREW (C/161) rejoined
from leave.

16.6.19 2/Lt. A.J.A. STUBBS (A/161)
rejoined from leave
2/Lt L.W. LYKYN (D/161)
rejoined from P.
The 161 Bde RFA Concentrated
at NIEDER PLEIS in accordance
with instructions from
3rd Bancho's Inf. Bde.
in order to be prepared
to advance in the event
of the Germans not
signing the Peace Terms.

20.6.19 2/Lt C.G. CHAPPELL (A/161)
rejoined from leave.

21-6-19 & 23.6.19 Batteries ← HQ/161
still at NIEDER PLEIS. Much
rain during this time.

24-6-19 Lt. B.B. HATCHORN MC (C/161)

posted & joined 4/61.

25-6-19 The Brigade was inspected by Maj-Genl H REED VC CB CMG Maj. Genl. in C. JEUDWING, KCB (Cmdg Lanco Divn) and Brig-Genl 2/Lt F. KTRINDGR Bgd Cologne Trior Ret. frm FP.

27-6-19 13/6/61 + C/61 left MERER PLESS and Lüdenscheid Gutersloh billets vacated by them in KILICH MULDORF and BEUEL respectively and BEUEL respectively Lt R.D. RUSSELL (C/61) proceeded on short leave to U.K. Lt E.J. LAWSON (13/61) Proceeded on leave to U.K. Major C.E.F. GAITSKELL profn r joined HIGHLAND D.A.

28-6-19 News that Peace had been signed received at 16.00 received.

29-6-19 30/61 returned to BEUEL + footstep billets vacated to 'J'mins 1 day.

4pm 2 Lt O.H.MACKFORTH JONES MC (A/Adjt) proceeded on leave to U.K.
2/Lt C.G.CHAPPELL (HQ/161) assumed duties as a/Adjt.
Lt. BRANTCHORN MC (A/161) att. HQ/161 + assumed duties of Bde Ord. Off.

30-6-19 A/161 + B/161 returned to SIEGBURG MULLDORF — + occupied billets vacated by Hers on 1" minus/day

JULY 1919.

1-7-19. 2/Lt. PIRIE (219 Coy RE) att: D/161 Instruction.
Lt. M. G. BARNETT (B/161) rejoined from leave to U.K.

3-7-19. Major E. SHERLOCK MC (D/161) proceeded to U.K. on leave.
Lt. R.D. RUSSELL MC (C/161) rejoined from leave to U.K.

4-7-19. 2/Lt. A.L. WHITE (B/161) att. R.A.R Camp Cologne.

5-7-19. 2/Lt. R. HICKS (B/161) on leave to U.K.
Lt. M.G. BARNETT (B/161) proceeded to England under Rhine Army letter A.563/4 (O3) 10-6-19

7-7-19 Col. R.G. KEYWORTH DSO proceeded to PARIS in Command of Rhine Army R.A Detachment in Peace March.
Mr. J.M. TAYLOR (D/16) evac: to England (sick and struck off strength)

8-7-19. Lt. K P SAWYER MC (A/6) proceeded on leave to U.K.

10-7-19 Lt. P W ALLEN (D/6) proceeded on leave to U.K.

12-7-19. 2/Lt. L W EYKYN (D/6) proceeded on leave to U.K. Capt (A/Major) G.A.K WISELY MC (C/6) proceeded to PARIS on leave, also Lieut. B.B NATCHORN MC (A/6). Lieut. E.G. SINNOTT R.E. (att. HQ/6) and Lt. J.E. GOODE (Ox Buck LI att HQ/6) until 15-7-19.

15-7-19. Lieut. E.J. LAWSON (B/6) rejoined from leave in U.K.

16-7-19. Lt (A/Capt) H.C. TERRY (D/6) rejoined from leave in U.K. and ad. S/O/Ranca Rn. as A/ Brigade Major.

19-7-19 Capt (A/Major) G. L K WISELY MC rejoined from leave in PARIS.
Lt. (A/Capt) + Adjt. O.H

HACKFORTH JONES M.C. rejoined from leave in U.K.

16.7.19. Lieut. B.SMATCHORN M.C. rejoined A/161 from att: HQ/161. Colonel R.G.KEYWORTH DSO rejoined from PARIS (Peace March)

21-7-19 Major E. SHERLOCK MC (B/161) rejoined from leave in U.K.

22.7.19. 2/Lt. R.HICKS (B/161) rejoined from leave in U.K.

23-7-19 Lt. K.P.SAWYER MC rejoined from leave in U.K.

25.7.19. Lt. R.D.RUSSELL MC (A/161) posted & joined C/161. Lt. PIPE (/219 Coy RE att A/161) rejoined unit.

26.7.19. Lt. P.W.ALLEN (B/161) rejoined from leave in U.K.

27.7.19. 2/Lt. B.B. WATHORN MC (A/161) proceeded to attend BC's Course at SHOEBURYNESS.

27-7-19 2/Capt. T HOGAN (2/16) proceeded on leave RUK (Cadr)

28-7-19 2/Lt F.J. VINCENT FERNIE (2/16) rejoined from leave in BELGIUM

29-7-19 2/Lt L.W. EYMAN (2/16) rejoined from leave in UK
Major E. SHERLOCK MC (2/16) proceeded on leave to UK prior to proceeding to CONSTANTINOPLE

30-7-19 Lt. J.T. MACKENZIE (2/16) proceed on leave to UK

AUGUST

Nothing of interest to report during August. Slept:-

15-8-19 An successful Impromptu Race Meeting was held at MANGELAR.

WAR Diary
161st Brigade RFA
1 April 1917 – 29 Sep 1918

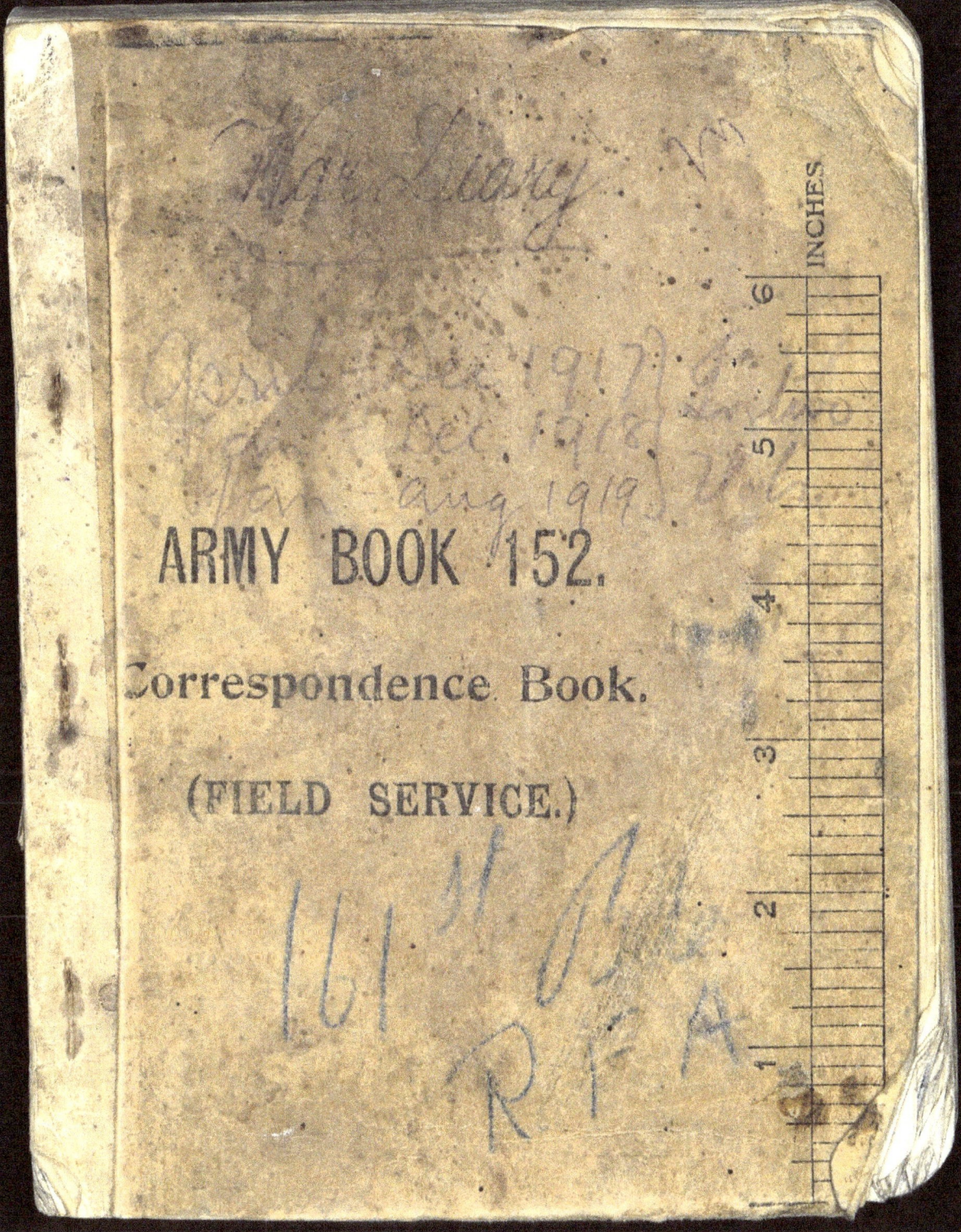

War Diary

Oct–Dec 1917 book two
Jan–Dec 1918
Jan–Aug 1919

ARMY BOOK 152.

Correspondence Book.

(FIELD SERVICE.)

161st
R F A

Opened on _____

Closed on _____

The Squares in this book are ¼ inch.

(700) Wt.7082—M891 180m Books 1/17 B.M.&S. E.646

APRIL 1917.

(1)

In the early morning the 21st Infantry Brigade attached and captured the Village of Savy with the 11th Borderers and 17th H.L.I. Artillery support to this operation was given by the 161, 152 & 168 Brigades consisting of a heavy barrage on the village. Later the 2nd Cav. Div. Infantry advanced. Information received as well as the Prisoners confirmed that enemy was in the open, as whereas that they suffered heavy losses when retiring from the village.

The 161st Brigade sent forward an officer with the 17th H.L.I., who kept in communication with the Brigade ending back the progress of the Infantry.

Later in the day the 9 b.n. Infantry Brigade moved through the 21st and captured Savy Wood. They reached [ ] failed to occupy point 136, their final objective, when fighting was on through the night.

At 10.0 pm the 181st Brigade moved their Head Quarters from Château to Pommery to Savy Village, and during the night the Batteries moved forward and came into action at 2.0 am South of the village opening fire at 5.0 am

4/4/17 Sgt. Ruston   Killed
G". Holt   wounded
 " Gilroy   "
Dr. Strogd   "

30/4/17 3 Howrs
G" Donald Reed
Pte. Ivonia wounded
G" Flanagan "   } A/161
Dr. Galen "
 " Whildon "
 " Mc Swent "
 " Wadmore "
Cpl. Yatturall "

2)

The 14th Infantry Brigade came up during the night, and at 4.25 am work forward the 2nd Manchesters & 1st H.L.I. Their objective being to capture the villages of Hulouch, Selency & Francilly. Support to their operations were given by the two Companies of Artillery and covered by a couple of Lances lying on the Infantry advanced. Little resistance appears to have been given by the Enemy & the three Villages fell into our hands without heavy losses. About 11.30 there was × heavy losses. About 11.30 there was Captain Francilly a German Field Gun Battery of 2 guns was captured by the 2nd Manchesters, the Enemy returning to surrender but fighting the guns till all the detachments were shot down. With a view to recapture this guns the Enemy counter attacked at the [?] from our Infantry to retire a few hundred yards on a tracing the guns in the [?]. The Enemy were however unsuccessful in their attack on the position we held commanded the guns and made it impossible them to approach the Battery. On [?] our attempt was made by the 1st Brigade to bring in the guns. At 5.30 pm a party of [?]

× Two Companies of the Dorsets
G. Engineers, wounded
S. Berwick "

2.

men from each Coy/Batty, under Lieut Lloyd were to man handle the guns out of their pits ready for teams which were found to arrive a few minutes later. It appears however that the Enemy had a listening post closer in, or an enemy scout, which with such a heavy firing, as soon as they attempted to approach, that it was thought advisable to withdraw until the following night.

Sjt Young } Killed 4/1/44
Cpl Smith }
Gnr Hiscock wounded

3.

Under Major Saunderson I.S.O. and Lieut Lloyd a fourth party from the 161st Brigade went out at 8.30 pm to bring in the guns. From the experience of the previous night it was thought advisable to approach the position from a different direction and that a covering party from the infantry was also necessary.

In spite of heavy shelling the party reached and pulled out of the pits and in and away as soon as possible to the town (under 2 hours from the start)

In this way four of the guns that were in were filled in and got back

3.)

Guns however as No 5 gun had been
withdrawn a large part of the Enemy
advanced over the crest, and Treatry
through the covering party pushed the
position forcing our men to abandon its
gun help out and this not yet
prevented from its pit. Desperate
fighting took place in the dark, and
the Enemy after destroying the breech
block of No 6 Gun, was forced to
retire with heavy losses. Both Guns
were safely withdrawn.
2nd Lieut Lawrence &/HQ wounded.

4th.

Battery commanders went forward during
the day to reconnoitre positions for
their Batteries to move forward into
during the night – unfortunately the day
was most unfavorable – visibility very
imperceptible owing to snow falling heavily
all day – Positions chosen were. A tair
distance on Halom to the N.E.of the
village, just the runway between Halom
about half a mile away to the South
B + C Batteries cross roads South
East of Halom and D on the Railway
where it cuts the Hotton – Barry Road.
During the night Batteries moved
forward into their positions and

Came into action the following morning

4th
S.S. Hospital Patient A/14
Sgt Pickernam Sinion "
Gr Barnell   "
 " Swain   "
 " Sayler   } 4/14
 " Young
Peter Bully

6th
Head Quarters of the 161st Brigade which was still in Savy, moved up to the Battery and occupied dugouts in the Railway Embankment close to D Battery. A Battery when we got there was heavily shelled to bring 1 Officer & 5 men. It was thought advisable for the two sections to move back where they had more cover as soon as possible. In the evening Colonel Cotter sent a party of men from H.Q. assisted in our handling of A Battery guns through the Billets of Hohon to where he ordered the section was to return.

D withdrew
without loss in 151st to the line

Sgt Peter Bateman 2/60 wounded
G/ James Garrard wounded 12/14
Sgt Adams, O/d Ellicom, Bdr Horsley, Dnr Rielly
Cr Rothwell wounded A/14

2/Lieut Buckman wounded 8/14.

B. Batty had two Lieutants wounded
2nd Lieuthson + 2nd Sypher B/1/4

The following Officers joined the Bn/RFA
and were posted as follows: 2/Lieut E Coates
to A; 2/Lieut Grier D; and
also 2/Lieut Shurer A.S.

12th
Captain Crow commanding A Battery wounded
2nd Stephenson B/1/51 2nd Martin C/1/51

13
An Officers Patrol went out at midnight to
see if Largé was occupied, and returned
with the news of no Officer finding the
enemy holding the village

14th (Being the 18 H.I. & KOYLI)
At 4.30 am the 97th Infantry Brigade
who were on the line attacked and captured
the Village of Largé without much resistance
in the paths of the enemy. Colonel Cotton D.S.O.
who was in liaison with the Infantry Bd
at the disposal of three Brigades of Artillery the
161, 159 and 168, and had arranged
Barrage in support of the attack Given in

8.12.1915 which had previously been much
carefully regained. The crossing of the
Infanta in September. This belongs with
such small losses, appears to be greatly
due to the excellent support of the Artillery, as
it held a point of great advantage.
After capturing the outlying works included
in to their second objection the Infantry pushed
the taking of Apex Farm and also the
Sunken road running north from it.
After hard fighting the farm fell into
our hands; but the troops on the left
were not so fortunate as heavy enfilade
M.G. fire caught them from the Tower
Copse. It was thought thought advisable
to retire our Infantry and deal with
the woods first. In the afternoon
after the Artillery had bombarded the Tower
Copse to help in been & make apparent
and occupied the two woods. It appears
that the enemy had been greatly shaken
by our bombardment in little to no
resistance was offered the enemy fallen
[14th Martin]
fleeing away to the far side of
Lenny put to death & own with
than hands up. During the day
over 379 prisoners fell into our hands
including 4 officers. All supports
the enemy from the Infantry spent with

14th

the highest praise of the support given by
the artillery, and say the fire was so
accurate and prompt that it gave the
troops the greatest confidence.

At night the 149th Russian? guard
forward the Batteries coming into action
in the following positions. A Battery
N E of Nelson B in the village of Selney
C in the valley west of Roit des Reies
and D in Nelson village and opened
fire on the enemy.

15th

C Battery who were reconnoitring a way forward
position had one Gunner killed & two wounded
and a Gun knocked out of action.

Genl Scarff C Battery 17th

20th

The 32 D Divisional Infantry was relieved
by the 61st and went out of the Line to night.
C R A 32 D Div handed over to the RE24
and horses lent to Engineers.
The 161 Brigade RFA covered the

20th
139th Infantry Brigade
C. Battery went Eastwards in [?] to
M.G posted close to Battery in case of an
Enemy attack

23rd
Recent word was received the Gueudecourt Carre
On the night of the 22nd went be [volunteer?]
to take out a party to [enter?] from Carre Battery
to bring in the Captured German guns
which were out in [front?] of our Gun Pits.
By an [oversight?]. Owing to heavy mortar
fire the attempt had to be abandoned for
the night. Again the next night the
officers [volunteered?] to go out again with
a party and worked [open?] heavy Battery fire
succeeded in bringing in all the guns.
When less [than?] [last?] two [guns?] the
Enemy attacked our party forcing them
to retire leaving the guns behind. In
spite of this event had returned and later
in the night and succeeded in recovering
the [remaining?] guns.

D Battery 141st Brigade came in
Section ground to the Rear old Gun
In Carre Battery went in with [us]

26th

At 7.20 pm S.O.S. signals were sent up by our own Posts close to Epy farm in response to which the Artillery fired at men on their protective barrage. The enemy it appears tried to rush a post back but were held up by the barrage and M.G. fire, having to retire with considerable losses. Enemy S.O.S. presence was also sent. Later in the evening a report was received from our Reserve Coys.us that the enemy were in Epy farm, the Artillery were therefore turned upon it from 10.0 to 10.10 pm and then lifted for the enemy to retire. No enemy were found. The Infantry report that there was very pleased by the prompt Support received from the Artillery fire and the accuracy of their fire.

Bdr Randall & Gnr Walther, B. Battery Service Gun. Pinxton /A Battery served

26th

At 4.30 in the morning a successful raid was carried out by a Company (half of the 2/3 Oxfords on the crater in N31 a.o-6. Enemy trenches to Curatis wood - Supported by an Artillery barrage from 1st & 16th Brigades R.I. the Infantry gained the Crater where a machine gun was captured, the detachment & occupants showing little fight and escaping captive by running away. Our the same time a further party of our Infantry were working North attacking Curatis wood, when two men M.G.

28th

was captured, Him also the Enemy apps himself and appear to have been quite taken by surprise at our flank attack. After completion the operation our Infantry returned with two of the M.G and our prisoner

29th

Guns B.C Trafficx Lewes M.C C/141 wounded.

At 9:30 the 161st Brigade bombarded Cepy Farm for 10 Minutes, after which a Patrol was sent out by the Infantry and found it unoccupied. Later in the night an Infantry listening post reported that the Enemy had sent out a party which was then occupying the farm. Again the Artillery were called upon to shell it & for ten minutes, after which a further patrol was sent out and found the farm empty.

Guns D/151 Brigade B. Battery run service
Guns Chaplin B. Battery

MAY 1914 2nd

The R4th Infantry Brigade was relieved
by the 163rd
C. Battery 163rd issued a Section back to
the position previously occupied by B.168.
Which division by A161 m Rifles Pits.

Gnr Thornburn wounded A. Phillips

3rd

1. The Sergt R.H. Wheel slight wound in wrist
B.W. etc., C Battery 101st Bde went out to rest at Couplain
gunfire

4th

183rd Brigade relieved the 164th Brigade

5th

during the night the 161st Brigade was called
upon to fire when Capt Lynn 5 minute Bombardment
after which the infantry sent out a patrol tonight

7th

One Section of A & D Batteries came out of action
after dark and were relieved by sections from 168
Brigade, and returned to their lines in Courplain

May

9th
During the night of the 9/10th the two remnants sections of D/161 were relieved by D/146 and B/161 by C/168 withdrawing to their wagon lines

10th
H.Q /161 were relieved by D/165 and withdrew to their wagon lines at OLMOT. After dark the two remaining batteries of /161 were relieved B/C/161 and retired to their wagon lines

14th
The 161 Bde (less C Battery) and 2 section 4th D.A.C + /161bty, H.Q Coy. 46 Div) marched to CURCHY + ETALON via VOYENNES + NESLE

15th
The Brigade left CURCHY at 5.30 am and marched to BOUCHOIR via FOLIES

at 5.30 & M.G. Coy & left
BOUTOIR and proceeded to HAILLES
via AMIENS - Bury Busses were there
the Brigade marched as a Brigade and
the weather was very fine

16th – 23rd
The Brigade bivouaced at HAILLES.
21st 2 Lieut STEVENS reported
for duty + was posted attached to A/IH.
20th 6/1/H billeted at HAILLES
having been relieved by the model, Co.
the night of 17/18th the Battn – Brigade
marched into 169 Brigade – Brigade
Staff.

23rd
The 169th Brigade Entrained at MARCELCAVE
and travelled via AMIENS, ABBEVILLE
BOULOGNE, CALAIS + ST OMER to
CAESTRE near BAILLEUL –
Ration carried no water + only 1½ hours
A/IH 9.40 am
H.Q. 4.50 pm
B/IH 5.40   "
C/IH 8.05 "
D/IH 8.3 "

May 1915 24th
6th H.L.I. Brigade reached
CoESTRE where it entrained
and marched to a camp 6/m
to BAILLEUL

25th
Work was commenced for the Bullery
positions which were in the open and
only seven hundred yards to hold the
German front line.

27th
Battery each sent a gun up into the
positions this was to fire by

30th
2 further guns of C/151 went up into
action

31st
All remaining guns + howitzers were
up into action
Bombardment began.

June 1917

1st Bombardment
2 Lt A.S. Blackamore reported for D.A.C.

2nd
Battalion reorganised

3rd
Further registration was carried out.
At 3.6 p.m. heavy artillery fire
raid was carried out on the German
front line resulting in the capture of
60 prisoners
Captain McCormack typs H.Q and
joined C Battery
B.M.

5th 6th Xth Bde
H.Q 1st & Bde moved to this
Battle level Quarters at Wulpen Duynda
to 6B

Trial Bombardment
7th
Attack of 2nd Army at 3.10 am Capture
of Messines. Wytschaete ridge by 12 noon.
Further attack at 3.10 pm & capture of
OOSTAVERNE LINE.

Lt Shaw & 30 P wounded &
[illegible]

Lt [illegible] slightly wounded

36th Division of Art[ille]ry supplied by
Army Fd [Arty] Bde by 2 Inf Bdes, each 2 Bties
front line support. 1 in reserve.
At Wicres – very little resistance – Kinuls –
7am FOO – Lt HAEFENDEN

8th
Counter attacks repulsed at 12 noon
at 9.15pm — ammunition Rgtl dumps.
Liaison officer – Lt Johnson
High Command to Lt [illegible] by Church Morlau
7th   ambo to
                                 DAC
Galvados warst week of action – halt drawn
to issue limes. Ammo trains at 4am drawn
to FO.B released

10th
Bde HQ and Bties in Gas Lines
At DENNISTON a interpreter went on to billet. First
town since Bde left HAILLES.

11th
1st Bde marched to GODESWAERVELDE via BAILEUL &
FLETRE. Start 8:30am.
Weather cool our 1st march pleasant.
Some few congestion along main roads. Bottleneck
Billeted in farms about 1 mile from village HQ in village
itself.

12th
At GODESWAERVELDE found heavy canal
east by 11th Brigade. Wading any MT. Attacker
Stana by enemy prevented officers Refr.
The 32nd Division is transferring from XIV Corps to
XV Corps in DUNKERQUE area

13th

Daybreak in bivouac. Scout Sturges with party
in reserve. Scout Sturges with party
was sent to WORMHOUDT to arrange billets
for the 18th Brigade who were to march
the following morn.

14th
                                                          large issue of
At 6 A.M. the 18th Brigade E & C Batteries
GODESWARWLDE and marched to WARMHOUD
about 9 ousks on a good road.
The day was very fine and the route
taken by STENVORDE free from any congestion
of traffic

15th
arrival having attached an officers' mess.

15th
Colonel Cotton &C.S. with two Officers
from each of his Battery Left H.Q.s
at 7.0 A.m. in a motor lorry to
inspect Battery positions on the front
Remounts arrived and were distributed
between Batteries. Lieut Drinkle went forward

& away billets at CAPELLE

16th.

At 11.15 a.m. the Brigade left WORMHOUDT for CAPELLE moving via BERGUES, where it spent the night in billets. The day was very hot and several of the men fell out on the way. Lieut Buckle + Barrage reced on to ZUYDCOOTE with Telephone Cart and H.Q. Signallers to prepare billets.

17th

The Brigade marched out of CAPELLE at 9.35 am. reaching Zuydcoote 12.30 p.m.
One section A B + D batteries moved up into action on night 17/18 coming under orders of various French Groups of 29th French Div. Arty. in positions vacated by French.

18th

One Section A B D + two of C moved up into action C into the open.
Bde H.q at Oeste DUNKERQUE Bains.

19th

Remaining guns came into action.
Battery wagon lines in vicinity of Coxyde.

20th

9 am Col Cotter D.S.O. took over command of Brigade covering 96th Inf Brigade (& to 0056 Dunkirque) (taking over from Col. GIVIERGE D.S.O. of 55th D.A.R. The Germans raided 16 N.F.'s (all Scotch) & took 11 prisoners. (12 missing)

23rd

96 Bde relieved by the 1st BDE 1 DIV. 161 Brigade R.F.A. moved their lines of fire so as to cover the front they were to remain in permanently, as 25th Brigade R.F.A. covered their own infantry in NIEUPORT Sect.

24th

Lt. Col Lewin (25th BDE) took over command NIEUPORT Barns sectn Lt Col Cotter LAMBARTZYDE. Groups 14 Inf Bde. (B.G. Lumsden VC DSO) HQ 161 Bde. moved up to A.C.D.

25th

Headquarters moved to B'rs Triangulaire 2 K. A.G.B.

26th

97 Inf Brigade (R.B. Blackleel) taken over from 14 Inf Bde. Two Bat: in line (HQ NIEUPORT 2nd Lr A9 bryland primes Brigade then asbd R.M.A replaced.

28th
The German Artillery showed considerable activity, bombarding the our front line systems.
Also shelled 60pr Battery in rear of A/161's position.

Sept 29th
The Germans shelled 60pr Battery all day intermittently. Practically no shelling in the trenches. A+D batty position almost completed

30th
—
1st

July.
2nd

2Lt 75 Harper B/W wounded in trenches on his
way back from inspecting forward gun &
Maxim team (admitted to hospital).
2 Lt W.R. Goodman slightly wounded in back.
Remained at duty. (S/6d)
L/21/4 Cpl Cammish TR wounded, hosp & hys remained
at duty.

3rd

Bosch Artillery very active all day
on trenches in Back Areas also on
Bridge at Ytricourt. O.P. Struisier
hit several times. Aeroplane wrecked A.C.Rec
kept him

4.5

11.45am raid was carried out by
the Border Regt. Bangalore torpedoes
& enfilade till 12.15 being held him
L A.M. hun barraged hus parapet &
Maltor Moore wood to get hun & was killed & mainder
A/TD battrous fired on the front & entry of
the trench and back in our line.
1.45 am 18 N LL Raiders in L myes expense
to the front of the brigade, strong A in
occupied & bombed several dug outs
by enemy & captured (Prisoner they had

D Coy Sidi Saleh
with Hun Mekhaten harass aa/t 2.30am
5 of our up 15 batmen pnd/w
45 minutes.

5
C Batty lost sir Lyons killed & two
men(?) & a pilot sent in the bag up
& CO Devours with Ammunition & two Sappers
who went to their assistance. Lieut. Pelham
& the three drivers wounded.
CPL Carter killed in L.A.D. Lorry Lorry Rodrigues
& Lapueho had. Lieut Pelham taken
to B.M. command.

6
Possibly Artillery because own actions him
hoset.

Bosch artillery + M.G. action
Shelled A tks up of ch. Hartbeer
all day with one Zeppelin gunner
Motor also shelled Kurkan +
back areas.

10.8

C/s shell the 1st & 32 previous
prior no thank. Then started
to shell the [?] left behind (2nd Brigade)
day. Bivouac-ranged to cup 66
Cahal. own right full in the Rwd cts
[?] (16.H.29) Lt. Lt left South (Brooker)
and no (2.Lt. [?] The [?]
[?] in m22b.
Lt. Barlington cave up to
one buy [?] shell also
Lt Gotta found an [?] scored
[?] of Res. Prato the two
killed. [?] OP to farm while
[?] fixed up Sirhind troops.
Pm.] Ryder
St Irwin & came both left back
Lt Hume Shuldup. high fire
snuiled.
Col Scales 14 NF. left [?] for
Lt Braham of A. st. k. W.
Capt. N. Lacour AVC embdud Blackight
tr

very quiet - quiet all day
except in darting overly up
feel about a Brigade point
with S.O.S. [?] there at
[?] of [?]
Rep. Battalion en chanomoned t

Battalion in [?]

Jeff said could not adopt his system
+ how he proposed to ABTC
to form two Brigades viz
14th Brigade withdraw to Ayth
Ruinada consisting of Artly Corps
in to action by 9 of 14/12
22 Brigade + 14 Bde RHA Corps
under command of 13 Brigade.

12th
Met Ackrill on the Bodapart wished
all the Bridge buy 9 a.m. asked by Colt
of all communications by pontoon. Same
Brigs only standby
72 Brigade registered by C Batt 5
lost 7 high & quick Quick 32 but
lucky the same were in the chat
oft 1st a/t of a 15 it
13.
Bought quick quit Our hourse
visited church the afternoon & our
Chaplain was very clear
Col Orton returned from leave & took
r took on Command

1.4.17

Enemy Barr. effect's opened in bn's trench
bomb'g junction with Rose avenue & its
Junction with her Lane in his Support
bomb its & Junction with Rose Alley & its
Junction with her bone no parapet
to its junction with Buchloch
the sap in rubies our post M22 to 8.
the hole at curb'g of the Orleck Steam
up We've Brought this enclosed armt to
capture & held this part of her
trench her Support. her Lane in
preparation of a diversionary from a defensive
flank on her Lane.
3.2 Siw Art. will assist with sp[oradic]
Bn's art, 2 LG will attempt to break
12.15 Lt. Col. attempts [telephoned?]
Lt. B Hill who attempting to establish
bn 15 failed on the left. Lt. Marriott
17. J. left to find the line in the night
& his pat'l right ceased.
16/4

An attempt has been to arise
at an enemy post in U of ?
was tapped in Bomb put down a heavy
barrage in about a quarter of an hour when
casual? bir'n to our Counter barrage
which slacked at 9:45 a hour in tell
9:15 the night became quiet up to
that.

14/8/14 9th Division relieved the Inf Bgs in the lines in Lombartzyde Section.

17th
Bad batt. in the evening. In an hour we loosed 14 wounded, bombs being thrown & even trench (trench lines) during such bombardment.

18th
The Boch tried to get into our line at about M22c9015 1st one of our pat' ran into a left hd. bd. with about mly 5th Bomb into & leaving heavy a number of casualty. M11 Bn bch & M2 Bde mc at the SOS line at 2-40 + continuing on & off till abt 6am.

19th
A him Enterprise was carried out by the left Battalion 4/5 KOYLI's at the pt. occupied by the Enemy in the Gallois Trench in M 22 a 47. A pt. in the pat hd led the OC Miller + Cam had eight Germans were seen & seen a full hurried down the gweiti. 5/16 pined in the Maxim. On reach. C/18 covered the back of the British trench. In there a hand went in & to it to clear of occupier it but

at 16 enemy put up a fairly heavy barrage shelly 16/7, 17/8 Bns reply'd firing the SOS.

20th
Day very quiet: afternoon & evening - night only quiet also.

21st
The Enemy was very active firing & shelling the Bns & regular B/16 Batty Posit's & the Back areas. His aeroplanes were very active dropping a lot of bombs & on one landed well down the

Enemy shelled heavily with Gas shells of a new type pretty heavy men out of action. Aeros very active by night

22nd
Enemy Aeroplanes very active during morning, two being up flying very low our own line all the morning. Enemy shelled his time to shelling back areas.
Major Kay A Battery, 2/Lt. Minter sent to Hospital. (Shock)

23rd July
Day normally quiet. At 11.7pm S.O.S.
Rockets went up on left Co Left Battn
front. 16.1.72 Bayonets had in the S.O.S.
lines / our Lewis advanced at
Travail. The enemy did not make an
line.
At 3.15am S.O.S. two reported on Right Battn
front. The Brigade had in the S.O.S./our
Lewis at a slow rate. Appears to have
been a false alarm.
Newpot shelled with gas shells.

24th
The Bosch action on back areas shelled.
at Rum Brigades & B/161 heavily fm
3.35pm to 8pm our fm of B.S put d/
of action. to Cashalli Carnival.
the night was very quiet. Newpot shelled
with tear shells. 16 tots Rhema 49ch in line

25th
Day exceedingly quiet.
Night very quiet John May P. Watts command
outgoing infantry long th bombarded much
26
Col Cotter attended a conference at P.C Armin
Newpot tot shelled intermittently during day
Bat night as well Okumin th sealer
Negative

27th

Col Cotter took Cr. other of the Oxfordshire
round at front line
hopeful but shelled intermittingly
D.R. to the hills was laying a wire
Saw was to have been and out but was
cancelled

28th

161 Bde & 72 Bde were detailed to
carry a raid on German Post at
M22 b83 Req Lt 17 Ken Riding High
Zero hour 12 Midnight.
One B & an S.O.S 2 yds long went
up has a corporal it had line
He said did not type flare it
ready but with order.
Sm has snapped the sent over W.
It was cancelled.
The German shelled my front pretty heavily
throughout & one train-Plan received
attention fm Jan Skull.
16/17/2 Bot Barry Tested by Col Cotter

29th

Raid which was taken token place
last night-took place bright-part
failed bread than objective tape ?
than were killed
16/17/9 shelled with gas shells

30th.
Division Baragwanath Tested at 8pm
fired for 12 minuts.
The enemy replies by road
rifle fire.
31st
Private Thomas Jones 3/161 killed at Bly
position by hostile artillery fire.

1st August 1914.
Day & night very quiet.
Rained.

2nd
At 9 am. enemy under cover of his Practice Barrage 1991f Rugged Reserve Enemy pits M22 t8521 + M1226 8637. also front line between M302526 & M1234338.
B, C & A Groups fired under instruction.
C.V. Cyler Barrage continued in belts an hour.
Rain still continued

3rd
Artillery Barrage — Rain still continuing.
Smith battery 9cm (Kent line super) in [G] 426 at 6.25 am. Smith pm.
BX gas on. SOS fired at 6.40 pm
CRA 32 Div & turned off [illeg] as incorrect.
[illeg] Rocket from [illeg]
Lt A.W. DENISON went sick (500")

4th
4th Nov & Dec
Weather improving. Lived with battery
5mn SOS fired at 6.5 & 20mins and 6.45 pm
5th
Retaliation
Weather fair and bright. Artillery activity increased.
Enemy shelled NIEUPORT & Bridges in the evening
2/LT F.S. HARPER 73/161 wounded by shell pm

At NIEUPORT hit in the stomach. Stretcher-bearer Jilks dealt have been admitted to hospital suffering from effects of gas shell bombardment of the 29th —
Since 18th of July 161477 B'ees have been firing continuously 130rds per day per gun & 60 rds per at 320 BX or 410 BX — on various tasks on enemy front lines in perpetual bombardment.

5th
Weather clear. Heavies continued bombardment.
C Bty lost 6 men from shell fire.

6th

7th
Weather grey & thing to night.
B group supported a successful raid carried out by 5th West Riding Regt 147th Bde on enemy post + dug out's in front of LOMBARTZYDE. Raid took place at 10.50 under Box barrage. 5 prisoners & 1 M.G. being captured. Counterbattery?

8th
This night a gas attack was made at 1.30am on bombardsyde by 'K' Special Coy R.E. with projectors and Stokes mortar gas bombs. B group cooperating with artillery fire

9/161 were slightly during the day fairly our
Mark wounded (slightly)
9th
161 Bde HQ were relieved by HQ 72nd Infy Bde
161 HQ with ours to Eaux Wir Battezies
9:30 am . . . Lt Col Cotton DSO & Lt Bradln
to hospital - suffering from gas (burnt)
10th
Lt Creasy came down
11th
HQ 161 moved to VILLA MARTHA LOUISA at
COXYDE BAINS
12th
Q.161 moved to Coxyde
15/16
Brigade Commander to rest to think
home. D/161 leaving this June in
letting parties.
16/17
Major Peace brother P.C Hunt,
Lieut Henderson, L. Turner & Campbell
& Bradle proceeded on leave
10th
ADMS Cotton DSO & Lieut Bradln
proceeded to Cass Major Chandler came

Awards during the month August 1917
MC
Captain Richardson AVC (281161) Bar to MC
Lt Bowles A/161 Lt TUNA(9/161)
Lt Coke A/161

D.C.M. Bar to M.M.
4/75780 Sgt H HOLMES C/161 Lt nightingale D/161

m.m.
4/235210 Cpl C Nightingale D/161
4/15771 Bar L.M. MASKREY B/161
4/9768 Cpl John SPANETT C/161
4/102284 " Bar T Eland 9/161
4/102366 Dr E S Howard D/161
4/102284 Bar A Gull B/161
4/92131 D' L Taylor 9/161
441769 St. W. H. Hiscock 161
4/102253 Sgt T. F. Boggs A/161
4/143413 Sgt P. A. Dodson P/161
4/19607 Sgt S Foord P/161
28-278 Cpl S.C. Roett 9/161
{ 1 Bar to MC
3 MC
1 DCM
1 Bar to MM
12 MM

During the 10 days spent at Allain wagon lines, the Brigade had time for a thorough overhaul and a certain amount of training – guns were inspected & repaired & in some cases calibrated at the gun range; opportunity for leave to officers was taken; daily officers rode under 2/Lt Hook, instructors for 97th Inf Bde riding school were provided.

27th/28th, 22nd/29th (August); 14th Inf Bde in Bombarzyde sector, & 97th div St George.

32nd Div relieved 33rd on the night of 29th Bde Sutcliffe & Met wounded.

30th 2/Lt Campbell returned from leave –

25th
Battn wagon lines to the certain area under the Command of Lt Col. Pickburg. 72 Brigade. Signal Arrangements.
to Bde. T.
2/Lt S.C. Cole
2/Lts Moore & Ross

D/161 Wagon lines shelled & 2 shelters on Appelle No 2 cleared.

28th
Major C.H.P. Watkins D.S.O., Major Hunt, 2/Lts Hindmarsh, Tilman, Campbell & Rowles returned from leave.
3 Sgts & 1 Gunner wounded in 9/161

29th (to B)
Captain Cross & 2/Lt Clift rejoined the Bde from England. Capt Buckley 2/Lt Dommiston 2/Lt Johnson went on leave. 2/Lt Massy rejoined from T.M's –

30th
HQ moved up to Bois Triangulaire. Weather has been very stormy these last few days & in the absence of our aeroplanes, enemy artillery activity increased especially on back areas e.g. Coxyde etc. Front appears to be normally quiet. A number of our heavy batteries have moved out recently.

31st
2/Lt Ashton & 2/Lt Watson & 2/Lt returned off leave. & 2/Lt Hindless

Sept 2nd.
During the morning batteries had a practice barrage on their S.O.S lines for 8 mins. Lt R T PEACH killed at gun position.

Sept 3rd.
Lt Col A S CATTER D.S.O. took over command of "B" group from Lt Col RITCHIE (72nd F.A. Bty) "B" group now consists of 161 Bde alma — Bty following group also covering the front of Left Brigade 32nd Div — C group (Lt Col FURNIVALL), SYKES group (2nd N.Z. A F A Bde)
PHIPPS S.O.S Sect
(   ) OC B group in liaison with 1/4th Hy Bde (Brig General LUMSDEN VC D.S.O), a battery supply by liaison officer was left by Bde.

Sept 4th.
C/161 moved their battery position to neighbourhood of BOIS TRIANGULAIRE into position recently vacated by a 6" how battery. This position provides dug out accommodation for personnel of battery.

Sept 5th
D/161 spotted an enemy T.M firing and claim to have silenced it.

Sept 6th.
A/161 were engaged in wire cutting. For this shoot (and for the report which led to it) the Brigade received the thanks of the G.O.C Division.

Sept 4th — ADD
D/161 wagon lines were shelled by a 6"gun during the night but no casualties were inflicted beyond 1 horse slightly wounded. Wag lines subsequently moved to LA PANNE.

Sept 5, 7th
C.B./ 32nd Division
The artillery covering 32nd Div.
Div. in wire cutting in front of
enemy post at GELEIDE
Sept 6th

Night firing + Day firing on special orders had
ceased. an endeavour being made
to break off the fort ilery duel.
6/9/16 on wire cutting in front of Geleide Post.
The front line quietted down considerably
though food areas and ways firms are
still shelled

OC 107m Special Companies RE.
carried out a gas projector and other
mortar attack on enemy trenches. 3/1/61
fired in cooperation.
Sept 9th.
8/9/16 on wire cutting in front of Geleide Post
Sept 11th.
A raid was made by the 5/6th Royal Scots
on GROOTE BAMBURGH Farm. Raiding
party left our trenches 9pm + proceeded
across Yser Polder; an entrance was
attempted made through the german wire (a machine
gun with screw of 2 being disposed of en route).
A dugout was bombed and two men taken
prisoners (unfortunately Pte Potter R.S. being
disposed of on the return journey). On the
order to withdraw a captured rocket was fired

and the artillery barrage came down, under which the party succeeded in regaining our own lines. Two men were killed and 13 wounded of the raiding party; of the enemy at least 8 were killed in dugouts, and more probably in the ensuing fighting. Lt Ellis to St Pol Cd. - Jaundice.

Sept 12a
Sgt A v. Dormston returned from leave.
Qa Inf Bde relieved 14th Inf Bde in the left subsector of the Divisional front.
2/Lt Halfpenden awarded MC for work as F.O.O. at Neuport. C/161 shelled with 21cm gun for 1½ hours - no casualties.

Sept 13th
At 10.45pm Special by RE discharged for a the Divisional front. B/161 had no communication with Hiss.
Major Grow (A.S.C.) to hospital.

Sept 14th
At 5.15pm the enemy put up a practice barrage for 20 min on our front system. Nieuport, Rue du Purr, etc. Our artillery retaliated. Otherwise all quiet.

Sept 15th
No 72611 Dr W.H. BLOODWORTH & 726359 Dr H.E.E. DEIGHTON both of D/161 awarded the Military medal for gallantry on Sept 4th when D's wagon lines were shelled.

Sept 17th
Early ... to arrange a ... to raid
the trenches of the Right B.t.Coy. up S.A.S. signal
was sent up at 5.13am and our
artillery barrage was in full swing by
5.15am. The enemy appear to have
noticed our barrage & were some men were
shot. The wire when turned ... kill and
eld. Their wire in trenches captured an
officer & 23m.
The COL Struben reaches # A B & C
battery positions.

Sept 17th - 22nd
Nothing of particular note occurred. Enemy
T.M activity increased and the following
plan has been adopted to cope with them.
By day A/161 Ayre guns laid out on known
emplacements, by night D/161 or D/172 -
If T.M are observed firing but not spotted
retaliation is fired & where known position,
if however they are spotted the howitzers deal
with them.

12'534 Dr LOCKEY & 125499 CY J.H BROOKSBANK
awarded Mily medal.

Sept 23rd
/Capt & Major E.A. CHISHOLM awarded Mily Cross.

Sept 24th
During the night B Coy HQ in BOIS
TRIANGULAIRE was subjected to 20 min
gas shelling at a rapid rate. Four

Sept 19th
1 officer from 2nd 14th 14 Bde ...
attached every two days to Batteries.
Sept 19-21 Capt Patterson   B/161 5/6 Royal Scots
21-24   Major Wheston   C/161 1 Donals
23-25 Lt Pasha & Snell   B/161 2/3 ...
25.27   C/161 15A H.L.I
27.29 Lt G.B. DALLAS A/161 ... 14 H.L.I.
29-1st LT A.K JAMES B/161 5/6 Royal Scots
1st-3rd Capt W/ SNELLIE   1st Dorsets

slight casualties resulted which can be traced to an attack with S. That earlier as [illegible] lines (in one case by boat) of a [illegible] exposed to B. Coy.

Sept 26th.

From 12 noon to 1.30 pm today [a] practice was held for communication between artillery units was die; communication being maintained by runner, wireless and visual -

At 4 pm a practice Counter Preparation was fired until 4.11pm - from 4.11 pm to 4.14 pm a practice S.O.S. on the whole of the Divisional front. The enemy did not did done his artillery contenting himself with retaliating for 6 min at 4.30 pm on our trenches a NIEUPORT.

Sept 27 St.

HQ B & C Battcoms were shelled by a 6" gun - from 8 to 10 am - no casualties, but two dug outs smashed in.

At 6.15 am an S.O.S. was reported on the LOM BART 2YDE sector. Rockets were opened fire until the situation was clearly shown to be a false alarm. Infantry reported very favourably on this barrage.

A practise Ll call was a failure owing to message from the air being jammed.

Sept 28.
LT. F. TURNBULL rejoined the Bde from England and was posted to D/161.
2LT W.B. GOODMAN rejoined C/161.
An LG call was received during the afternoon and enemy target engaged. The 97th Inf. Bde relieved the 96th Inf. Bde in the Lombartzyde Sector.

October 1st.
During the afternoon the tide began to flood out parts of the Right Bttn front and at one time it appeared it might be necessary to withdraw part of the garrison under cover of Smoke barrage: this however proved unnecessary.

October 2nd.
The Corps Commander inspected wagon lines in neighbourhood of COXYDE, and expressed himself well satisfied.

October 3rd.
Test of S.O.S. rockets on Left Brigade front was held at 6pm to 6.30 pm; this was not a success.

October 4th.
Weather broke in rain & wind which continued during the 5th. Trenches are mostly flooded out.
Capt. Bozzelt Major HUNT (OC B/161) went

Officers from 141 A Inf Bde were attached to Batteries of this Bde for 'instruction' as under.
Oct 1st - Capt W.A. SMELLIE - 1st Dorsets - C/161.
Oct 3rd - 2Lt B. McSHERRY - 2nd Hamd - B/161
Oct 5th - 2Lt J. MUIR - 15 H.L.I. - C/161

on a months leave to England.
Night 5th/6th 42nd Division (less artillery) commenced relief of 32nd Division (less artillery) in the AREA. The 125th Inf Bde (5th 6th 7th & 8th LF) Brig General HFARGUS NG DSO relieving the 97th Inf Bde in the LOMBARTZYDE Sector.
6th.
15th Hy Seige B. Relief completed on St Georges Sector
6th/7th.
Summer time ceased at 1am tonight
During the 7th & 8th the weather continued extremely unfavorable to operations — high wind & rain necessary.

Oct 10th.
Hostile artillery activity increased somewhat. 168 Bde pulled out of action.
Oct 11th.
Lt Col A.S. Cayon DSO assumed command of 41st Divisional Artillery. Major E.H.P. PEASE-WATKIN DSO took over 161st Bde, Capt Bucurey adm. command of 2/161
1 section per battery relieved by sections of 211th Bde RFA 42nd Div Arty. 161st Bde withdrawing to wagon lines
Oct 12th.
Remaining sections of 161 Bde withdrew to wagon lines after dark on completion of relief.

During 5th. S.O.S rocket lane reported again a full ww from the same cause.

Oct 13th
161 Bde marched to GHYVELDE & after
dark. Weather very wet.

Oct 14th, 15th
Brigade rested at GHYVELDE.

Oct 16th
Brigade marched to WORMHOUDT via BERGUES,
starting at 5am and being settled in by
12 noon. Weather was clear during the
march with a cold wind.

At 7am Battery Commanders and
a small staff left WORMHOUDT by motor lorry
and proceeded to YPRES, reporting to
18th Div Arty Hd qrs prior to relieving 255
Bde RFA.

Oct 17th
Brigade marched from WORMHOUDT to
neighbourhood of POPERINGHE, starting
at 9am & arriving at 3pm. Traffic was
very heavy and march consequently
disjointed and uncomfortable.

Gun detachments travelled by motor
lorry to YPRES area and relieved
detachments of outgoing brigade in
neighbourhood of POELCAPPELLE. Guns
were exchanged.

Oct 18th
Lt Col AG ARBUTHNOT CMG DSO took over
command of the Brigade from Major E.H.
PEACE WATNEY DSO.

161 Bde form part of D Group (Lt Col
PARRY DSO) - 34th Bde RFA of 18th
Div Arty Group.

Oct 16th

Wagon lines of 161 Bde moved to Bréa.
Vacated by 255 Bde RFA.
HQ 161 took over at 10am from HQ 255.
During the day the Brigade took part in a bombardment of enemy works NE of BELLACOURT viz a defensive 18pdr barrage being substituted for the infantry who went down into dugouts to escape the hostile 4 cases but close shooting.

Oct 19th

Above programme was continued B & C Batteries lost 2 guns destroyed by enemy shell fire and 2 guns slightly damaged. Ammunition was taken up to batteries by pack during the day. The batteries were intermittently shelled during the day very in fairly heavily. Shelling from 12 to 2 pm. Some 200 shells were fired during the night A Battery being the chief sufferers.

October 20th

Brigade field barrage and bombardment programme from 5.30 am to 11 pm.
Major E.H. PEASE WATKINS DSO commanding D Battery wounded by shell fire and evacuated.

Oct 21st

Bombardment programme continued.
Enemy batteries less active than usual.
2Lt F.G. STEVENS (A/161) died of wounds received in action this morning.

---

16 Casualties

4/12315	Sgt. Riddell J.W.	A/161
44588	A/Bdr. Barrett A.	"
4/18861	Gnr. Cooper W.	"
4715	" Gooney R.	"
common 4893	" Bradbury G.	"
825284	" Walker W.J.	"
68438	" May A.	C/161
106278	" Bilsbury W.A.	B/161
4/27647	" Martin Q.H.	"
4/11945	Bdr Argile H.A.	B/161 slightly wounded, remained at duty 18/4

19 Casualties

Died 19/7 → 4/25421	Sgt. Cooke H.	C/161	Shell Shock 19/4
	85390	Gnr Brennan J.S.	B/161 Wounded 19/4
Died 20/4 ← 4/5524	" Green H.	C/161
	110060	" Jeffrey W.	"
	12534	Dr Lockey W.	"
	4/12415	A/Bdr Evans G.T.	B/161 Wounded Gas 19/4
	4/45391	Gnr Ruddenham J.	"

20 Casualties

Major E.H.P.W. wounded

21 Casualties

Please see entries opposite.

2/Lt Stevens died from SC

Died of Wounds 21/4 → 4/5525 Sgt Watkins F. A/161 Wounded

22.

Course of the day yet to be determined. Major Cross, Captain Ward, Lt Col. Henderson, Lt Morton, 2/Lt Crow, AG, Captain Cuiward MC & Capt Cook MC Norton sent down to 1st Battery from orch of 5/161 all but suffering from shelling (remained at duty).

We all were fine, but ground showed little sign of drying. A machine barrage was fired in the course of the afternoon to check lines & switches, under Brigade arrangements.

Oct 22nd

At 5.35 am an advance was made on the front of XIV & XVIII Corps to reduce the salient held by the enemy in the form of the northern houses of POELCAPPELLE - attack on XVIII Corps front was carried out by the 8th NORFOLKS & 10th ESSEX of the 53rd Inf Bde 18th Division.

Under cover of a creeping barrage, objectives were gained, the advance extending to a depth of a thousand yards.

The 161st Bde formed part of the artillery supporting the advance. The Barrage was intended to be arm en grade, but was only rarely so, for the batteries of the Brigade. This entailed greater difficulties from the gunners point of view and more or less shooting. Considering the mud and general conditions under which the work had to be carried out, the success of any

22/10 4/1212 Cpl Dawson AW. 6/161 Slightly wounded remained at duty
24529 Dr Neville J. 2/161 Killed 22/10
91266 Gnr Moore A. " Wounded "
2/Lieut C A Norton 4/161 Admitted hospital wounded - GAS
4/12362 Dr Talbot " — ditto
213994 Gnr Shepherd W. " — ditto

protection of the field artillery infantry under the enemy barrage in most gratifying.

23rd

Day passed quickly and Batteries were able to get some rest and sleep.

D/161 withdrew their guns and took them in neighbourhood of Canal Bank preparatory to a further advance. The guns were successfully withdrawn in spite of considerable hostile shelling.

Weather continued showery with Brighter intervals.

24th

Bombardment & enemy front lines and rear positions recommenced in conjunction with heavy artillery.

Enemy shelled vicinity of Battery positions especially during the morning. Enemy bombing machines caused some casualties in D Bty in the early afternoon.

25th

Bombardment continued.

D/161 commenced work on new forward positions etc. an advanced wagon line of 6 teams per Battery was formed on Brandys

---

23rd Major J. Crow MC A/161 Admitted Hospital wounded (GAS)

24th Casualties:
2/Lieut. D.W. Bowles A/161 Wounded (seriously)
584445 Sgt Dickinson A. B/161 "
119458 Bdr Winn J.R. " } Wounded
119464 a/900 Jefferson W. "
119449 Gnr Hildyman W. " " Killed
1/40483 Gnr Stevens W.A. "
665655 " Sutherland J. " } Shell Shock
1/24639 " Lightfoot C. "
18839 " Whitwam W. C/161 Wounded

2/Lt C.E. Hattenden wounded slight by bomb
831420 Gnr Badham J.C. D/161 Wounded by Bomb.
Lt. Hindmarsh to hospital (wounded -Gas 22/7)

was back of coral Bank to save time in
cashing up ammunition to (forward) positions
13th D.A. relieved by 58th D.A.

25th Casualties:-
4/19538 Dvr Bagnall A. A/161 Killed

26th " " " " 26th " " " :
Enemy attacks. An attack was made along the
Divisional + Corps Fronts: the 161st Bde supporting
the left Bttn of 173rd Inf Bde (58th Div) The
situation still appears very obscure + the
objectives still appear to have been gained and
then lost under pressure of counter attacks.
The weather throughout the day was
undescribably bad - rain falling continuously
Teams to withdraw Guns preparatory to a pullout obviously ordered up
but the situation remained to obscure
to enable any movement to be made.
2 Hows of D/161 moved up to new positions +
a certain amount of ammunition was
got up in spite of enemy shelling heavy + close.

26th Casualties:- 30485 Gnr Hanniaway C. C/161 Slightly wounded remained at duty.
201338 Gnr Slater R.E. B/161 }
85084 " Symonons F.M. " } Wounded
2640 Dvr Turkinson G. D/161 }

27/10/17

About 200 prisoners were taken in yesterday's operations but no advance was made on the Divisional front. Enemy S.O.S. some guns of ground were made to our north & on the South. 2 more hows of D/161 went up into action.

28 × 17

A 4.5 hows bombardment commenced again at 6.30am. Workers for Somme were not arrived till 4.45am.

Lt Col Apple Wolfe Cole DSO (161 Bde) took over command of D Group on relief of 34th AFA Bde by 126th AFA Bde.

29 × 17

Continued bombardment.
Batteries were shelled during the day by 5.9 shells causing a number of casualties as mentioned. We are also digging a C 15 hole in the ground at present occupied.

D/161 reported from Somme forward position

30 × 17

An ack ack was handed in at 5.50am.
The enemy's front exhibited now to be on the usual exception and bombing camps were fired. The situation remained very obscure all day and still is so. Officers seem to have taken the same course as on the last attack, namely an advance

---

27/7 Casualties
L/18903 Bdr Gabbitas H. B/161 - Killed
26710 Gnr Lunford B.C.   — slightly wounded remained at duty
103760 " Everton F.J. A/161 - Wounded

28/7 Casualties
L/58818 Gnr Furniss G. 18/161 - Wounded (Gas)
44790 Gnr Fayell A. D/161 - Wounded
94657 Gnr Rhodes F. " - "

Missing
Gunner Ellis 18 Bar RMS

29/7 Casualties
311594 Cpl Reed N.J.
254944 2/Cpl Ladvu H.G.A. } 118/161
58884 Gunner Fitzmaurice H.J. } Wounded (Gas)
311607 Gnr Midgley J.
1/12231 Gnr Burbery G.
50147 " Lincoln G.W. } A/161 - Wounded (GAS) 2/11
152224 " Stagshawe F.
4/5854 " Wright A.
4/19414 Gnr Greene A.
125952 Gnr Ryott R. } 15/1/61 wounded
190404 " Chadwick J.W.

30/7 Casualties
2nd
4/1114-722010 Beals J. A/161 wounded
L/5495 Sgt Whittles B. 18/161 wounded (GAS)
1553 Gnr Deacon H.W. wounded slightly remd at duty
89137 Bdr Jayne J.C. A/161 wounded (GAS)

success, but was and subsequent withdrawal due probably to machine gun fire and loss of direction.

F.O.O.s were supplied by 126th Bde & 161 Bde but information were not obtained to cut satisfactory as before.

31/10/17

Day passed quietly. batteries re-registered 9/161 continued work on forward position with a view to occupation very shortly.

31/10/17 Casualties.

2/Lieut F.W. Hook. 2/161 Slightly wounded remained at duty.

88630 Bdr. Woollard G. } 3/161 Wounded
1998 Gnr Hodges W. } 3/161 Wounded

Nov 1st

During the night B/161 pulled 2 guns
guns into action and one was taken
down in wagon lines that had been damaged
by shell fire. B/161 exclusive of a gun
from their position and C/161 took 2 guns out
of action preparatory to moving into
advanced position during the night.

B & C Batteries moved into "new wagon lines"
at BRIELEN.

Day was marked by a certain amount
of hostile artillery activity: harassing fire
was carried out on enemy communication.

Nov 2nd

Day passed uneventfully until 11 pm enemy
appeared to attack divisions on our right
during the night, and artillery fired some
minutes on S.O.S. lines and the situation
appeared clearer.

Nov 3rd

Day passed quietly, a bombardment
was carried out by D Groups on close support
and suspected enemy strong points in
Square 9019.

HQ 161 moved into mission huts
near GOURNIER FARM. There were
no bombardments we carried out
shelled during the night but no casualties

2nd Casualties:
110598 Gnr Adjacent J
11052 Gnr Aspey J. Other wounded

Nov 4.
Enemys barrage was fired as S.O.S. break at 4.40am for half an hour. No Tanks dropping after coming forward to attack any enemy who might be expecting an infantry attack.

Nov 5.
Barrage as above was repeated at 4.50am. S.O.S alarm at 5.30am.

Nov 6.
Barrage as above repeated at 6am in conjunction with an attack by the Canadian Corps on our right on PASSCHENDAELE. All objectives were gained in this attack. Enemy action on our front confined to isolated strides and irregular artillery activity, enemy using a considerable number of long range H.V. guns against rear areas.

Nov 7.
A barrage was fired again at 5.30am. At 1pm a practice barrage was fired on area to the S & South zone on which enfilade fire could be brought to bear—a barrage being creeping and then enfilade.

Nov 8.
Preparatory barrage was fired on the above front as on previous days 5am & 5.15am and 5am with bursts of fire at 4pm. Harassing fire was also continued on enemy tracks and approaches.

4. Casualties –
110593 Gnr Hurst J. 5/11/17 Wounded.

6. Casualties
196200 Gnr Baker G 13/11/17 }
4/18873 Dr Harvey J 3/11/17 } Wounded
265110 Dr Mason W 3/11/17 }
4/36319 Gnr Pitts AE 13/11/17 } Killed
4/1553 " Dixon S.W.   }
181039   Dr Haylock A J "Slightly wounded
                          remained at duty"
148281 Gnr Farnham WH } Wounded 6-11-17
189174   " Alee W   }

Major Hunt returned from leave & being on command of Bty from Major Gosselin who took over A/161

5. Add A/161 recommenced road & firing positions near RETOUR CROSS RDS & OB.

Nov 9th.
They made no serious move from their position
4.20am and 6am were quiet and continued
on toward position
May 10th.
Bn moved down with 1st Brigade of
the 1st Division the Brigade Group
supply by 2nd Norfolks, Northumberland
ponies, 2 Sections RFA, 2nd K.R.R.C., 2nd Strode
(Part of 1st Brigade of the 1st Division
and the 1st Cav Brigade coming in may
to drive the Turks to the offensive & to
have the completed with the remainder
the heavy Bde to give on effect & set
by the enemy. Day was cold.

Nov 11th
The Brigade spent preparations
barrage at 6am, and barrage
We had a very heavy fire & we
was was continued a very heavy.

Nov 12th
A fine clear day with host 6/xc
moved 2 more guns up in front
position Bde fired a properly
barrage at 4.45am.

Nov 13th
C moved 21 guns who action in forward
positions and at 8:00 am C R A
inspected the positions and expressed
his appreciation of the work done by

10th Casualties
1/19595 Bdr C.E. Featherstone 6/161 Killed
1835 Sgt. W. Alvis 9/161 Killed
44045 Gnr Freeman C.H. 13/161 Wounded

11th Casualties   Nil

12th Casualties   Nil

13th Casualties
27046 Dvr Lowden R.H. A/161 wounded by
     left splinter
95383 Dvr Adamson B. B/161 slightly wounded
     remained at duty

Nov 13.
Enemy counterattacked Canadian division on night of PASCHENDAELE but were repulsed - 2 attacks being made during the day by this Brigade. Day was misty and work progressed.

A preparatory barrage was fired at 5.15am.

A move 4 guns forward. Occupied position with 1 section; also A. remainder of these Batteries being withdrawn to waggon lines. R remain in action as before. B & D being in action, active batteries in the Brigade only. A & C being silent.

Nov 14/15th

A preparatory barrage was fired at 6.15am and harassing fire continued.

A Have now 6 guns in position at forward positions as well as C. 1 Section of each of B were in action in case of S.O.S. Battery being nearly shelled in the early morning. B was damaged by shell fire during one gun of C the night.

Nov 16th

Barrage at 7.15am fired this morning.

Nov 17

At midnight 16/17 orders were received for personnel of the Brigade to relieve detachments of 36th Bde 2nd Div Arty on the divisional

14th Casualties
L/12140 Gnr Rudgworth H.   6/11/01 Killed
61054   "   Harringer S.   "   Killed
L/19607 Sgt Ford G.   "   "
101468 L/Bdr Adams WO   "   Wounded
L/19710 A/Bdr Cope H.   "   "
L/12147 A/Bdr Horsley W.   "   "

15 Casualties
105307 Gnr Minore P. 13/11/01 Killed
24671   " Malone M.   "   Shell Shock
78735   " Hickman F.   "   Wounded
31853   " Bartholomew A.   "   "

16th Casualties
Nil

14th Casualties
89634 Gnr White F.6   } Nil
L/12526 Gnr Smales H.
126334 " McFord A.   } Wounded
86629 Gnr Watts J.
88633 " Wigginton R.   } Slightly wounded, remained
205193 Gnr Sissmore R.   duty

front immediately on our right.
A B C withdrew detachments and took over positions of 15th & 64th & 71st Batteries during the day. They now form part of a group under OC 168 Bde near ST JULIEN
D161 withdrew detachments to batteries W.L.
Guns were left in position under a guard no advance of wagon lines took place, and HQ did not move.

Forward positions were shelled fairly heavily at 9.15am, causing casualties to other batteries and infantry working parties.
20 mins after detachments and G.S. wagons of 161 Bde G.a.s cleared; also the forward exchange handed over to 126 Bde was flown in just after relief had been completed.

Nov 18th and 19th
Nothing of significance occurred. New positions seem quieter than the old front and ammunition supply enough so the roads are in better condition.

Nov 20th
HQ 161 withdrew to wagon lines near Vlamertinghe vacated by 36 Bde RFA
Nov 21st
HQ wagon lines moved to new billets - Today the weather broke and everything is once again a sea of mud

18th Lt H. W. TILMAN M.C. Rifle Bde.

18th Casualties
424412 Dvr Morcom F.H. Bty 161. Wounded

Nov 22nd

A/161 moved 2 guns forward to positions near TB161. C/161 commenced to withdraw a detached section to rejoin remainder of battery. (2/Lt W.E. WILSON joined 4/161 21-11-17)

Nov 23rd.
Weather was fine, and ground drying. The d[ivisional] Colonel Cmdg inspected B161 wagon lines.

Nov 24th.
BBt 32nd Division Arty relieved 1st Division R.A. Artillery.
Command of Divisional artillery Group passed to CRA 32nd Div at 10am A/161 moved remaining 4 guns into action at forward position.

Nov 26th.
An S.O.S alarm was raised at 7.14pm and batteries opened fire, no infantry action was reported.

Nov 26th.
A/160 relieved B/161, who withdrew to their wagon lines.
2/Lieut V.J. HORTON (SR) reported for duty from 39nt D.A.C. & was posted to D/161.

Nov 29th.
Lt Col A.C. ARBUTHNOT CMG DSO wounded and admitted to hospital Command of the Brigade passed to T/Capt of Major F.A. Chisholm. Enemy shewed considerable

Sgt PARIS B/161 awarded M.M.

24th Casualties:
238905 Gnr Turner S. A/161. Wounded

25th Casualties:
230285 Gnr Ling A. B/161. Wounded

26th Casualties:
419386 Gnr Brough Y/32 T.M.BTY. attd B/161. Wounded

28th Casualties
nil

29th Casualties: Lieut Col A. Arbuthnot C.M.G. D.S.O. Wounded
19955 Gnr Oram J. B/161 Wounded
425198 " Collier W. A/161 "
114981 " Bartram G. " "

activity against back areas, shelling VLAMERTINGHE and POPERINGHE with long range H.V. guns.

Dec 2nd. At 5am Sgt Sgy Bde attacked plus two Bde's of 1st Div to attain to original objectives. Corps was employed but our own side were shelled in continuously. We act as our infantry advanced. The first push did not succeed with our artillery fire at all.

Our own infantry captured all their objectives. But at 4.15pm a strong enemy counter attack developed and we were compelled to withdraw to our original line.

The Divis'n on our right were similarly forced back. 51 prisoners were captured on Div Front.

Dec 3rd.
2/Lt Y.J HORTON R/Jd reported at W Bdy HQ. Day passed quietly — original trenches & watch line being reestablished.

Dec 4th W.B & ___

Period handed ___ ___ G ___ ___
6th OPS R.C.B battery recommended.

30th Casualties.
2/10/17 7501/75 L/Cpl Wilson F. } slightly wounded remained
         4/11962 Gnr Sellens S } at duty.
         8/1962 Sgt Ellison P.L. Wounded

2/12/17 2/Lt W.G Launder admitted hospital sick

Battery positions at 1st Div Arty on the STROMBEKE (preparatory to taking over on the 10/11 & 11/12.

Dec 7th.
Sledt Lad W/P FORD assumed Command of Brigade.
During the night the enemy crossed the PADER BEKE which had frozen and dug in between our Bty RHQ and the Dot of our Regt. They were eventually repulsed with very few casualties to us.
Comms & rations in our hands.
Weather clear and frosty.

Dec 9th.
BC & D Batteries relieved personnel of 114th 46th & 40th Batteries respectively.
1st Divisional Artillery on the STROMBEKE and zerom part with 32 DA Group
A/161 to B Group &
Lt B Bindloss to R.A. HQ, 1st Cor MS.
D/161 HQ vice Bindloss.
11th Major CHISHOLM MC on leave. Major LOCKHART to 32 DAC, Captain M. K. French took over command of A/161.

Dec 10th.
Relief was completed.
13th CAPT: WARD MC took over command

10th Casualties.
— 15499 Sgt Mashney J.M. : m.m. 13/1/61. ? Wounded.
D — ? 186543 A/Sdr Smythe J.A. "
220141 Gnr Mackie R. sustained injuries caused by collapse of dug-out due to enemy fire
Lt W.G. Hudson from 6/1/61
to A/161.

11th Casualties
4/194452 Gnr Harrison J. A/161. Wounded (Gas)
Died 12-12-17.

10TH

A/161/ which shifted guns to a new position
close Dec 12th

161 Bde HQ opened today over Gam he
3 group at CHEDDAR VILLA, ST. JULIEN.

Dec 13th.
D/161 and B/161 withdrew one section
from positions in the STROMBEKE.

Dec 15th
C/161 were relieved by personnel of 32nd
Bty. D/161 withdrew remaining hours,
and B/161 one more section.

Dec 16th
161 Bde Ammoned to ALBERT A + a
long concrete battalion command 18
hut - very comfortable.
Personnel of C, B, forr/section, and
D Batteries relieved personnel of
A C + D/84 at SPOT FARM
B still retains forward section in
STROMBEKE.

Dec 17th
B/161 (three 2 sections) took over C/161
position C/161 moved 8 guns into
their original position

Dec 18th
Weather clear and frosty. HQ 161

Bde moved out D to CHEDDAR and OILY
Bn ALBERTA to move up to the Infantry Bde HP the Infantry Bde HP.

Dec 19th
Day & night firing
Harassing fire was kept continuously during the 24 hours. The Bty Battery about 170 rounds in 24 hours out of the 24
S.O.S also being rigged in and 100 rounds of bang cartridges were continued

Dec 20.
HQ 161 Bde moved to CARRION from CHEDDAR to ALBERTA to be in close touch with the 3rd Inf Bde.

Dec 22nd
Protective barrage was put in straightening our line & cutting across the movement by a source of fire. This was not a surprise owing to enemy artillery and M.G. fire.

Dec 23rd
A message was captured bearing orders for enemy relief. Batteries barraged approaches and tracks at times of their "relief" night & am.

2/Lieut C.A. Weiler (SR) posted from 32nd SAB & attached

18/12/17 Casualties
121599 Fitter Thorpe A. 6/161. to hospital shell shock

19/12/17 2Lieuts R.L. Blake (SR), F. Addison (SR), & A.G. May (SR) posted from 32nd A.B. & attached to B/161, A/161 & 6/161 respectively.
Capt C.W. Ward M.B. A/161 authorized to wear badges of rank of Major.
Lieut JP. 6 Grubbes Lomax M.B. C/161 authorized to wear badges of rank of Capt.

Authy:
32nd Bur No A/100/
No A/100/
201 d.f.
19.12.17

20/12/17 Lieut L. Gilkess B/161 Granted Leave to U.K. from 23.12.17 to 5-1-18
2/Lieut from M.F.J.J Mossy A/161 Evacuated (sick) to OBS

24/12

Casualties.
5221 Gunner Bowsher G.W. A/161
Wounded (Gas)

14th Dec ... Dec 5 ...
B&c ... ... Dec 17th ...

Dec 25th
Quiet day. Weather wet and misty.
...marched from the Divl ...
...journal...
R.S Corps D.S.O Gts or Lts. Geo...

Dec 28th
Snow fell incessantly on the night
... enemy had ... Brigade moved
Enemy bombs of our line (2nd Batt.)
6.45 am a.a. the Divl. in & rev...
light rain 7.40 with 5am
... of the ... ... 2nd DSO received
on a course ... ... F.C. Hunt
to try for ... ... of the Brigade
...
Major E. A. CHILCOTT Reng ... hav-
...

Dec 29th.

Lieut-Col Lord Wynford DSO attached to R.5
Squadron R.F.C. from 27-12-14 to 31-12-14
Major F.C. Hunt B/161 assumed command
of Bde. vice Lt-Col Lord Wynford DSO
Lieut B/6 Trapper Loman H.C. C/161 posted to
Band assumed command of B/161 vice Major
F.C. Hunt.

At 7.40 p.m. enemy sniper's rapid fire opened on [first?] by [?] Swedenorp on our right. Battery fired in S.O.S. lines R.E. 45mm fire supported by machine gun fire Bde.

"A" reported as present.
"B" reported as present. Ammunition of Bn. was good: well distributed and with B in the heaps at battery posn.
Rations could not have been better placed 6 cm of protective paint of view

During the night a 4.5 gun fired [?] under our enemy with fair effect up to 1.00 am. A close defence gun has also been pushed forward covering the period from 8.30 to 12. [?] and of B/161 took place between 1 and 2 am.

Dec 28th

Snow still covers the ground and weather remains clear. B/161 were shelled between 12 noon and 2pm, about 200 5.9s falling in vicinity of battery position but no damage was done.

Dec 29th

0 [illegible] [illegible] white breeze reviewed to the
30°

Dec 31st

14th July Bde were relieved on night 30/31 by 117 Inf Bde 39 Div – On 32nd Div

29/12/14 Casualties – 1 O.R. wounded (gas) (654490 Gunner R.C. Mason A/161

Lieut R.E.T. BELL (S.R.) posted from 36th X A + A. attached A/161 (30.12.17)

28/12/14 Casualties.
281146 Bdr. Boothroyd W. C/161 wounded.
88011 Bdr. Stenning R.C. C/161 slightly wounded remained at duty.

* Harassing fire on communications, tramway points + tracks has been continued day and night; and a sniping gun been to Bijsi has taken every opportunity of firing available on the enemy. A close defence gun has also been pushed forward covering the period from 8.30 to 12 [?] and of B/161 has been manned by two [?]. The work of salvage has been pushed on, some hundreds of thousands of empty cartridge cases being returned as well as ammunition, equipment and miscellaneous. Construction of better shelter for detachments has been hindered by the snow and cold weather. Reserve positions for defence of Corps Line have been marked out and work started.

Throughout, work has been very seriously hampered by shortage of men. An average of 40 in hospital, 60 on command, and 60 under strength seriously depletes the

Authority:- H. Corps No
8/H.R/32/3-11 & ABRO
16.12.17. 32md BRO
26532 d/16-12-17

Honours & Awards – December 1917.

Major E.A. Chisholm M.C. Awarded Bar
6/161 to M.C.

Capt. J.W. Buckley 5/161. Awarded
Military Cross

2/Lieut. A.G. Blacklaws 3/161 do

26563 Bdr Fox J. 3/161 Awarded
D.C.M.

T/Captain H.L. McCormick mentioned in Despatches
Brigade D.S. Bolton DSO "

Our artillery sent a barrage as per
and training.

Dec 31st

The enemy put down a 20 mm
strafe of all calibres on front line at 6am
a few rounds falling on battery position
areas. The S.O.S. was sent up and the
Brigade fired accordingly - no counter
infantry action developed.
A & B Batteries moved their wagon
lines to 30th + 31st to Staples near D + H.Q.
East of the Canal.

Strength of the Brigade. There is a shortage
of N.C.O's, and the work of training
gunners, never more urgent than at the
present moment, is thereby seriendered
difficult. It is hoped that an opportunity
of resting, training and overhaul may
shortly be ours.
In spite of the losses and hardships
suffered in the recent campaign, it is
in the sure confidence of victory and
with a set determination to extend
our reputation that the 161st Brigade
enters upon another year of the war.

Casualties:- 42544? Gnr Sellers F. + 163017 Gnr J.R. Ackerman
   A/161 - wounded (Gas)

31/17
2/Lieut E.A.Tew (SR) posted from 32nd S.A.B.
+ attached C/161.

48699 A/Bdr W.G. Sweyart) wounded (Gas)
104203 Gnr F. Faidlow)
Casualties: 31/17 131924.. G. Vicars

January 1918

1st C/119 marched to new Wagon lines with the rest of the Brigade East of Wieltje. "A" & "B" Bde. four. det. to V/V & D/59 returned command. Vice Major Hunt on return from attachment to R.E.C.

2nd Enemy shelled C battery slightly - a stray shell causing 4 casualties inside the dugout.

3rd Enemy was confined with orders from enemy relief a approaching, at were carried accordingly.

4th Weather continues good & cold, enemy aircraft active one Eng. 200 ft above Bay HQ. Raining apparently lost its way in fog & major C/118. WAPD Mc to England on 8 d.a. Capt. Tuam M.C. Jan 8 assumed command of A161.

5th Day (very) quiet and very quiet. No harassing fire was carried out.

6th Day passed quietly, nothing to report. Relief of 166 by 174 Bde 39th Div Duty commenced.

7th Enemy shelled area of B.Y tery positions.
- 2 guns of D/161 were knocked out, 1 officer
- 1 O.R. slightly wounded

16th Relief completed.

Casualties 1/8. Nil
201229 Gnr Bridges.

Casualties 2/8.
201229 Gnr Bridges W.H. C/161 Killed
640238 " Campbell " Killed
4/12143 " Midgley J. " Slightly wounded
45459 Sapper Wakeford E.J. Batt C/161 remained at duty
554 Jd J Cory. R.B. ditto
229486 Gnr Lewis A.J. B/161 ditto

16. E.H. Bombs approached H.Q. & Wagon lines but.

a) Capt 93 G.S Murphies Lomax M.C attached to 71st Squadron RFC.
b) with the 2nd line attached "R" A. Bty Lost. Budd.

7/18 Lieut. C.R. Cliff C/161 on leave until 21-1-18

8/18 Snow all during the morning and weather turned bad again
    Lost sgt. A.C.D. Stewart (19911 Sgt Holmes A.) returned to duty A.S.C 83 R.g.a. R.D. 39 to Div Buty. Passed to command of Div Cdr.

C.R.A. 29th Division

9/18 Runr Raimsay 25 class A.C.D. Wire returned to duty. 2/18 Bde. & Hors drawn in.

10/18 Lieut. Col. Lord Wynford D.S.O. assumed command of 32 D.a.
    vice Brig-Gen J.A. Tyler C.M.G. on leave. Major C. Chisholm M.C. C/161 assuming command of Bde. & Capt F. Bennett assuming command of C/161.

12/18 a/Capt. B.C. Trappes-Lomax M.C. rejoined from attached to 7 squadron R.F.C.

Casualties 7/18
2/Lieut A.S. Blacklaws M.C. B/161. Killed
19911 Sgt. Holmes A. B/161 Slightly wounded, remained at duty
18342 Gnr Harding E. A/161 — ditto —

Casualties 8/18
210020 Gnr Savage W.L. B/161 Wounded

Casualties 9/18 19832 B/dr Moores J.W. B/161 Slightly wounded remained at duty.

16/8 Lieut-Col. Lord Wynford D.S.O. relinquished command of 32 D.A.

17/8 Lieut-Col. Lord Wynford D.S.O. proceeded to attend R.A. Senior Officers Course at Shoeburyness commencing 20-1-18.

17/8 Lieut. C.F.W. Huffenden M.C. rejoined Bde. & was posted to 28/161.
Capt. & Adjt. R.L. Creasy M.C. granted leave from 17/8 to 31/8

18/8 Capt. J. Filmes 9/161 assumed duties of Adjt. vice Capt. R.L. Creasy on leave.
Capt. J.T. Heffernan R.A. M.C. 9/a Field Ambce. relieved

1918
19/2 Capt H.F. McCormick R.A.M.C. who had been
      granted leave from 20-1-18 to 3-2-18
20/2 90th Infantry Bde. moved into Hospital Farm area
      2/Lieut W.C. Wilson A/161 attached 6/161
20/2 97th Infantry Bde. moved into Langemarck
20/21/2 3 guns Jan Bty. Taken up into action in N.3 areas
      CHEDDAR VILLA, a Guard being placed in rear of
      Battery's farm taken by II Corps Defence line over the guns
2/2/18 32nd Div. H.Q. (less Artillery) moved from
      Camp X c/o CANAL BANK. C.25.d. O.O.
      114th Infantry Bde. moved to Hospital Farm area
      96th   "   "   "   "   "   area east of
                                          CANAL
29/2 - 29/2 32nd Division (less Artillery) relieved
      18th & 1st Divisions (" ")
30/2 2/Lieut W.G. Laynder A/161 struck off strength Medical
      Board obtained
30/31/2 Section by section moved up into
      new positions covering 3rd Div. Inpts.
      taking over sector newly on
      Artillery forn'd sector newly on
      82 & 83 Bde RFA
3/1 Remained in actions for pnts.
    made up into 4 gun
                    (8)   II 15.18.2 (2)
    A/161 U.16.a.9.1 (8) II 15.18.2 (2)
    B/111 U.22.a. 27.99 (3) U.16.a. 18.33
    C/161 U.21.c.65 (4) U.21.a.6.4. (2)
    D/161 U.20.6.93 (4) U.20.6.51 (2)
    123 Bath ✱ 6.5 B⁵⁹ Cam. under Cdn
    ✱ 161 Bde. 11am 1-2-18
    Lieut F.J. Phillips posted 161 Bde. from Fourth
    Army + attached to A/161
    Owing to illness A/161 proceeded to attend A.6's Courses
    Capt of Gilmore at Shoeburyness commencing 3-2-18

23/2 Lieut B. Bakewell rejoined B/161 from
     "R" AA Bty.
24/2 Major E.A.J. Sease-Watkin D.S.O. posted to
     + assumed command of Bde. Major to A.
     Chisholm M.C. resuming command of 6/161
     Major E.A Chisholm M.C. 6/161 granted leave to
     Major J.W. Buckley M.C. 29/161 PARIS from 25/2
     2/Lieut R.G. Johnson B/161 to 29/2 Both dates inclusive
25/2 Major Left J. Sease-Watkin D.S.O. with Battery
     Commanders reconnoitred positions occupied by
     82nd & 83rd Brigades R.F.A.
26/2 Major P. Crow M.C. posted from Base +
     assumed command of A/161.
✗   2/Lieut E.A has rejoined 6/161 from Hospk/Anti-Gas School
29/2 Lieut C.R. Cliff rejoined 6/161 his leave
     having been extended by W.O. from 21-1-18
     to 29-1-18
✗   Lieut B Bakewell 15/161 on leave until 12-2-18
✗ 29/2 2/Lieut H.C. Dryland B/161 on Course at Fourth
        Army Anti Gas School
     Capt M. King-French A/161 on leave until 1-2-18

41 Reinforcements received during Jany 1918.

February 1918.

1st — Headquarters moved from W.K. into action at LAPIN FARM

Command of Right Group Artillery passed from Major W.E. Connolly Comdg Right Group (282nd&305th RFA) to Major E.H.P.
PEASE-WATKIN D.S.O. Comdg. 161st Bde. R.F.A. at 11 a.m.

Capt & Adjt R.L. Greally M.C. returned off leave & proceeded to H.Q. 32 di Divisional Artillery to study duties of Bde Major vide G.H.Q. letter 0.48/1911/3 dff 19/8/17.

× 2nd Lieut R.A. Wynter-Birch 6/161 assumed duties of Adjutant.

1/2 — 114th Infantry Bde relieved 97th Infantry Bde in the HET SAS sector, the 97th Infy Bde being in Divisional Reserve in BOESINGHE No 2 Area with H.Q. at ZOMMERBLOOM

2nd —

3 — Orders received that Divisional front would be re-adjusted so as to hold Divisional front with all Infantry Bdes in the line, each on a front of one battalion. The 14th Infy Bde will be on Right Bde Sector, 96th Infy Bde. in centre Bde Sector and 97th Infy Bde on Left Bde Sector.

4th — Raid on GRAVEL FARM. by 105th Infy Bde (on night) at 4/5 a.m. A/161 B/161, 123rd Bdes fired in support (P.T.O. for result)

4/5 — 97th Infantry Bde. (less 17 H.L.I) relieved 14th Infantry Bde. in Left Bde Sector.

5th — Lieut F.J. Philips A/161 & a party of 1 N.C.O. & 10 men proceeded to Calais to draw remounts from No 5 Base Remount Depôt

---

1st — Lieut A.W. Sennington H.Q/161 & Lieut F.J. Jaddion A/161 proceeded to Fourth Army Artillery School on course.
× 2nd Lieut R.A. Wynter-Birch 6/161 assumed duties of Adjutant.

(2 Lieut J.H.G. May Fourth Army Artillery School.
2 Lieut F. Midgebrook A/161) on leave until 17-2-17.

3/18 — Lieut. J.A. Dryland rejoined B/161 on completion of Course at Fourth Army Anti-Gas School.
Capt. W. Long-French A/161 attended 4C's Course at Shoebuzyness commencing on this date.

4/18 — Capt. F.J. McCormack R.A.M.C. returned off leave & Capt. G.T. Heffernan R.A.M.C. rejoined of the field Ambulance

Lieut-Col. Lord Wynford D.S.O. proceeded on leave on completion of Course at Shoebuzyness

Result of raid of 14th on GRAVEL FARM. V.8.a.0.0.
Complete success.
Gravel Farm & neighbouring posts destroyed.
Large shelter destroyed & 9 enemy killed by
bangalore which was pushed through loophole.
29 enemy actually killed by our Infantry &
1 O.R. (wounded) of 14th Cavy. 94th I.R. brought in
for identification. 1 MG was destroyed by bombs.
Our casualties were 3 O.R. slightly wounded.
Message was received expressing excellence of
our Artillery fire.

4/8 2/Lieut from 2/T J.D.Mason A/161 - leave extended
to this date on medical grounds.

5/6 14 Infantry Bde. (less 2nd Manchester Regt) relieved
96th Infantry Bde. in Right Bde. Sector.

6th 2nd Manchester Regt was transferred to 96th Infy. Bde.
& 16th Northumberland Fusiliers & Disbandment of 1st
commenced.

7/8 96th Infantry Bde. relieved 14th & 94th Infy. Bdes.
in Centre Bde. Sector.

8th Lieut. W. Ellis on leave until 22-2-18

9/8 Wagon lines of 161 Bde R.F.A. near Bridgetown C.19.d.
handed over to 39th Bty RHA, A/g. v Batteries of
161 Bde taking over the wagon lines of 25th Bde
R.F.A. at A.12.0.0. & B.7.a.
1st Divn.

9/18 Lieut. G. Turnbull 9/1/61 to RFC as Balloon Observer on probation. & struck off strength.

10/18 Casualties.
36594 Gnr H. Blackley 6/1/61 Wounded

10/18 14 Reinforcements received from S.R.B.

11/18 At 10 am 2/1/61 & 13/1/61 came under the command of 35th Div. Artly. & form part of Left Bde. 35th Div. Artly.
Composition of Bde. R.F.A. —
A/28 Bde RFA & B/28 came under orders of O/C 16/13 de.
From of Right Group 32nd D.A. along with 6/1/61 & 5/1/61
2/Lieut. S. Murphy posted from 2nd Army Art. School to 10/Bde RFA. & was attached to 5/1/61.
2/Lieut. A. J. Meakes posted from Base & was attached to 29/1/61.

11/7/18 2/Lieut J.A. Clayton posted from 1/32 T.M. Btly & attached to 6/161.

13/7/18 Major G.A. Chisholm M.B. 6/161 proceeded to attend B.C's course at Shoebuyness, Lieut O.R.Cliff assuming command of 6/161.
2/Lieut Hon. T.F.J. Massy's leave extended to this date on Medical Cert.

14/7/18 Reinforcements arrived from 32nd L.T.C.

15/7/18 2/Lieut. R.L. Blake 9/161 admitted hospital sick.

18/7/18 Lieut-Col. Lord Wynford S.O. rejoined on expiration of leave & resumed command of Bde. Major L.A.O. Page Watkin S.O. resuming command of 2/161. Major C.W. Ward M.C. rejoined & resumed command of A/161.

12/7/18 4/27668 Lce Bd+ Cuthbert A. A/3/161 wounded. Accidentally wounded.

18/19. 96th & 94th Infantry Bdes. under cover of Artillery Barrage carried out raids on enemy Pill Boxes, posts etc. the object of raids being to kill, take prisoners & obtain identifications. Batteries of 161 Bde R.F.A. fired in support of raid by 96th Infy Bde. During the operations 27 prisoners & 1 M.G. were brought in. Severe losses were inflicted on the enemy in killed. Our casualties slight.

19/20. 14th Infantry Bde. relieved 94th Infantry Bde. in Left Sub-Sector.

20th 2/Lieut. J.G. Creighton posted from Base & attached to C/161.

21st Lieut. E.N. Thornton posted from 32nd D.A.C. to C/161.

21/22 Enemy raided Belgians on our left. Batteries of 161 Bde R.F.A. opened days rate of fire in accordance with Mutual Support Scheme.

22nd Lieut. F.J. Phillips A/161 & 1 N.C.O. from B/161 proceeded on 2 days course at Salvage of Fy. Products Depot Calais.

23/24. 16 Lancs. Fusiliers relieved 2nd Manchester Regt. in front system of forward Zone, 2nd Manchesters moving to ABRI WOOD & becoming No 3 Battalion. 15 Lancs Fusiliers relieved 16 Lancs Fusiliers in support system of forward Zone & became No 2 Battalion.

x
23/8 2/Lieut. R.W. Johnson B/161 granted leave from 24.2.18 to 10-3-18.
2/Lieut S. Murphy D/161 attended course commencing today at II Corps Anti-Gas School. (P.T.O)

19/8. Lieut. B. Bakewell's leave extended to his stay on Medical Course.

x
22/8 2/Lt. Hon. T.F.J.D. Massy D/161. Struck off strength — Medical Board ordered.
2/Lieut. F.W. Hook D/161 admitted hospital sick.

23rd Capt & Major P.W. Buckley M.C. 1/161 on leave from today until 26-3-18

25th Casualties.
92561 Gnr G. Today 6/161 wounded

26th Lt. & Capt. P. Crews M.C. attached to No 9 Squadron R.F.C. for instruction.

27th Raids on Maréchal Farm & neighbourhood carried out by 14th and 96th Infantry Brigades. All objectives captured and 12 prisoners taken, also 2 M.G's. Large number of enemy killed. /Batteries of 161 Bde R.F.A. fired in support of raids.

(P.T.O.)

28/2/18 Batteries of 161 Bde RFA fired in support of Raid by 35th Division. Enemy retaliated during the night by shelling Battery positions & vicinity with Gas Shell.

21. Reinforcements arrived during the month.

Honours & Awards

84899 Sgt. M.A. Gillyons A/161 — Awarded Belgian
4/28048 Sgt. E.H. Ashmore C/161 — Croix de Guerre.
4/19516 Sgt. Giles R.G. C/161 Awarded Chevalier
de l'ordre de Leopold II

Authy. for above :- M.S.1/A/7591 d/- 27-1-18;
32nd DRO 2761 d/ 3-2-18.

March 1918

1/18 1/4 Reinforcements arrived from 32nd I.A.B.

2nd Information received at 7.40 p.m. that enemy would raid COLOMBO HOUSE at 8.20 p.m. Batteries warned accordingly. Concentrated fire brought to bear on above front. No enemy action materialised.

3rd 2/Lieut. S. Murphy D/161 posted to 168 Bde R.F.A. on completion of course at II Corps Anti-Gas school. Lt. Col. P. Curos M.C. rejoined B/161 from attached M.G. Squadron R.F.C.
2/Lieut. R.A. Myrtley Birch ceased to perform duties of Acting Adjutant & assumed duties of Orderly Officer.

3/4 9nd Infantry Bde relieved 96th Infantry Bde in Right Bde Sector.

4th Lieut. A.B. Traders-Lomax M.C. B/161 attached to H.Q. & assumed duties of Battery Offr. Acting Adjutant.

5/3/18 At 3 a.m. Batteries of Brigade fired in support of raid carried out by 35 Division on our Right. Results – We reached objectives but found no enemy – Casualties Brig. nil.

6/3/18 Afternoon received in the evening gun that the enemy aircraft raid COLOMBO H.S.E. – have came off.

7/3/18 at 1.15 a.m. C/161 x D/161 Bde in support of a raid by the 35th Bde on our right – results nil.

8/3/18 5 Reinforcements arrived. Lieut. A.W.Denniston A/B + 2 Lieut. F Addison 2/161 rejoined on completion of course at Fourth Army Artillery School. 2/Lieut. R A Wynley-Birch ceased to perform duties of Orderly Officer & was attached to A/161.
At 2.05am an enemy raid on our front and fired shot the 10th A.S. on a SOO front. Planning were in pyjamas.
At 9.20a.m. 1/1 Beds and 168 Bde assisted by 157 Bde fired a barrage (creeping) for a counter attack by the 2nd Royes (1 coys) on the right and the 2nd/4th 6th Royal Scots on the left. The enemy

11/3/18 2/Lieut R.G. Johnson 93/161 returned off leave

12/3/18 5 Reinforcements joined from Base

13.3.18. 7.85 P.m. Enemy opened a heavy
bombardment (17mm, 10"5cm & 6cm
T.M.s and B.Bs.) on our front
of HEPT COCOABO KEEP. About
30 germans were seen advancing.
A.C.O.S was put up by Rifle Gr. & Lewis
Guns & by Artillery. (They did not reach
our Barrage) (They did not reach
our lines.

14.3.18 12. LAZZENDEN P.C.
Bombed by T.B.G. on Fg.
Gr. C.R.S. 15. 3.16.
6 Reinforcements arrived for 2nd

15/16. Divisional front re-adjusted so as to be
held on a one Brigade front.
Following reliefs took place:-
96 Infantry Bde relieved 144th Infantry Bde.
97th Infantry Bde. becoming 2 Bde (next to
go into the line) & the 144th Infantry Bde.
becoming No 3 Bde in reserve.

16.3.18. The Division had a heavy
AM & GAS Shell bombardment
of our right Battalions and
C.O.'s Scout East of 2 Bde.
Lines in support of enemy the
Hot Graich on Lens (the Lochres)
at 3.0 P.M.

17.3.18. At 5.0 am the enemy heavily
shelled the Battalions and M.G.
with [mustard] gas. The Infantry
action ceased.

18.3.18. At 10 am the Battalion to M.G.
were again subjected to a heavy
gas Shell Bombardment.

Lieut F.J Phillips admitted hospital sick.
19.3.18 Lieut [Fischer] wounded in confusion
[Jeuvre] & Lens
1 OR wounded (QRs)

18/3/4 5 OR wounded (QRs)

20/3/16 Left Neuf Berg. Intermittent shell
fire all day night.

21/3/16 Heavy back area bombardment all
day. 161 who shelled also Slow dump Roclincourt
R Maroeuil — Previous Brest broken. No attack
followed — (enemy known S boundaries)

22/3/16

23/3/16 Relieved around district C
1st Aust Bn C.O. reports arrangement
A/16 reported to this HQ + to 2/3 R A I.
2 Coy C Coy + Mortar Pls. to D/16 + HQ + 2 Mddsx
2/3/F Aust A/16 - 2 L.Gs. wounded
+ 2 L.Gs. half-buried in N.C. reg'd D/16
7 [illegible]

24/3/16 Great G. Crayton attached to R A s' Army
7 Div area Plan given A/16 on completion

25/3/16

26/3/16 Lt-Col CW Mandy reports A/16
died C.E. Leach N.F. attached to O.C. Coys

29/3/16 Belgians arrived either were to take
over 2nd & 4th Brigade Bulgar. Infantry took
our line we went —
Capt J.W. Buckley M.C. returned off leave &
D/16 MSR WR gunshum — 26/3/16.

28/3/16. Very quick Belgian again
guns and Battery positions.
Col. said my 2nd wk & CRA 12 Jun
Maj Pead 17 Jun 17 LdS train - O/C 161.
Lt Mortin came H.Q. of Brigade H.Q.

29/3/16 B/16 & C/ in Belgian arty festemen
Belgians had a few guns during war)
Belgians had 4 guns D + 4 guns C.

30/3/16 161 Brigs handed [?] and
Belgians & moved down to
B/16 at SIEGE CAMP
2 Bars. hives at SIEGE CAMP

31/3/18 C+D Batteries returned to
Billets for SAVY BERLETTE
Major Estheral at 2.30 at
PROVEN arriving at SAN DENNETTE
11.0 pm
Billets or Billeting style night in
field at BELEER HEADING

April 1918

1.4.18
Scalping took place and farriers detained
at SAVY and TINCOURT which also bore
the night at HARBICOURT
2.
One section now for Thy, returned one
section of 152nd Sqn REA
3.4.18
HQ 161 Bde returned HQ 15th Bde at
ENSUENT
Bombarding actions
Every Battery Comd with W.L at ENUDIENTRE
4.
They had mapped for accommodation of 6
Battery Commanders and ammunition
has been up
A161 moved antitank gun to forward
position [illegible]
5. Capt (+ Adjt) R.C. CREASY MC returned
from course of instruction at R.A HQ
3 D.Div Lt DENNINGTON rejoined 6 cm
A161 moved 15 inch Rest one, one
section now arrangeables moved forward
Day quiet
6.d Registration commenced
Remaining guns moved forward

5.L   3 O.R wounded, 1 O.R killed

6.d   2/Lt P.A. Rothwell posted to
       A161 from D.A.C C.O Capt KING
       2/Lt J.B Boardman ditto

7th Bn Dwd wood gave it forward OP'. Shrow and hvy shelling scattered

9d Bn HQ B/6 and Bde moved out of BAVINKT. Enemy quiet except for gas shelling of ADINFER WOOD

9th 3/16 Brig'n Bn relieved in ADINFER WOOD

10th 3/16 Brig'n Bn had to position up to get some rest. She was affected and sank down to sleep mostly in E.80

11 Having the Bde continued during the period between 7th and 6am, mapping and registering dury the day. A concentration was put during the day on hostile BATTN though to be active.

An enemy attack is thought possible at any moment. New positions and routes have been reconnoitered and arrangements made for ammunition supply. O P's are kept in visual comm

---

4th 1 TM round

9d 2 Other rounds (B.M.)

9th 3 TM rounds K.F.3

10th 8 O.P. mounded (G.A.)
    45 Returned from 9 a.e

12th. Day passed quietly; very warm and fine; great F.A. activity. Enemy shelled back areas with long-range guns with some pertinacity.

12th. "72nd Army Bde R.F.A. (Lt Col RICHEY) came into action as a subgroup under OC 151st Bde. Day quiet.

14th. HQ 161 Bde moved to valley near JJ in Bde HQ. (Mennot Galley) As new zone 4000 away!); a cold wind made tents rather a chilly change. Day was quiet. J/2nd Bde registering.

15th. Continued reports of short shooting have lead to the discovery of some bad ammunition; this has caused a great deal of trouble. Day was quiet.

16th. Day quiet. nothing to report. 2Lt FREAKES wounded at D 151 position. A 161 made a "silent Battery" firing on Sr. S.O.S. a counter preparation.

17th - 18th passed quietly - Under orders from CRA B/161 Accoms a 2ndLt. Battery was R/61.

19th Gas Bombardments by How Batteries. Dick carried out on an average of one every two nights. The enemy's gas shelling has died down to the front is in all respects normal except for leaking - no message on the enemy's front.

21st Ammt B/161 was engaged by a 15cm How during early afternoon - forward appears to have been the old gun pits used by the battery as a marker. One man slightly wounded. No casualties to equipment.

22nd Day passed quietly - a slight burst of shelling near D.R.S. at 5.30pm. During the night D. assisted in a gas bombardment of support line enemy HQ.

23rd Enemy artillery rather more active, several area bombardments being put down, but none near the batteries. Several reports of hostile movement received

19th 1 OR joined from reinforcements from field.
19th 1 OR wounded
21st 1 OR wounded
22nd 1 OR wounded (Gas) Lieut G Trumbler M.O. posted to Brigade from 372 Bde.
23rd Lieut J Campbell posted to Brigade from 372 Bde. as Sig O.

23rd 1 OR wounded

24th Day passed quietly

25th 1 OR wounded

25th A bright clear day. Enemy shelled ADINFER WOOD rather heavily, & enemy artillery was considerably more active.

26th A dull day with some rain. Gun Shoot & Lingering fire. Command of 37th Div on formation to command of Corps.

27th Day passed quietly. One section of one battery 161 & 168 Bde. relieved one section of 7.4 & 75. 80th Guards Brigade relieved one section during the night 27-28. The left group of the 2nd Division who were on our left.

28th HQ relieved the HQ of the Guards Artillery, taking over command of one Section that went in night 27-28, were registered. Remaining 2 sections of each battery took over during night 28-29 & were all in action by 10.30 p.m. There was some shelling during the relief

28th Had no casualties

29th A dull quiet day. Problems were heard during the day

May

1st. Began lines on mow near BAILLEULMONT and BAILLEULVAL in open. Quiet front material are arriving. Guns and huts arrange and large Canas near Artillery positions and they are getting settled etc. Built some Richican observatories with Quads D.17 Headquarters at BLAIREVILLE nearer.
6th Inf. Bde. 2nd Division under 41st DA. H.msn. is'd 168 one. Un Loft anti Gray.

2nd. Day passed quietly - at 2.30 am Group fired in support of raid by 2nd Canadian Division on our left. 8 prisoners were captured. Light 5 mags and many of the enemy were otherwise accounted for. Artillery fire lasted for 35 minutes for 161 Bdl and

2g 15 pm see 163 Bde - Bn Battery engaging
and 2 local convoys

3rd   Rather increased hostile arty activity
      Neighbourhood of A161 being engaged
      during night of 2nd/3rd by 5.9 Bty. Some
      bombing (a/c) on BLAIRVILLE in the
      evening.

4th & 5th Nothing of interest - some counter
      battery work on A161 and neighbouring
      batteries; a cap[tured] wood 3 inch battery
      + 106 fuzes being used.

6th   At 9.10pm the S.O.S. was reported
      on the left of the 2nd Bde on our
      right. The group fired for 30 mins
      in support of the group on our
      right - no infantry action was
      reported.

7th   Headquarters of 761 moved to
      quarry outside the village - occupying
      2 mizzen huts and some dugouts.
      These have been constructed by 6, 6th
      Inf Bde of 2nd Division for us.

8th. A test of all means of communication in other than telephone was carried out to day with on the whole satisfactory results. There was a good deal of artillery activity during the night.

9th. Nothing of interest. Some counter battery work on B/161. unfortunately causing few casualties.

10th. Day passed quietly. A battery having moved from old position having been shelled rather heavily during the last few days. D battery carried out a bombardment with in[c]endiary shell on a large dump of ammunition boxes, setting it well alight, to the great joy of the infantry.

11th. Increase in activity of hostile artillery on both sides. Our Inf Brig[adier] Gen Hart-Synnot had left us. Known away of his Brigade Major Wright killed by some shell whilst walking through BLAIRVILLE.

12th. A quiet dull day. Our Divisional infantry relieved the 2nd Division last night. But our divisional RA HQ are not leaving over yet.

13th & 14th Nothing of interest.

15th A Lothian's forward guns were shelled heavily and out moving Mobile artillery caused us several casualties to-day.

16th A Lothian's forward guns moved forward to a position in the roadway close to D battalion position.

17th Last night in conjunction with the Canadian Corps on our left we fired a Piping Hot barrage NE of BOYELLES. Mobile artillery is becoming noticeably more active and has started on counter battery work.

18th Nothing of interest. Lt. 32nd Divisional artillery HQ relieved Lt. 40th to-day.

15th 1 O.R. wounded

19th There has been practically no case in enemy fire actually as regards Brandon-hoffling work. Both B + D batteries receiving attention.

20th Enemy artillery actively on howe
21st Last night we occupied in two raids one on the Right Angle front the other by the left with the cadre group. The other by the Right Group Canadian Brigade assisted by the Right Group Canadian artillery and D/161.

22nd Hostile artillery carried out an effective distribution shoot on D/161. The afternoon Major Pease-Watkin was wounded and Lt Filtness was badly wounded and died in hospital in the evening. Four men were kd and 3 other had wd at section.

23rd D Battery raised their position to the position on the outskirts of Ebin forward section.

24th–26th Enemy artillery very active counter battery work throughout this period A/161 and C/161 have each had a gun put out of action.

27th At 2.0 a.m enemy put down a very

19th 1 OR wounded

20th 1 OR wounded

21st 7 ORs wounded

22nd Major E.H.P. PEASE-WATKIN D.S.O } Wounded
      Lieut. J. FILTNESS
      Lieut. J. FILTNESS died of wounds
      2 ORs wounded
      1 OR wounded or remained at duty

24th 11 Reinforcements from D.A.C.

25th 1 OR wounded

26th 5 OR killed
      P.T.O

Lieut B. BAKEWELL } wounded & adm. Host.
2/Lieut. T. CAMPBELL }
2 ORs killed
1 OR wounded

28th 23 Reinforcements from SAC.

27th(cont) heavy barrage on our out post line and shortly after no info any quarter. Shelled B Sound HQ & C Battery signal dugout killed 5 signallers. To the burned a direct hit on B Battery Officer mess wounded Maj Ward, 2/Lt B. Cadwell and 2/Lt T. Campbell. Two of the servants were killed and another wounded. Maj Ward was only slightly hit and did not have to go to H8 dressing station.

28th Enemy artillery activity has died down considerably.

29th Batteries are registering for a raid to be carried out by the 17th Lancers it was The has since been cancelled

30th 155th Army Bde were taken out of the line from the group on our right. The group now consists of our own batteries viz 110, 85 & C/1A and D/186.

31st A quiet day very little shelling

June 1918

1st C Battery Forward section in Bois-beau our Mont were shelled to-day and Lieut Cliff wounded. One gun was badly damaged by shell fire. They are moving to a new position in the Aisne Valley.

2nd Gas concentrations were fired in the valley behind our batteries. The detached section of D battery had 2 men hit by HE's, three men gassed by a shell that burst in the mouth of one of the dugouts.

3rd The Canadian division on our left carried out a raid. We put down a barrage for 10 minutes do cover their attacks.

4th & 5th The 72nd Army Brigade R.F.A. relieved the 186th in this sector. The 16 M Battery CFA are no longer in this group. B/161 Bow and Howen do BRETENCOURT becoming the Mobile battery of the group. There has also been taken over by A/72. Lieut T Cowan joined the Bde

6th A/161 forward section to day 2 killed again to-day & 2 Lt Addison wounded.

1/6/18
Lieut. C.R. CLIFF wounded & admitted hospital
2/Lieut R.E.T. BELL proceeded to Lieut Army Sch of Instn on horse

2/6/18
2 OR. wounded
3 OR. wounded (GAS)

3/6/18
1 OR. wounded 2/Lt D/161 MAY 3/Lt brought back to USA

4/6/18
Lieut. E.J.S. ROBINSON wounded and admitted hospital
Lieut T. COWAN joined Bde and posted D/161

5/6/18
1 OR. wounded
Lieut W.E. ELLIS returned from leave

6/5/18
2/Lieut. F. ADDISON wounded and admitted hospital

7/6/18 OR wounded (nerve splinter) and remained at duty
1 OR wounded

9/6/18 8 Reinforcements from Base

10th 2/Lt G.S. CAMPBELL posted to England (wound)

11th Lieut O.R. CLIFF transferred to Reserve (wounded)
Lieut G.O. d'I VRY gazetted acting Capt and posted 13/M

12/6/18
Lieut G.O. d'I VRY K.P.M.S. posted SIBBALD MITRY & me army
[illegible]

June 1918

7th The Divisional Commander & CRA visited the O.P.'s & battery positions to day. An aeroplane dropped a bomb close to C/161 forward section. Lieut P.R. Hamilton MC joined the Bde posted to A/161

8th & 9th Nothing of interest. The front is known to be [illegible] quiet. 8 reinforcements from D.A.C.

10th Major V.A. Hellman joined the Brigade as Horse advisor. 2/Lt G.J. Cooney joined the Brigade posted to C/161

11th A quiet day

12th Last night the 9.6" Infantry Brigade carried out a raid on enemy posts and secured 3 prisoners. We fired a protective barrage of which the infantry spoke in high praise. 2/Lt A.H. Godley & 2/Lt J.W. Britten joined the Bde posted to D/161 & B/161 respectively

June 1918

13ᵗʰ Nothing of interest

14ᵗʰ T.M. heavy arty carried out a concentration on trench mortars in Bozelles this afternoon. Our batteries also fired on the same targets.

15ᵗʰ, 16ᵗʰ Ex cept for trench mortars firing on star front & outpost lines there has been very little activity on our front.

16ᵗʰ 17 reinforcements joined from D.A.C.

17ᵗʰ 2 Lt W S Kirk & 21ˣ L A joined the Bde posted to B/161 & C/161 respectively.

18ᵗʰ With a view to discovering the enemy on the Ghl frontier of our S.O.S. line our S.O.S. was sent up at 4.0 a.m. this morning & we fired on our Defend. S.O.S. barrage line to the north of our S.O.S. lines.

13/6/18 J.K. wounded

17ᵗʰ/18ᵗʰ Kynock & T Boswynd in completion of course at Ind Army Artillery School.

18ᵗʰ Lieut P H J Mills wounded the course of ambulance on the "Ironwood" Owen Gibb. On my flight at VI on this defend

13ᵗʰ 21ˢᵗ A C PRYND proceed on leave to England

June 1918

20th — The 9th T.I. C.S. carried out a raid with 300 men in for to in and near Ossylles. Very few of the huts were found occupied but identification was obtained & prisoners wounded was taken. We found craters & flank barrage for the operation.

21st — The Canadians on our left carried out a raid last night. 20 prisoners were taken & but few of the enemy seen. We fired a flank barrage for the operation. Nothing of interest.

22nd — Nothing of interest

23rd — Slight shelling of forward areas

24th — A quiet day

25th — The Canadians carried out a raid on a large scale on their right front. 22 prisoners were taken & machine guns and 1 trench mortar. We fired a flank barrage on a division

26th — Our front is now held on a one battalion frontage.

Reinforcements from B.A.B.

22/6/18 — 1 O.R. wounded
23/6/18 — 2 O.R. wounded
24/6/18 — 2/Lt. P.N. ALLEN injured may his
  L. Davie & Osisnisky in the forward
  area. Onlv Davie Ayt of St hosp. to base
25/6/18 — Lieut. G. DUNDAS M.C. awarded
  to Third Army Gas School as
  Brinne...

June & July 1918

27th Nothing of interest
28th A/72 Battery were heavily shelled to day and two hit or on fire. Luckily there were no casualties.

29th

30th Brig. Gen Girdwood 96th I.B. ascended a cut of the observations of the Bde as a mark of appreciation of good work done by the Bde whilst on the HOULTHUST FOREST front.

1st & 2nd Nothing of interest

3rd Two sections (for batteries) were relieved by 74th Bde. (guards Trench Artillery) This evening and proceeded to Hunebeæcourt.

4th Headquarters & the remaining section for batteries were relieved to day and marched to Hunebecourt.

5th The Brigade is now at rest but is in readiness to move at 1 hours notice from dawn to 9.0 a.m. and 4 hours notice from 9.0 a.m. onwards.

20/6/18 2nd Lieut T. S. M. Moseleyh to British Army Hidden School
  on pass & leave

3/7/18
1 J.R. wounded

17/7/18 2nd Lieut A.G. DRYLAND rejoined from Leave

2/4/16

6th Major Chisholm reconnoitred the position we should have to occupy in case of attack. B Battery's guns went to "cowher" to-day for calibration

7th Batteries are carrying out "draming" in driving drill, marching & setting up drill, gun drill & drill orders

8th D Battery's guns were calibrated at the calibration range

9th Mar Gen Haldane the Corps commander inspected the Brigade dismounted in the courtyard at Brigade HQ to-day. He afterwards went round the Horse lines and Gun parks.
A & C Battery's guns were calibrated to-day

10th
11th Batteries are continuing with their
12th draming

13th a Test Emergency turnout was ordered
15 Divisional RA HQ and carried out successfully

7/4/18 2 Lieut. R.ROTHWELL A/161 proceeded to Vth Corps Gas School on course
6 Reinforcements posted to 161 from 32nd DAC.

12/4/18 6 reinforcements posted to 161 from 2nd DAC

12/4/18 2 Lieut. L.A. MOULD C/161 proceeded to Third Army Arty School on course.

13/4/18 2 Lieut. R.ROTHWELL A/161 rejoined on completion of course at Vth Corps Gas School

July 1918

14th
15th
16th The first half of the Brigade sports were held this afternoon
17th There was a Brigade skeleton drill order this morning & in the afternoon the second half of the Brigade sports were run off. The Divisional band playing for the occasion
18th Orders received to entrain
19th The Brigade entrained at DOULLENS, BOUQUEMAISON and MONDICOURT.
20th The Brigade detrained at WEVENBERG + PROVEN + marched about 2 miles to good billets on the HARDINGE WATOU Road. During the afternoon batteries moved on a advance for hostilities into reserve positions close to LA LOVIE aerodrome to cover the Blue line.
21st A reconnaissance of the Blue line and OP's was carried out
22nd } Batteries are carrying out training
23rd } of personnel under Battery arrangements. Two NCO's & four men are remaining with the ordnance in position

10/7/18 2/Lieut. F.A. POHL joined Bde. and posted
17/7/18 2/Lieut H. JONES G.F. joined Brigade and posted B/161
18/7/18 12 reinforcements posted to Bde. from 32nd D.A.C.

23/7/18 2nd Lieut R.A. WYRLEY-BIRCH D/161 on leave until 6-9-18

July 1918

24th Brigade + Battery commanders proceeded by bus to reconnoitre positions in the neighbourhood of RENINGHELST.
Gen Buckle RA inspected our horses this afternoon.

25th Batteries and working parties to XIX Corps area to prepare positions

26th
27th } Nothing of interest
28th
29th

30th 168th Brigade held their sports meeting.

31st Nothing of interest.

27/7/18 Lieut. N.E. WILSON. A/161. proceeded to II Corps Signal school on course

28/7/18 2/Lieut. J.G. CONEY, C/161, on leave until 11-8-18
2/Lieut. L.A. MOULD C/161, rejoined on completion of course at Third Army Arty School.
2/Lieut. A.G. DRYLAND, B/161 proceeded to Second Army Arty School, on course.

August 1918

1-6 Battere reconnoitred positions
     to cover the East POPERINGHE line
     the WATOU line and West POPERINGHE
     line. We cover the 32nd Div. 30th
     American Division and Belgian
     Belgians respectively.
     Brigade hp WATOU Bivouac

7th Hostmoor & hiding out in bivouac.

     Ch WAAYENBERG.

8th HQ and A Battery disposed as
     VILLE-LE-MARCHAL. Reconn.
     orders received and were taken in to
     action and were taken on to
     AMIENS & SEDLES. The Brigade
     marched to LONGEAU and billeted
     in the vicinity

9th Bde marched out clearing
     Amiens to TEMUIN crossing
     late in the evening. Bosche were
     bombed with high [?] and hydrane
     our horse lines whilst the Bde was
     crossing billeted A hidden led ore
     men & two horses killed and
     three men wounded

10th Orders received to march to
     LE QUESNEL at 3.0 am. Brigade

Aug 1918

10 Relieved guns East of L. OUESVE Eu, and
    Battery Commander's + 2 Subs went
    back to Ronville + up from
    Batteries moved up into action
    East and North East of BOUCHOIR
    in the early morning + covered
    the 96th Bde + 3rd Bde advance of the
    3rd Canadian.

11 The 32nd Div took the old front
    line West of PARVILLERS. The 32nd Div
    was relieved by the 3rd Canadian Division
    during the night 11/12th. Maj Ward
    B/161 wounded by M G fire on battery
    position.

12 The 7th Canadian Inf Bde who are
    holding the front of our sector advanced
    their line to slightly to-day by means
    of peaceful penetration.

13 The advance on DAMERY WOOD +
    PARVILLERS was held up by M.G. fire
    but there was a till heavy M G fire from
    PARVILLERS. The French on our
    right attacked DAMERY but were
    forced to retire.

15 The 9th Canadian Infantry Bde
    went through the 7th Bde and under
    a heavy barrage attacked [...]

16/8/18 1 OR wounded
17/8/18 Capt C.W. WARD M.C. wounded
         [...] detachment [...]
         1 OR wounded
         4 OR wounded

12/8/16 Major REAMES joined Bty
         from the Base R.A.
         1 OR wounded

19/8/16 2nd Lt [...] wounded [...]
         [...]

14/8/16 2nd Lieut EATON joined
         admitted hospital [...]
         3 OR wounded [...]

15/8/18 1 OR killed [...]

August

15" DAMERY & PARVILLERS. Enemy counter-attacked with 2 battalions but were caught in our barrage & beaten off with very heavy casualties.

16" A Battery moved to new position near BOIS EN EQUERRE.

17" C Battery moved to new position close to A Battery. Infantry have advanced the line East of PARVILLERS.

18" Brigade moved northwards to the Australian Corps area. Batteries were to have taken over from 4th Australian Bde R.F.A. One section per battery to where the night order was cancelled and batteries remained for the night at the wagon lines.

19" Batteries East of VAUVILLERS were reconnoitred and occupied. Batteries remaining silent.

22nd Aus Aus'n Corps attacked on the front HERLEVILLE - CHUIGNES. 96th M.I. Bde on the right covered by the 161 Bde / the 4th Aust Bde R.F.A. All objectives gained & 2,500 prisoners taken on the Corps front. Our front only advanced slightly & a straightened out.

23rd Enemy reported to be retiring and our infantry ordered out to hold to keep touch. F reach on our right were ordered to CILLETTE

24th Our bns advanced to VERMAND - VILLARS. Enemy has retired except for a few MG posts.

25th Enemy's adv retiring our patrols failed to maintain touch (a heavy hostile gas barrage during the evening in the neighbourhood of Battn HQ caused several casualties to our infantry. I was strengthened by Pervis Battn of H.L.I.

26th B.attns moved up to support advance of Infantry. C.battery to the right covering 4th /8th Border L/N covering A/L 1/5 Borders Cd S.O.A.R. Infantry advanced Franchise Aa Lattery on the under cover of an artillery barrage ABLAINCOURT creation at 7,500. Battns are moving up A+C Battery in close support of the advg front line battalions, B+D batteries in reserve

27th

August

28¹ 96th Inf Bde advanced under a barrage at 5.0 a.m. By 7.30 a.m. Infantry had advanced to a line 1000 yds east of ABLAINCOURT.
A & C Batteries moving up in close support encountered mines in the road at ABLAINCOURT. A Battery had 3 men wounded 2 horses killed and one gun put out of action. C Battery had the whole blown off 1 gun. Batteries are avoiding the village and using a very bad cross country track.
All Batteries in action by 4.0 p.m.
French are reported to have reached the SOMME in our right.

29" Batteries moved up again to positions to cover crossing of the SOMME. Infantry held line within 500 x of SOMME. 97 th Bde relieved the 96 Bde during night 29/30"

30" The whole front has now been taken over by the 97 th Inf Bde, the 2nd KOYLI holding the original 96 th Bde front and the 1/1/5 th Borders ac 2000 yds of the front on the north. We are covering the 2nd KOYLI B and D

August

The Nor*** close to HORGNY. Infantry now hold the West bank of the SOMME

31st Quadraluvns or our left have crossed the SOMME and are advancing on the PERONNE. Our infantry attempted to cross the SOMME but have held up by M G fire A ∼ C Batteries are further sending orders forward.

September

1st Batteries remained in the same
    positions throughout the day and
    carried out harassing fire on M.G.
    strong points in St Christ, and
    at V9d & V3b.

2nd a) B Bty again attempted to
    cross the Somme in the morning by
    the bridges at V16b. 00.5. C/161 Battery
    were informed to once, with
    a horsed Bty, the 3000 rd, as had
    for 710 attack was unsuccessful,
    however but was withdrawn
    throughout the day on roads in
    V5, V11 & 10.83 gun was engaged
    by D/161 on the Wachau edge of
    FOUR SHEAVES WOOD under cover
    of A/161 firing H.E. from C
    forward to sunken road in U8C
    A/161 remained silent

3rd A/161 moved to a new position
    in T18a last night. This is forward
    gun — he took hut out of
    action by hostile M.G. fire
    & being withdrawn during night.
    other batteries remained in
    their own position.

September

4th D/161 moved 1 how to V1a45 and
cut wire along the Brigade front Gape
were cut as follows U9c6015
V15a55 to U15b03, V15b01,
V15c8525, U21d35 to V21b44
V17a79, V3d63, V3a5085
V3b90, V3b6015, 350 rounds
were fired. All distances were
employed on firing as movement was
observed in the country were observed in
trench. U15 A & C. German artillery
other of individuals or small arms
between 9 a.m. & 12 noon. 4.2 hows.
was fired on the enemy in V9c59.
Harassing fire was carried out
by all batteries during the night
& two hostile M.G.s hard on tread of
enemy activity.

5th 9b × 7 of B.ty after several attempts
crossed the river SOMME by BRIE &
CIZANCOURT bridges and cleared
S E CHRIST Batteries on the hill
movement during the day D/161
advanced a 4.2 how firing from
U16 b 4.5. In the evening 97" 14
B.a established the line U24b50-
U12d50 thence along ATHIES-
PERONNE Road. Orders were issued

September

6th No bombing at 7.0h. to advance on
morning 6th Nch Affroux i attack
Bailly & St CHRIST was in
completed with 6.30 a.m. dividing
the Somme. B/61 crossed the Somme
by BRIE Bridge & followed up in
close support of 1st/5th BORDERS Bn
11th A.E. & D & Wings carried by
9.0 foot bridge

Troop were pushed ford through
Villecourt & Fenal dividing
B/Somme A/161 VIIIc2, B/61 VSCSS
C/61 4 guns VISC 85 2 guns V 92 A7
F/161 & C87, D guns 16 A 33. Coys
covering advance D# moved to
bothine 7.0b to Vrela Mhardus 2
V/161 H/61 took 3 prisoners
C/161 2 prisoners

7th Advance continued this morning
and all divisions reached by 10.0 a.m.
B/61 & C/161 moved up in close
support Dorset & Green Howards
on Q 35 c 66 & W.5 a 85 respectively
with a section of C forward at
W 17 c 95.

2
A/161 sent forward & section
in close support of Yorkshires
and his in an ambush which covered

September

Nothing gone but seen holding up
the intervening ridge in Sqdn A Pl with
2 H[?] 2 M[?] guns had been withdrawn

A/161 3 guns W11 b 52. 1 gun W12 a 20
B/161 Coys into action at W14 a 88
and outer's moved and traced in
the evening to W10 c 58.
Line shown not observed to days.

Batteries are now located

A/161 3 guns W11 b 51
       1 gun W12 a 20
B/161 6 "   Q 3 b d 62
C/161 2 "   W 22 b 86
       2 "   W 22 b 35
D/161 4 (less W10 c 59
       2 "   W 16 d 53

6th Australian A.F.A. Bde recommenced
and continued firing on W12 a 45
& W 5 a 74, forming a rear-guard
do the Bde.

During the day the batteries
fired 50 nds per gun on MG emplacements
Vide Appendix 65 attached

9th   Batteries still exactly the same
      position. Vigorous harassing
      fire has been carried out on

September

DEAD WOODS Sunken road in vicinity of ATILLY & atos X15 central OR W5 respect of the French high ground in X16C was also harassed

10th 96th TJ Bde relieved 97th TB to-day. Batteries harassed the high ground in X16C and fired on movement east of ATILLY C/161 moved to a new position at W12 d 55.30. situation Vide Appendix 6 attached.

11th B/161 Btys moved to new positions in 2 guns X7C60, 2 guns X7a54 & 2 guns X13 a 9.9. C/161 moved to a new position at W12 d 47. B/161 were shelled out of the position. they had suprally included & had two men slightly wounded, and moved to position above. Very little firing was done on the situation was obscure throughout the day.

12th An attack by the 96 & 1B supported by an artillery barrage by 161 Bd LRRAM Cunstalarion AFA Bd of 2.3.22 AFA Bd & 168 Bd RJa due to take place at 5.30 am was cancelled at 3.00 am as the infantry had reached the final objective unthout opposition. The Bde was relieved by the 23 AFA Bde & withdrew to wagon lives during the afternoon & evening. Vide Appendix 7 attached

13th Btns noted at their wagon lines. It being contemplated to withdraw the Btns to ATHIES for a period of rest and training, a reconnaissance of wagon lines was made under the direction of the Adjt. In the afternoon before the Btns moved, instructions were received cancelling the move. (We appeared to)

14th Btns remained at their wagon lines under orders to be ready to move into action at a moments notice.

15th An Attack with the view of driving the enemy towards the main HINDENBURG LINE being contemplated the Bde received instructions to reconnoitre positions in X.4.a. &c. This reconnaissance was carried out by the C.O. & Bty Commanders in the afternoon, when positions were allotted as follows:—
A: X.4.c.6.6   C. X.4.c.30.65
B. X.4.a.43.00 D X.4.a.92.15
In the evening Btns brought up ammunition to these positions to make up dumps of 400 per gun & 300 per how.

16th Btns moved to their positions during the day and at night they brought up their guns & had them in ST QUENTIN WOOD and adjacent copses, and got up the remainder of their ammunition

17th Relieve worked on their position and on right flank their guns in position and arrangements for the barrage to be fired the following morning (Vide appendix 9+11)

NB moved to X 3 d 4

18th Attack by Infantry (164 IR) supported by Artillery took place at 5.50 am the Brigade (attack LEFT GROUP under Command of Col Weber DSO) supported 2/ Y + L R (A. B. & D. Buns.) C/2 were Land Mr. KEEPER'S HOUSE 1 at about M 25 d and a Forward Intelligence Officer with a joint commission with the object of gaining information of the progress of the Infantry (Vide Appendix + 10) — the Infantry (1st Objective) after reaching (their first objective) after reaching the final objective the opposition became not serious and they met with arm resistance on the line of consolidation on the left The position on the right was along the line (being attacks) to be in HOINON VILLAGE It had been arranged that our Artie should form the barrage as far as the GREEN LINE and that the two Coys during what the barrage remained on this line, should be utilised in moving forward the Tanks to positions in R.36.a where they were to lay up till the Barrage again and continue up to the final objective. Before the 2 Coys had started all Wire were in position and all were in telephone communication with Bde. H.Q.

At 8 night owing to the change in the situation 'C' & 'D' Btns were instructed to the position they had occupied earlier in the day. (Vide appendix 12)

19th 2/Lt HERN & 2/Lt MAWER both of C/161 were wounded during the day.

2 am by Group H.Q. to prepare for a barrage in support of the Infantry who were to make another attempt to reach the final objective of the previous day. The Infantry advance at 5.30 am, but enemy M.G. held them up & the line remained stationary. Orders were received to A. & B. Bties to withdraw at

dawn the previous day, all patrols
towards the enemy (appendix 13) claiming the night

20th. The Infantry spent the day
consolidating on the line :- M.21.a.32
along road in M.27.a.v.c. to the old C.T.
about M.27.d.1.3. then to the T of CHAMPAGNE
TRENCH to the junction of DOYEN TRENCH
& AMERICAN ALLEY

Orders were issued regarding
the action of Battery Commanders in
the case of a successful Counter attack
by the enemy (vide appendix 14)

21st. Quiet day. At the request of
the Infantry who reported that the
enemy were in the French Trenches
at M.28 & C.05.85 the point of the
Armoured Car Trenches were engaged
by B's Forward Section. the 6" Sur-
"Sim- Sapps" to the right and the
lanes of Battery had carrying parties
to be depôts. (Vide appendix 15.)

22nd. The enemy put down a heavy
fire on the PCHQ & in the vicinity
of PCHQ between 3.30 & 5.15am
& the enemy SOS was brought up
15.00 rds of ammn. to new front up
position & the operation before the
next attack as follows —
A/ R.36.a.8460 C/ R.36.a.93.14

had ask brought me food & this new positions at night. A reconnaissance of Wagon Lane at MORVAL LA GREAT was made during the afternoon. Wandering fire during the night on the Quadrilateral in S 3 & 4. Instructions were issued to Battns regarding the action to be taken in the event of counter preparation being ordered. (This afternoon 16 Divis: orders.)

23rd   We moved this Hqrs line K
MORVAL LAGACHE. Orders were issued by GROUP for the Brigade to be first in support of an attack by the Infantry the following morning. Hrs moved up their forward position in R 32 & did hand-over at night (see appendices 17 & R)

24th   At 5.0 am the attack by the Infantry commenced. The front objective of the IX Corps & the French was the ship known MANCHESTER HILL - FRANKLIN SELEREY - QUADRILATE RAL - M34 b c d - M38 b d - M16 b d. Our brigade was to support the 16th Infantry Bde whose first objective was S 4 a 5 & 8 (NORTH ALLEY) along RIDGE TRENCH to M 25 c 65 a and the second objective was the

22nd 2/Lt K J Allen 8/10/16 returned from leave

23rd Capt 6.E.W Stallindon 8/10/ Granted leave to UK terminated 4/10/16

24th 2/Lt W. B Wilson 27/10/16 returned from leave

frontier of BRETON ALLEY with the
6th Hunts (?) at SYLBOSCE along the
new trench & three Wings ARGONNE
TRENCH & PERONNE TRENCH to TREAT
From the M28 & 35 15 2 the dead line
between 1/KSLI on right & 2/Y & L
(which the bn was supposed to have had
AMERICAN ALLEY
The attack was not directed at the
first two objectives being found in the
left & third objectives not heavily held
at the QUADRILATERAL which the enemy
held firm with a barrel added to
the French line in possession of FRENCH
SELENCY & the line found with the line
of the infantry being in front of
DOUAI TRENCH as far south as
Sq a D as made an attempt to come
the QUADRILATERAL by bombing down
As trial, but it put into life
circular. They established a post in
"HAZ NELOOP - ST QUEATIN Road at
S8d 95 95 but had to withdraw
to take H. SELENCY at the time
being in the hands of the enemy. The
early hours of the following morning
a fresh attack was made on the
QUADRILATERAL which we found present

A R.O.B was sent forward
t view form a first hand information of
information of the progress of the attack
the applies & kit of the
from & between the bring taken in
ignored this effort
At 10 pm instructions were
issued to the bn, notifications of
the relief there was at [?] early
around their bivouac at [?]
from the [?] following morning
(an attempt on 19.)

www.ingramcontent.com/pod-product-compliance
Lightning Source LLC
Chambersburg PA
CBHW081424300426
44108CB00016BA/2296